Gender, Development, and Globalization

Gender, Development, and Globalization is the leading primer on global feminist economics and development. Lourdes Benería, a pioneer in the field of feminist economics, is joined in this second edition by Günseli Berik and Maria Floro to update the text to reflect the major theoretical, empirical, and methodological contributions and global developments in the last decade. Its interdisciplinary investigation remains accessible to a broad audience interested in an analytical treatment of the impact of globalization processes on development and well-being in general and on social and gender equality in particular.

The revision will continue to provide a wide-ranging discussion of the strategies and policies that hold the most promise in promoting equitable and sustainable development. The authors make the case for feminist economics as a useful framework to address major contemporary global challenges, such as inequalities between the global South and North as well as within single countries; persistent poverty; and increasing vulnerability to financial crises, food crises, and climate change. The authors' approach is grounded in the intellectual current of feminism and human development, drawing on the capability approach and focused on the importance of the care economy, increasing pressures faced by women, and the failures of neoliberal reforms to bring about sustainable development, reduction in poverty, inequality, and vulnerability to economic crisis.

Lourdes Benería is Professor of City and Regional Planning and former director of the Gender and Global Change Program and of the Latin American Studies Program at Cornell University, USA. Her work has focused on gender and development, paid/unpaid work, globalization, labor markets, and structural adjustment policies, particularly in Latin America.

Günseli Berik is Professor of Economics at the University of Utah, USA. Her research and teaching is in the fields of development economics, gender and development, feminist economics, and labor economics. Berik is co-editor of the journal *Feminist Economics*.

Maria S. Floro is Professor of Economics and co-director of the Program on Gender Analysis in Economics at American University. Her publications include *Credit Markets and the New Institutional Economics, Women's Work in the World Economy*, and articles on time allocation, unpaid work, finance, informal employment, vulnerability, and poverty.

Gender, Development, and Globalization

Economics as if All People Mattered

Second Edition

**Lourdes Benería,
Günseli Berik,
and Maria S. Floro**

Routledge
Taylor & Francis Group

NEW YORK AND LONDON

First edition published 2003
by Routledge

Second edition published 2016
by Routledge
711 Third Avenue, New York, NY 10017

and by Routledge
2 Park Square, Milton Park, Abingdon, Oxon, OX14 4RN

Routledge is an imprint of the Taylor & Francis Group, an informa business

Library of Congress Cataloging in Publication Data
Benería, Lourdes.
  Gender, development, and globalization: economics as if all people
  mattered / Lourdes Benería, Günseli Berik, and Maria Floro.
  pages cm
  Earlier edition published in 2003.
  Includes bibliographical references.
  1. Feminist economics. 2. Women in development. 3. Globalization.
  4. Economic development—Social aspects. I. Berik, Günseli.
  II. Floro, Maria. III. Title.
  HQ1381.B46 2015
  305.42—dc23
  2014045153

ISBN: 978-0-415-53748-3 (hbk)
ISBN: 978-0-415-53749-0 (pbk)
ISBN: 978-0-203-10793-5 (ebk)

Typeset in Minion Pro
by Florence Production Ltd, Stoodleigh, Devon, UK

To our sons and daughters who are inheriting a difficult and unequal world, hoping that their actions will contribute to the huge task of constructing just societies and a sustainable Earth.

"This new edition of a book that has already proved invaluable for those interested in gender and globalization from a development perspective will be on interest to an even wider audience. It provides an overview of the impact of globalization on gender relations in different regions of the world, expanded and updated to consider recent financial crisis. It synthesises the key contributions of feminist analysis in the field of economics, exposing both stated and hidden assumptions through which it is able to construct a world that is apparently free of injustice. And it reminds us that the politics of redistribution must be combined with the politics of recognition in feminist efforts to create a more just and sustainable international order."
—*Naila Kabeer, London School of Economics and Political Science*

"Lourdes Benería, Günseli Berik and Maria Floro provide an indispensable compendium of the research on gender and development and a comprehensive road map to feminist economics thinking today. The authors unmask the neoliberal, market-driven policy agenda that has dominated development policy for decades and offer feminist, people-driven alternatives that promote democracy, economic well being and ecologically sustainable development."
—*Randy Albelda, Professor of Economics, author of*
Economics and Feminism: Disturbances in the Field

"Drawing on the latest thinking in feminist economics, this book provides a powerful critique of neoliberal globalization as well as of the way gender has been mainstreamed in development policy. It is the ideal text for a course in gender and development, a provocative complementary reading for courses in development studies more generally, and pivotal to all those concerned with building a more gender equitable society."
—*Carmen Diana Deere, Distinguished Professor of*
Latin American Studies and Food & Resource Economics,
University of Florida

"*Gender, Development, and Globalization* is a remarkable book. It encompasses and highlights the best of innovative thinking in the field of economics. Policymakers will benefit from novel framework for promoting human well-being. The authors go well beyond the boundaries of traditional economics to consider care work, the environment, and the challenges posed by class, gender and race inequality. This revised edition could not be more timely, in a world in which so many are seeking new ideas on how to understand and address problems of growing inequality, tendencies to economic stagnation, and intergroup conflict."
—*Stephanie Seguino, University of Vermont*

"*Gender, Development, and Globalization* is an excellent introduction to critical feminist analysis of the changing patterns of global employment, wealth, and well-being. Particularly concerned with the state of the world's workers, and among them, the most disadvantaged, it makes strong contributions to pressing debates about inequality, neoliberalism, unpaid labor, and the goals and design of development policy."

—*Julie A. Nelson, University of Massachusetts, Boston*

"This book is a very rich and up-to-date source for teaching in the areas of globalisation and gender and development. Its theories range from the recognition of women's paid and unpaid economic roles in the 1980s to the human rights based framework developed in response to an instrumental policy approach to the MDGs in the new millennium. In particular, the book signals a new developmentalism in which heterodox economics engages with feminism and in which social movements push an agenda based on social solidarity practices across the world."

—*Irene van Staveren, International Institute of Social Studies of Erasmus University Rotterdam*

Praise for the Previous Edition:

"Lourdes Beneria is one of the leaders of thought on gender economics as well as development studies. In this wonderfully interesting book, Beneria discusses and critically assesses the recent trends in the analysis of gender and development issues. It is an accessible and very engaging account and enlightens both the fields as well as the challenges of globalization in the contemporary world."

—*Amartya Sen, author of* Development As Freedom and Poverty and Famines

"Behold 'Davos Man,' symbol of the international elite that meets regularly in luxurious fortresses to advance its global interests. This book strips off his gilded three-piece suit to reveal a lifeless, brittle piece of molded plastic. Lourdes Beneria's feminist deconstruction of mainstream economics urges us to look in new directions toward a more generous, sustainable, and democratic model of global development."

—*Nancy Folbre, author of* The Invisible Heart: Economics and Family Values

"Beneria's ideas about what to do if we agree that 'we cannot continue today on these lines' offer a positive sense that another way of thinking, at least, is already possible . . . Informative reviews of 1) the history of feminist influences on the field of economics, 2) the dominant ideas shaping development thinking during the late 20th Century and 3) the literature on labor dimensions of globalization and industrial restructuring make this book additionally useful as a reference."
                    —Journal of Planning Education and Research, *Gwen Urey*

Contents

Figures

Tables

Preface

The first English edition of this book was published in 2003 although some parts had been written in the late 1990s. Given the rapid changes that have taken place since then in global economics, politics, and overall social life, it is no surprise that the book was in need of an update. The central focus of this new edition continues to be the extent to which economic and social change under globalization has been shaping the dynamics of gender inequality and women's condition across countries. One major event that required analysis for the new edition was the Great Recession that began in 2007 in the US and spread quickly, particularly to Europe. Its effects continue to be felt across the globe, with consequences for the world economy and for many people's lives. In this sense, a difference between the two editions is that many development issues such as unemployment and poverty have become crucial to the global North as well. More specifically, the ensuing policy responses to the crisis have had a variety of gender-differentiated effects that are very relevant for the analysis in the book.

A major concern in the first edition was the legacy of the debt crisis in developing countries during the 1980s and 1990s, particularly the lost decade in Africa and Latin America. Interestingly enough, this second edition comes at a time when the effects of the financial crisis of 2007–08 still linger on in the global North, while the South has also suffered its consequences. Both crises are part of the discussion in different parts of the book, with emphasis on their gender dimensions.

The book is written more specifically from our perspective of the field of gender and development, which has been rapidly expanding during the past decades. The different chapters emphasize the ways in which globalization and neoliberal policies have been shaping many aspects of development and in particular women's place within it. Empirically, the book pays special attention to developing countries although also emphasizing the important connections and new parallels between North and South. The field of gender and development did not exist before the 1970s nor was the different impact of "development" on men and women questioned and discussed in teaching, research, and policy circles. The shift towards the new field can be viewed as a consequence of the questions generated by the women's movement since the late 1960s but especially since the 1970s. In more recent decades, women have become even more central in our understanding of development, policy, and action. The field's phenomenal growth has moved in many directions some of which—such as the political aspects—are beyond the scope of this book. This growth and subsequent influence makes us wonder how "development" was ever viewed as gender neutral.

Much has been accomplished in the field during these decades and this is part of the analysis in the book. We have much to celebrate in terms of higher levels of gender equality but much still remains to be done. The book provides extensive discussions of the progress made and the problems still remaining or unfolding anew. We have kept the same chapter structure as in the first edition, with the same central topics, although with a variety of changes in their content and analysis.

Written mainly from a feminist economics perspective, the book is intended to reach an interdisciplinary audience. It is inspired not only by the work of feminist economists but also by the large body of social science research that has been dealing with issues of gender, globalization, and development during the past few decades. In comparison with the first edition, some topics have been expanded while others have been added, dropped or updated. The two new co-authors have been a wonderful addition to the task. Being very knowledgeable of the field, they have brought new energy and a wide range of work and experience to the initial book's effort. Given that the three co-authors have used the first edition of the text in our teaching and for other purposes, we have been very aware of the initial text's contributions as well as its shortcomings. The new edition takes all of them into consideration and hence should be a much-improved version. For this, I am much indebted and grateful to Günseli Berik and Maria Floro, and to Routledge for being flexible with the expanded number of pages and with our delays in meeting deadlines.

Lourdes Benería

Acknowledgements

This book includes inputs from many people who have helped or inspired us directly or indirectly. Many of their ideas and work are necessarily reflected in the book, which is in fact the product of an enormous collective effort of many years, based on exchanges at many levels that are not always easy to identify. While we discuss the specific work of many researchers, which amounts to an extensive list of the literature used, it is difficult to identify all the work that has contributed to the making of this book. We thank our communities for exchange of ideas, sharing of knowledge and information and support in many ways. In particular, we want to thank Rose Batt, Zişan Berik, Cihan Bilginsoy, Carmen Diana Deere, Valeria Esquivel, Kimberly Fisher, Lina Gálvez, Maria Dolors García-Ramón, Caren Grown, Tom Hungerford, Dolores Juliano, Ebru Kongar, Neema Kudva, Cecilia López, María Martínez-Iglesias, Mieke Meurs, Porus Olpadwala, Iñaki Permanyer, Nohra Rey, Carmen Sarasúa, Shahra Razavi, Yana van der Meulen Rodgers, Stephanie Seguino, Gita Sen, Verena Stolcke, Diana Strassmann, and Christine Verschuur. We are also grateful to our students over many years for their questions and comments and the many opportunities for us to discuss, explain, and clarify many of the ideas synthesized in this book. Finally, we want to acknowledge the various women's organizations around the world with whom we have collaborated in the past three decades and whose work and actions continue to inspire us.

Our deep gratitude goes to Diksha Arora, Valeria Esquivel, Ebru Kongar, David Kucera, Julie Nelson, Iñaki Permanyer, Marilyn Power, Shahra Razavi, and Carmen Sarasúa, who read one or more chapters of the draft and provided useful comments—all on short notice. Many others responded to our questions, provided comments and suggestions on specific issues, suggested sources—also on short notice. In particular, we thank Anıl Aba, Haimanti Bhattacharya, Engin Dalgiç, Simel Esim, Polly Morrice, Codrina

Rada. We alone are responsible for the ideas expressed in the final version of the book.

We thank Diksha Arora, Greg Seymour, Mungunsuvd Terbish, Smriti Tiwari, and Maria Wahlstrom for assistance. We thank Routledge for supporting the updated and expanded edition of the book. In particular, we appreciate Michael Kerns's support, flexibility with the expanded number of pages, and patience over the long writing and editing of the book and the efforts of Emily Davies and Lillian Rand in seeing through the completion of the project. Special thanks are due to our children, Jordi, Marc, Alev, Mehmet, and Maria, and to Cihan Bilginsoy and Tom Hungerford for companionship and support.

Introduction

This book is about the multiple gender dimensions of development, globalization, labor markets, and women's work since the 1970s. With an analysis springing from feminist economics but using also an interdisciplinary approach, the book includes theoretical/conceptual as well as empirical and historical analysis of these themes. In so doing, it makes a contribution that challenges mainstream economics in many respects. An important part of this challenge came from feminist research in the field of gender and development, which provided valuable insights on the diversity of women's lives and new standpoints from which to construct knowledge.

The structure of the book reflects our feminist economics perspective and vision for social change. We lay the conceptual groundwork for analyzing economic development and globalization questions from a gender perspective in Chapters 1 and 2. Chapter 1 provides an overview of the policy-oriented field of gender and development from the critical GAD perspective we adopt in our analysis. Chapter 2 presents a history of feminist economics; its emergence and development out of engagement with the different schools of thought in the discipline of economics and with feminist theory and research in other disciplines. Chapters 3, 4, and 5 evaluate how processes of contemporary globalization have affected workers' ability to generate livelihoods through paid and unpaid economic activities and their well-being. Chapter 6 takes us to questions of policy and action, in order to reset the development process on a course that prioritizes people's livelihoods and well-being. We focus on issues particularly relevant to economic development in general and gender and development in particular and outline alternative agendas for change from a feminist economics perspective. We describe the content of the chapters below in greater detail.

Our aim in this book is to be useful to teachers, researchers, activists, policymakers, and general readers who are interested in the ways in which a gender perspective can offer important insights into development and globalization issues and to the dynamics of gender inequality. We address readers from many disciplines and explain terms in order to be understood broadly. Each of the six chapters can be used as a standalone piece but they also contain common themes—such as the neoliberal reforms or the 2007–08 financial crisis—that are approached from the perspective of the different chapters. Specific chapter sections on such cross-cutting themes can be read selectively to gain a broader understanding of a theme. In each chapter we provide a historical perspective on a variety of debates, particularly as they have evolved in the literature since the 1970s. We seek to provide sufficient detail and context to communicate the importance of the topic under discussion and provide sources for readers to pursue further research if they wish to get into greater depth.

Capitalist development is an uneven process that unfolds in the global North as well as the global South. Therefore, we draw upon evidence from a variety of countries and regions, and highlight the connections of the economic processes across regions. We seek to identify the geographic and social context of the evidence we present and avoid generalizations to low-income or high-income regions. Given the broad scope of the book, however, there is unevenness in the extent to which we are able to represent processes in different regions of the world. In addition, while gender and class have been consistent lenses in the book, we have been less attentive to how their intersections with race, ethnicity, and sexual orientation shape advantage/disadvantage in different parts of the world.

* * * * *

Chapter 1 provides an overview of the policy-oriented field of gender and development and the conceptual shifts and innovations it experienced since the early 1970s. The field has come a long way from its beginnings in Ester Boserup's work, its research agenda having expanded in many directions through critique, debate, and action. We examine the contributions of WID, WAD, and GAD frameworks and the challenges raised by postmodernism and postcolonialism. A different challenge that came from neoliberalism has also shaped the oppositional discourse of GAD, and the emergence of human rights and capabilities approaches. While acknowledging the impressive integration of gender issues in development policy agendas, we are also concerned about some of the ways in which this integration has proceeded. Chief among our concerns are the instrumentalization of women in policy design, the mechanistic approach towards gender mainstreaming in policy, and the promotion of gender equality without regard to other social inequalities with which it intersects. These features of gender mainstreaming constitute a barrier to advancing an agenda that promotes equitable well-being for all. Despite these signs of strong neoliberal influence on the field, we believe that the critical GAD perspective, in combination with the capabilities and human rights approaches and the social provisioning approach in feminist economics, provides a promising oppositional discourse for research and policymaking.

In Chapter 2 we tell the story of the origins, central principles, main contributions, and emerging research agendas of feminist economics. The study of gender in economics has evolved through critique and engagement with different schools of thought—orthodox economics, Marxian theory, institutional economics—as the distinct heterodox strands in the discipline. By the early 1990s feminist economics emerged from the accumulated body of critique as well as developments in feminist thought. The chapter first examines the making of feminist economics and the central tenets in its critique of the mainstream. Second, we examine the social provisioning approach that comes closest to providing coherence to feminist economics as an intellectual project, and from our perspective, a tool to build progressive policies and social change. Briefly, this approach conceptualizes the economy as involving a wide range of market and non-market activities aimed at human provisioning; emphasizes that economic processes must be evaluated on how well they support the overarching goal of sustainable human development; and is attentive to multiple social differentiations among people on the basis of their class, race, and ethnicity. Third, we focus on the contributions of feminist economics to the analysis of provisioning activities and household dynamics. Fourth, we examine the contributions of feminist economics to engendering macroeconomics and ecological economics, which are central to envisioning alternative economic policies to build sustainable economies.

The overarching themes of this book—on gender, globalization, and development—are examined at length in Chapters 3 and 4, which analyze the dynamics of globalization since the 1970s and its profound effects on economic relations and on people's and, more specifically, women's lives. In Chapter 3 we scrutinize the widening and deepening of markets, together with the rise and consolidation of neoliberalism across countries and regions. The chapter first provides a historical view of neoliberalism and its theoretical underpinnings and a discussion of the neoliberal policies introduced since the 1970s, both in developing and high-income countries. It examines the links between the global expansion of markets and its conceptual roots in orthodox economics, such as the assumptions around economic rationality and "economic man." Second, we examine the intrinsic features of capitalist development: capital accumulation through the expansion of markets, concentration of capital, and proletarianization. The post-1980 period has been characterized by growing inequalities and the concentration of wealth; financialization and commercialization of everyday life; and accelerated proletarianization of labor in many low-income countries. Our analysis emphasizes the gender-differentiated nature of these processes. It focuses particularly on the feminization of the labor force—in general and in specific sectors, including manufacturing, agriculture, the services—and the rise of human trafficking. Finally, it discusses the patterns of women's integration in paid employment, including gender discrimination, and women's location in the lower echelons of the labor market hierarchy and changing gender relations. We review the contradictory tendencies of women's increasing participation in paid work, pointing out the co-existence of empowering effects as well as the continuation or reappearance of practices that constrain women's capabilities.

Chapter 4 provides a close up on the labor market processes underlying global economic integration. It focuses on labor market restructuring associated with firm restructuring and reorganization of production, which were driven by the twin engines of globalization: technological change and neoliberal policies. With a gender lens, we examine the trends that affect workers' ability to make a living and to improve the well-being of their family members: the loss of power on the part of labor relative to capital, symbolized by the decline in unions in the global North; rising employment insecurity; rising inequality and polarization among wage earners, and deterioration of working conditions; and informalization of work in high-income countries, especially since the 2008 economic crisis. The chapter also pays special attention to the main characteristics of the informal economy in developing countries and the different forms of informality and vulnerability, and we analyze the ways in which they affect women, together with their primary involvement in domestic work and childcare responsibilities. Finally, we provide an overview of the recent history of international and national strategies to counter the downward harmonization of working conditions: the attempts to come up with internationally enforceable labor standards; ILO's *Decent Work Agenda*; corporate social responsibility schemes; the organizing work done by both women factory workers and informal workers, such as the Self Employed Women's Association (SEWA) of India. While the playing field between labor and capital is very unequal in the new millennium, we consider worker organizing efforts linked by international solidarity activity as key to improving labor standards both domestically and globally.

Moving from women's paid to unpaid work, Chapter 5 explores another important issue regarding women's labor, namely, the significance of their traditional concentration on unpaid domestic work and family care responsibilities. The chapter examines the conceptual challenges and statistical questions involved in what we call the "Accounting for Women's Work Project" and how it has evolved substantially over time. We explain this evolution starting with the conceptual and practical neglect of unpaid work in national income accounts up until the 1970s and 1980s when feminists began to question the economic and social meaning of unpaid work and its measurement. The Accounting Project problematizes the neglect of not only domestic and care work but also volunteer labor and different forms of informal and family labor in farms and small enterprises. The Project has been carried out with the help of many actors, including academics, researchers, women's advocacy groups and networks, and international institutions such as different branches of the UN and of national governments. We emphasize the importance of the effort to make women's work more visible and we explain the variety of difficulties that the Project has been encountering as well as the considerable amount of success achieved. We believe that the empirical and theoretical contributions made through this Project have enhanced our understanding of gender inequality, poverty, and of well-being in general. The chapter ends with a discussion of policy debates around the issue of reconciling paid and unpaid work—or family and labor market work.

Finally, Chapter 6 takes us to broader questions of policy and action. We refer especially to the most salient problems affecting our globalized world, including the multiple crises of capitalism, growing inequalities, and climate change, and the problems preventing progress towards equitable and sustainable human development. First, we identify three obstacles that affect policy and action: the tendency to view poverty reduction as a development issue separated from issues of overall social inequality, distribution, and sustainable development; the fact that increasingly devastating financial crises have produced stronger power for capital and more entrenched neoliberal solutions; and the processes of gender mainstreaming in development agendas that have resulted in women being used as instruments serving the neoliberal goal of maximizing economic growth. Second, this chapter focuses on the question of alternatives for policy and action, pointing to agendas for change from a feminist economics perspective. These efforts include engaging in a dialogue with other heterodox perspectives on economics and alternative views on how to build sustainable development and shape progressive social change.

This agenda implies a strong emphasis on environmental, social, and economic sustainability and its connections with the reduction of income inequality, poverty, and labor market instability. We emphasize that global regulation and global governance reforms are necessary to move this agenda forward. And we underline the importance of agency and of social movements —including by many existing women's groups—that press for transformative policies regarding these questions at national, regional, and international levels.

CHAPTER 1

Gender and Development: A Historical Overview

We have moved from viewing women as victims to seeing them as essential to finding solutions to the world's problems.
Speaker at the UN Conference on Women, Beijing 1995

Introduction

Until the publication of Ester Boserup's book *Woman's Role in Economic Development* (1970), the notion that economic development might have a different impact by gender—or even that development had anything to do with women—was unthinkable. To be sure, in the 1960s, women anthropologists such as Eleanor Leacock, June Nash, and Helen Safa had considered women in their work on different communities and in their concerns on socio-economic change. And, earlier, Margaret Mead had showed how gender roles differed across small communities in the Pacific, challenging the prevalent notions that Western gender norms were universal (Mead 1958). However, Boserup's book represented a turning point in shining the spotlight on the specific ways in which colonialism and "modernization" had affected women differently from men. It came at a historical moment when there was intense interest in taking stock of development policies pursued by newly independent nations and at the height of social movements, notably the women's movement, in the rich countries of North America, Europe, and in many parts of Asia, Latin America and the Caribbean, and Africa. The 1970s thus gave birth to the policy-oriented research field of "women in development," what we now call "gender and development." In this chapter, we present an overview of this field and the conceptual shifts and innovations it has experienced.

The United Nations (UN), through its World Conferences on Women (1975, 1980, 1985, and 1995) and through its different agencies, served as a catalyst for creating the institutional frameworks for research and policy in national and international institutions. The passage of the Convention on the Elimination of All Forms of Discrimination Against Women (CEDAW) in 1979 and additional key international conferences in Vienna (1993) and Cairo (1994) buoyed continued international policy interest in women's well-being and gender inequality questions. The policy interest culminated in the Millennium Declaration of 2000 that reinforced the message that there could be no development without pursuit of women's equality with men. Indeed, since the late 1990s the predominant policies to fight poverty globally—including microcredit and conditional cash transfer schemes— have featured women as the main agents. Over the years the policy interest spread from the UN agencies, international donors, and non-governmental organizations to the World Bank and the IMF, the premier international institutions behind economic globalization and neoliberal policies. Even the World Economic Forum, which represents global elites, has felt compelled to deal with gender issues, albeit these institutions differ in their emphases on why gender equality matters.

The research and teaching on gender and development has evolved since the 1970s to encompass an expanding range of topics that are studied using a number of social science frameworks, including economics. The field has also experienced a number of conceptual shifts. The original Women in Development (WID) and Women and Development (WAD) perspectives that appeared during the 1970s have largely given way to the more encompassing Gender and Development (GAD) perspective generated from the important theoretical changes that transformed feminist theory in the 1980s.[1] While WID emerged from liberal feminist circles that incorporated Boserup's analysis of women and development, WAD emerged precisely from a critique of liberal feminism and orthodox development theory. Proponents of WAD pointed out that women's disadvantaged position is also a result of the way the economic system recreates gender inequalities and precarious types of employment, thereby raising questions about the type of development that women are to be integrated in (Benería and Sen 1981; 1982).

Over the years, GAD has incorporated both WID and WAD perspectives, given that a degree of convergence between WID and WAD took place around the notion of gender as a central category of analysis. The emergence of postmodernism, with its emphasis on difference and attention to particular contexts and identity issues, contributed to this convergence. Yet, there is a wide range of feminist scholarship and action that falls under the GAD umbrella; in particular, a general differentiation can be made between those who are closer to liberal feminism à la WID and those who represent extensions of WAD. The distinction between the two shades of GAD turns on the degree of critical thinking among GAD feminists with regard to key issues such as gender and globalization, class inequality, the nature of capitalism, and the role of markets and their regulation. While there are differing interpretations of what GAD represents, in this book we identify the GAD approach with this second strand—the critical perspectives in the field of gender and development.

The field has come a long way from its origins, theoretically, empirically, and in terms of policy and action. Now there are gender-differentiated datasets, gender-inclusive measures of well-being, and gender concerns and empowerment goals are integrated in the development policy agenda. Despite the enormous progress in the inclusion of gender issues in international organizations and development agencies, gender integration in development policy remains problematic in a number of ways that we view as a barrier to advancing an agenda that promotes equitable well-being for all.

First, there is the danger of its instrumentalization, that is, the inclusion of gender in program activities and projects for purposes that do not necessarily serve goals of gender equality and enhancement of women's well-being or that might even conflict with them. Feminists have long been wary of instrumental approaches to women's issues (Benería and Sen 1981; Moser 1989; Elson 1991a). The examples are numerous, such as programs of population control whose objectives reflect not so much a concern with women's well-being or gender equality than as a way to use women to achieve demographic targets. Similarly, short-term employment programs for women can be aimed at toning down the negative effects of male unemployment rather than promoting women's long-term interests. The World Bank, and regional development banks, donor agencies, and government ministries have provided many examples of instrumental arguments for gender equality, for instance by emphasizing the importance of women's education as a way of increasing productivity in the household and the market. Their concerns have often focused on women's contributions to economic growth rather than the importance of women's education as a means for empowering women and enhancing their capabilities. Upon release of the World Bank's *World Development Report* (WDR) of 2012, feminists have criticized this "efficiency" or "smart economics" approach, pointing out that the primary goal should be the promotion of women's well-being while economic growth should be seen as a means rather than an end in itself (Global Social Policy 2012; Razavi 2012).[2] This critique emphasizes that the efficiency concerns should not eclipse the goals of gender equality and promotion of women's rights as primary ends in and of themselves.

A second concern with gender integration in development policy has to do with the practice of "gender mainstreaming." This refers to the effort to integrate gender issues across programs and projects of national and international programs, organizations and donor agencies, attentive to planning, implementation, and monitoring activities, which normally did not include them. While the term gender has been integrated in development policy discourses, gender mainstreaming in policy and organizational mandates has often resulted in a simplification of gender equality and empowerment goals, turned a feminist process of social transformation into a technical process to be overseen by bureaucracies, and became depoliticized (Rai 2002; Mukhopadhyay 2004; 2013). It has produced policy approaches that lack a comprehensive understanding of the gender dimensions of the issues at hand. This is so particularly when policy measures overlook the range of gender constraints and naively seek to empower women by simply supplying what is perceived as the missing ingredient (e.g. credit or business skills).[3]

A third concern is that, well into the twenty-first century, in the development policy agenda gender equality is being pursued as a standalone goal, women and men being considered as homogeneous groups, and without regard to reducing other social inequalities such as class, race, and ethnicity. The broad acceptance of gender equality objectives likely owes to the fact that standard strategies such as increasing women's participation in labor markets or in microenterprises, or making them property owners, do not necessarily challenge the prevailing socio-economic order. Undoubtedly, positive transformations have taken place for those women who have benefitted from new opportunities afforded by economic change, but not so for those who have been marginalized and excluded as a result of their position in the national and global economies. Gender equality appears to be less politically threatening to the hegemonic system when isolated from other social inequalities. As many proponents of the GAD perspective have long argued, however, we cannot speak of gender without also speaking about these inequalities with which it intersects. Gender equality is only a part of the overarching fundamental goal of social equality. Yet, neoliberalism appears to have taken on board feminist concerns that are narrowly focused on gender equality, leading commentators to argue that feminism has been coopted in this process (Eisenstein 2009; Fraser 2013).

In this chapter we problematize the state of the dominant gender and development discourses and examine the history of conceptual and policy shifts that have brought the field to its current state. We focus on the frameworks that have been most influential for research, policies, and action, starting with the WID perspective and the contending GAD approach. Second, we examine two disparate developments that have shaped the research agenda of the field since the 1980s: the critique of WID framework by postmodern writers, feminists, and women's organizations in developing countries and the rise of neoliberal economic policies that continue being implemented in most countries. We review these developments and three counter discourses to neoliberalism, which provide the conceptual tools for transcending these policies: feminist critiques, the capabilities approach and the human development paradigm, and the more recent human rights approach that emphasizes economic and social rights.

In the Beginning There Was WID . . .

Until the early 1970s, women were invisible in economic development analysis and ignored by policymakers, except in their roles as mothers and wives. Policy sought to make women better mothers through child-focused health and nutrition and family planning programs. As Moser (1989) pointed out, this "welfare approach" to women in developing countries was characteristic of the late colonial and post-independence era. No doubt this identity of women had its counterpart in the male breadwinner ideal underlying the characteristic Keynesian macroeconomic policies and welfare policies of the 1940s–1960s, whereby women and children were considered to be dependents of the male wage earners who were entitled to social security and unemployment insurance (Elson and Çağatay 2000). These women-only programs in developing countries were in sync with traditional gender norms in most societies and not threatening to the social order. While in the early twenty-first century, policies continue to pay attention to women in their role as mothers, most notably in the conditional cash transfer schemes, in the 1970s there was a dramatic shift in women's perceived and ideal role in the policy discourse as a result of the women's movement and the rise of feminism. Advocates, practitioners, and scholars drew attention to women's productive roles, and to what women contributed to the economy. This new identity of women became the hallmark of the emerging interdisciplinary and policy-oriented field of women in development and the associated WID perspective. WID advocates promoted women's integration into the economy on an equal footing with men as the means for improving women's status in developing countries.

The WID approach characteristic of this period and tied to liberal feminism challenged the notion that women were unproductive members of society. A number of contributory influences were at work in the emergence of the field and shaping its concerns. First, women practitioners in development agencies, notably USAID, provided their experiential knowledge for the WID argument (Tinker 1990). They had first-hand knowledge of the work women did in fields and factories in developing countries and the differing impacts of development policies on women and men. Second, the Population Control Lobby of the 1960s and 1970s drew attention to the connection between women's work and fertility; increasing women's education and employment, it was argued, could potentially reduce fertility rates that would then decrease the population growth rate.

Third, the shift in identity of women from mothers/wives to economic agents in the development policy discussions also resonated with the second wave of the women's movement in the 1970s. The liberal feminist agenda and call for action, particularly in the US, traced the source of gender inequality to the gender norms and stereotypes that confined women to the home and to their roles as mothers and wives. Accordingly, the solution for gender inequality was to remove the legal and institutional barriers to women's education, training, and employment. Activists emphasized equity as the key goal of the women's movement and this was pursued on many fronts through legal changes.

Fourth, shifts in economic development thinking in the 1970s also contributed to the reshaping of the gender and development research. These shifts emanated from the realization that pursuit of economic growth implemented through industrialization policies in the 1950s and 1960s did not improve the lives of the majority of people in developing countries. The search for alternative approaches produced the Basic Needs Approach (BNA) spearheaded by the International Labour Office (ILO) in 1976, which drew attention to alleviating rural poverty through investments in social and physical infrastructure. The BNA brought attention to rural women's poverty and catalyzed research on rural women's work and gender division of labor in agricultural households. It also raised issues of redistribution and the need to combine economic growth with equity objectives. This emphasis also resonated with the equity and efficiency argument of WID proponents in shaping development policy.

Fifth, Ester Boserup's *Woman's Role in Economic Development* heavily influenced the emergence and growth of the field. Boserup rejected the narrow view of women as mothers and wives and highlighted the wide range of productive work performed by women in developing countries and called for policy attention to increase women's productivity. As Tinker (1990: 30) put it, Boserup "legitimized efforts to influence development policy with the combined argument for justice and efficiency." Boserup's book became an inspiration for much of the work that followed on these issues in the 1970s and early 1980s. She raised the major problems affecting women's condition in the developing world—from questions related to the gender division of labor across sectors, countries, and regions to the undercounting of women's work in domestic and unpaid activities, and the exclusion of women from industrial employment.

Boserup's contributions are encapsulated in two themes that run through her book: she sought to show that (1) gender division of labor is a social category that varies by place and changes over time; and (2) women were harmed by the process of modernization; they were either left behind relative to men and/or experienced an absolute loss in status over time. With respect to the first theme, Boserup produced a sector-by-sector examination of gender division of labor based on the very limited data available. In agricultural production she distinguished between the farming systems in Sub-Saharan Africa and South Asia. Through her discussion of what she referred to as the "female-farming system" in Africa she challenged the assumption that men everywhere are the providers of food. She also examined how the gender division of work changed over time, highlighting how growing population pressure on land and colonial administrations' prejudices on who should be the farmer resulted in a transition from female- to male-farming system in many parts of Africa.

Boserup's diagnosis of the forces underlying this change also illustrates the second theme in the book: that the modernization of farming (or industry, services) did not benefit women. For her, women's marginalization in the development process was the only shortcoming of an otherwise beneficial process characteristic of the colonial and postcolonial era.[4] Guided by their own gender values, she argued, colonial policymakers introduced plough agriculture and cash crops to men, trained men, and gave land titles to men. As a result, men became the farmers and women became helpers and lost status.[5] In her view, the cause of economic inequality between women and men was productivity differences: the less productive the work one performs, the lower one's income will be.

Boserup noted that a similar process of marginalization occurred in the course of industrialization, whereby women who lost their jobs in traditional manufacturing were not hired in modern manufacturing enterprises. Hers was a comment on the track record of the inward-looking strategy of import-substitution industrialization that drew upon the male labor force, with the exception of a few industries, such as textiles and food processing. Recent evaluations of this history support Boserup's observations on the gender effects of early industrialization across countries, for example, Chile, Uruguay, Malaysia, Taiwan, and Korea (Berik et al. 2008). Boserup's analysis showed the decline in women's share of employment with industrialization—a process commonly referred to as "defeminization" in the contemporary gender and development discourse. With the increasing reliance on women's labor in export manufacturing in developing economies after the late 1970s Boserup's argument was replaced by the feminization U-hypothesis that posits a decline first and subsequent increase in women's labor force participation with the rise in the average income level of a country. This hypothesis continues to be examined in the economic histories of the US and Western Europe as well as in contemporary developing country contexts (Goldin 1995; Çağatay and Özler 1995; Humphries and Sarasúa 2012; Kucera and Tejani 2014). More recently, defeminization of industrial labor has reappeared in contexts where industrial upgrading took place or there was a large inflow of low-wage male labor, such as for example the decrease in the proportion of women in Korea's and Taiwan's export sectors or in Mexico's maquiladora industry.

In her discussion of rural–urban migration Boserup also discussed its effect on women's work. In urban settings women were unable to continue subsistence work, which was replaced by a narrower range of domestic tasks. She problematized the omission from labor force statistics of subsistence activities, which led to the statistical invisibility of much of women's work. The questions she raised initiated subsequent feminist work on the "Accounting Project" that extended the concerns about undercounting from subsistence work to domestic labor, volunteer work, and informal work (Benería 1981).

The upshot of Boserup's analysis of changes in gender division of labor was that in all sectors of the economy men advanced in modern activities, while women were left behind in the traditional, lower productivity sectors. As a result, women's and men's productivity, income, outlook, and attitudes diverged. Boserup called for state attention to integrate women in development. Her emphasis was on education and training of women so that they would close the gap with men in productivity.[6] She argued that the failure to utilize women's productive work would amount to inefficient resource use. This line of thinking later evolved into the "efficiency" approach that characterized the work of some international organizations and became mainstream at the turn of the twenty-first century. For example, the 2006 World Bank Gender Action Plan (GAP) argued the "business case for expanding women's economic opportunities . . . [which] is nothing more than smart economics" (World Bank 2006: 2).

Institutionalization of WID: The UN, CEDAW, and the Equity Agenda

The women's movement was the force that propelled the institutionalization of the field of gender and development in the 1970s and beyond. It has continued to influence the work of grassroots non-governmental organizations and generated the multiple international networks that contributed to the impressive increase in awareness regarding women's condition and gender inequality across countries. The movement was instrumental in shaping the pioneering WID-inspired foreign assistance programs of the US that included the condition that US foreign aid be used to promote integration of women in development. Also far reaching was the UN's role in the institutionalization of research on gender and development. The UN spearheaded research efforts through its agencies, particularly through the Division for the Advancement of Women (DAW), United Nations Fund for Women (UNIFEM) and UN International Research and Training Institute for the Advancement of Women (INSTRAW) (Pietilä and Vickers 1990). These agencies were integrated into a single organization, UN Women, in 2010.

Perhaps the UN's most visible effort reflecting the pressure from the global women's movement at the international and domestic levels was the organization of the UN Decade of Women conferences that sprang from Mexico City in 1975 to Copenhagen in 1980, Nairobi in 1985, followed by Beijing in 1995. These conferences served as powerful mechanisms for consciousness raising to discuss women's condition and concerns worldwide and to set agendas at the international level. They provided important venues for women activists, feminists, scholars, and practitioners from different backgrounds to discuss and debate the priorities and direction of economic development. Amidst these debates, the 1995 UN World Conference on Women produced the Beijing Declaration and Platform for Action that provided an overarching agenda to serve the goal of "empowerment of all women" and "the full realization of all human rights and fundamental freedom of all women" (UN 1996: 21). These conferences also helped strengthen the combined argument for efficiency and equity, as equity arguments faced resistance by national bureaucracies (Razavi and Miller 1995). Gender issues were also at center stage at other world conferences organized by the UN, such as the 1994 Cairo conference on population, and the Vienna conference on human rights in 1993. By the end of the twentieth century, practically all UN agencies had incorporated gender-related research and programs in their specific areas of work—from the ILO to UNFPA, UNRISD, FAO, and the UNDP.

Similarly, the UN was the forum that brought countries together to adopt the Convention on the Elimination of all Forms of Discrimination Against Women (CEDAW) in 1979, which entered into force as an international treaty in 1981. CEDAW represents the culmination of decades of efforts to elaborate from women's perspective the Universal Declaration of Human Rights adopted by the UN General Assembly in 1948. CEDAW reflects principles consistent with the equity emphasis of WID. Often described as "a bill of rights for women," since 1979 CEDAW has served as the main vehicle for promoting gender equality internationally (Simmons 2009; Byrnes and Freeman 2012).

Unusually for an international convention, CEDAW covers not only rights in the public sphere but also those in private life: the right to non-discrimination and rights related to marriage and family relations, which asserted the equal rights and obligations of men and women with regards to choice of spouse, parenthood, personal rights, and command over property. CEDAW also pioneered the reproductive rights of women, which specify what it means to have equal rights with respect to family formation and planning. The Convention's preamble emphasized that "the role of women in procreation should not be a basis for discrimination."[7] Family planning and fertility control was an area of rights that became the subject of much debate in the UN International Conference on Population and Development in Cairo in 1994.

CEDAW upholds equal rights of women and men before the law—formal equality—as the prerequisite for achieving equality of outcomes. In doing so, CEDAW promotes the same values of equality everywhere and does not leave policy open to cultural interpretation that may restrict women's rights. However, CEDAW goes beyond a call for formal equality. Some articles specify the means to achieving equality. Article 11, for example, points out that to achieve gender equality, creating a non-discriminatory legal environment is not enough; state policies have to support couples by providing access to childcare and paid maternity leave so as to remove pregnancy and childcare as obstacles to achieving equal opportunity in employment. The concept of equality underlying CEDAW is thus based on recognition of the biological difference of women and men, but one that seeks to ensure that this difference is not a basis of unequal treatment. Article 4 stipulates that any affirmative-action type measures—referred to in CEDAW as "temporary or special measures"—that will necessitate different treatment of women and men should not be considered discriminatory to men, making explicit that these are measures on the path to equality and they are implemented to make up for the effects of past discrimination against women. In addition, CEDAW Committee's General Recommendations to national governments are important in raising attention to issues on broader aspects of the treaty, even though they are not part of the treaty, for example, violence against women raised in its General Recommendation No. 19 of 1992.

By ratifying CEDAW countries commit to a process of bringing their national laws in conformity with CEDAW. However, CEDAW's reach beyond the usual political, economic, and education areas and into the realm of family and cultural practices resulted in many countries placing "reservations" on certain of its articles and some have yet to ratify CEDAW.[8] As of late 2014, 187 countries had ratified the Convention and the remaining seven are an odd group consisting of Islamic Republic of Iran, Somalia, Sudan, South Sudan, Tonga, Palau, and the US.[9] A reservation on an article meant that the country is not able to comply with that aspect of CEDAW, which in some cases are contrary to the Convention itself.[10] Despite the reservation loophole, the CEDAW process—the regular reviews of country performance on

CEDAW articles—has put countries under the international spotlight, and opened up the political space for local activists to push for change in national laws and to raise awareness about gender equality questions. As a result, several countries have changed their national laws to reflect principles of gender equality and lifted reservations on CEDAW. Recent evidence finds support for a positive "CEDAW effect" in the area of political and, to a lesser extent, social rights of women (Engelhart and Miller 2014).

Ultimately, the effect of CEDAW depends on the enforcement of these laws and the implementation process at the national level. Since governments are responsive to majorities and will rarely take steps that will upset their values or sensibilities, a key roadblock to implementing CEDAW or other international treaties is the persistent patriarchal values and norms that permeate economic, political, and social life. As with any example of the legal approach towards social change, to attain significant progress towards gender equality a critical mass in a society has to embrace the ideals underlying the laws. Thus, critical to making its principles a reality is to promote "CEDAW literacy" and consciousness raising, which entails making sure that women and men even in remote areas become aware of their rights and of their being equal under this UN Convention.

With regards to the agenda-setting efforts carried out by the UN over the years, the 1993 international conference on human rights in Vienna was another important event. Under the slogan of "women's rights are human rights," it became a comprehensive step to emphasize women's rights in general. As in the case of the passage of CEDAW, the debates on gender issues in the Vienna and Cairo conferences were a reflection of the influence that feminism and the women's movement had acquired over the years with regards to the discourse on human rights affecting women and the call for equality.

The WID agenda of the 1970s and 1980s also set in motion the establishment of "WID units" and programs by national governments. These units tended to focus on women-only projects isolated from the regular policy agendas of government ministries. The women-only economic activities that were often implemented with donor funds tended to "misbehave" in the sense that they were marginal efforts that ended up not being economically sustainable (Buvinić 1986). The efforts to "mainstream gender" were partly a response to these problems.

From WID to WAD to GAD

In contrast to the WID perspective, a more critical view of the development process, both from a socio-economic and a feminist perspective, unfolded in the late 1970s. Focusing on questions inspired by feminism, Marxism, and the New Left, this perspective represented a critical view of both mainstream economic analysis, its economic growth model and modernization theories, and capitalism and class inequalities. This approach, referred to as "Women and Development," or WAD, was not only concerned with raising productivity and earnings of women but also in laying bare the socio-economic exploitation that affects women and men, albeit in different ways (Deere 1977; Croll 1979; Elson and Pearson 1981; Benería 1979; Benería and Sen 1982; Sen and Grown 1987). Proponents of WAD pointed out that the WID arguments were often made without questioning the economic system that generated gender inequalities. In contrast to the WID approach, the WAD approach saw the need for structural change and transformation of the development process itself, for example, through redistribution of wealth and creation of decent employment, in order to attain gender equality.

The systematic evaluation of Boserup's work by Benería and Sen (1981) illustrated the methodological differences of this critical perspective from the WID approach, and partially laid out the conceptual foundation of what would become Gender and Development (GAD) perspective in the field. Benería and Sen argued that Boserup did not explain colonialism's impact sufficiently. Colonialism was more than a value system; it was an economic system designed to promote capital accumulation, which caused class differentiation. This process, which Boserup saw as beneficial to men, for example the introduction of cash crop agriculture, in fact left many men behind as well. It was colonial policy that confined Africans to small areas, which made it difficult to produce enough food and forced them to either work the land more intensively or migrate to search for work. Moreover, Boserup's sole focus on changes in the sphere of production (farm work) was insufficient to explain how women's social status changed with capitalist development. And in a context where whole families were becoming landless and being pushed off the land her proposed solution to close education gender gaps was insufficient. What good would teaching better techniques to women subsistence farmers do, they argued; this solution was like "treating cancer with a bandaid" (p. 287).

Benería and Sen (1982) articulated an alternative conceptual framework to generate a more adequate explanation of how and why the capitalist development process affects women and men differently. Using some of the conceptualization at the time, they called for framing the explanations in terms of the concepts of capital accumulation and reproduction. The concept of capital accumulation would provide insights into the uneven and disruptive social (class) differentiation process underway in a given society undergoing capitalist development and help identify the uneven effects on the gender division of labor. Development, in this perspective, is not a linear process of growth, but one that dispossesses a large majority from their means of livelihood, except for their labor power, and concentrates wealth in the hands of the few.

In addition, Benería and Sen argued that the concept of reproduction was needed to draw attention to the reproductive labor of women and its relationship to paid labor. Reproduction encompasses activities that go beyond childbearing to include childrearing and the provisioning of care to ensure the daily and intergenerational reproduction of family sustenance and of the labor force. Given that historically women have been concentrated in these areas, they argued that the different ways in which the processes of capital accumulation and production impinge upon the sphere of reproduction are highly relevant to understanding women's status in society, gender roles, and inequality.

The concept of reproduction was part of the framework of the social reproduction approach that dated back to Frederick Engels and was especially developed by feminists in the 1970s. In the Preface to *The Origin of the Family, Private Property and the State* of 1884, Engels emphasized the two-fold character of social life. He argued that the analysis of social change would be incomplete if it only focused on production of goods and services for subsistence or the market, without analyzing the evolution of institutions concerned with reproduction, such as the family and the division of labor in the household (Engels [1884] 1981).[11] Along these lines, feminist theory has contributed extensively to emphasizing women's key role in social reproduction and the care economy (Picchio 1992; Folbre 1994).

Methodologically, WAD and early GAD theorists insisted on a contextual analysis of impacts of capitalist development processes on women's lives that did not allow for easy generalizations. Benería and Sen, for example, argued that general conclusions could not be reached on whether development intensifies women's work, brings loss of control of land, generates migration, or weakens patriarchal control. These questions required a specific analysis of the nature of capitalist development in context. Similarly, Elson and Pearson (1981) examined the impact of work in export factories on women's subordinate social status in terms of a framework that allowed for contradictory effects.

Beyond the broad concepts of capital accumulation and reproduction, Benería and Sen (1981) argued that an analysis of the development process had to be attentive to gender and social class differences. In the early 1980s researchers' emphasis was on the intersection of gender and social class, which later expanded to include race/ethnicity and other forms of identity such as sexual orientation. The category women, central to the WID approach, concealed the diversity of experiences of women and left out of consideration the experiences of children and men. Gender relations needed to be part of the focus, whether captured in terms of gender division of labor or of resources. In addition, Benería and Sen argued that women's (as well as men's) experiences vary by social class and give rise to the concrete meaning of gender. In turn, these differing experiences result in differing interests, which have implications for political organization. If poor women's lives were marked by overwork and undernourishment, the authors asked, how could these women be assumed to share similar experiences with well-off women and unite around common goals?

According to Benería and Sen (1982), the strategy to address the inequalities generated by capitalist development is to tackle the ill-health and overwork consequences for poor women. Through self-organization poor women could fight for immediate policy changes to benefit themselves in their daily lives (such as infrastructure investments). Pursuit of goals to alleviate immediate hardship is a prerequisite for questioning broader inequalities in the social order and long-term radical transformation of society (to create more egalitarian institutions and economic system). GAD theorists further fleshed out the short-term policy goals and long-term goals of social transformation by differentiating between "practical" (more immediate) gender needs/interests of women and the "strategic" (long-term) gender needs/interests (Molyneux 1985; Moser 1989).

This strategy for change was emphasized by Sen and Grown (1987) who articulated the vision of a group of developing country scholars, practitioners, and activists who formed Development Alternatives for Women for a New Era (DAWN).[12] The DAWN perspective went beyond the goal of gender equality to question the nature of development and the domination of developing countries by rich economies. These authors argued that development policies must be conceived, revised, and evaluated from the perspective of poor women in the Third World, since this group of women is the largest and most disadvantaged group.[13] In addition, they argued that change that improves the lives of this group of women can only come from such a bottom up mobilization of Third World women's organizations and global activism.

The Challenges from Postmodernism and Women of the Global South

Can there be a homogenous group of "Third World women" or "poor Third World women," who in turn can push for changes in the strategy of economic development? This was the challenge posed by Aiwa Ong (1987) and Chandra Mohanty (1988) and other feminists from the global South to those engaged in issues of gender and development. The answer of both groups was a resounding "no," but their arguments differed.

The postmodern critics argued there could be no general, coherent category "Third World woman." They also challenged structural approaches and the 1970s paradigms that relied on general categories such as "patriarchy" and "capitalism." They rejected essentialism in the concepts used, and questioned the use of general concepts—such as "labor," "gender division of labor" or "production"—and the previously assumed connections between economic structure and the socio-economic conditions affecting women and men.

The unfolding of postmodernism was a key turning point in feminist theory. The postmodern challenge had its sources in the profound changes that feminist theory underwent in the mid-1980s. One influential source was feminist theorists' call for a deeper understanding of the social construction of gender. Scott (1986) argued that gender involved culturally available symbols, normative concepts that set forth interpretations of gender meanings, kinship systems, and subjective identity. The all-encompassing nature of these elements led her to argue that "gender is everywhere." Scott's emphasis on the notion of gender as a way of denoting "cultural constructions" became dominant in feminism's shift towards cultural studies. Another influence was the feminist emphasis on intersectional analysis, which emphasized the connections between gender and other dimensions of identity, including social class, race, ethnicity, and sexual identity, which GAD researchers increasingly emphasized.

When their work engaged with countries of the global South, many postmodern critics identified as "postcolonial" theorists, albeit another entry point to postcolonialism was a critique of Western conceptualizations of gender and gender equality. The work of feminist postcolonialist scholars such as Zein-Elabdin and Charusheela (2004), for example, assessed the predominantly Western perspective in the developmentalist and feminist approaches' interpretation of non-Western women's situation and experiences. They argued that Western (or Western-influenced) women tend to adopt the modernist organization of society as the norm for development and such an approach fails to provide appropriate solutions to the problem of gender subordination in non-Western societies.[14]

In this vein, Ong, Mohanty, and later Parpart and Marchand (1995) questioned the WID and critical gender and development studies of the 1970s and 1980s for their Western, middle-class feminist presuppositions. The feminist critics of WID (that is, the proponents of WAD) were also lumped together in this postcolonial critique, despite their attention to class differences among women. Mohanty argued that the writing on women in developing countries gave rise to a coherent image of Third World women with certain negative attributes. Accordingly, the Third World woman was a poor, dependent, passive, oppressed, uneducated, helpless, tradition-bound victim. Her implicit counterpart was the First World/Western woman, a representation that was similarly homogenized: she was independent, well-off, educated, autonomous, liberated. The dichotomy was characterized by the superiority of the First World woman. She was the norm, the role model by which progress for the Third World woman could be gauged. Mohanty argued that this image was generated discursively, via common textual strategies used by WID and WAD researchers. For example, whenever authors referred to the impact of some factor on women—such as economic development, Islam, the family structure—this, according to postcolonial critics, reduced Third World women to object status, taking away their agency.

Postcolonial critics also problematized the attempts to document the extensiveness of Third World women's powerlessness through the "arithmetic method." For example, based on their wearing the veil and the presumption that the veil denoted powerlessness, veiled Muslim women were assumed to be oppressed and powerless. In addition, Mohanty and other postcolonial theorists argued that the use of general concepts in gender analysis, such as labor, gender division of labor, and justice, created a distorted image of Third World women's experiences. Such theoretical entry points presumed universal explanations and a reality that was not necessarily one experienced by any particular group of women.

Postcolonial critics argued that these representations have consequences. The generalizations do not do justice to the complexity of Third World women (that is, differences among them by class, ethnicity, nationality, age, and cultural differences). Moreover, the characteristic images "colonize" Third World women; they stifle Third World women's agency and knowledge and perpetuate the domination of the West over the Third World. The images, they argued, are used to legitimate the need for rich country interventions in the affairs of developing countries and to promote control by and dependence on rich country experts and technical aid (Parpart and Marchand 1995; Parpart 1995). These images bolster arguments in favor of policies to educate, civilize, and liberate women, for example, through Western models of development, foreign interventions, and foreign aid, which can be harmful, according to postmodernists. In addition, given the messages of superiority of Western women and inferiority of Third World women implied by the imagery, Mohanty (1988) also argued that these representations make it more difficult for Third World women's groups to form political coalitions with Western women's groups and thus they stand in the path of global feminist activism.

Postmodern critics favored a research approach that was more characteristic of the discipline of anthropology—ethnographic research—that is attentive to the concrete realities, indigenous knowledge, and local expertise of women. They called for the discovery of the experiences of Third World women through careful, locally grounded, small-scale case studies with due attention to power, meaning, and differences. This meant emphasis on differences among women and the multiple identities that shape women's lives. Mohanty held Maria Mies's study of lacemakers in Narsapur (India) as exemplary in this regard, in its focus on a specific caste of women, in a specific location (Mies 1982). Yet, while Mies's study fit many features that are attractive to postmodern critics, as Udayagiri (1995) pointed out, it defied other postmodern tenets, such as the use of a Marxist-feminist framework and associated general categories of analysis. Even the book's subtitle engages in the dreaded totalization of women's experiences in India and posits an essentialized world market by referring to "Indian Housewives Produce for the World Market."

While agreeing with many postmodern critiques of WID, many women scholars from the global South raised doubts about the promise of post-modernism in helping forge national and international political movements and in bringing about social change. Of particular concern was the post-modern focus on deconstruction and struggle in the terrain of representation. While useful regarding issues of identity and corresponding struggles, such as within the gay and indigenous movements, struggles over representation did not help in addressing the immediate crises and social problems experienced in either high-income or low-income countries. Udayagiri (1995) raised the difficulty of building coalitions on the basis of a theoretical position that views women's experiences as local and contextual. A prerequisite for feminist political movements, Udayagiri argued, is Third World women's mobilization around a shared sense of injustice. She also pointed out that postmodernism was not the only approach to guide understanding of local and contextual experiences of people, and that many scholars and activists from the global South were already emphasizing attention to difference and context.

Indeed, as early as the first UN Conference on Women held in Mexico City, feminists from the South highlighted the importance of differentiating women on the basis of their locational setting and background. Feminists from Africa, Latin America and the Caribbean, and Asia sought to understand the dynamics of gender within the context of their countries whose socio-political and economic structures were shaped by colonial legacies (Ahmed 1992; Berger 1995; Mills and Ssewakiryanga 2002). Hence, women's situation in the development process and their struggle against patriarchal norms needed to be understood as part of the broader struggle against the forces of colonialism and neo (post)-colonialism. Zein-Elabdin (1999), for example, noted that there are significant historical and cultural contrasts between women and men in Ghana, Somalia, and South Africa, which require careful application of feminist concepts and development frameworks in each case.

There is need to take into account the diversity of women's experiences on the basis of their class, ethnicity, race, and nationality. Some Southern feminist scholars have brought particular attention to the need for understanding the local interpretations and meaning of gender and have enriched the gender and development discourse.

Another concise response from the South to postmodernism came from Maria Nzomo (1995), an activist in Kenya's democratic movement. Nzomo argued that, contrary to postmodernism's insistence on generating knowledge from the particular local level, Kenyan activists should be able to appeal to universal ideals of democracy in their fight for equality and to adapt them to the Kenyan context, rather than reinventing democratic ideals. Having universal ideals is important, she argued, to show that Kenyan women are demanding what is accepted as goals everywhere.

Nzomo also cautioned that postmodernism's insistence on attention to differences among women can undermine collective action, which Parpart and Marchand (1995) concede is a danger. Nzomo argued that emphasis on difference would fuel divisions among women who come from different backgrounds and have different interests, rather than uniting them around shared goals. Relatedly, Nzomo was concerned about postmodernism's objection to representing poverty as a key concern of Kenyan women on grounds that all Kenyan women are not poor. She argued that one could make the case that poverty is the most pressing problem affecting most women (even women married to rich husbands, should their marriages fail).

Other critics argued that postmodern rejection of universal moral principles could lead to condoning questionable age-old practices that are harmful to women (Udayagiri 1995). In a similar vein, Moghissi (1999) problematized the relativist positions that emerged from postmodernism in the context of Islamization of societies. As they sought to validate women's experiences, she argued, postmodernist critics softened the harsh daily reality experienced by women, colluding with Islamic fundamentalist views about women's lives as culturally authentic. The irony of speaking on behalf of Third World women and criticizing their colonization in WID and WAD writings while writing in opaque prose also did not escape the critics of postmodern critics (Udayagiri 1995).

In spite of these shortcomings, postmodernism has strongly influenced not only the humanities and literary fields but also the social sciences. The undermining of formerly stable categories of analysis, such as labor, gender division of labor, reproduction, opened up new questions about the most effective way of theorizing, doing research, and promoting action on gender inequality. Most notably, postmodernism shifted the emphasis from material to cultural issues. As Barrett (1999) pointed out, the role of the material in feminism was replaced by the new emphasis on culture, meaning, and identity, which implied that the social sciences lost out to the humanities in academic work. In Nancy Fraser's terms, issues of "representation"—such as identity, discourse analysis, and citizenship—took priority over economic questions, including issues of redistribution (Fraser 1997).

At the same time, recognition of the importance of understanding "the material" did not diminish, despite the postmodern influence within feminism. This interest, in fact, explains the growth of feminist economics with the birth of the International Association for Feminist Economics (IAFFE) in 1992. Even so, postmodern sensibilities influenced many feminist economist critics of mainstream economics. As discussed in Chapter 2, feminist economists sought ways of integrating the different streams of feminist thought, a task that has required an important effort to develop interdisciplinary analysis by finding commonalities between the disciplines and the crossing of boundaries with respect to gender analysis (Ferber and Nelson 2003a; 1993). The influence of postcolonial thought was also felt in feminist activism. For example, in Latin America where feminism had originally been connected to leftist parties, there was a shift away from political parties and towards more specific feminist politics that made gender inequality at all levels more central. Understanding gender relations and gender constructions, the emphasis on identity and cultural norms, together with North–South differences, became the target of a strong re-affirmation of feminisms from the South (Kapadia 2002; Saunders 2002).

The postmodern influence continues to be felt, and is "mainstreamed" in contemporary commentary on representations of Third World women. With increasing violence against women globally and increasing awareness of extreme constraints on lives of women in various parts of the world, in countries such as Sudan, Afghanistan, India, and Yemen, the postmodern caution against sensationalizing women's lives is ever present, while at the same time serving as reminders of the differing concerns and priorities of women. But do these cautionary notes downplay the harsh realities experienced by women? Where do they lead in terms of the political agenda for promoting well-being in an equitable manner?

One highly contentious area that continues to have political implications is the veil, in its various forms, that is worn by Muslim women. Echoing Mohanty's critique, in "Do Muslim Women Really Need Saving?" Abu-Lughod (2002) problematized the use of Afghan women's dress in arguments to justify the US invasion of Afghanistan. In the post-9/11 era the oppression of Afghan women under Taliban rule was prominently featured as one justification for the Afghan war. Abu-Lughod argued that the veil, in and of itself, did not represent the unfreedom of Afghan women. After enumerating a number of arguments on what the veil does and represents[15] and explaining the mode of its use in the pro-invasion discourse, she proposed an ethic of respect for different gender norms.[16] For Abu-Lughod the veil is a trivial matter; Afghan women do/did not need to be "saved" on account of the veil; any strategy for improving women's lives in distant lands had to address the crushing conditions of daily poverty that is the most pressing problem and the product of the history of the country. Her argument thus prioritizes alleviating the constraints of poverty in women's lives while downplaying the constraints associated with the veil; this position discourages activism on all goals other than poverty reduction and issues of representation.

A similar argument is made by Kabeer (2004) who presents an argument that foregrounds the power of representations of Third World women. In her critique of the representation of women export workers in the US media that are used to justify implementing international minimum standards on working conditions, she calls for examination of women workers' own views of the meaning of export factory employment. This "view from below" shows a more complex picture of benefits for women in a context where women have virtually no job alternatives. Sure there are problems with working conditions, Kabeer argues, but the jobs in question offer benefits for women that should not be overlooked and these jobs should not be endangered by any scheme designed to improve their quality. Similar to Abu-Lughod, Kabeer emphasizes poverty reduction as the goal for action in low-income countries; short of that, she suggests, not much can be done to alleviate the problem of poor working conditions, without hurting women's employment. While Kabeer promotes policies to reduce poverty (through funding a universal floor for incomes), postmodern authors tend to not problematize conditions of poverty or other deprivations experienced by women. Nor do they take up how these deprivations might be reduced. This type of argument shirks from applying a universal yardstick to identify what is wrong with the conditions observed; and its paralyzing effect on solidaristic international political action is one legacy of postmodernism.

Nonetheless, postmodern and postcolonial feminism has had an important influence on recent gender and development research. Now, researchers address economic problems that affect the lives of women and men in developing countries with greater sensitivity to postmodern critiques. Specifically, there is greater caution in making generalizations, greater attention to the local context, and the voices of women themselves, and greater sensitivity to explaining experiences and goals from a variety of perspectives. We believe that these features of the postmodern/postcolonial critique are invaluable if they are combined with a normative framework for evaluating well-being in order to strengthen the potential of gender and development research in promoting social justice. As explained below, the capabilities approach complemented by the human rights arguments provides such a normative framework. In addition, as discussed in Chapter 2, with its roots in the WAD approach, feminist economics provides the key conceptual framework necessary to guide policy to promote gender equitable livelihoods and well-being. Specifically, feminist economists' attention to issues of social reproduction and the sustainability of human life provides an important framework with which to approach multiple crises—financial, economic, political, ethical, and ecological—facing the world today.

The Rise and Rise of Neoliberal Policies[17]

The end of the 1970s and early 1980s marked a shift away from the Keynesian approach in macroeconomics to a free-market approach in mainstream economics that was favored by ascendant conservative political and economic forces. With the arrival of neoliberal economic policies on the global scene, a good proportion of the gender and development research, in particular from a GAD perspective, focused its attention on the gendered impacts of these policies.

Keynesian economics entailed reliance on fiscal and monetary policies and government regulation to promote employment, economic growth, and stability. This approach was influential in guiding development strategies in many high-income and low-income countries in the 1950s and 1960s, in the latter through an emphasis on import-substitution industrialization and public investment. However, Keynesianism appeared to be unable to address the inflation and unemployment problems in high-income economies in the aftermath of the oil-price hikes of the 1970s. In addition, ascendant conservative voices in the North deemed it responsible for the unsustainable domestic and external debt amassed by low-income countries.

These perceived failures ushered in the policy shift to what are variously known as "supply-side," "free-market," "neoliberal" policies. The shift also had a strong ideological component. The proponents of neoliberal policies argued that economic growth was impeded by the heavy-handed role of the government and that the solution was to give free reign to markets in operating the economy. The standard neoliberal policies consist of deregulation of the economy, privatization of public enterprises, government budget cuts, trade liberalization and export orientation of the economy, together with openness to foreign investment and financial flows. Each of these policies was intended to reduce the balance of payments problems faced by developing countries and to rein in the runaway domestic debt and associated inflation problem. In developing countries, their implementation through Structural Adjustment Policies (SAPs) resulted in recessions and stagnation everywhere, adversely affecting the livelihoods of low-income groups and increasing poverty. In Latin America and Sub-Saharan Africa, it resulted in the "lost decade" of the 1980s and 1990s. Proponents argued that stagnation was only a temporary effect that would give way to vigorous growth once the economy adjusted to the new rules.

In high-income countries neoliberal policies were first adopted in Anglo-Saxon countries such as the US, UK, and Canada, after the election of conservative governments in the 1980s. In low-income countries the early adopters were Argentina (under the generals), Chile (under Pinochet), and the Philippines (under Marcos) in the 1970s, Mexico and Bolivia in the early 1980s, while other countries followed soon, mostly under the pressures of the "Washington Consensus." In many African and Latin American countries SAPs were imposed as a solution to the debt crises of the 1980s. In some countries, such as Turkey and the Philippines, the suspension of democratic rule and declaration of martial law proved to be a prerequisite for their implementation. In some Latin American countries, austerity measures were adopted by governments during and after the end of military rule, which justified them as a way to accompany pro-market reforms. Even as the debt crisis lost its importance towards the end of the twentieth century, neoliberal policies continued and became the new normal in macroeconomic policy regime for developed and developing countries alike, with global financial institutions—the World Bank, the IMF, the European Central Bank—acting as enforcers of these policies.

Feminist Critiques of Neoliberal Policies

As soon as the social costs of SAPs began to be felt in Asia, Latin America, and Africa, it became clear that they had specific gender dimensions. Along with critics such as Cornia, Jolly, and Stewart (1987), feminist economists provided critical evaluation of the social costs of adjustment from a gender and class perspective (Elson 1991b; Benería and Feldman 1992; Çağatay et al. 1995). In fact, the effort to understand the specific effects of SAPs on women led to a new understanding of macroeconomic policy as non neutral with respect to gender. Studies of SAPs showed that the social costs of adjustment were not shared equally among different social groups, and by women and men in particular (Elson 1991b; Sparr 1994; Benería 1999a). For women, SAPs and austerity policies have often generated an intensification of their unpaid work when budget cuts result in diminished public services or their deterioration while family income decreased. Given that these policies also tend to increase women's participation in the labor force, they also contribute to the problems of reconciling unpaid workload with labor market work. Likewise, analysis by feminists of the post-2008 crisis has showed similar gender effects (Benería and Martinez-Iglesias 2014; Elson 2012a; Antonopoulos 2013; Albelda 2014).

In addition, as we discuss in detail in the chapters that follow, the feminist literature produced critical information about the effects of globalization and a range of macroeconomic policies, such as trade and fiscal policy (Seguino 2000a; Berik 2000; Van Staveren et al. 2007). These studies gave impetus to work on measurement of unpaid work and gender budgeting initiatives (Floro and Messier 2010; Floro and Komatsu 2011; Budlender 2000; Sharp and Broomhill 2002). Some UN organizations, such as UNICEF, the ILO, INSTRAW, and UNRISD, have also provided critical analysis of neoliberal policies. Much of this research bears the hallmarks of the GAD approach, which questioned the predominant distribution and redistribution of resources and also placed emphasis on social policies that deal not only with gender inequality but also class, ethnic, and other forms of inequality.

At the same time, the feminist literature has subjected these policies to the scrutiny of human rights criteria. Balakrishnan and Elson (2011) use the economic and social rights enshrined in the Universal Declaration of Human Rights of 1948 and subsequent international human rights covenants and conventions to construct alternative criteria for assessing the effectiveness of macroeconomic policies.[18] Key economic and social rights are the right to work; right to rest; right to adequate standard of living; right to education, by which all governments have to abide.[19] The principles necessary to uphold these economic rights involve commitment to promoting them in an equitable manner by raising adequate funding for programs to ensure the government's compliance with its international obligations.[20] Balakrishnan and Elson evaluate macroeconomic policies—fiscal, trade, and monetary policies—to determine whether a government is promoting the right to health.[21]

When economic and social rights are used to assess macroeconomic policies, Balakrishnan and Elson (2011) and Elson (2012a) show that Mexico, the US, and the UK are doing poorly in meeting their international obligations. Elson (2002a; 2012a) argues that the evidence flies in the face of the neoliberal presumption that reducing the role of the state while expanding the private sector would boost efficiency and growth and give substance to human rights. Quite to the contrary, she argues, the most basic economic rights provided in the UN Declaration and later covenants ratified by many countries have suffered from the results of deregulation of markets, privatization, austerity measures, and the implementation of other neoliberal dictates.

The most recent entry point to the feminist critique of neoliberal policies has been provided by the literature that focuses on the 2007–08 financial crisis and its consequences, particularly in countries where the crisis has generated high levels of unemployment and where austerity policies have been adopted. This includes several European countries and, to a lesser extent, the United States and developing countries. The literature points out the gender effects of the crisis, including the dismantling of the welfare state through budget cuts, particularly in health and education, the reversal of policies regarding for example policies to reconcile family and labor market work, and the differential effects on women's and men's labor force participation.[22] We will return to these issues in later chapters.

In contrast to feminist critiques, the hegemonic neoliberal discourse has viewed the expansion of globalized production processes and global markets as positive for the empowerment of women and gender equality. The basic neoliberal argument with regard to gender equality is that the free market and deregulation at the national and global levels are important means in the pursuit of gender equality. And looking at the record of the 1980s and 1990s, it is apparent that in some respects feminist discourses and actions regarding women's needs and rights are compatible with the neoliberal order. Neoliberal globalization buoyed the trend towards feminization of the labor force in developing economies. Women's share of employment rose across sectors, most prominently in the informal sector and manufacturing sectors that produced for the world market (Chen and Carr 2004; Chen et al. 2005; Standing 1989). Women became the desirable workers for the export sector. In addition, women entered professions from which they had been largely absent, albeit they continued to face discrimination, glass ceilings, and new forms of employment segregation (Anker 1998; Seguino 2000b; Salzinger 2003; Rio and Alonso-Villar 2012). Women have also experienced much progress in education, including in countries where their educational levels had been traditionally low such as in the Middle East and North Africa. Although decline in gender education gaps was slow in translating into changes in the jobs most women held, some women have reached positions never held before—becoming country presidents, CEOs, legislators, and top administrators. At the same time, the large majority of women have remained at the lower levels of the labor hierarchy, earning poverty-income levels (see Chapters 3 and 4).

From a political perspective, the neoliberal approach has been accompanied by hegemonic discourses that associated "the market" with "democracy" and with the discourse of "freedom to choose" (Friedman and Friedman 1980). Since the 1980s there was fresh evidence for this association in many developing countries where political democracy or some form of electoral voting system was introduced along with neoliberal policies. Such was the case in Latin America where pro-market reforms were introduced by governments that followed the military regimes of the 1970s and 1980s, and where in some cases the transition to formal democracy was accompanied by continuation of neoliberal policies, such as in Argentina, Brazil, Chile, and Uruguay. For women, the new democracies ran parallel to their greater participation in economic and political life during the 1990s, a tendency that became particularly visible in the 2000s with the election of women presidents in Chile (2005), Argentina (2007), and Brazil (2010).

Thus, within the mainstream framework of neoliberalism, a number of feminist goals around women's autonomy, participation, and representation have been partially fulfilled and gender inequality has declined in some sectors and occupations as well as in some key dimensions, such as property rights for women (Deere and León de Leal 2001a; World Bank 2011). Gender mainstreaming was introduced in multilateral institutions and programs, even though their work has not always reflected feminist objectives. In general, the goals of gender equality have been promoted but without supporting agendas to reduce other forms of social inequality such as class.

Specifically, according to the neoliberal framework, gender equality is a goal to be pursued within the existing social structure and international economic order. In this respect, neoliberalism is consistent with liberal feminism, which does not question class differences and patterns of income and wealth distribution and their impact on political power. In the gender and development field, this position has been exemplified by the WID approach. The WID approach has been attentive to gender inequalities mainly in markets, for example, the gaps in labor force participation or unequal access to productive resources, and emphasizes market solutions to these inequities.

The Case of WDR 2012

An interesting illustration of the way mainstream economics has dealt with gender issues is provided by the World Bank's *World Development Report 2012, Gender Inequality and Development* (World Bank 2011). The WDR 2012 represents the culmination of the Bank's efforts to incorporate gender issues in its programs and is an extension of the "gender equality is smart economics" approach fleshed out under the World Bank's Gender Action Plan, which was carried out in 2007–11 to address gender concerns (World Bank 2006).[23]

The WDR 2012 represents a massive compendium of information on issues that are very relevant to analyze gender inequality—ranging over the links between development and gender equality, women's voice and agency, gender norms, employment, trade and globalization, public policy and "the political economy of reforms for gender equality"(p. 35). It takes a broad view of development by addressing its social dimensions and recognizing the role of cultural norms and social practices in the different positioning of women and men in society and in determining economic outcomes. But the report also illustrates the limits to addressing gender inequality within mainstream economics and a liberal framework. Typical of the mainstream approach, the report does not problematize nor mention the neoliberal macroeconomic policies that have increased class inequalities—with consequences for men and women—since the early 1980s. At the same time, the report views the forces associated with globalization very favorably on the basis that they "have operated through markets, formal institutions, and informal institutions to lift some of the constraints to greater gender inequality" (p. 256).

The WDR 2012 presents the Bank's most well-articulated argument to date in favor of reducing gender inequalities to achieve economic growth. It makes the standard two-fold case on the benefits to be gained from promoting gender equality: that it matters intrinsically and it makes economic sense. On the intrinsic argument, that gender matters "in its own right," the WDR 2012 references Amartya Sen's definition of "development as freedom" and emphasizes that this notion calls for the gender equitable expansion of freedoms. It also reminds readers that the pursuit of gender equality is part of international commitments of governments that are party to CEDAW and the Millennium Declaration.

Not surprisingly, given the World Bank's principal mission, the Report's emphasis is on the instrumental argument. In making the "gender equality is smart economics" cause the Report draws upon the rich gender-aware economics research, much of which was produced by feminist researchers in the 1990s and early 2000s, and supplements it with the World Bank's own research and commissioned background papers. There are four strands in the Bank's instrumental argument that gender equality makes economic sense. The first two emphasize direct efficiency gains. Accordingly, the Report argues that equal access to endowments (resources) and economic opportunities will increase productivity in both the short run and the long run. In the short run, output would increase if discrimination against girls and women in education, employment, and access to land and other productive inputs is reduced. Echoing Boserup, the Report suggests that more educated women, better equipped women farmers, and a greater number of women employees will contribute to greater efficiency and growth across economic sectors.

In the long run, gender equality is deemed important for improving the capabilities of the next generation. The WDR 2012 argues that if women have greater control over household resources, they are more likely to invest in children's health and education, which would boost future economic growth. Moreover, improving women's own education and health would improve child health and survival; educated mothers (and fathers) are more likely to seek immunizations for their children, provide better nutrition, and thereby improve the survival chances of their children. In addition, mothers who have more control over their lives are less likely to experience domestic violence; hence their children would be less likely to be exposed to violence in the home, which in turn reduces the likelihood of lifetime adverse consequences of this exposure for the next generation (for example, alcohol abuse, greater susceptibility to intimate partner violence, health problems).

The third argument in the World Bank's case for reducing gender inequality involves the value of the feminine touch in governance. The WDR 2012 recommends actions to reduce the gender gaps in power, particularly in decision-making in various institutions. It envisions benefits from individual or collective agency of women in making institutional change. This component of the argument also represents continuity from World Bank (2001), which anticipated positive impacts on governance of women's greater participation in political decisions. As a striking example, the Report points to evidence on the effect of political quotas at the village level in India whereby women representatives are both less susceptible to bribery and more likely to support the provision of public goods. While the examples of positive effects on governance are clear signs of win-win possibilities for promoting gender equality, nonetheless there are also other examples across countries that show that having a woman leader does not necessarily change the status quo policies—examples with which the Bank does not engage.

While the instrumental argument for investing in women and girls is always cast in terms of a win-win scenario, feminists point out that the efficiency argument threatens to eclipse the intrinsic argument for gender equality and for ending gender norms oppressive to women (Chant and Sweetman 2012). They question the extent to which promoting gender equality and women's empowerment is a priority, rather than facilitating "development 'on the cheap' and/or [promoting] further economic liberalization" (Chant 2012: 202). There are reasons to be skeptical: first, the WDR 2012 presents a limited agenda for change that focuses on micro- or sectoral-level policies, without regard for macroeconomic policy. Yet, neoliberal macroeconomic policy has not only been complicit in aggravating gender inequalities in the home and the market and destroying jobs, but also stands in the way of implementing the World Bank's own narrow agenda for reducing gender inequality (Berik and van der Meulen Rodgers 2012; Elson 2012b).[24] Second, the win-win rhetoric of the Report contrasts with the actual lived experience of women in poor households and communities (Chant and Sweetman 2012). Poor women's work burdens are on the rise as they are asked to bear more responsibilities with minimal or no public support. Third, the emphasis on girls' well-being, while an important priority, seems to neglect the contributions and needs of older women. It seems women and girls are worthy of investment only "if they can fix the world" (Chant and Sweetman 2012: 527).

Currently, the strategic win-win argument is pervasive. Feminist researchers in multilateral organizations often settle for and rely on this justification in their quest to prioritize funding flows or policy attention to women and girls, even as they are aware that the funding organization has little interest in gender equality (Chant and Sweetman 2012). And the smart economics argument is very much in sync with arguments that promote other contemporary win-win scenarios, as evident for example in the increasing prominence of social entrepreneurship: social entrepreneurs profit while investing in a project that they deem will improve the lives of the disadvantaged. Only if the investor can count on profits can the disadvantaged become the beneficiary and only in ways deemed appropriate by the investor. The scale of benefits the disadvantaged can derive from the business plan or whether they actually benefit are not relevant considerations. In such instances we witness the corrosive effects on moral causes of the expansion of the market and decline of public funding—only if private returns can be guaranteed is a moral cause worthy of attention.

To what extent has the neoliberal approach taken over the field of gender and development? There are reasons to argue that the field has been highly influenced by the hegemony of neoliberal discourses and policy during the past two decades. This influence has not only been manifest in the field of gender and development; Hester Eisenstein (2009), referring to feminist scholars in general, and to feminist economists in particular, has argued that feminism has been "seduced" by women's accomplishments and positive changes in gender equality during the neoliberal era. This has resulted, she argues, in giving too much ground to neoliberal hegemony. Fraser (2013) has also argued along similar lines, pointing out that "in a cruel twist of fate" feminism "has become entangled in a dangerous liaison with neoliberal market society." Although both authors are referring to feminism in general, we concur with the notion that, in the field of gender and development, a significant proportion of the work during the 1990s and 2000s could be viewed as lacking a critical view of neoliberalism. However, even if there is evidence that feminist analysis has accommodated to this era, as we discuss in Chapter 2, in feminist economics there has also been a large amount of critical thinking during the period. Many studies have analyzed the negative effects of neoliberal policies from different perspectives. In addition, we emphasize that first the capabilities approach and more recently the human rights framework, both empirically rooted in problems of gender inequality in developing countries, have provided theoretical and empirical foundations for the critique of neoliberal policies.

The Capabilities Approach and Human Development

The strongest counter discourse to the neoliberal approach since the 1980s has been the capabilities approach developed by Amartya Sen and Martha

Nussbaum. This approach gained prominence in economic development circles in large part through its operationalization in the *Human Development Report* (HDR) of the United Nations Development Programme (UNDP), which launched its Human Development Index (HDI) in 1990. The capabilities approach provides a normative framework for evaluating the well-being of individuals and the effectiveness of policies. Its central idea is that development entails (and policies should aim for) the expansion of people's capabilities, defined as what each person is able to do and be. Proponents of this approach have argued that capabilities provide a more adequate yardstick for measuring individual well-being (how well people are doing) than the income-based or preference-based measures of mainstream economics. The approach calls for policies that seek to remove obstacles in people's lives "so that they have more freedom to live the kind of life which, upon reflection, they find valuable" (Robeyns 2003a: 6).

Capabilities represent the multi-dimensional potential of individuals. A capability is the ability to be and to do what an individual wants to be and do. Capabilities range from the most elementary, such as being able to ride a bike, to those that are central to debates in economic development policy, such as the ability to be well nourished, to be educated, or to be free from discrimination. The framework distinguishes between capabilities and functionings: the former represent what an individual can do or what is possible and desired while the latter is what s/he actually achieves (Nussbaum 2004; Robeyns 2003a; Robeyns 2005).

As Sen and Nussbaum argue, the expansion of national income is a means to the expansion of capabilities, but not an end in itself. Engaging with cross-country evidence and a comparative discussion of growth records of a selected number of countries for the early 1990s, Sen (1999) argued that a higher level of national income is not sufficient to expand the capabilities of a country's citizens.[25] Higher GNP may not even be necessary for citizens of low-income countries to enjoy the most basic capabilities. Sen's basic point is that a country's capacity to improve the capabilities of its citizens depends on the utilization of the proceeds of growth, hence its institutional arrangements and policies concerning distribution. Further, Sen argues that even low-income countries can prioritize improved health and educational achievements, rather than awaiting the attainment of a higher income level. Because health and education are labor-intensive services, investment in these sectors not only delivers vital services to improve the basic capabilities, but also generates employment, which in turn can set off a virtuous circle of development. While the capabilities approach does not spell out the nuts and bolts of the policies that are necessary to support the livelihoods of people that, in turn, enable their capabilities, it emphasizes the imperative of doing so. Thus, the capabilities approach offers a people-centered notion of development that contrasts with the mainstream focus on expansion of output.

Nussbaum (2000a; 2003; 2004) has gone beyond Sen's more general approach. She developed the capabilities approach as a theory of justice and made the case for promoting women's capabilities universally. She identified a list of ten capabilities as an irreducible list that should be promoted everywhere, although she argues that desired capabilities might differ according to specific circumstances related to socio-economic conditions and cultural factors. The list ranges from "life" ("being able to live to end of human life of normal length . . ."), "bodily health" ("being able to have a good health . . ."), to "bodily integrity" ("being able to move freely from place to place . . . and to be secure against violent assault . . ."), and others such as "control over one's environment," which includes political participation as well as control over material aspects of people's lives such as being able to hold property (Nussbaum 2003: 41–42). The list is premised on the notion that to be human entails being a bodily entity, being cared for, and being capable of caring for others.[26] The list is gender aware in that it includes capabilities that are particularly important for women, such as the capabilities to be safe from domestic violence and to have reproductive choice.

Delineating a list of capabilities is invaluable in that it can be used to design indicators of well-being and to set social goals and design policy. Benería (2008), for example, develops a capability-policy matrix in the context of Bolivia based on discussions with local women's groups to identify policies that would help balance unpaid family work with market work and to alleviate the work burden of women.[27] Similarly, lists can be used as a "capability diagnostic" framework to describe the capability deprivations experienced by women and the forces that contribute to them. For example, so-called honor killings (an example of deprivation in capability of life) or poor health of women (that is deprivation in bodily health) in specific contexts can be examined from the perspective of the capabilities approach to map out their causes and to examine their potential solutions.[28]

By her insistence on the universality of capabilities, to be upheld every-where as constitutional guarantees, Nussbaum strikes a moral stance that could raise skepticism among many post-postmodern era gender and development scholars. Critics could argue that these norms articulate goals on behalf of (some) Third World women. However, Nussbaum's is a list of capabilities, which means that each individual can choose whether or not to pursue these capabilities.[29] Nussbaum's basic point is that as long as women (and men) have the freedoms to choose the lives they lead, it is up to them what they choose—whether it be cloistered or segregated lives or public participation, or whether they wear the veil or not.[30]

Alternative Frameworks of Well-being Require Alternative Measures

Once we recognize that well-being entails more than income and that aggregate average income per capita conceals inequalities, including gender inequalities, then it is important to identify gender-aware measures to assess progress in meeting goals towards gender equality and women's empowerment. In the early twenty-first century, researchers are faced with an abundance of cross-country composite gender-aware indices from which to choose, ranging from those that measure well-being outcomes (such as UNDP's Gender Inequality Index) to those that measure institutional obstacles to gender equality (such as the Social Institutions and Gender Index (SIGI)).

The pioneering efforts in creating gender-inclusive measures began with the UNDP's Gender-related Development Index (GDI) and Gender Empowerment Measure (GEM), which were introduced in 1995. These measures grew out of the UNDP's Human Development Project, which was inspired by the capabilities approach. The UNDP launched the Human Development Index (HDI) in 1990 to assess the extent to which countries were making progress towards building people's capabilities in a few key areas. The HDI included indicators for health and education, and income level to represent the means for achieving capabilities in a country.[31] The HDI showed that countries with the same level of income did not necessarily have the same level of human development, which allowed for evaluating policies and economic regimes that were more effective in promoting well-being.

In 1995 the HDR introduced GDI and GEM in order to provide some degree of quantification of gender inequality that would enable comparisons between different points in time or across countries or regions.[32] While such composite indexes represent only a crude and limited way to assess gender inequality and women's empowerment and cannot match the value of textured information on gender relations generated from small-scale qualitative studies, the effort has important benefits for policy analysis of gender inequality. Composite measures that highlight countries' relative performance call the attention of policymakers to the problem of gender inequality in a direct way that other more detailed information and indicators cannot do. Moreover, such measures can be used in cross-country or country-level research to assess the impact of various policies or economic growth on gender inequality and to examine the correlates of this inequality. These evaluations, in turn, enable design of policies to reduce gender inequality and promote women's empowerment.

While this path-breaking effort of the UNDP was welcome, the GDI and GEM were problematized on various grounds. Chief among these was that neither the GDI nor GEM was a measure of gender equality (Dijkstra and Hanmer 2000; Dijkstra 2006; Schüler 2006). In addition, use of a constructed income measure and inclusion of an income component that rewarded high-income countries in rankings were subject to critique. Criticisms have also been leveled at all composite indices in that each is a summary measure that is not transparent and conceals differences across the various indicators and dated information for some countries. For these reasons, there has been a flurry of suggestions to improve the measures (Benería and Permanyer 2010; Klasen and Schüler 2011).

Partly in response to these critiques and as part of its overhaul of the methodology of HDI, in 2010 the UNDP introduced a new measure of gender inequality, the Gender Inequality Index (GII), to replace GDI and GEM. The new index has three components: an entirely new, women's reproductive health component; empowerment; and labor market. However, as Permanyer (2013) argues, the GII introduced more problems than it solved. At the conceptual level, one problem is the lop-sided nature of the index as a measure of gender inequality. By choosing women's reproductive health as its health component GII settles for an absolute measure that has no counterpart for men, whereas the other components are relative measures. Moreover, the problem of rewarding high-income countries with a better (lower gender inequality) rank continues with the GII, which means country rank is not entirely reflecting discriminatory norms and practices against women.[33] One solution to these problems is to revise the GII (or create a new index) so that its components all measure women's relative standing compared to men, for example, measuring the health component by women's and men's life expectancies at birth, and using a simple average of the components (Benería and Permanyer 2010; Permanyer 2013).

Several other gender-inclusive measures are also currently available for researchers, thanks to the increasing availability of comparable cross-country data. As Irene Van Staveren (2013) shows, however, not all gender indices are created equal. Focusing on the five best-known, high-coverage, and easily accessible gender indices, including the UNDP's GII, Van Staveren shows that country rankings differ depending on the index used, which makes these indexes not interchangeable, and that understanding the conceptual and methodological underpinnings of each is important for proper use in analysis.[34] The choice of the gender index depends on the researcher's objective. The indices emphasize different aspects of gender inequality in the capabilities approach, ranging from resources and institutions to capabilities and functionings. Most measures gauge achievements (outcomes) for women in the absolute sense or relative to men (as in the case of the Gender Inequality Index (GII)). Distinct from this group is the Social Institutions and Gender Index (SIGI) of the OECD that measures legal and informal institutional barriers to gender equality, providing a useful complement to outcome measures (Branisa et al. 2014).[35]

Despite the flourishing of gender-inclusive measures there are still data gaps that hinder the measurement effort. Lack of individual income or wage data for many countries is one obstacle. There are also limitations in obtaining information on intra-household processes of income use or prevalence of violence. Another shortcoming of the current gender indices is that very few include indicators for unpaid work, such as care work. In addition, we need to be aware of the fact that measuring is an important but insufficient condition for design and implementation of policies for transformative action that increase gender equality.

The Human Rights Approach: Economic and Social Rights

While Nussbaum's elaboration of the capabilities approach in more gender-aware ways strengthened the potential of the approach for gender and development scholarship, the capabilities approach has had limited practical effect in altering neoliberal policies. In this regard, the project of Balakrishnan and Elson (2011), focused on human rights, has greater potential. Their work reclaims the human rights approach for their evaluation of neoliberal policies, putting the critique on firmer ground than the capabilities approach. The value of the human rights approach is that it forces governments to prioritize their human rights obligations in designing macroeconomic policy, in a way that the arguments of the capabilities approach do not: governments have to find ways of achieving economic growth in a human-rights-compliant manner; they have to avoid becoming party to international treaties or the IMF stand-by agreements that violate economic and social rights of their citizens. If they fail to do so, they can be held accountable in international, regional, or national fora.

Focusing on economic and social rights in the Universal Declaration of Human Rights makes the human rights criterion for evaluation of policy effectiveness commensurate with the standard economic criteria. Contrary to the mainstream approach in economics that focuses on economic growth, the human rights approach insists upon the essential minimum levels of economic and social rights that must be maintained in the performance of economic processes, whether it be in commodity production, social reproduction, allocation of government budgets, or international trade. The human rights approach puts forth what we may call a "provisioning" criterion—which is more compatible with the goals of feminist economics, as discussed in Chapter 2—while the mainstream criterion focuses on efficiency.[36]

There is substantial overlap between, indeed complementarity of, the capabilities approach and the human rights argument for economic and social rights (Nussbaum 2011a). Both approaches promote similar goals and cover a comprehensive domain of activities that encompass those pertaining to the provisioning for human needs (Balakrishnan and Elson 2011; Elson 2002a; Nussbaum 2003; Robeyns 2003a). For example, the right to health has a counterpart in the capability to be healthy. The right to work, likewise, has a counterpart in the capabilities approach's emphasis on the means (institutions and resources) that enable people to pursue their capabilities. Second, while the human rights language provides a more authoritative and urgent discourse that identifies the deprived as active claimants of rights, the capabilities approach provides some notion of a basic social minimum so that all people, women and men, are actually able to lead a life worthy of the dignity of the human being (Nussbaum 2003). Third, there is complementarity in foci of the two approaches: the human rights approach provides a new criterion for judging the effectiveness of social institutions, such as markets, in allocating resources and economic policies to ensure or satisfy the minimum essential levels of economic and social rights. The capabilities approach, on the other hand, guides the development of alternative measures of well-being or social welfare that go beyond incomes and GDP per capita growth, such as the HDI, and can be used for comparison between groups and across countries and for monitoring progress.

The overarching objective in both frameworks is to ensure and expand the capability (right) of each and every person to live a dignified human life based on the economic goal of provisioning for human life. Both frameworks treat each and every person as an end and not merely as means to an end, or as tools for the ends of others.[37] The justification in both frameworks therefore involves weighing the alternative uses of resources and manner of allocation in terms of meeting the essential level of economic and social rights of each and every person (above a critical threshold) and thereby to guarantee the substantive capabilities that the members of that society can enjoy. This reasoning differs from the mainstream economics framework that focuses on the weighing of costs and benefits to satisfy individual objectives such as the maximization of utility, income, or output.

While Articles 23–26 of the Universal Declaration are not intrinsically gendered, the principle of nondiscrimination and equality that is integral to the human rights framework can easily incorporate gender awareness. The framework thus allows evaluation of government commitment to gender equality in the promotion of economic and social rights and, whenever possible, measurement of the gendered outcomes of policies. The framework can thus help evaluate and prevent implementation of policies that increase the incentives to deceive and distort rules, and cause financial disaster for a large proportion of the population, as has happened since 2008 in countries hit by the economic crisis. One advantage of the human rights over the capabilities approach is that the proponents of the former have shed light on and problematized instances where a narrower gender gap has been a result of deterioration in men's/boys' achievements without any improvement in women's capabilities.

Thus, the combined human rights and capabilities approach provides a powerful counter discourse to neoliberal economic policies and an alternative approach to rethink economic policies. It opens the boundary of economic analysis to go beyond the preoccupation with output and incomes and to include a deeper examination of the nature and constraints that restrict an individual from realizing her economic and social rights or that impede her ability to enjoy substantive capabilities—such as freedom from hunger and starvation, or from violence. The combined approach views basic economic and social rights (capabilities) both as ends and means; fulfillment of rights (capabilities) of women and men serves as a basis for evaluating economic and social progress and the effectiveness of economic policies. We believe the combined capabilities–human rights approach has immense potential that can be developed for the integration of gender into economic analysis in a manner that is both transformative and empowering.

Conclusion

The gender and development field has come a long way from its modest beginnings in Boserup's pathbreaking work. The themes laid out in Boserup's book continue to define and inspire the research agenda: gender division of work, women's education, access to land rights and other inputs, women's contribution to the economic activities in developing countries, and women's economic power relative to men. At the same time, globalization and its concomitant developments have raised new questions that are being taken up by gender and development researchers. These questions emerge from the unfolding of capitalist development on an international scale, the enhanced power of capital to move globally, the ongoing commoditization and proletarianization of the labor force, and rising income inequalities. In the context of increasing income inequalities globally, improvements in women's relative wages in some contexts may mean that women are getting a slightly bigger share of a shrinking pie that goes to labor. Other new topics range from the intensification of international migration, to land grabs (that is, corporations or rich countries taking control of land in poor countries or from poor groups), the transformation of post-Soviet economies, increased risk to livelihoods of most inhabitants of the planet posed by the inherent financial instability of the deregulated global economy, and the unfolding of the climate crisis. Similarly, new economic development models, such as those being implemented in some Latin American countries, bring up interesting new questions about the connections between institutional change and gender inequality.

The competing frameworks that emerged in the 1970s and 1980s—WID and GAD—still shape the approach of researchers of these issues, if not in name, at least in orientation. The gender and development research exemplified by the WDR 2012 bears many of the characteristics of WID, while the GAD perspective continues to shape an oppositional discourse. This critical perspective now includes the theoretical innovation of the capabilities approach and the human rights approach in its critique of neoliberalism and a good proportion of work in feminist economics.

The mainstreaming of gender inequality concerns and integration of much feminist research in the international policy agenda in the first decade of twenty-first century have been important developments. While this was a goal sought by gender and development researchers, we view the nature of this institutionalization with skepticism, since the neoliberal macroeconomic policies that underpin gender inequalities continue to be implemented. There is also a tendency in the development policy agenda to take up gender issues in isolation from the discussion of more general political issues and macroeconomic policies. At both the theoretical level and in policy discourse, neoliberal policies have to (continue to) be challenged, particularly after the financial crisis of 2007–08 that has generated multiple adverse effects on livelihoods in many countries. The next chapter will examine the project of feminist economics, its critiques of mainstream economics, and its trajectory in shaping the discipline. This evaluation will provide a more detailed discussion of the contributions of feminist economics in topics related to economic development.

Notes

1   We refer to WID and GAD as distinct perspectives in the field that started out as "women in development" and later came to be called "gender and development."
2   The following quote by World Bank President Jim Yong Kim typifies this smart economics approach: "We know that reducing gender gaps in the world of work can yield broad development dividends: improving child health and education, enhancing poverty reduction, and catalyzing productivity" (Foreword, World Bank 2014a: ix).
3   This problem is illustrated, for example, by the view that "empowering women to compete in markets" through microcredit programs and an enabling business environment for working women is key to attaining Millennium Development Goal 3 of promoting gender equality (World Bank 2006: 4).

4   Boserup viewed the basic principles of economic development to be the same everywhere, as a process driven by technological change that responds to population growth.

5   As Razavi and Miller (1995) point out, Boserup's marginalization story in African agriculture implies a gender-equal past (not only in productivity but also in status), which is not supported by evidence of patriarchal norms in precolonial societies.

6   She appealed to planners via standard development concerns: far from creating further unemployment, integrating women in development would increase food production, reduce urban unemployment, and raise labor productivity.

7   CEDAW defines discrimination in its Article 1, "as any distinction, exclusion of restriction made on the basis of sex in the realm of the political, economic, social, cultural, civil or any other field" and sought to eliminate it in all areas of life (UN Women 2014).

8   As Andrew Byrnes and Marsha A. Freeman (2012) report, 29 of the 187 countries that had ratified the convention by 2011 had not fully endorsed Article 16 (which calls for the elimination of discrimination in all matters relating to marriage and family).

9   While President Carter signed CEDAW on behalf of the US in 1980, the US Senate has not ratified it. The principles of gender equality and fairness are embraced by the majority of the US population. Yet, the sentiments in the US Senate appear to have reflected the backlash against women's rights in the 1980s and subsequently the resistance against the US becoming signatory to any international convention that could threaten its sovereignty. Nationally, ratifying CEDAW could strengthen US efforts to support the struggle for gender equality in a number of areas such as pay discrimination, education, domestic violence, and sex trafficking. Moreover, the absence of the US from CEDAW leaves it with little credibility as an advocate for the rights of women and girls around the world.

10   For example, a reservation on Article 2 means that the country cannot abide by its obligation to remove discriminatory laws or to promulgate gender equality in laws. Other reservations have put crucial areas of social life in the countries in question beyond the reach of CEDAW, such as the reservations placed on Article 16. Here CEDAW has run into conflict with the national "personal status" laws that reflect religious law or norms.

11   The use of the concept of reproduction in feminist analysis goes back to the late 1970s when it was used to analyze questions around the gender division of labor and women's involvement in the reproduction of the labor force (Benería 1979). Over time, the focus of analysis of reproduction shifted from unpaid domestic work towards childcare and it came to include the continuous marketization of unpaid care work (Folbre 1994). This type of analysis has expanded into a large body of literature concerned with care work, the care economy, welfare regimes, and social policy.

12   DAWN was formed at the Third UN World Conference on Women in Nairobi in 1985 to express dissatisfaction with the WID formulations and to articulate the Third World women's perspectives.

13   A similar articulation of the standpoint perspective is by Nancy Hartsock (1983) who drew on Marx's argument that only the working class had the most complete perspective on the workings of capitalism. Hartsock formulated the argument that women who engaged in care tasks due to the gender division of labor had a unique understanding of the workings of the capitalist form of patriachy.

14   In addition, some postcolonial theorists identify themselves with postmodernism. In our discussion, we identify the overlapping positions of postmodern and postcolonial critics as postcolonialism, even as we acknowledge their different analytical starting points.

15   Abu-Lughod's list includes both the practical benefits of the veil (a form of "portable seclusion"; symbolic separation of women and men; a sense of belonging to a particular group and upholding its moral ways) and a caution against jumping to conclusions about lack of agency or freedom of women who wear the veil.

16   While Abu-Lughod claims that she is trying to steer clear of cultural relativism and is not condoning the government-imposed restrictions on women in Afghanistan, she seems more concerned about the agendas of pro-invasion groups than furthering the cause of alleviating constraints on women's lives.

17   The dominant responses after the 2008 crisis indicate the striking resilience of neoliberal economic policies that warrants this characterization, which is our take on Ruth Pearson's "The Rise and Rise of Gender and Development" (2005).

18   These are the International Covenant on Economic, Social and Cultural Rights (ICESCR), the ILO Declaration on Fundamental Principles and Rights at Work (1998), and regional conventions.

19   These rights are articulated in Articles 23–26 of the Universal Declaration of Human Rights adopted by the UN General Assembly in 1948.

20   The key principles are: progressive realization (whether the government is engaged in ongoing pursuit of the rights); use of maximum available resources (both within the country and from international cooperation; and government attempts to mobilize domestic funding to meet its obligations); avoidance of retrogression (undermining of rights by cuts to public expenditures or by cuts in taxes necessary to fund these programs); satisfaction of minimum essential levels of economic and social rights (to the poorest and most vulnerable groups, regardless of the extreme resource constraints); non-discrimination and equality (commitment to formal and substantial equality for all groups); and participation, transparency, and accountability in the pursuit and promotion of human rights.

21   The assessment compares the US and Mexico's performance to countries at comparable income levels (OECD and Latin America, respectively) as well as examining changes in the US and Mexico over time. Balakrishnan and Elson also compare how different social groups fare in each country.

22   The impacts of these policies in producing the 2007–08 financial crisis and the subsequent stagnation are evaluated from a feminist economics perspective by several contributions in a 2013 *Feminist Economics* special issue, that focuses on Canada, Spain, Turkey, UK and US and examines cross-country and regional (Latin American) impacts.

23   The Gender Action Plan (GAP) sought to accelerate the implementation of Millennium Development Goal 3 by "making markets work for women (at the policy level) and empowering women to compete in markets (at the agency level)" (World Bank 2006: 4). Thus, GAP emphasized the creation of incentives to increase women's market participation and measures that reduce transaction costs, such as infrastructure investment, and improving the policy and institutional environment for women in land, labor, finance, and agricultural product markets (World Bank 2006).

24   For instance, the WDR's solutions for improving maternal health (such as investment in infrastructure) will likely run into financial constraints imposed by the neoliberal approach to government budgets.

25   Sen pointed out that while Brazil and South Korea both experienced high growth rates of GNP per capita, Brazil's growth did not guarantee improvement in life expectancy comparable to that of Korea.

26   This notion of human nature is very different from the disembodied one in liberal theory that underlies mainstream economics (Jaggar 1983).

27   Based on the list of capabilities drawn up by Robeyns (2003b) and discussions with local groups, Benería identifies six relevant capabilities that are associated with inequalities in time allocation and time poverty and that represent the expressed needs of the local population. In turn, in collaboration with local groups she identifies a set of public policies that could promote these capabilities.

28   In the case of honor killings in Pakistan, for example, multiple capabilities of women are severely constrained by institutions and tribal norms that defy Islam and national laws (Appiah 2010). This diagnosis points to changing the norms as the solution. What is needed is to reshape the meaning of what is honorable by engaging—in solidarity with international groups—in national organized action against the institutions that condone or encourage the killings.

29   The question of lists has been subject to debate among capabilities researchers.

30   Nussbaum (2004) anticipates likely critiques that insist on the cultural roots of certain practices that constrain the capabilities of women. First, she argues that cultures are neither monolithic nor static, and one particular norm/tradition cannot be taken as representative of a country's traditions. Second, traditional practices that hinder one or more capabilities, specifically harm a person (for example, his/her bodily integrity) should not be maintained. Third, she argues that her list of basic capabilities could not be construed as a paternalistic imposition either, because she is calling for broadening freedoms, rather than restricting them, and is arguing against voices that seek to restrict women's freedoms.

31   These components initially were measured by life expectancy at birth, adult literacy and school enrollment ratio, and the real GDP per capita. There were subsequent changes to the education and income measures.

32   The GDI measured gender differences in the same dimensions included in the HDI, thus measuring loss in human development represented by gender inequality in a given country. GEM was constructed to examine the extent to which women and men are able to participate in decision-making in economic and political life and have access to certain levers of power.

33 Another problem owes to the methodology of the construction of the index: due to the symmetric construction of the GII, the rank of a country can be more favorable in cases where disadvantage for women in education and labor force participation components can be compensated by disadvantages for men in these components.

34 Van Staveren's evaluation focuses on the GEI (Gender Equality Index) of the Institute of Social Studies, GII of the UNDP, SIGI (Social Institutions and Gender Index) of the OECD, and WEOI (Women's Economic Opportunities Index) of the Economic Intelligence Unit, all four of which were first published in 2010, and the GGGI (Global Gender Gap Index) of the World Economic Forum, available since 2006.

35 SIGI's components measure five institutions: family code and norms, civil liberties, physical integrity, ownership rights, culture of son preference.

36 The provisioning criterion, however, raises the difficult and legitimate question as to what kind of coordination and system of entitlement relations would enable the realization of human rights, given limited resources. Inevitably, the approach requires a system of setting priorities for resource use and a framework for evaluating potential trade-offs between the attainment of different needs of people, for example, housing, food, education, medical services, mobility, self-expression.

37 For example, they criticize the view and the practice of treating women as adjuncts to men and their labor as a resource for reproducing and maintaining the labor input in market production processes (Sen 1999).

CHAPTER 2

The Study of Women and Gender in Economics

What if . . . economic theory creates myths that strengthen the hands of the most powerful, greedy, and short-sighted economic actors, while needlessly undermining normal human ethical sensibilities and normal human aspirations for a society that is prosperous, just, and sustainable?
Julie Nelson[1]

Introduction

Since the 1970s, feminist scholarship has had a profound impact on many academic disciplines. In the humanities and much of the social sciences it has challenged definitions and expanded the boundaries of knowledge by confronting and addressing gender issues that were previously excluded from accepted knowledge. These efforts have transformed the disciplines by altering many of the basic androcentric assumptions behind traditional knowledge. In economics the feminist critique has yet to have a transformative effect on the core tenets of the discipline, despite the presence of feminist voices since the 1970s and the attention that mainstream economics has given to questions about the division of labor in the family and about labor market-based inequalities. Unlike other fields, economics is largely characterized by a single orthodox core—also known as neoclassical economics—which has shut out heterodox alternatives and proved resistant to feminist critiques.

Despite this resistance, feminist economics has flourished, largely in a parallel universe, and can claim a substantial body of innovative work while at the same time maintaining its critical stance towards the discipline. Feminist economics is not a distinct school of thought in economics, but rather represents the use of gender lens for doing economic analysis. Born out of multiple intellectual traditions, feminist economics continues to be a pluralistic field. The big tent of feminist economics encompasses neoclassical economists and heterodox economists of different perspectives, together with feminist researchers from other social sciences who examine the socio-economic aspects of gender inequality. Included are scholars who work with the "master's tools," as Audre Lorde would put it, some using these to critique the master's work and continuing the conversation with the mainstream, while others use them to build gender-awareness in the discipline; and yet others eschew these tools as they continue on alternative paths to doing economics.

This chapter tells the story of feminist economics, its origins, central principles, main contributions, discourses, and emerging research agendas. This review starts with the established approaches in the discipline—neoclassical economics and the primary heterodox alternatives of Marxian and institutional economics that provided the starting point of feminist critiques. A strong impetus for the development of contemporary feminist economics was its critique of the neoclassical mainstream—its assumptions, models, methodology, methods, and pedagogy. These critiques drew upon epistemologies and methodological developments in feminist theory in other disciplines. Much of the empirical evidence that challenged mainstream economics was generated by researchers dealing with developing countries, who provided valuable insights on the lives of women in diverse settings and new standpoints from which to construct knowledge.

Second, we examine the turning point in economics in the 1980s and early 1990s when feminist critiques achieved coherence and stronger consensus, building on the parallel efforts of many feminist scholars since the 1960s and 1970s. The founding of the International Association for Feminist Economics (IAFFE) in 1992, followed by the launch of its journal *Feminist Economics* in 1995, marked the growing feminist challenges to the discipline—what Albelda (1997) has called "disturbances in the field." The 1993 book *Beyond Economic Man*, edited by Marianne Ferber and Julie Nelson, captured some of the different aspects of the moment (Ferber and Nelson 1993). The capabilities approach, rooted in economic development discourses, was also articulated during this period, providing an example of an emerging feminist alternative framework. *Feminist Economics* created the space for conversation among feminist economists and other gender scholars from different intellectual traditions and disciplines.

Third, we examine the contributions of feminist economists. Drawing upon heterodox economic approaches and feminist research in other disciplines since the 1980s feminist economists have begun to reconstruct economics as the study of social provisioning for human life, through interdependent paid and unpaid economic activities mediated by markets, households/community, and the government. This approach has led to the development of a body of knowledge that is more accountable to the diversity of the lived experiences of women and men. Using this social provisioning approach has led to a substantial body of research on gender inequalities in the key provisioning activities that use paid labor and unpaid labor, and on the key sites of these activities—labor markets, households, and communities. Feminist research efforts have also focused on macroeconomic policies that frame how (and how well) people are able to secure their livelihoods and to meet their needs. Our examination includes feminist analyses of dominant neoliberal macroeconomic policy and the relationship between economic growth and gender inequalities, and feminist ecological economics.

We conclude with comments on the extent to which gender analysis of the economy has altered the established economics traditions, including heterodox work that has a substantial theoretical and methodological overlap with feminist thought. We consider the fragmentation of heterodox approaches as a weakness that prevents the emergence of a coherent alternative to the dominant mainstream economics. We argue that the next step in the agenda has to be a greater engagement among heterodox approaches. We hope that closer partnerships in developing analytical frameworks to address the multiple crises and problems that face the world today—including the jobs crisis, the climate crisis, food crisis, and various forms of injustice—will result.

Gender and Economic Analysis: A History

Feminist economics as a lens has emerged from disparate histories of engagement with gender questions in the discipline. Mainstream (neoclassical) economics, Marxian theory, and institutional economics are distinct strands that contributed to the questions raised by feminist economics. While historically Keynesian or post-Keynesian economics has not engaged with gender questions this approach could also well complement feminist economics, as recent engagements with this question argue (Danby 2004; Van Staveren 2010). In what follows, we briefly review the evolution of these approaches, bringing the discussion up to the 1980s and 1990s when feminist critiques in economics gathered significant momentum.

Neoclassical Approach

Mainstream economics has a history of inclusion of questions pertaining to inequalities between women and men that goes back to the nineteenth and early twentieth century.[2] The discipline, born out of the classical economists, was further developed in the late nineteenth century in the context of capitalist industrialization that had moved production from the household into factories and amidst the dominant Victorian gender norms and strict gender division of labor. This context and the privileged class and gender position of the mainstream economists shaped what they thought was worth studying as an economic problem with respect to women (Barker and Feiner 2004). Early neoclassical economists subscribed to the views that women belonged in the home, the work they did was unproductive, and if they engaged in paid work, they were not worthy of pay equal to that of men (Pujol 1992).

Neoclassical economists' interest in women's role in the economy increased in the late 1950s and early 1960s as a growing number of married, middle-class women in the US and Europe began leaving their socially assigned domain (home) and joining the workforce. The phenomenon in some sense was puzzling, since family (husbands') income was rising at that time and thus a decline in women's paid labor supply might have been expected. In a radical departure from the ideological stance of early neoclassical economists in analyzing women's economic status, the new generation used their economic theories to explain gender inequality. Jacob Mincer's explanation was that the rising educational level of women and increased demand for labor raised the opportunity costs of staying at home (Mincer 1962); that is, women's incentive to enter the labor force was stronger than the incentive provided by the rise in husbands' income to stay at home. In economics-speak, this was a classic case of the "substitution effect" offsetting the "income effect." Mincer formulated this analysis at about the time Betty Friedan wrote *Feminine Mystique* (1963), which detailed the multiple problems facing full-time homemakers in America's growing suburban society (Friedan 1963). Friedan's description of women's oppression and stifled yearnings and aspirations was in sharp contrast with the simplistic economic analysis of opportunity costs in Mincer's model. The contrast was symbolic of the tasks ahead if the feminist questions raised by Friedan were to be taken up by economic analysis. Much more than narrow economistic explanations would be needed to explain women's experiences in the home and the paid labor force.

In the 1960s and 1970s neoclassical economics produced an explanation for the observed specialization of women and men in household and market work, respectively, and gender wage inequalities. In the human capital theory formulated by Nobel-prize-winning economist Gary Becker, women were said to earn less than men because they chose low-paying occupations, and had fewer years of and different kinds of schooling compared to men, since they prioritized their work in the family, wanted flexibility, and did not plan continuous attachment to the labor force. Thus, wage inequality was said to be due to women's own choices. Neoclassical economists also attempted to explain differences in educational choices and attainment, job training, and unemployment (Benham 1974; Lloyd 1975; Blau 1976; Beller 1979; Lloyd and Niemi 1979).

Economists' growing interest in using neoclassical economic analysis to understand the sphere of the household gave rise to New Household Economics (NHE). This approach applied key concepts and models of mainstream microeconomics to household production and decision-making. Gary Becker modeled "A Theory of the Allocation of Time" after the theory of comparative advantage and specialization used in describing the logic of international trade (Becker 1965). Accordingly, countries are said to specialize in goods they can produce at the lowest relative cost, or in which they have a "comparative advantage," and trade them for goods from other countries that specialize in different goods. Becker applied this analysis to the gender division of labor, that is, the pattern of certain household members engaging in paid market work while others specialize in home production. Relative productivities were said to make it rational for women to specialize in housework while men specialize in wage work, since women's earnings were less than men's on the job market. These choices, made within an assumed harmonious household, it was claimed, would promote collective household well-being in the form of a larger total household output.

The NHE analysis opened up new theoretical and empirical inquiry into other issues such as the economics of marriage, choices around labor supply, education, the number of desired children, and fertility rates. Methodologically, however, these neoclassical models followed what feminist scholars call the "add women and stir" approach. From a feminist perspective, the gender questions were "trapped" within the constraints set up by the orthodox analytical framework and its basic assumptions: individuals with given preferences seek to maximize well-being within their means (a resources or endowments constraint). Applied to the household, this framework was not conducive to asking, let alone answering, the kind of questions that the women's movement had generated about gender socialization, inequality, and asymmetric power relations. The framework treated preferences as exogenous, assuming away any discussion on how these are shaped.

In his *A Treatise on the Family* (1981) Becker introduced different preferences in the household by assigning altruistic motivations to the (male) head who gives transfers to other selfish family members (wife and "rotten kids") to induce them to act in his interest (Becker 1981). The model thus ruled out intra-household conflict as well as consideration of gender socialization in shaping preferences. It took as given beliefs about gender skills—such as that women are better than men at cooking and childcare while men are better at market work—just as feminists were questioning these.[3] Thus, taken together, the human capital theory of the gender wage gap and the NHE analysis of division of labor in the household provided strong justification for gender inequality: given the wage differential, the household division of labor made sense; given the household division of labor, the wage differential made sense. The orthodox theory had explained away the problem of gender inequality!

The hegemony of the NHE within the profession and the dominance of unitary household models continued through the 1980s (and until the present, despite the development of alternative household models). Despite these trends within the profession, feminist concerns were often present in the work of women economists who raised many questions about the narrowness of the standard models and criticized them for their assumptions about exogenous preferences, individual ability to make choices, and the role of the market in producing optimal solutions for everyone (Ferber and Birnbaum 1977; Sawhill 1977). Bergmann (1974) used the supply and demand framework to construct a new model to explain gender inequality in the labor market.[4] Bergmann (1981) also provided a powerful critique of Becker's household model, emphasizing the adverse consequences for women of the traditional division of labor. Part of the disadvantages of specialization had to do with the loss of economic power for women who specialized in housework and who would suffer serious decline in economic well-being in the event of a divorce. The drawbacks of being a full-time housewife had to do also with gender socialization that contributed to male domination, and women's low level of autonomy and self-confidence.

Marxian Approach

At the height of the second wave of the women's movement in the early 1970s some feminists adopted the Marxian approach in their search for a framework that argued for the transformation of political, economic, and social relations that would distribute wealth and power more equally, including along gender lines. In particular, the Marxian focus on exploitation, inequality, and the systemic tendency for capitalism and market forces to generate class inequalities seemed to be more conducive than the neoclassical framework to answering questions about inequality. It seemed more appropriate for analyzing social relations and power inequalities between men and women and more open to interdisciplinary approaches. There were also feminists who were socialists or part of progressive social movements and adhered to the international political economy school of thought, who sought to extend these frameworks to incorporate feminist concerns in their analysis of unequal social relations and gender subordination.

The Marxian tradition has a history of engagement, albeit short lived, with the role of reproduction activities organized around the family. In his Preface to *The Origin of the Family, Private Property and the State* Frederick Engels argued that production and reproduction activities were equally important for the maintenance of economic systems (Engels [1884] 1981).[5] His book was partly an attempt to address the lacuna in Marx's writing. Although Marx referred to the role of women in reproduction and to problems when they are drawn into wage labor (for example, in *Capital* Volume I, Chapter 15, section 3), he focused mostly on the capitalist production process, and assumed that the livelihood of the worker was mostly secured by men's labor market work (Marx [1887] 1967). Thus Marx left out of consideration the family and unpaid labor, which are necessary for the reproduction of the very labor power he felt was central to accumulation and the maintenance of the capitalist economic system. Despite Engels's emphasis, the unpaid life-sustaining activities in the household dropped out of the Marxian scholarly focus until the domestic labor debate of the late 1960s and 1970s, which focused on the functions of domestic labor within the economic system. More specifically, participants in the debate examined the ways in which unpaid domestic work contributes to lowering the costs of maintenance and reproduction of the present and future generations of workers (Himmelweit and Mohun 1977). While this debate helped to legitimize feminist questions within the Marxian paradigm, feminist critics also pointed out that this extension of the Marxian framework failed to identify and analyze gender relations inherent in domestic work and the household division of labor (Molyneux 1979; Benería 1979; MacKintosh 1978).

A similar extension of the Marxian framework was applied to the role of rural women's subsistence work in low-income economies where men were engaged in wage labor in the capitalist sector of the economy (Deere 1976). The analysis underlined the crucial contribution of women's unpaid work to both social reproduction and lower wages of male workers engaged in the capitalist sector. Similar to the domestic labor debate, this effort introduced gender issues into the Marxian framework in development economics; and, similar to the New Household Economics, it represented a new application of economic analysis to the previously ignored areas of unpaid work. However, once again, the question posed within the framework—what function women played within the capitalist economic system—constrained an understanding of the dynamics of gender relations and their complexity in the household and in subsistence economies.

Within the Marxian framework the debate about the nature of gender relations in the household was also sparked by the focus on the history of working-class struggles of the late nineteenth and early twentieth centuries (Humphries 1977; Hartmann 1979a). According to Jane Humphries (1977), the struggle of the English working class to reduce the length of the working day and seek a family wage was an attempt to prevent proletarianization of all members of the family and the erosion of the wage. Underlying this argument was a notion of the working-class family and kinship network as a unit of solidarity against the capitalist class. While emphasizing the well-being effects of having fewer family members in the labor force, this perspective downplayed the adverse consequences of the family wage on women: women ended up dependent on men and, if they were engaged in wage labor, they were only entitled to lower wages as the secondary earners. By contrast, Hartmann (1979a) emphasized gender interests of working-class men as the motivation underlying the historical struggles over the family wage and hours legislation; they sought to reserve better-paying jobs for themselves and to confine women's labor to services in the household.

The shortcomings of the notion of the family as a unit of solidarity led some feminists to integrate Marxian categories within a feminist framework (Hartmann 1981; Folbre 1982). Hartmann (1981) posited the family as a "locus of struggle." The emphasis thus shifted from the household as a harmonious unit to a unit of conflict. Further, Folbre (1982) examined the extent to which the concept of exploitation can be applied to work carried out at the domestic level. Her analysis raised the question of commensurability of work at home with market work. At a more general level of analysis, harking back to Engels, a Marxian framework was also used to produce explanations for gender inequality, invoking the connections between capitalism and patriarchy, reproduction and production, and between patriarchy, the household, and the labor market (Hartmann 1979b; Benería 1979).

The development of the Marxian analysis of women and gender issues has been uneven. In the United States, feminist engagement with the Marxian framework developed with little interaction and insufficient dialogue with liberal feminists, since the Marxian paradigm in general and feminist analysis within it was relegated to the margins of the economics profession.[6] This was not the case in Europe and Latin America however, where feminists applied a Marxian framework to understanding the gender dimensions of capitalist development (Deere 1977; Safa 1986; Saffioti 1986; Deere and León de Leal 1987). As Albelda (1999: 539) points out, "Marxist methodology provides a powerful springboard for thinking and theorizing about gender relations." Methodologically, the Marxian approach contributed to subsequent framing of gender questions within the workings of the capitalist economic system, focusing attention on social relations of production (as opposed to market exchanges) in shaping people's daily lives, considering interrelationships between unpaid and paid work, and emphasizing attention to differences among women and men in terms of social class (Benería and Roldán 1987; Picchio 1992; Power 2004; Folbre 1994). More recently, feminists have applied a Marxian framework to understanding the gender dimensions of crises of capitalism, including the 2007–08 financial crisis (Eisenstein 2005; Fraser 2009; Roberts 2012; Ezquerra 2012).

Institutional Economics

Institutional economics provided another avenue for feminist analysis that is increasingly recognized and claimed by a variety of economists. Since the 1980s theories of institutions have evolved and gained prominence in development economics. They focus on the nature of the interaction between institutions, defined as social rules and conventions (laws, regulations, norms) that guide the interaction of individuals and organizations, and economic processes.

The institutionalist school of thought was first introduced by Thorstein Veblen and John Commons in the late nineteenth century with their examination of the economy as a social organization aimed at human provisioning. Veblen recognized the importance of power and ideology, in particular gender norms, in affecting the economic process of provisioning. Institutionalist thought has since evolved into different strands, under the umbrella of New Institutional Economics (NIE). Two strands, in particular, became influential in modern economic thinking: the transaction costs approach that draws from the work of Ronald Coase, Oliver Williamson, and Douglass North to name a few; and the school associated with the theory of imperfect information developed by George Akerlof, Joseph Stiglitz, and William Spence among others.[7] The former strand has to do with the presence of transaction costs and the development of institutions, which reduce the uncertainty of social interaction and thus prevent prohibitive transaction costs, thereby shaping human interaction (Williamson 1985; North 1990).[8] North (1990) and Elinor Ostrom (1990) argued that the presence of transaction costs provides the impetus for the development of institutions shaping human interaction, which they considered as key to understanding economic change.

The NIE strand associated with imperfect information emphasizes the presence of asymmetric information faced by the transacting parties as the rationale for institutional arrangements and contracts (Hoff et al. 1993). In this approach, the design of economic contracts reflects the strategic behavior of market agents under conditions of asymmetric information, moral hazard, and pervasive risks. These approaches challenge the separability of efficiency and equity, a principal result in mainstream economics. Institutionalists demonstrate that when transaction costs and imperfect information are important, the terms and conditions of economic contracts, for example in land, labor, credit markets, which directly affect the resource allocation efficiency, also crucially depend on ownership structures and property relations (Bardhan 1989).

A third, political economy strand extends the idea of Marx ([1904] 1967), which explores the underlying power relations in the rules of the game. This approach examines how changes in the material productive forces and in the conflicting interests and shifts in power among groups can bring about changes in institutions or rules of the game to favor the powerful (Harriss-White 2003; Bardhan 1989). Harriss-White (2003: 489) elaborated on this point, arguing that "market exchange is better understood not in terms of allocative efficiency but rather as a mechanism of extraction of surplus by one class from another." Hence, according to this perspective, the outcomes of market processes of buying and selling, such as wages, prices, output, are also outcomes of political processes.[9] The social and political power involved in market exchange that is emphasized in this approach can lead to maintenance of or change in institutions governing surplus appropriation by a dominant class (Bardhan 1989).[10]

All proponents of institutional economics emphasize the importance of institutions that shape human interaction in understanding economic processes and outcomes. Of particular interest to feminist economists are the socially constructed norms or rules and societal attitudes that are learned and internalized pertaining to the roles, codes of conduct, and acceptable behavior of women and men. These gender norms regulate market exchanges through the ideology of subordination and rules of market that are prejudicial to women (Harriss-White 2003). They include both what women are prohibited from doing and under what conditions they are permitted to undertake certain activities. Another important aspect of institutional economics that resonates in the work of feminists is the notion that power relations are embedded in market exchange. Not only are gender roles socially constructed as part of the rules of the game in societies, but so are the economic and social advantages and disadvantages, entitlements and penalties associated with those gendered roles.

Institutional economics is also featured in the work of labor economists in the United States who during the 1970s and early 1980s combined Marxian and institutional approaches to describe labor market stratification/segmentation and its relationship to class, racial and gender inequalities (Edwards et al. 1973; Gordon et al. 1982). This approach allowed them to discuss the historical and contemporary processes of labor market segregation and discrimination, which implied a critique of the competitive labor market model of the mainstream. It also provided an alternative perspective to the understanding of wage inequalities and other differential labor market outcomes. Labor market segmentation theory had many implications for an analysis of gender inequality (Reich et al. 1980).[11] Feminists made use of this approach by drawing the connections between labor market segmentation and sex segregation and by emphasizing how both were linked with gender stereotypes and socialization processes outside of the workplace where they were reproduced and transformed (Hartmann 1979a; Strober 1984).

Other contributions from institutional economics have emphasized the notion that social processes are not governed by universal laws and do not have universal meanings, hence the importance of placing feminist analysis within cultural and historical contexts, including changing institutions in order to explain disadvantages faced by women (Jennings 1993).

Feminist Economics: A Critique of the Mainstream

In the 1980s and early 1990s feminists joined other heterodox economists in examining the biases in neoclassical economics. With a strong influence from postmodernism and postcolonialism, discussed in Chapter 1, this was also a period when there was some convergence of approaches in feminist scholarship around the category of gender, the importance of paying attention to varied experiences of women by race and ethnicity, and in particular, the move away from the use of universal and general categories in scholarly research (Benería 2003). The confluence of these intellectual developments gave strong impetus for feminist critiques of economics. For example, they identified masculine, or androcentric, biases in the self-definition of the discipline, the models used, topics, methods, and the teaching approach. Nelson (1992; 1995) argued that the discipline is permeated by a dichotomy of gender values that privilege stereotypical masculine traits over stereo-typically feminine ones. Accordingly, the characteristics that are most highly valued in the practice of economics are associated with masculinity and men (in US/Western capitalist society), such as objectivity, detachment, logical consistency, individual accomplishment, use of mathematics, and lack of emotion (Nelson 1995). An important moment for feminist economics had begun.

Critique of Homo Economicus

Much of the feminist critique of the discipline has focused on the core assumptions behind mainstream analysis and the characterization of the economic behavior of individuals. Mainstream analysis assumes that the economic system comprises self-interested individuals (*homo economicus*) each of whom makes autonomous decisions by engaging in maximizing (more generally, "optimizing") behavior based on their preferences and their capacity to meet them. Their calculating behavior—economic rationality—refers to weighing different options in light of income and time/resources constraints and expressing their preferences and choices in consistent ways. Individual preferences—the likes and dislikes for particular consumer goods or activities—are assumed to be stable, not comparable to others' preferences, and not influenced by family, friends, community, or advertising.[12] The maximizing individual is assumed to interact with others in markets through the mediation of price signals and engage in voluntary and harmonious exchanges (England 1993). This concept of human nature is assumed to characterize all behavior in markets and, in the absence of any other interaction admitted by mainstream theory, its concept of society is the agglomeration of millions of autonomous, rational individuals. The choices of each of them underlie the operation of markets, which for the mainstream is the key institution for the promotion of human well-being, understood in terms of consumption of goods and services.

The discipline's defense of this starting point of economic analysis is that it is a simple, useful approximation of representative economic behavior, whereas feminist economists see flaws in it. As Power (2004: 4) has put it, "starting points matter," since they tell us what will be included and what will be left out of the analysis. This "separative-self" model of human agency "presumes that humans are autonomous, impervious to social influence, and lack sufficient emotional connection to each other to make empathy possible" (England 1993: 38). Furthermore, it is an unbalanced conception of human behavior, focusing on only one side of implicit dichotomies: autonomy (vs. dependence), reason (vs. emotion), self-interested (vs. caring) behavior, competition (vs. cooperation) (Nelson 1992; Strober 1994). England (2003) further pointed out that, in contrast to the separative selves in the market, the theory presumes "soluble selves" in household interactions, where the harmonious household is presumed to have Becker-type unity of interests.

Historically, women have been viewed as being motivated by non-maximizing objectives, their choices and actions often associated with love, cooperation, empathy, norms, traditions, and the division of labor within their households.[13] This is of course subject to change, influenced by factors such as women's incorporation in the labor market, socialization, and changing traditions. On the other hand, many people, women and men, also behave in ways quite different from those assumed by mainstream models. Frank (2004), for example, has investigated this issue extensively, showing that many individuals and even firms do not behave in purely self-interested ways but can instead be motivated by other objectives such as altruism, cooperation, and the "moral high road." In addition, he as well as other authors have argued that self-interest and individual choices are also socially constructed (Skidelsky and Skidelsky 2012).

Furthermore, the economic individual of the mainstream is a "mushroom man," who has no childhood or old age, and springs into optimizing behavior as an adult (Nelson 1995). This individual does not care for nor is cared for by anyone. By definition, care labor has been left outside of the starting point of economic analysis. Thus, for example, standard labor economics has historically started its discussion of human capital and wage determination with the individual choice of whether or not to invest in more education, for example a college degree; care of children and the imparting of skills through the unpaid work of caregivers is not part of the analysis.[14] Similarly, another foundational assumption is that the world is characterized by scarcity, which then leads to optimizing behavior as the characteristic economic behavior. Strober (1994) problematizes this characterization as it overlooks the human-made nature of scarcity caused by either maldistribution (for example, the hunger problem is a result of uneven distribution of food supplies, rather than not enough food being produced) or advertising, which creates wants and induces scarcity. And the mainstream's emphasis on scarcity and optimization behavior may only exacerbate true scarcity in a world of finite resources.

The Rhetoric of Economics

Feminist economists also have deconstructed the rhetoric of economics and its tendency to obscure questions that matter and to silence non-mainstream ways of conceptualizing economic behavior. These efforts at deconstruction, which cut across heterodox approaches, reflect the influence of postmodern critiques emanating from the humanities, whereby meaning, rather than causality, is the focus of the analysis (McCloskey et al. 1989). For example, Strassmann (1993) questioned the "disciplinary authority" through which the mainstream has imposed its views about what constitutes economic analysis. Blank (1993) has questioned the rhetoric of choice. As she stated, the assumption of an empowered individual in economic models does not leave room for the fact that an individual might "feel dominated, repressed, passive, stuck, ill, unsure about his or her abilities, or unaware of alternatives" (p. 141). Women's ability to enter the labor market, for example, is often hampered by tradition and sexist norms and institutions. Similarly, feminist economists have examined the tale of Robinson Crusoe, a common character in economics textbooks as the quintessential economic man. He is seemingly self-sufficient when in fact he depends on the labor of another. He lives outside of society and has no obligations to anyone. As Grapard (1995) and Hewitson (1999) argue, this powerful image does not reveal relationships of power and unequal exchange in society and ignores elements of domination and exploitation while avoiding engagement with issues of race, gender, and sexuality.[15]

What Are We All Striving For?

Feminist economists have also questioned the pursuit of efficiency as the criterion of economic success (Elson 1991b; Barker 1999). According to the mainstream, successful economies are ones that promote efficiency, not equity, equality, or fairness. The beauty of market-provided solutions, according to mainstream economics, is that they are efficient, which means they have come about as the result of the optimization efforts of millions of individual entities—businesses, consumers, workers—and offer the best possible solution for the well-being of market participants. Efficiency, whether in terms of maximum output or minimum cost, is measured in terms of marketed resources. The concept of efficiency does not take into account spillovers of market transactions into the household or other domains, that is, the externalities. Efficiency may have been achieved as a result of downloading of costs onto the household or reliance on resources that were not paid for (Elson 1991b). For example, the public health services system may achieve efficiency (in terms of reduced budget deficit) through cuts in spending or introduction of user fees that result in increase in women's unpaid work caring for the ill in low-income households. Such spillovers that adversely affect the well-being of women will not be captured by the use of market-based measures of efficiency.

Moreover, Pareto optimality, which is the gold standard of efficiency, can only be achieved under very restrictive simplifying assumptions that do not reflect the nature of most contemporary economies. Pareto optimality refers to any arrangement between two individuals where it is not possible to make one person better off without making the other worse off.[16] Yet, mainstream economists argue in favor of market solutions as if efficiency actually characterizes the outcomes of the operation of markets. Thus debates over government intervention in the economy often turn on the efficiency that needs to be sacrificed if policies were to regulate markets, the classic example being the setting of (or raising) the minimum wage or other labor standards. The standard mainstream objection focuses on the loss of jobs that such policy would bring about. The trade-off that this argument sets up between higher pay for some workers and loss of jobs for others prevents exploring how the trade-off might be overcome or whether a trade-off even exists; regulating the market is ruled out as inefficient.

Pareto optimality also constrains discussion of distribution questions in economics since any policy that redistributes income from the rich to the poor will make the rich worse off, and hence, will not be Pareto optimal (King 2008).[17] As a result, the mainstream perspective is only interested, at most, in promoting equality of opportunity (for example, the chance to seek education or employment), and not in lessening inequality in outcomes (for example in wages, income, or wealth). And on this view, equal opportunities can only be promoted by fostering market competition through removal of legal barriers.

The capabilities approach pioneered by Amartya K. Sen in the 1980s provided another entry point to critique the mainstream's concept of well-being and contributed to the development of feminist economics. Sen and philosopher Martha Nussbaum argued that the income or output approaches to understanding well-being and their underlying utilitarian frameworks are not adequate for evaluating the efficacy of a successful economy or a good life (Nussbaum 2003; 2004; Sen 1999b). First, inferring well-being from income (and consumption) levels is flawed. One's income level (or ownership of resources, or the capacity of the economy to produce goods and services) can at best be a means to a good life, but it does not define that life. The income-based approach, which measures economic success by aggregate or average measures such as GDP per capita, tells us little about people's well-being. It does not take into consideration inequality in the distribution of that income. Nor does it take into account differing needs of groups and the fact that the same income level can generate more well-being for one group/individual than another. In other words, the ability to convert a given income level into well-being is contingent on personal, social, and environmental factors, what are termed "conversion factors." For example, to achieve the same level of well-being, a physically disabled person (group) would require more income than an able-bodied person (group). Similarly, Nussbaum (2004) argues that in order to overcome a history of discrimination society has to devote more resources to historically disadvantaged groups to achieve the same level of well-being as the groups who have not experienced such discrimination.

Second, the utilitarian underpinning of the income-based approach, which asks individuals how well-off they are, is also problematic. Sen and Nussbaum highlight the inadequacy of our subjective declarations of well-being, arguing that our pronouncements invariably reflect "adaptive preferences," that is, how we adapt to our circumstances. If one does not see any possibility of improving one's life options, then one may declare contentment with one's lot, when in fact any outsider could see shortfalls of well-being (for example, malnourishment or the inability of women to leave the house due to restrictions on their physical mobility).[18]

Nussbaum and Sen also argue that "freedom of choice" touted by the *homo economicus* model can only be an abstract, "suggested feasibility" of choice, unless one considers the material and social preconditions that impinge on that choice. For example, a woman who has a "feasible choice" to start a business may not be able to do so due to social conditions and economic circumstances that make it very difficult or impossible. Although she has the freedom in the sense that no law prevents her, she may actually be prevented from enjoying that freedom by prevailing patriarchal norms, the enormous burden of caregiving and household maintenance responsibilities she faces, or by simply lacking assets or access to affordable credit.

What is Economics?

The discipline's self-definition has also been another focus of critique by feminist economists. Mainstream economics defines the discipline principally in terms of optimizing the behavior of individuals: where there is exchange, it can be analyzed in terms of choices and markets. For example, the field of New Household Economics incorporates the family and women in its analysis by representing the household as a domain of exchange (that is, unpaid labor exchanged for upkeep provided by market labor). In addition, the discipline celebrates the application of its standard choice-theoretic methodology beyond markets (for example, the economic problem for a rational couple is to optimize their time allocation and specialize in different household tasks at least to some degree). Such extensions to mathematically formulate a broad range of questions in many other disciplines as optimization problems are viewed by the gatekeepers of economics as a strength of the discipline's analytical power (for example, Lazear 2000). Yet this approach marginalizes or obscures the importance of social provisioning, that is, how societies organize the activities involved in making a living. It also assumes away questions of "how much is enough," assuming that human wants are limitless and should be satisfied though market exchange. Feminists have joined established heterodox critiques that have questioned this neglect of the process of provisioning (Nelson 1993) and the discipline's "extraordinary indifference" to shortfalls of provisioning as represented by problems of poverty, lack of healthcare, and deteriorating social conditions (Heilbroner and Milberg 1995).

How Do We Know What We Know?

Feminist economists have criticized the discipline's emphasis on mathematical modeling to the exclusion of other methodologies, such as analytical description and qualitative analysis. Until recently the only valid, and still the most valued, methodology in mainstream economics, is the use of a formal, or mathematical, model that is then tested through econometric analysis.[19] According to its practitioners, formalism accompanied by econometric testing (and more recently, experimental methods) imparts the semblance of rigor and precision, and context-free generality to the analysis. That it can also produce "thin" analysis, which has little relevance to explaining or solving major economic and social problems, is of little concern to the core of the discipline.

The arm's-length treatment of the data used in most empirical work is a related shortcoming of the mainstream approach, which also underlies the mainstream's skepticism of qualitative research methods. Such a stance, practiced in the name of producing unbiased analysis, can conceal arbitrary judgments performed in the selection of underlying sample and choice of variables and prevent generating reliable insights from empirical analysis (Nelson 1995; MacDonald 1995; Berik 1997). This is the case, for example, with the recent economics literature on gender and risk aversion. Nelson (2014; forthcoming) shows that analyses supposedly supporting the broad claim that women are more risk averse than men are in fact based on weak empirical foundations: they tend to exaggerate and overgeneralize findings of sex differences as these studies are mainly based on samples of specific subgroups of the population in particular contexts. A more careful interpretation of the results, she argues, indicates that differences in risk attitudes and behavior between and within the sexes are more likely due to researcher biases, rather than sex difference per se.[20]

In addition, feminist economists have vigorously opposed the mainstream's claims that their preferred quantitative methodology offers unbiased analysis. This opposition has been based on developments in feminist theory around standpoint theory and the notion of situated knowledge, which recognize that values can be part of good, rigorous science. Feminists argue that knowledge is often constructed, not discovered, and knowledge producers are embodied and have values that are reflected in the research (Kabeer 1994; Harding 1995; Robeyns 2000). As Barker and Feiner (2004: 11) expressed it, "a view from nowhere" is impossible. "Every view is a point of view, and every point somewhere." In reality, economic methodologies are value-laden and certain standards are used by the dominant paradigm to "discriminate against or empower specific social groups" by turning "the experiences of everyday life into categories of people . . . that reflect prevailing political arrangements" (Harding and Norberg 2005: 2009).

Standpoint theory has been used by feminists to critique mainstream development economics—its concept of economic development and its preoccupation with GDP growth. For example, Sen and Grown (1987) argued that economic development must be evaluated from the perspective of poor Third World women who are the most disadvantaged group, and development strategies must be reconceived so as to transform the lives of those who are at the bottom. Similarly, Kabeer (1994) demonstrated the underlying hierarchy of knowledge upon which the dominant notion of development is constructed. She argued that the development establishment favors certain kinds of knowledge (produced by formal models that rely on decontextualized universal concepts) over others (local, contextual, experiential knowledge), which leads to budget priorities that disadvantage poor people. She argued that the use of the seemingly neutral criterion of GDP growth obscures the bulk of work performed in developing countries that is unpaid and this criterion is not of much use in assessing the impact of policies on the groups who perform unpaid labor. Furthermore, the methodological reductionist approach to knowledge construction separates economics from politics, culture, and the ecosystem and leads to neglect of the important interactions between different spheres of knowledge. This fragmentation of knowledge obscures the interests served by maintaining the development policy agenda that promotes economic growth; it also obscures the extent to which those who command material resources and wealth also exercise enormous power over the lives of others and over the ideas of their times. Kabeer argues that, by reversing the standpoint and assessing development policies from the perspective of poor Third World women, a different development agenda is possible.

The feminist methodological critiques thus emphasize pluralism in research methodology, validity of variety of standpoints, and challenge the notion of value-free knowledge production.

A Methodological Convergence

While feminist economics emerged from multiple critiques of mainstream economics, the project continues to have a big tent approach and is still evolving. Feminist economists accept the possibility, and indeed desirability, of different paths of analysis into the research agenda. This pluralism applies to their visions of social change and political action as well. While some feminist economists use mainstream frameworks, most eschew these, and others are on the continuum in between.

Given this pluralism, what is distinct about feminist economics? Our working definition draws upon Alison Jaggar's definition of a feminist theory—a theory that seeks to explain and to change women's subordinate position in society—as a starting point (Jaggar 1983). Thus, feminist economics has two central goals: to produce explanations for the causes, nature, and role of gender inequalities and to strive for a society that is more gender equitable, where women's subordinate position is eliminated. Feminists (and feminist economists) tend to interpret the goal of gender equality in the sense of equality of outcomes, albeit equal outcomes require the presence of equal opportunities (Phillips 2004).[21] To these goals we add the third goal of disciplinary scrutiny to reduce androcentric biases and produce more adequate explanations of economic life. Given the interdisciplinary nature of this effort, disciplinary scrutiny can contribute to feminist work in other social sciences as well. Many feminist economists believe that producing economic analyses will lead to progressive visions of social change that shape policies for a better world for women, men, and children (Longino 1993; Nelson 1995; Robeyns 2000; Benería 2003; Barker and Feiner 2004).

This working definition of feminist economics makes gender a central category of analysis. Beyond this central concept, since the early 1990s a commonality of approach emerged from feminist critiques of both mainstream and established heterodox theories and the WID approach in the gender and development field. Power (2004; 2013) refers to this common ground as the "Social Provisioning Approach" and identifies five areas of agreement that characterize it: the need to value caring labor, the use of human well-being as the yardstick for economic success, the belief in the importance of social agency, of ethical judgments, and of the relevance of various social stratifiers that differentiate among women and men. Critics in the gender and development field—the proponents of the GAD approach—discussed in Chapter 1, have also generated research that bears similar methodological features, as identified by Young (1992). We believe that these principles come the closest to providing coherence to feminist economics as an intellectual project and, from our perspective, a tool to build progressive policies and social change. While some feminists draw upon neoclassical economics in their work as we pointed out, we believe that embracing a social provisioning methodology means fundamentally rejecting neoclassical economics, and that the main tenets of neoclassical and heterodox economics cannot both be accommodated within feminist economics.

Gender as a Central Category of Economic Analysis

Gender is a key category of analysis for feminist economists, who commonly examine gender divisions of labor and gender inequalities in access to resources in the household and in labor markets, while seeking to promote gender-equitable provisioning and expansion of capabilities. The economic agent of feminist economics is gendered. Gender has been incorporated in the analysis based on insights from interdisciplinary scholarship in women's and gender studies and the concept has evolved in tandem with developments in feminist theory. Gender conveys what it means to be born female or male in a given society at a given point in history. As such, the gender difference shapes the experiences, options, and economic outcomes of individuals. However, the gender systems, or the gender value systems, which define the ideal behaviors, attitudes, and activities for women and men vary by society and are subject to change. The notion of gender as a social construct, constantly shaped and reconstituted, reflects the rejection of essentialism by feminist theory—the idea that there is an essence to being a man or woman that transcends time and place.

The gendering of individuals occurs through the process of socialization, that is, individuals who are born female and male become women and men in the context of family, schools, communities, workplaces, and under the dictates of social norms and the threat of social, sometimes legal, sanctions. The process entails as much conformity to norms as active creation of gendered behaviors. This conceptualization of gender as a product of individual agency opens up the possibility of multiple gender identities that defy the gender (man–woman) binary. While there is room for various forms of non-conformity, the rewards for gender conformity (and sanctions against non-conformity) often lead individuals to "do gender," that is, to live up to the ideals appropriate for their gender in a given social context. Evidence supporting the doing gender hypothesis is seen in situations where women or men appear to be deviating from gender norms. For example, feminist economists are finding that, in cases where husbands are unable to conform to the male breadwinner norm due to unemployment, women with full-time jobs are taking on a greater share of the housework (Bittman et al. 2003; Sevilla-Sanz et al. 2010; Baxter and Hewitt 2013).

Moreover, feminist research on gender norms has shown that gender is not a static category that defines women's and men's experiences throughout their lives. Over a life course as women (men) assume different positions in the household and in society the meaning of gender changes. This variation is prominent in parts of the world where classic patriarchy prevails, namely the region that runs from North Africa through the Middle East and South Asia. For example, woman's power in the household increases as she ages, if she has sons, and when she becomes a mother-in-law (Kandiyoti 1988).

Inspired by both feminist scholarship and institutional economics, since the 1990s feminist economists have increasingly analyzed gender as a hierarchical value system that is embedded in the workings of all institutions, indeed as we discussed, in economics as a discipline. This conceptualization of gender enables the systematic analysis of gender aspects of economic phenomena or gender implications of policy and the conveying the power relations, structures, and mechanisms that make and sustain gender relations. Such analyses set off from the premise that gender norms permeate all aspects of social life, and are central to understanding the functioning of the economy; for example, how labor markets operate in gendered ways (Elson 1999). Researchers have also made gender norms the object of analysis to explain how, even when a particular norm is gender-symmetric, it might produce disadvantages for women in a context where it is dominated by asymmetric norms enshrined in customs and laws marked by gender inequality (Van Staveren and Odebode 2007).[22] Close examination of gender norms can thus provide insights into why an apparent increase in bargaining power of women (for example, when their assets or income increases) may not alter gender-unequal outcomes, and how gender equality policies cannot solely focus on improving women's fallback position.

In contrast to feminist economic research where gender figures in the "thick" sense, which goes beyond the characteristic disaggregation of data by male and female, in mainstream economic analysis gender is often used in the "thin" sense, and mentioned in a "token" or "by the way" manner (Robeyns 2000: 13).[23] This type of analysis that does not go beyond gender disaggregation of data is also likely when feminist economists conduct econometric analysis with macro-level data (at national or cross-country levels). For example, when investigating the relationship between gender inequality in education levels and economic growth the gender concept tends to be reduced to the sex difference as recorded in official datasets and gender inequality is assumed to have the same meaning across countries. Moreover, in the absence of wage data, it may be not possible to sort out the transmission mechanism between gender equality in education and growth. What fuels economic growth? Is it the higher productivity of more educated women or the added advantage of wide wage gaps?[24] And in cross-country statistical analysis it is difficult to strengthen the gender content of the analysis, given the challenge of using insights from interpretive data (compiled using interview, participant observation methods), and analysis of secondary sources from country case studies.

The Economy as Constituted by Provisioning Activities

Feminist economists have shifted the subject matter of the discipline away from exchange towards provisioning activities, which are broadly defined to include both unpaid and paid activities aimed at generating the basic necessities of life (Nelson 1993). As reflected in this book, what is distinct in the feminist focus on provisioning is the emphasis on the importance of unpaid caring labor for provisioning individuals and communities on a daily basis and reproducing the labor force in an intergenerational sense, thereby contributing to social reproduction. Feminist economists argue that wage work and unpaid work are both important in determining the well-being of individuals and families. While in contemporary economies paid employment is the predominant mode of securing a living for oneself and one's family, considering solely paid work as economic activity overlooks important non market activities—care work, subsistence production—that undergird labor market activity.

Feminist researchers have problematized the invisibility of unpaid subsistence work in national statistics since the 1970s, when Ester Boserup (1970) remarked on the importance of unpaid work by women in subsistence production and as family helpers in farming in developing countries. An extensive body of research was launched on the issue of invisibility of and accounting for women's work. For example, Devaki Jain's work in the 1970s on time allocation by women, men, and children in India provided some of the earliest data that demonstrate the substantial amount of unpaid work provided by women, especially among the poor (Jain and Chand 1982). Bennería (1981) called attention to the underestimation of women's economic activities and to the need to re-conceptualize the labor force. Deere (1982) showed how the population censuses undercounted women's farm labor in the Andes. Bhattacharya (1985) analyzed the Indian data collection system and statistics and problematized its failure to capture all the relevant work activities performed by women and children. Similarly, Nash and Safa (1985) provided evidence on how unpaid work in the daily lives of peasant women in the Andes and those of female factory workers in Brazil, Mexico, Puerto Rico, and Jamaica, affects the manner and terms in which they engage in paid work. These studies also imply that if policies do not take account of the extensive amount of unpaid work women perform, and assume women have unlimited time on their hands, they may adversely affect the well-being of women by increasing their workloads.

In sum, by identifying the economic agent as an individual who is interdependent in a network of social relations in and outside of the household, feminist economics parts ways from the mainstream's isolated individual or unitary household. And by identifying the economy as the domain of interdependent provisioning activities, feminist economics thus transcends the monetary–non-monetary dichotomy and defines economics as the study of social provisioning.

Human Well-being as the Central Measure of Economic Success

Over the course of the 1990s and 2000s, the focus on gender analysis of the economy moved from concern about economic experiences of women at home and in the labor market to broader questions of well-being that affect men as well as women. Instrumental in this move were not only feminist critiques of development economics using for example standpoint theory but also the development of the capabilities approach, mentioned earlier, and other theoretical and practical approaches such as the human rights perspective (see Chapter 1) that challenged the mainstream concept of well-being. Many feminist economists have adopted the capabilities approach as the normative complement to their work and define well-being in terms of capabilities of individuals, rather than average or aggregate measures of income and wealth; feminists agree that the latter measures are at best inputs to human well-being and often are not sufficient for meeting human needs.

According to the capabilities approach, the goal of economic policies and social arrangements should be to promote the well-being of individuals defined in terms of capabilities. A good economy or a good life, then, is one that expands what people are able to do or to be. In this approach, capabilities represent the valuable options from which one can choose. A basic list of capabilities includes the capability to be healthy, to lead lives free of violence, to be free from discrimination, to participate in decision-making in society.[26] Some of these capabilities can be the means for promoting others; for example, the ability to be educated helps promote the ability to make informed choices for family well-being or in elections.

Much of Sen's and Nussbaum's work includes illustrations of capability deprivations experienced by women, especially in developing countries (Sen 1990a; 1990b; 1992; Nussbaum 2000a; 2000b). Sen's work on "missing women" examines the sources and underlying causes of deprivation of the ability to live. As Nussbaum (2004: 241–42) articulates the gendered well-being problem, "Women in much of the world lack support for fundamental functions of human life [. . .] [U]nequal social and political circumstances result in women's unequal human capabilities." She proposes a basic list of capabilities that are relevant for women's lives universally. Nussbaum insists on the notion that the goal of policy should be the promotion of capabilities in the form of constitutional guarantees in all countries (Nussbaum 2000a; 2011b). The approach allows for individual choice in leading one's life: The actual outcomes for individuals represent their "functionings," that is, their achievements, given the capability options. Thus, someone might choose to go into a violent sport and put their health in grave danger and end up with poor health (or worse) due to that choice. A life cut short or damaged due to that choice represents that person's functioning, but it is the result of a choice made in the context of the capability to lead a life free of violence.[26] By contrast, if a woman is subject to her spouse's violence, not only is her functioning impaired but also we can infer that her capability to lead a life free of violence does not exist. Capabilities or functionings are typically measured at the group level (for example, the maternal mortality rate for a given geography rather than one mother's pregnancy and childbirth outcome).

What enables capabilities? Individual or household income is an obvious means but often it is not sufficient. The logic of the capabilities approach flows from means (resources for provisioning) to capabilities to functionings. The means include endowments of each individual (labor power, assets) that generate the income to support livelihoods (or an individual's entitlement to a share of household resources) plus the entitlements that are guaranteed by the state or community. The capabilities approach views it as imperative that governments make sure that adequate means (resources) are available for promoting capabilities of all and that social restrictions creating unequal access for certain groups are removed: if the capability in question is health, then the resources (mostly financial) have to be generated and devoted to promoting the capability to be healthy, for example, in the form of clean water, access to medical care, basic health knowledge, immunizations, sanitation. In addition to resources, promoting capabilities requires institutional arrangements to support them: for example, establishing a system of health clinics, or in the case of other capabilities, institutions that guarantee political and social freedoms, provision of a social safety net, transparency in public office. Since the capabilities approach is only a normative framework to assess well-being and to infer the efficacy of social and economic arrangements in providing well-being, it does not elaborate on how these means for promoting capabilities can be developed or strengthened (for example, what kind of macroeconomic policies or development strategies should be pursued).[27]

Thus, the capabilities approach has been instrumental in extending feminist economists' focus from gender inequalities in provisioning activities in the household and labor markets to gender inequalities in well-being, and to examine the connections of well-being to inequalities in provisioning. The approach has also made ethical questions more explicit in feminist writing in economics.

Human Agency is Important

Feminist economists are as interested in the process that generates economic outcomes as in the outcomes themselves. This position implies that attention to agency underlying the outcomes is relevant for research. For example, typical outcomes of interest for feminists are gender inequalities in wages, assets, unpaid hours, or consumption levels. Feminist economists are interested in examining how these inequalities come about, which groups are involved in maintaining (or benefit from) them, and how inequalities might be reduced. Attention to process and agency, in turn, has methodological implications. In some instances it entails complementing statistical analysis with analytical description of the workings of the household, the labor markets, and the state. This stance implies paying attention to quantitative as well as interpretive data. In other instances, it calls for moving away from the discipline's preferred data sources and crossing method boundaries in generating data (Nelson 1995; Berik 1997; Starr 2014), for example through interviews or small-scale sample surveys. In general, feminist economists hold that the choice of method depends on the research question, which gives rise to methodological pluralism. This position implies that feminist economists are not averse to formalization as one possible approach to economic analysis. If gender inequality is to be examined for its connections to macroeconomic outcomes—to examine, for example, whether gender inequalities help or hinder economic growth—reliance on formal modeling of the macroeconomy and econometric testing can be very useful.

In order to generate information on human agency and process however, feminist economists tend to use evidence generated by other social scientists or collaborate in cross-disciplinary research projects.[28] Certain topics that concern power, domination, or oppression may require analytical description or theoretical discussion and research methods such as interviews, focus groups, participant observation, and primary surveys to generate the relevant data. These interpretive methods also fit closely with the feminist goals of giving voice to women and gaining insights into how to make change to promote socioeconomic justice (Esim 1997). In addition, such data can be used to formulate hypotheses that are to be examined through formal methods (Van Staveren 1997) or to provide validity to quantitative analysis or interpret results of statistical analysis (Berik 1997; Olmsted 1997).

Ethical Judgments are Integral to Economic Analysis

Arguing that there is no value-free analysis, feminist economists reject the distinction between positive and normative analysis. Instead, they tend to make explicit their values (for example, the pursuit of gender equality or social justice), while adopting a rigorous (though not necessarily formal) analysis that produces insights relevant to solving the economic problems identified. These positions emerge from feminist critiques of orthodox thinking, and they emphasize that each researcher is a product of his/her social circumstances—social class, gender, race, as well as his/her professional training. The social and historical location of the researcher shapes the research process from the selection of the research question to the method used, and it produces "situated knowledge." This position implies that at the level of the individual researcher one cannot speak of objectivity. Instead, feminist economists have argued that the goal of good science should be to achieve "strong objectivity" that emerges at the level of the research community, through interaction and debate in the larger research community by researchers who bring a variety of perspectives (Harding 1995).[29] To achieve strong objectivity in her/his research efforts, each researcher should make explicit her/his perspective and examine the values and hidden cultural assumptions in existing theories.

The shift in the definition of economics from the study of individual choices to the study of social provisioning entails a shift in values, which feminist critiques make explicit. Contrary to the mainstream's pretence of value-free science, it should be noted that an economics that views well-being in terms of the fulfillment of unlimited wants of individuals is narcissistic and potentially destructive as it encourages unlimited extraction of resources to satisfy the unlimited wants (Strober 2003). On the other hand, making provisioning the centerpiece of economics invites concern about the levels of provisioning being achieved by everyone, and a willingness to address shortfalls in provisioning by state-based entitlements, and to regulate production and trade to ensure adequate quantity and quality of goods and services.

Intersectional Analysis

Feminists agree that it is not possible to speak of gender differences in isolation from other social stratifiers such as class, caste, race/ethnicity, national origin, sexual orientation, and age, which further differentiate options for provisioning one's self and family and may compound disadvantages for subordinate groups. This position calls for intersectional analysis that is attentive to differences among women (and men), which is another legacy of the developments in feminist theory.

Attention to race/ethnicity/sexuality and other social differentiations produces a rich analysis, sometimes with unanticipated results. For example, the effect of sexual orientation often differs by gender. Badgett (1995a) shows that in the US gay and bisexual men earned considerably less than equally productive heterosexual men (on the order of 11 to 27 percent), whereas among women, the effect of sexual orientation was less precisely estimated. On the other hand, lesbians' earnings were only about two-thirds of those of gay men, indicating that gender is more important than sexual orientation in determining earnings for lesbians. Likewise, analysis of the 2007–08 US financial crisis shows that racial/ethnic differences and family type were more important in shaping the impact of the crisis than gender alone (Fukuda-Parr et al. 2013). The groups in the US that were most adversely affected were people of color and single mothers across racial groups.[30] In the aftermath of the crisis, poverty rates for single mothers rose in all racial groups, whereas examining the trend in incomes by gender shows a more positive outlook for women compared to men.

In practice, however, most feminist economists do not engage in empirical research that is attentive to all these stratifiers. Researchers are often hampered by lack of data on some dimensions of stratification. For example, sexual orientation often is left out of the analysis, even though it is clear that gender analysis is not sufficient in explaining economic outcomes of lesbian, gay, bisexual women and men (Badgett 1995b). When researchers wish to consider how sexual orientation differentiates economic outcomes by gender and race/ethnicity, they rely on special surveys (Badgett 1995a). Another common obstacle in the path of intersectional statistical analysis is the lack of datasets with samples that are large enough to examine economic outcomes of multiple groups, which may prevent consideration of, for example, race/ethnic breakdown of gender-differentiated data.[31] Data constraints thus may render invisible the diverse experiences of women (men), unless alternative research methods are utilized, such as small surveys, interviews, and focus groups.

Gender Inequalities in Provisioning Activities

Most people provide basic necessities for themselves and their families on the basis of income or output generated by their own labor: wage labor, income based on informal activities, self-employment, subsistence or market-oriented agricultural work. However, unpaid labor in the household is necessary to transform the proceeds of this work into family well-being. Feminist economists have shown the interdependence of both paid and unpaid forms of labor in producing livelihoods. In this section, we focus on contributions of feminist economics to the analysis of labor markets (wage labor and informal activities), non-market forms of labor such as unpaid family labor on market-oriented farms, and the dynamics of household relations.

Wage Labor

Feminist analysis of inequalities in capitalist labor markets has moved the field beyond the conventional work on discrimination and occupational segregation. As we pointed out earlier in this chapter, feminists began with a critique of human capital theory that posited women's secondary position in labor markets as the outcome of their own choices. Accordingly, women are choosing the amount and type of education and training and occupations that destines them to lower pay. Feminists contend that this argument overlooks discriminatory practices that exclude women from well-paying jobs and the societal discrimination in the socialization process of boys and girls that produce the different preferences. Moreover, the labor market discrimination against women—whether in hiring or on the job—also shapes women's occupation or job choices.[32] In other words, women's choices are endogenous, feminist economists argue, with plenty of discrimination in play, contributing to gender wage inequality.

In empirical analysis, the debate with human capital theory boils down to attempting to identify the relative contributions of labor market skills and discrimination to the gender wage gap (Blau et al. 2014). Human capital theorists argue that data shortcomings stand in the way of a full accounting of the productivity differences between men and women (for example, there is rarely data available on motivation, work effort, and other relevant job qualifications); if these productivity differences were to be properly measured, they argue, they would show that women are less productive than men. Feminist critics, by contrast, argue that much of the gender wage gap that is unmeasured (also referred to as "unobserved" or "unexplained") in empirical analysis actually reflects discrimination against women. The two positions have different policy implications for closing the gender wage gap: an emphasis on closing the education gaps as sufficient condition versus addressing discrimination through equal opportunity legislation and greater scrutiny of gender socialization, especially in schooling prior to higher education. Even when human capital theorists acknowledge discrimination may be at work, they expect market competition to eliminate it over time by making employers realize that discrimination is not good for their bottom line.

Empirical studies of labor markets in developing countries have also been framed in terms of this methodology of differentiating between discriminatory and productivity-related sources of wage inequality. Much of the research finds a sizable unexplained component attributable to discrimination, lending support to strengthening equal opportunity policies. In addition, a flurry of research, mostly on developing countries, has shown that discrimination does not disappear with increased market (international trade) competition (Kongar 2007; Oostendorp 2009; Menon and van der Meulen Rodgers 2009; Gunewardena et al. 2008). In fact, discrimination may intensify (Berik et al. 2004). This is not surprising, of course, when one brings into the picture the low bargaining power of women workers vis-à-vis employers, and discrimination as a practice that benefits employers in their quest for lowering labor costs.

Stepping outside the mainstream framework further shows that the debate is built on questionable mainstream assumptions: that wages are an objective measure of individual labor productivity and discrimination is the differential in wages over and above the productivity-determined wage (Albelda and Drago 2013). Also this type of empirical analysis tends to use gender as a dummy variable, stripping the concept of gender of much of its content (Figart 1997). Dissatisfaction with this type of analysis has led to alternative feminist formulations which are more consistent with heterodox economics and feminist research in other disciplines. These formulations recognize that gender norms (for example, the undervaluation of women's labor or traditions that predetermine the gender division of labor) are embedded in the workings of the labor market, which makes it more difficult to root out discrimination via equal employment policy alone (Elson 1999; Figart, et al. 2013).

Moreover, feminist research has shown that legislation on equality of opportunity has not been sufficient to improve women's labor market position in any society (Strober 1984; Power and Rosenberg 1995; Trzcinski 2000; Rubery et al. 2001; Blau et al. 2014). Active labor market policies, such as work–family reconciliation policies, social security, welfare rights, and other institutional changes are necessary (Laufer 1998; Rubery et al. 1998; Bruegel and Perrons 1998; Antonopoulos 2013; Razavi et al. 2012). Some of these policies were introduced in the European Union in recent decades, though the 2008 economic crisis has stalled or reversed these policies in many countries (Benería and Martinez-Iglesias 2014). Feminist economists have also engaged in debates about policy initiatives regarding increases in the minimum wage and the promotion of basic income guarantee schemes, both of which would disproportionately benefit women (Bernstein et al. 1999; Kabeer 2000; McKay 2001; Rubery and Grimshaw 2011; National Women's Law Center 2014). Tackling labor market inequalities also requires framing these policies in a macroeconomic policy framework that is conducive to the growth of decent jobs. Otherwise, improving women's access to good jobs may come at the expense of men, and thus not only face policy opposition but also fail in terms of the feminist goal of expanding livelihoods and well-being in an equitable manner.

Beyond Wage Labor

As will be discussed in Chapter 4 in more detail, in developing countries, a large proportion of women engage in agricultural and informal sector activities and most of this labor is not performed under regular wage relations. Since the 1970s, feminist scholars, including economists and development scholars, have challenged development studies, agricultural economics, and labor economics in their assumptions that men alone are the farmers and informal sector participants. They have also challenged conventional labor force data collection, which supported the notion that agricultural systems in Asia, Africa, and Latin America and the Caribbean are based on male labor. They amply demonstrated the substantial agricultural activities of women, whether in performing certain tasks such as weeding, harvesting, and milling or in cultivating food or subsistence crops. For example, Jain and Banerjee (1985), Croll (1985), Deere and León de Leal (1987), Agarwal (1994), and others noted the diversity in the gender division of work and women's participation in agriculture, by region, and according to race, ethnicity, and caste.

The nature of women's and men's activities in the informal sector has also been examined by feminist economists. As in agriculture, the early research on the informal sector tended to overlook the gendered aspects of these activities. But such neglect was addressed by the work of Caroline Moser (1981) on market sellers in Ecuador, the study of lacemakers in India by Maria Mies (1982), and the study of homeworkers in Mexico City by Benería and Roldan (1987). These studies helped pave the way for feminist re-conceptualization of the informal sector. They also provided evidence on the gender bias in measurement of labor force participation that consistently underestimates women's economic activities. The gender analysis of the informal sector showed the importance of women's economic contribution to household earnings, for example, in the case of the Mexico City study, through subcontracted activities from a variety of sources that included plastic polishing and toy assembling. These studies also demonstrated inequalities in access to means of production, credit, technology, and market information that constrained the incomes of women. Given that the household is the locus of production of many self-employed activities, feminist studies of self-employment brought attention to the intra-household inequalities in resource allocation and well-being. And they raised the question of whether women's income has more beneficial effects on the family, particularly for children, than men's income, an issue that has been emphasized by studies that show the long-run economic growth impacts of household-level gender inequalities, discussed below.

Asset Ownership, Credit, and Risk

Assets are one of the main endowments of individuals, besides their own labor, that can contribute to individual and family livelihoods and in turn enable capabilities. Gender differences in ownership or control of physical and financial assets thus have important implications for well-being of women and their families (Deere and Doss 2006). Women's ownership of land or a house has been shown to increase children's capabilities to be well-nourished and increase women's decision-making power (Allendorf 2007) and to affect the incidence of physical violence against women (Panda and Agarwal 2005; Bhatla et al. 2006; Bhattacharyya et al. 2011). In addition, where agriculture is important as a source of livelihood, ownership of farmland is important for food security (Agarwal 1994). Yet feminist research on gender asset inequalities is relatively recent compared to the attention devoted to gender earning inequalities (Deere and Doss 2006; Deere et al. 2013). The main reason for this lag in attention is the lack of gender-disaggregated data on asset ownership, which is slowly being remedied as surveys include questions on individual wealth.

As farmers, women in many countries have fewer rights over land compared to men. Land rights refer to use rights enshrined in customary law or formal rights to own and manage property backed by laws. While women's formal land rights have improved since the early 1990s in Latin America and

Sub-Saharan Africa, there are many obstacles to women's land ownership.[33] Even where women have legal rights to own land, in many parts of the world they are still unable to exercise these rights, handing control over land to male relatives (Agarwal 1994). On the other hand, the introduction of private ownership of land has undermined women's customary use rights over land in some parts of Sub-Saharan Africa (Lastarria-Cornhiel 1997) while strengthening women's land rights in other parts of Sub-Saharan Africa (Behrman et al. 2012).

Feminist researchers have traced the inequalities in asset ownership to a number of sources: women's lack of property rights renders them unable to inherit property; low earnings and limited access to credit can hinder purchase of land by women; and gender norms and legal regulations prevent women from promoting their interests. For example, marital regimes that govern the sharing of property within marriage and upon its dissolution are fairly common and can contribute to gender inequality in assets. In a comparative study of individual asset ownership in Ecuador, Ghana, and the Indian state of Karnataka, Deere et al. (2013) show that there are major differences in married women's ownership of wealth depending on the type of marital property regime and inheritance laws which prevail.[34]

Credit, along with savings, is one route through which women can acquire assets and establish a small business. In recent years, much attention has been given to women's access to credit and its role in promoting women's self-employment. In fact, a voluminous literature on microcredit and its role in reducing income poverty and empowering women has emerged. The complexity of the relationship between access to credit, productivity, and empowerment has made this subject contentious. While many donor agencies and international organizations have touted the benefits of microcredit programs that target women, many feminist scholars have cautioned against viewing microcredit as a policy for either reducing poverty or empowering low-income women. Evaluations of microcredit programs have raised a number of concerns about its role in providing income security for women borrowers. Microcredit may not generate a sustained increase in income because women's activities are typically low-return and unstable activities while the size of loans might be too small (Mayoux 2000); only if women are able to rely on other income sources can microcredit provide a pathway to increase women's income (Jahiruddin et al. 2011). The group lending feature of microcredit, especially in the context of commercial (for profit) loans, ties low-income women's and their families' livelihoods to the uncertainty and risk of financial markets (Karim 2011; Wichterich 2012). In addition, microcredit studies focus almost exclusively on production loans, ignoring the consumption debt to meet health emergencies, etc. (Floro and Messier 2010).

With regard to the questions of agency and empowerment, the feminist debate has focused on whether women control the loans or the income from the microenterprise (or are simply a conduit for the loan that their husbands use) and how empowerment should be measured (Goetz and Gupta 1996; Kabeer 2001; Parmar 2003; Garikipati 2008). Feminists have also been critical of the tendency to isolate evaluation of the impacts of microcredit from the prevailing social relations and type of economic environment, which can either strengthen or weaken its effect on women's well-being (Goetz and Gupta 1996; Adams and Mayoux 2001; Rankin 2002).

Feminist economists have also explored the gendered dimension of attitudes and behavior towards risk, which influence the returns to investment as well as business earnings, at least in the high-income countries. Feminist research builds on experimental research as well as empirical studies from other social and behavioral sciences, some of which found statistically significant differences in average risk preferences between the sexes (Hinz et al. 1997).[35] Some early research found that in retirement plans, US married women were, on average, more conservative in their asset allocations compared to married men (Sunden and Surette 1998), which led to lower average investment returns (Jianakoplos and Bernasek 1998).[36] The proposed explanations have ranged from sex difference in preferences in competitive situations and overconfidence on men's part, to a possible greater incidence of negative outcomes experienced by women, which make them more risk averse. However, there is debate about the extent to which these results may reflect the specific situations that frame the decisions and affect the behavior of individuals rather than actual differences between women and men (Nelson 2014; forthcoming; Filippin and Crosetto 2014).

The Dynamics of the Household

The household is one of the key sites of interest to feminist economists. It is the locus of unpaid caring activities and provisioning based on incomes generated by household members; it is also the site of gender inequalities in workload and resource allocation, and power relations that mediate well-being outcomes. As mentioned above, feminist frameworks of the household grew out of critiques of Becker's unitary and harmonious model of the household. In several cases, the impetus was provided by developing country research that challenged Becker's model. In addition, within the mainstream there was a methodological shift to game-theoretic formulations of intra-household relations.

A large body of literature on households in developing countries pointed out the unrealistic and simplistic assumptions of unitary models that do not reflect the variety of ways in which families and households function across countries and cultures (Dwyer and Bruce 1988). In her analysis of agricultural households in Africa, Koopman (1991), for example, illustrated how the assumptions of shared preferences and pooled resources were at odds with the separate productive enterprises of men and women within households. Moreover, presuming that households function according to the unitary model can frustrate the anticipated supply response to various agricultural policies. For example, due to the rigidity of the gender division of labor and non-pooling of incomes, cash-crop production may not rise when crop prices increase.[37] Or it may increase only if women have weak bargaining power vis-à-vis their spouses and end up substituting work on cash crops controlled by their spouse for work on food crops, which may undermine food security for women and children (Darity 1995).

The methodological shift away from the unitary household model came with the bargaining models of Manser and Brown (1980) and McElroy and Horney (1981), who used game theory to analyze intra-household allocation. These models assumed household members, invariably a couple, were individuals with different preferences and different options on which they could fall back if their relationship did not work out. The strength of those options—for example, having a well-paying job, divorce laws, effective control over assets, or absence of dependents to support or care for—gave different degrees of bargaining power to each individual, who in turn could bargain over the allocation of resources in the household. While bargaining models allow for differing preferences within the household with the potential for disagreement and discord, otherwise they are thoroughly within the neo-classical microeconomics mold: each individual is a *homo economicus* driven by self-interest, with a very clear idea about her/his preferences and options, and equally capable of bargaining.

An important contribution towards the construction of feminist models of the household was made by Sen (1985; 1990a), who argued that the household is a site of both cooperation and conflict, where conflict is subsumed under the appearance of cooperation. Sen's innovative formulation of the household as the site of "cooperative conflicts" advanced the analysis of the household beyond the earlier economic conceptualizations of the family: (a) the neoclassical view of a harmonious unit; (b) the Marxian view of the family as a source of unity and survival for the working class; and (c) the feminist view of the family as a locus of conflict and struggle.[38] Sen argued that gender inequalities in even the most basic aspects of life, such as survival, nutrition, health, and literacy were the result of differences in bargaining power. A long-time critic of neoclassical models, he argued that these models were incapable of explaining the systematically inferior social status of women in many societies; both the harmonious rational choice model and the game-theoretic bargaining models of neoclassical economics were flawed in capturing the nature of gender relations and inequalities within families, particularly in developing countries.

As an alternative, Sen (1990a) proposed a bargaining *framework* that included three factors relevant to the bargaining process: (a) the fallback position feature of the bargaining models, which he termed "breakdown well-being response" (what a person has to fall back on, were s/he to physically survive outside the family), and two innovative elements, (b) "self-interest response" (one's perception of her/his self-interest) and (c) "perceived contribution response" (one's perception of her/his contribution to the family).

Sen argued that these perceptions are relevant to understanding how gender inequalities emerge and how they are maintained. His reasoning was that women, especially in developing countries, tend to have limited perception of their individual well-being since they view themselves as part of the family unit and their care for others leaves little room for having an independent sense of their own interests, needs, and well-being. A weak sense of self-interest thus makes women more likely to go along with arrangements that leave them disadvantaged. In addition, Sen argued, in family-owned businesses or family farms, some of them in subsistence agriculture, women's contributions to the family enterprise might be less visible both to themselves and others around them compared to a setting of wage labor. Such weak perception of one's economic contribution would disadvantage women in the intra-household distributional processes.[39]

Sen has used his bargaining framework to explain the problem of "missing women," which continues to be prevalent in China and India (Sen 1990b; 1992). Accordingly, the lopsided population sex ratios in countries or regions within a country were the result of the low bargaining power of women in the household. The solution then was to increase women's bargaining power and agency by improving each of the three components of bargaining power (Sen 1990a). This, in turn, could be achieved by improving women's employment opportunities in paid work outside the network of kinship relations (in his words, "gainful work outside"), increasing women's educational levels, and consciousness raising.

Sen's formulation has been conducive to analyzing the factors behind women's subordination, powerlessness, and low bargaining power. As such, it has subsequently been developed by other economists with a more specific feminist lens (Katz 1991; Seiz 1991; Agarwal 1992a; 1997; Carter and Katz 1997; Kabeer 2000). For example, Agarwal (1997) focused on relatively neglected dimensions of Sen's bargaining approach, providing a rich analysis of bargaining power, informed by her empirical work on India. In her analysis, the factors affecting women's fallback positions and relative bargaining strength go beyond individual sources of power to include social norms, market institutions, the community, and the state, each subject to transformation through policy and action. Agarwal made the case for the interrelated nature of bargaining within and outside the household, given the embeddedness of households in a larger institutional context. Under-valuation of women's work in the labor market thus has feedback effects on women's bargaining power over family subsistence via both limited perception of their contribution and their low earnings. More recent empirical evidence also shows that women's ability to exercise the bargaining power they derive from employment and earnings is affected by gender norms, values, and inequalities at the institutional level (Van Staveren and Odebode 2007; Mabsout and Van Staveren 2010; Bittman et al. 2003).

Feminist economists have also engaged with Sen's bargaining framework. Agarwal (1997) argued against Sen's view that women lacked a perception of self-interest as well as the feminist arguments that women are more altruistic than men due to their gender socialization. Lack of protest against inequality does not mean lack of awareness of it, Agarwal argued; gender constraints often prevent women from acting overtly in their self-interest and may result in the appearance of compliance. She also argued that self-interest and altruism often coexist.

Sen's emphasis on paid work outside of kinship networks as an instrument for strengthening the three components of women's bargaining power has also been subject to critique. Critics argued that paid work is important but may not be sufficient to give women greater say in the household and to improve their well-being: women wage workers end up with the dual burden of household work and paid work; and low-waged work can have only a weak effect (Koggel 2003; Domínguez et al. 2010). Other studies show that participation in paid work is not necessary to ensure higher survival chances of females. Quite the contrary, the prevalence of unpaid family work in rural settings, which is extremely valuable for the viability of smallholder agriculture, is associated with higher female–male sex ratios among children (Berik and Bilginsoy 2000). The notion of the capitalist workplace as free of patriarchal relations, suggested by Sen's emphasis on "gainful work outside," has also been long challenged by feminists. Elson and Pearson (1981) emphasized how companies make use of traditional gender norms to organize the workplace and thereby reinforce these gender norms, which weakens the potential of large factory settings to raise women workers' consciousness. In addition, the trend in India's sex ratio at birth also challenges Sen's argument in favor of women's education as a tool for strengthening women's agency and bargaining power in the household. Indian evidence shows that while women's labor force participation is positively related to the greater survival chances of girls, women's increasing education level is associated with rising male–female sex ratios at birth, a sign of son preference exercised through sex-selective abortion (Mukherjee 2013; Srinivasan and Bedi 2008; Sen 2001).

Nonetheless, the cooperative-conflict bargaining framework continues to inform empirical analyses of intra-household bargaining, even though empirical studies do not always uphold its predictions. For example, based on experimental evidence from Uganda, Jackson (2013) finds limited support for Sen's framework. In a gender system that is patriarchal and patrilocal and where husbands formally have complete control over money management in marriage, there is no difference in women's and men's perceptions of self-interest, and monetary contribution-based power does not hold. Also since marital success is important for upholding masculine identities, wives end up having a stronger fallback position.

In terms of methodology, while both Sen and Agarwal argued for a broader approach unconstrained by formal models, the empirical analysis of intra-household allocation and decision-making has taken off in highly quantitative directions. The quantitative turn has been the result of increasing recognition of the importance of women's bargaining power for children's well-being and the interest in establishing causality in what drives child well-being outcomes (Doss 2013). The World Bank's "gender equality is smart economics" argument hinges on women's bargaining power in making decisions. The argument posits lower gender inequality as the contributor to economic growth, and the primary mechanism is women's spending patterns that benefit children. The growing empirical literature on intra-household bargaining can thus be attributed to the impact of feminist economics on policy circles, which have taken an instrumental interest in intra-household bargaining. Yet, as Cheryl Doss (2013) points out, neither bargaining power nor women's preferences for particular outcomes are observable and therefore any empirical research will have to rely on the use of proxies, such as women's earned income, assets, and education level. This literature has presumed that a positive effect on a desired outcome (for example, child educational attainment) reflects women's preference for that effect. The variety of proxy measures for women's bargaining power has sometimes led to different findings, thus stimulating a debate among feminist scholars and policymakers alike.

Moreover, the interest in sorting out causality, and unambiguously establishing the effect of women's bargaining power on a desired outcome (rather than vice versa) increases the bar for standards of rigor. Thus, nearly two decades after the feminist economic critiques of the hierarchy in research methods, a hierarchy is prevalent in research on women's bargaining power: natural experiments and randomized control trials are considered as the most rigorous sources of data, and the econometric studies invariably are expected to address the problem of endogeneity (that is, rule out reverse causality—when in fact most aspects of social life both shape another aspect and are shaped by it). Doss (2013) points out that less rigorous data provide important insights while Jackson (2013) argues in favor of combining evidence—from experiments, surveys, and ethnography—to provide external validity to the analysis. We agree with these views and believe that quantification for its own sake can undermine insightful gender analysis of socioeconomic relations.

Macroeconomic Policies, Provisioning, and Well-being

Parallel to the focus on labor markets and households where gender relations are visible, feminist economics has made considerable headway in engaging with the broader questions of how to bring about an economy that is equitable. This latter question, on the agenda of feminist economics since the 1980s, is based on the recognition of the crucial role of macroeconomic policies in shaping conditions for provisioning of livelihoods and well-being. The basic macroeconomic policy instruments of fiscal policy, monetary policy, exchange rate and trade policy are designed to address the problems of unemployment, inflation, and economic stagnation. However, until the 1980s, both the policy objectives and the instruments were assumed to be gender neutral, affecting women and men in a similar manner, and the impacts were assumed to be confined to the monetary economy. The implementation of structural adjustment programs (SAPs) in severely indebted developing countries in the 1980s and 1990s provided feminists ample opportunities to challenge this assumption.

The project of "engendering macroeconomics" grew out of studies that showed the gender and class bias of the SAPs and set the stage for integrating gender in macroeconomic models from the 1990s onward (Çağatay et al. 1995; Grown et al. 2000).[40] Feminist research examined both the impact of fiscal or trade policies, economic growth, and financial crises on gender inequalities and the effect of gender inequalities in the household or in the labor market on macroeconomic outcomes. In this section we highlight the contributions of both research projects.

Critique of Neoliberal Macroeconomic Policies

SAPs were designed by the International Monetary Fund (IMF) and the World Bank together with other international financial players as a condition for new loans to developing countries on the brink of default due to heavy indebtedness to international creditors.[41] The test case for the World Bank's structural adjustment lending (SAL) took place in the Philippines during 1979–82 (Broad 1988).[42] By 1982, the debt crises erupted in several developing countries starting with Mexico. A SAP was implemented whenever a country announced its inability to meet its debt payments, enabling these multilateral financial institutions to play major roles in the country's development process. Thereafter this program became the typical IMF/World Bank model that was implemented throughout the 1980s and 1990s in Latin America, Asia, and Africa, and in the Eastern European countries during the post-1989 period. In a nutshell, SAPs focused on cutting government budgets, privatization of public assets, deregulation of industries, and liberalization of trade and investment in order to bring about economic stability.[43] In the early 1980s these policies were also adopted in the US, UK, and Canada, under the label of supply-side economics. At the time, British Prime Minister Margaret Thatcher famously pronounced "there is no alternative" to these policies. Since then, they have been referred to alternatively as market reforms, structural reforms, austerity packages, or neoliberal policies. By the end of the 1990s, the IMF and the World Bank dubbed them "sound" macro-economic policy and they were mainstreamed. After the 2007–08 financial crisis several European nations also were subjected to strong austerity measures representing some variation of the SAP model.

Soon after SAPs began to be implemented, it became quite clear that the burden of adjustment was not equally distributed among the population. Studies showed that many countries registered an increase in poverty levels, income inequality, and social polarization (Cornia et al. 1987; ECA 1989; Commonwealth Secretariat 1989; ECLAC 1990; 1995). Furthermore, mostly based on country case studies, feminist research showed that these macroeconomic policies were gender biased as they had specific negative impacts for women.[44]

Building on evidence produced by feminists, Elson and Çağatay (2000) argued that inherent in these policies are three biases that disproportionately hurt the low-income groups, especially women among them: *deflationary*, *commodification*, and *male-breadwinner* biases. First, the emphasis on budget cuts puts the economy on a recessionary or deflationary path. The deflationary stance is manifest in the policy attention given to financial variables (inflation, budget deficit), rather than job creation, whereby the goal of policymakers is to signal to the financial markets that the real returns on assets will be high, and taxes and expenditures will be low. This austerity approach contributes to low employment growth and lay-offs for formal sector employees which, in turn, reverberate through the economy. Where formal jobs are mostly held by men, lay-offs are followed by pressure on women to enter the labor force, searching for jobs. The hardships generated by SAPs, together with export-orientation that generated jobs for women, contributed to the accelerated entry of women into the labor force in the 1980s and early 1990s (Çağatay and Özler 1995). The Asian financial crisis provided evidence for the gendered labor-market effects of deflation. Lim (2000) showed that unemployment rates of both women and men increased in the Philippines, but paid hours of women increased while men's hours declined. And because the increase in relative and absolute paid work for women came in the context of unequal unpaid care work, Lim (2000: 1305) concluded that there was "a tendency toward 'overworked' females and 'underworked' males."

Second, in the name of promoting efficiency and "getting the prices right," the World Bank and the IMF encouraged the privatization of public services and public firms.[45] The introduction of user fees for public services or their privatization contributed to the commodification trend in the economy. Every public service—hospitals, schools, utilities, health insurance, pensions— becomes available for purchase for those who can afford them. In addition, as quality of public services (healthcare, education) deteriorates due to shrinking budgets, families seek to send their children to private schools or go to private health clinics, thus putting poor families under pressure if they cannot afford the fees. As household budgets shrank, securing the resources to pay for these more expensive or new budget items meant increase in domestic work; women sought to make do, substituting home-prepared items for market-bought goods and services (for example, more food preparation or repairs done at home). Women served as "providers of last resort," bearing increased overall workloads, albeit these effects cannot be fully documented in the absence of time-use surveys. Intensification of women's work combined with a rise in the costs of keeping children in school often brought interruption of children's education—girls' education, in particular, as their help was needed at home—as well as increasing the risks to health of women. These costs of "getting prices right" are not visible in the macro-economic measures (the GDP growth rate) that are the basis of policymaking. The efficiency gains that are assumed to result from implementation of SAPs (for example, by balancing government budgets) are achieved because the programs focus on the market and the sphere of paid production while disregarding unpaid economic activities and the sphere of reproduction.

By contrast, groups that are (potentially) internationally mobile (TNCs, financial capital, and the wealthy who derive most of their income from asset ownership) either benefit from these reforms or are unscathed by their adverse effects. If they are unhappy with a country's economic policies, these groups can threaten to leave and move to another country. Moreover, this policy approach contributes to the increasing divide in many countries between the rich and the poor in terms of income levels, consumption patterns, and capabilities. The reforms are welcomed by the well-off, who can afford to send their children to private schools, obtain healthcare in private hospitals, and do not have to pay the taxes to support the public services. These deflationary and commodification policy biases clearly reinforce each other: budget cuts encourage privatization and, as privatization proceeds, the financial interests (rentier groups and financial institutions) and satisfied consumers of private services become more resistant to relaxation of the deflationary bias. As Elson (2002a: 15) points out, "[u]nder this pressure, social policy becomes a branch of financial policy and [. . .] the risks of liberalized international financial markets are compounded by funding social provision through financial markets."

Third, SAPs were often designed under a male-breadwinner bias, reflecting the assumption that men are the first to be entitled to decent jobs or first to be hired in economic recovery, while women are assumed to be secondary earners and economically dependent on men. To illustrate, in the 1990s when the IMF, World Bank, and policymakers in Latin America became aware of the difficulties facing poor households as a result of SAPs, safety nets with the name of Social Emergency Funds were designed as a way of dealing with basic needs; women were entitled to these safety nets but they were viewed as dependents of male family members (Benería and Mendoza 1995; Elson 2002b).[46]

In the late 1990s, the IMF and the World Bank softened the conditionalities placed with the policy packages and allowed for some debt relief to heavily-indebted poor countries. This shift was in response to the IMF's experience with the Asian Financial Crisis and the ongoing debt problem experienced by very low-income countries.[47] As of 1999, SAPs were replaced by Poverty Reduction Strategy Papers (PRSPs) as a condition for loans to low-income, heavily indebted countries. As part of the borrowing process, countries had to prepare, abide by, and take ownership of a document akin to a national development plan that is expected to address poverty reduction and facilitate growth (IMF 2001). While this innovative initiative emphasized country ownership, participation by local NGOs in the design of the PRSP, and poverty reduction as a goal, evaluations have shown that these features have not been realized in practice (Dijkstra 2011; Cypher and Dietz 2009). Importantly, PRSPs carried over the gender blindness of SAPs by their insistence on the same macroeconomic stabilization measures and structural adjustment as SAPs, which feminist economists had shown to be neither conducive to reducing gender inequalities nor fostering long-run economic growth (Van Staveren 2008; Elson and Warnecke 2011).[48] Thus, while SAPs may be history, their problematic features have continued in PRSPs and its successor program that has replaced PRSPs since 2010.[49] Feminist economists have argued that any new formulation of SAPs that does not reform the macroeconomic policies that create the problems in the first place is an ineffective response; instead, alternative macroeconomic policies are needed (Elson and Çağatay 2000; Elson 2002a; Elson and Warnecke 2011; Van Staveren 2008).

In addition to engaging with fiscal austerity, feminist research has examined the impact of economic growth, trade liberalization, and financial liberalization on gender inequalities, each of these being major determinants of the livelihoods of people. Feminists have questioned the synergistic argument that posits a win-win relationship between economic growth and gender equalities, posited, for example, by Dollar and Gatti (1999). Seguino (2002; 2008) showed that growth is not sufficient to reduce gender inequality. While methodological and data constraints hamper the gender analysis of trade reforms, feminists have produced substantial research that shows certain trends. Trade liberalization and expansion since the early 1980s has contributed to the growth of women's employment in labor-intensive export sectors in many countries, and reduced the labor force participation gaps between men and women; yet, women workers predominate in low-wage and low-productivity export sectors. The record on export sector-wage levels is mixed and does not support a general decline in gender wage inequalities (Berik 2011).[50]

Financial liberalization, on the other hand, has heightened market volatility, induced more unstable growth, and increased the incidence of financial crises and economic downturns (Singh and Zammit 2000; Floro 2005). Its resulting impact on business foreclosures and factory closedowns, job loss, credit availability, and social services is not gender-neutral; in the end, many women tend to shoulder the burden of economic downturns in terms of higher incidence of violence against women, lower earnings, and more unpaid work.

Feminist economists also examined the macroeconomic effects of gender inequalities in the household and in labor, credit, and product markets. This research has identified multiple channels through which gender inequality can affect macroeconomic aggregates. For example, unpaid caring work affects various macroeconomic variables such as labor supply, consumption, savings, and investment (Van Staveren 2010). Empirical studies show that gender equality can both be a stimulus to growth and hamper growth. Studies find that reducing gender gaps in education, labor force participation, and employment boosts economic growth. By contrast, Seguino (2000a; 2000b) showed that gender inequality in wages was a stimulus to economic growth in a group of semi-industrialized economies over the 1975–95 period. In this case, gender wage inequality boosts export earnings and supplies the foreign exchange to fund new investments. The key question raised by these contrasting results is whether gender wage inequality can be reduced without derailing the long-run growth of the economy and the productivity-boosting effects of promoting gender equality in education. Feminist research also made the case for recognizing the adverse effects of gender inequality on the sustainability of economic growth—the coveted goal of the IMF and the World Bank. For example, in agrarian economies of Sub-Saharan Africa gender inequality in access to inputs, training, and lack of land rights accounts for low productivity in food production, which leads to food imports, exacerbating foreign exchange shortages and fueling price inflation. Financing the programs to reduce these gender inequalities would thus boost economic growth.

Finally, drawing upon a range of social science research, feminist economists have shown that consumption patterns differ by gender and that these differences have macroeconomic effects. For example, research has established that a higher share of women's income tends to be spent on household consumption goods compared to the proportion from men's income, and women and men are often responsible for different categories of consumption expenditure (Dwyer and Bruce 1988; Hoddinott and Haddad 1995; Quisumbing and Maluccio 2000). These gendered practices imply that increasing women's relative income would result in greater well-being effects compared to a scenario where men's incomes increase. Improved well-being of children, in turn, contributes to economic growth. Thus, over the long term, gender wage equality can be good for growth.

Alternative Macroeconomic Policies

Feminist research has also produced the criteria for the design of alternative macroeconomic policies to bring about broadly shared development. Accordingly, putting people at the center of development requires taking seriously the burdens of adjustment, being attentive to social constraints that prevent easy adjustment of people who are displaced from their jobs or their homes due to the reforms, and avoiding disproportionate burdens for low-income groups. In general, policies have to be designed with attention to their immediate gender and class impacts as well as their hidden costs that may entail long-term losses.

The primary goal of alternative macroeconomic policies should be to promote the livelihoods and well-being of people, rather than getting the prices right or maximizing efficiency and economic growth. To promote livelihoods it is necessary to pursue full-employment policies. These, in turn, require increasing tax revenues that have shrunk under neoliberal policies.[51] However, creating more fiscal space (by moving away from fiscal austerity) is not sufficient to ensure gender-equitable outcomes. The male-bread-winner bias in the workings of institutions also has to be addressed. Thus, complementary policies are needed to ensure work–family balance, to cover providers of unpaid care under social protection schemes, and to create decent work for women and men. In some countries, gender-responsive budgeting has been a tool to achieve more gender-equitable public finance; through participation in the budget process, civil society groups have increased public awareness of gender, class, and ethnic biases in expenditure categories. One major issue of concern in this approach has been to assess the impact of fiscal policies on unpaid work and total work burdens. In this way, gender-responsive budget exercises have tried to reduce these biases, bringing about more accountability in the budget process (Budlender 2000; Sharp and Broomhill 2002; Austen et al. 2013).

At a different level, feminist economists have fleshed out broader strategies to make gender equality and economic growth mutually reinforcing by considering a combination of trade, industry, and financing policies (Seguino and Grown 2006; Berik and van der Meulen Rodgers 2010). Seguino and Grown have argued in favor of pursuing industrial policy in order for countries to move out of the low-wage export niches, which would in turn allow payment of higher wages to women workers in the export sector. Moving away from overreliance on exports as well as out of the low-wage export niche is also central to the international trade-linked strategy to improve working conditions that Berik and Rodgers identify.

As Çağatay (2003a: 36) argues, the ultimate goal of the project of engendering macroeconomics is to identify "macroeconomic policies that promote gender equality and types of growth that help reduce poverty and social inequalities in a sustainable and environment-friendly way." While the feminist macroeconomics project has made considerable headway as a critique of neoliberal macroeonomics and in fleshing out an alternative policy program, the policy responses to the 2007–08 financial crisis show that neoliberal macroeconomic policies are alive and well (Ortiz and Cummins 2013) and the gender blindness of macroeconomic policies continues (Esquivel and Rodríguez Enríquez 2014).

Feminist Ecological Economics

The overlap between feminist economics and ecological economics has been explored by several scholars since the late 1980s (Shiva 1988; Agarwal 1992b; Perkins 1997; Nelson 1997).[52] Both feminist economics and ecological economics increasingly recognize the interdependence of social provisioning and the environment and the links between the marginalization and exploitation of the natural world and women's labor (Perkins et al. 2005; Veuthey and Gerber 2010). And both share a common vision of sustainable and equitable development that addresses and maintains the balance between the provisioning needs of the current generation and that of future generations.

In recent decades, the evolution and development of each body of writing has been enriched by the ideas, methodologies, and insights from the other and led to the development of feminist ecological economics. Ecological economics, much like feminist economics, criticizes the manner in which standard neoclassical economic models neglect the contributions of ecosystem services as with the unpaid work contributions of women. The orthodox models' preoccupation with economic growth obscures the immense adverse impacts on the ecosystems, as in the case of the unrecognized unpaid work burden of women (Perkins 1997; 2007; O'Hara 2009).

The work of feminists and social science researchers on the valuation of unpaid care work links directly to the analysis of the value of ecological services. The work of ecology scholars has demonstrated that gender equality and social provisioning demands attention to the natural environment in which we thrive and live upon. As Nelson (2008) points out:

> As members of the human race, we may be concerned about future generations because we reason that such concern for humanity in general is fair and just. Or we may be concerned because we can imagine the distress we might be bringing on our own children and grandchildren by failing to address climate change . . . if we allow our economies to run along a business-as-usual path, we will bequeath to future generations a world whose life-sustaining capacities will be severely compromised. (p. 444)

Feminist ecological economics focuses on social relations in the household, community, markets, and societies, and interrelationships between people and nature, all of which underlie the functioning of economies. Its analytical approach demonstrates the deep linkages and connections between concerns for nature and concerns for equity, including interspecies and intergenerational equity. In an economy where social provisioning is central, production, distribution, and consumption are guided by a different set of principles than those that currently guide market-based economic growth.[53] The gender lens used in feminist ecological economics helps identify the structural causes of the systematic exclusion of both the natural environment and unpaid work in mainstream economics and policy discourses. The expansion of markets guided by neoliberal policies has had negative impacts on the provisioning of care by often stretching the demands for unpaid work to levels that undermine the well-being of the worker, and on ecological processes, which can reinforce each other. Feminist ecological economics sees the "add women and stir" and "add environment and stir" approaches that have been applied in gender mainstreaming efforts and in conventional environmental and natural resource economics evaluations as shallow and capable of leading to misguided or erroneous recommendations. Feminist ecological economists argue that a meaningful analysis of the material and social constraints at work in market economies that lead to care deficits and climate change involves a feminist and ecological lens and methodological tools.[54]

Centered around social provisioning of basic needs within and across generations, feminist ecological economic analysis shows the importance of women's unpaid work, ecological destruction, and material throughput without necessarily commodifying or monetizing these elements, which are regarded as externalities in mainstream economics. The work of creating sustainable economies, to the extent that it falls unequally on women and men, is considered to be ultimately unsustainable; hence, the promotion of sustainable development entails the promotion of gender equality. Finally, feminist ecological economics sees collective action and engagement in the process of social change as necessary in addressing gender and ecological concerns. Because of the importance given to collective and social processes, there is respect for diverse ways of knowing and valuing things, and methodological pluralism, thus allowing for the flourishing of the field in different directions.

Conclusions: Towards a More Inclusive Economics

Feminist economists have moved beyond the critique of mainstream economics and produced a rich body of literature in many fields; they have also contributed to research in other social science disciplines through collaborative research or use of a variety of research methods and methodologies that go beyond statistical analysis. Feminist work has been incorporated in contemporary development policy initiatives, such as those that emphasize the economic returns to reducing gender inequality, or anti-poverty programs that provide financial help to women rather than men on the basis that women tend to use funds in a way that is more beneficial to children (for example, conditional cash transfer schemes, microcredit).

However, feminist research has largely moved on a parallel track to mainstream economics. Despite the burgeoning feminist literature, the economics profession has proven to be the least open of the social sciences to the challenges raised by feminism. While mainstream economics has evolved since the height of the feminist critiques of the early 1990s, its fundamental features have hardly changed. Feminist and other heterodox critiques have hardly made a dent in the core tenets of the discipline. While economic models have become increasingly sophisticated, these innovations are not influential in undergraduate teaching in economics. It is the core of the discipline that is hegemonic in undergraduate teaching, popular and polit-ical discourse, and the market reforms that are widely implemented (Kanbur 2002; Ferber and Nelson 2003b; King 2013; Wade 2011). And macroeconomic policy, for the most part, continues to be gender blind.

Gender breakdown of categories in statistical analysis has become almost routine in many fields of economics, spreading beyond its initial base of labor economics. However, this step is not sufficient. The discipline has con-tinued to strongly privilege orthodox thinking and exclude heterodox alternatives through a variety of means: from the nature of graduate school programs to screening in economics journals and simply ignoring research findings that are contrary to mainstream research. The narrow definition of the discipline and strong emphasis on modeling and quantitative methods of analysis makes the discipline unreceptive to epistemological questions and interdisciplinary inquiry. For these reasons, it has been difficult to alter deeply ingrained practices and entrenched "ways of knowing," of theorizing and of "doing science." Yet the interdisciplinary nature of feminist economics has made it relevant to other social sciences, establishing mutual interests and useful exchanges for research, teaching, and action.

Within economics itself, we believe that there is much to be gained from greater collaboration across heterodox approaches towards the goal of toppling mainstream economics from its hegemonic position. While many feminist economists produce research that is in the heterodox tradition, other heterodox economists have often been unreceptive to engagement with feminist challenges to their schools or to calls for building on the considerable overlaps between them. For example, Danby (2004) and Van Staveren (2010) have examined the possibilities for progress towards a gender-aware post-Keynesian economics, while Fukuda-Parr et al. (2013) have argued for a more robust analysis of the 2007–08 financial crisis that draws upon feminist and heterodox macroeconomic perspectives.[55] Similarly, there are opportunities for feminist economists, ecological economists, and new developmentalists to engage in complementary work on development strategies that are both equitable and sustainable. A more robust economics is possible, for example, in addressing the environmental (climate) crisis by building on the contributions of two or more of these strands of thought (Nelson 2008; Power 2009; Floro 2012; İlkkaracan 2013b; Berik 2014). As feminists we have to keep the vision alive to create a more equitable and sustainable future.

Notes

1   "Poisoning the Well, or How Economic Theory Damages Moral Imagination" in *Oxford Handbook of Professional Economic Ethics* (ed. George DeMartino and Deirdre McCloskey, 2015).

2   Pujol (1992) evaluates earlier strands of feminism (and anti-feminism) in writings on the economic status of women.

3   Becker's analysis of the gender division of labor also had biological-deterministic leanings. His positions represented a sharp contrast with the social constructionist approaches emanating from feminist theory and empirical work in the social sciences and in economics (MacKintosh 1978; Benería 1979).

4   In contrast to the mainstream human capital theory explanation of occupational segregation by sex and gender wage differentials, Bergmann's crowding model

emphasized exclusion of women from a range of high-paying occupations and their crowding into a small number of occupations as the cause of the gender wage gap.

5 Engels emphasized both biological and social aspects of reproduction as well as attaching equal importance to production and reproduction activities. However, in the same essay Engels also articulated the call to integrate women into the labor force as a strategy to reduce their subordination to men. In other words, his solution to women's subordination in capitalism was to move them out of the home and into wage labor, thereby emphasizing the determinative nature of production activities.

6 In addition, the postmodern critique of "grand theories" and their tendency to essentialize what is not universal paralyzed further development and the potential impact of the Marxian framework. Although postmodern critiques of grand theory apply equally to orthodox economics, the latter has remained more immune to it, in large part because postmodern critiques emerged from disciplines other than economics.

7 The transaction costs approach can be traced back to Coase (1937), who argued that when it is costly to transact, institutions are created to reduce the costs.

8 Transaction costs include the costs of gathering and processing information, making negotiation or agreement, monitoring and supervision, coordination and enforcement of contracts.

9 For example in rural markets, the practice of interlocking market contracts for labor, credit, and output by landowner-lenders or trader-lenders gives the propertied classes the ability to benefit from a more dominant bargaining position with a farmer-borrower.

10 To give an example, an interlocking of transactions in credit and labor markets in the form of a loan to a worker provided by an employer-lender can be explained, using the transaction costs approach, as a means of reducing transaction costs and as a substitute for an incomplete credit market. This type of market exchange itself may also act as a barrier of entry to third parties and can be a source of additional power for the dominant partner in such transactions. As Bardhan (1989: 1389) points out, these personalized interlockings of labor commitments and credit transactions also "divide the workers and emasculate their collective bargaining strength vis-à-vis employers, who use this as an instrument of control over the labor process."

11 Initially, women were added on to the analysis as a way of describing their location and conditions of participation in the labor market, rather than as a way of explaining why segmentation was gendered (Benería 1987).

12 These are the foundational assumptions of neoclassical economics: the rational, self-interested behavior informing individual decisions; impossibility of inter-personal utility comparisons; the exogenous and static tastes in economic models.

13 See Benería (2003) for a more detailed discussion and references.

14 More recently, James Heckman has focused on early childhood education, highlighting its social as well as individual benefits. See, for example, Heckman (2000; 2011).

15   While the use of the Robinson Crusoe trope in introductory economics textbooks has declined over time, it has not disappeared. Mankiw (2012) uses Robinson Crusoe's activities to explain the importance of specialization, trade, and productivity. He states that it is rational for the "shipwrecked sailor who spends his time gathering coconuts and catching fish" (p. 54) "and his friend Friday" (p. 56) to engage in trade. And in the discussion of the determinants of Crusoe's productivity there is no mention of Friday's contributions (p. 241).

16   This moment of bliss, however, can only be achieved when both persons have perfect information about their options, the markets are competitive, and there are no externalities, that is, individual decisions do not affect other persons either adversely or positively.

17   As King (2008) reminds, the Pareto optimality concept encourages thinking of growth as a desirable goal so that the possibility of redistribution is not entertained. If the pie grows, then the shares of everyone can potentially grow and poverty can be alleviated without resorting to any redistributive measures.

18   On the same grounds, Sen and Nussbaum view the recent turn to happiness measurement with skepticism. There is, however, a recent attempt that combines happiness measures with objective measures of well-being in terms of capabilities or livelihoods in order to identify desirable policies to promote well-being. See the recent effort by the Gross National Happiness (GNH) working group, which differentiates between well-being (objectively measured as GNH and the subject of policy), happiness skills (that are the object of personal change) and happiness (measured by subjective surveys) (Graaf et al. 2013).

19   Increasingly, experimental methods are being utilized in economics, challenging the supremacy of econometric testing. In the early 2000s, conducting controlled experiments has emerged as a contending research method in producing know-ledge. Fashioned after medical trials, randomized control trials (RCTs) have been applied to an increasing number of research questions and viewed as providing definitive evidence on causality, i.e. the effect of one phenomenon on another. However, this methodology is designed to answer small questions and does not part ways with the foundational assumptions of mainstream economics (Basu 2013).

20   Nelson points to stereotyping and confirmation bias of researchers.

21   By equality of outcomes we refer to similar group distributions (for example, in women's wages vs. men's wages), and not equal means, even though within each group there might be inequality. Phillips regards equality of outcomes as a test of whether equality of opportunity exists.

22   Such is the case among the Yoruba in Nigeria where couples are expected to be financially independent and share contributions to the household. However, this egalitarian arrangement may not lead to increased well-being of women even when women's economic power increases. She may not be able to exercise bargaining power vis-à-vis her spouse since the gender-symmetric economic norm is undermined by men's stronger property rights and access to resources, symbolic value of male household headship, and patriarchal child custody rules.

23   Page number refers to the unpublished English version.

24   The empirical finding that countries that reduced gender gaps in education attracted more foreign direct investment, may be interpreted in two ways: either foreign companies are interested in employing highly productive women workers or there is the added draw of the lower wage rates of women workers which actually help reduce unit labor costs. If the latter is the case, then FDI may not generate secure livelihoods for women workers (Berik, et al. 2009).

25   See specific lists of basic capabilities drawn up by Nussbaum (2003), and Robeyns (2003a).

26   We borrow this example of the boxer and the woman subject to domestic violence from Robeyns (2005).

27   This means the capabilities approach has to complement a theory of economic development that focuses on how productive structures can be transformed to create the capacity to raise resources that ensure people's well-being. One promising approach is new developmentalism that has generated principles for economic development on the basis of experiences of East Asian economies (Khan and Christiansen 2011).

28   A third option is for the feminist economist to design and conduct her own research to generate primary data. While feasible, this option is potentially costly for the researcher in terms of time investment in learning the methods typically not taught in the economics graduate curriculum, acceptance of research results, and reputation in the discipline (Berik 1997).

29   Philosopher Harding (1995) has joined the debate on objectivity in economics, pointing out that models of scientific knowledge that are viewed as "objective," including in the social sciences, often "express and serve the projects only of dominant institutions" from which women have been excluded (p. 8).

30   The financial sector targeted these groups for subprime loans, putting them at greater risk for default and foreclosure as the financial crisis hit.

31   For example, it is impossible to carry out race/ethnicity- and gender-differentiated statistical analysis of training outcomes for the building trades in the US, which are dominated by white men. Statistical analysis founders due to the tiny numbers of Latinas or black women who are training for the trades.

32   One implication of this critique is that the demand side of the labor market (employer behavior) interacts with the supply side (women workers' choices), which violates the basic mainstream assumption about the workings of a market.

33   In several Latin American countries joint titling of land was introduced, making it possible for husbands and wives to jointly own land (Deere and León de Leal 2003).

34   Women fared much better in Ecuador where a "partial community property" regime prevailed, owning 44 percent of the couple wealth, while they owned only 19 percent and 9 percent of the couple's wealth in Ghana and India, respectively, where "separation of property" regimes holds.

35   Their results particularly noted that single women are more risk averse compared to single men.

36   In Sunden and Surette's 1998 study, the wealth holdings of single women are found to be relatively less risky than those of single men and married couples. Hence, investment decisions for retirement purposes are likely to be influenced by the interplay of gender and marital status rather than gender alone.

37   The price incentive may not translate into higher output, if the land for cash crops is controlled by men, the crops are sold by them and income is controlled by them, but at least some of the labor is provided by women. Under such conditions, women may prefer to work on their own plots rather than produce cash (or export) crops.

38   For more detail about these conceptualizations, see Benería (2009).

39   While Sen's primary focus is on the allocation of resources as the object of contention or bargaining in the household—for example, the amount and type of food consumption, expenditures on doctors' visits or children's schooling—the object of bargaining can also be in the area of labor allocation to household production; who does what work and when are often contentious issues.

40   For an accessible overview of the project of engendering macroeconomics see Çağatay (2003a).

41   This set of policies promoting market liberalization was later referred to, from 1990 onward, as the Washington Consensus.

42   The signing of the World Bank-Philippines SAL agreement took place in September 1980.

43   Although some details have varied from country to country, the basic characteristics can be summarized as being in four major policy arenas: (a) adjustments in the area of foreign exchange, often including a devaluation of the national currency; (b) drastic cuts in government spending and privatization of government-run firms; (c) deep economic restructuring and deregulation of markets, including labor and capital markets; and (d) trade liberalization and the easing of rules regulating foreign investment, thereby increasing the global integration of economies and shifting production towards exports relative to domestic markets. For an overview on SAPs, see Benería (1999a).

44   See for example Elson (1991a); Benería and Feldman (1992); Blackden and Morris-Hughes (1993); Floro and Schaefer (1998); Çağatay et al. (1995); Grown et al. (2000); Sparr (1994); Floro (1995).

45   "Getting prices right" refers to the setting of prices and quantities exchanged on any given market by the interaction of supply and demand, that is, without the government intervening to set minimum or maximum price levels.

46   The Social Emergency Funds were put in place in the mid-1990s partly in response to the evidence that SAPs were causing greater social stress than originally expected. These packages included some form of palliative for "the most vulnerable" and were sporadic, ad hoc measures aimed at alleviating the most extreme cases of distress and poverty and preventing social tensions.

47   The IMF and the World Bank began to insist that countries that borrow from the IMF have in place a social safety net (social policy) in order to prevent the

hardships generated for the most disadvantaged groups when deflationary programs are put in place. This shift was motivated in part by the experience of Asian countries that were forced by the IMF to implement SAPs when they had no social safety nets. As Elson and Çağatay (2000) argued, this add-on approach can be no more than a short-term palliative, unless the SAP-type policies are discontinued.

48   Van Staveren (2008) argues that PRSPs have not been gender aware, even when there is local gender expertise and commitment to pursuing gender equality goals. The problem lies in the gender-blind macroeconomic framework that is focused on monetary and fiscal stability and does not acknowledge the adverse impacts of stabilization policies for poverty in the short run and for underinvestment in human capabilities, which could undermine economic growth in the long run.

49   As of January 2010, the new Poverty Reduction and Growth Trust (PRGT) was created to extend new types of loans to low-income countries. The loan facility that funded PRSPs, the Poverty Reduction and Growth Facility (PRGF), was replaced by the Extended Credit Facility (ECF), which the IMF intends as a more flexible option than before for medium-term loans to low-income countries. While the new approach is more responsive to country needs, the conditionality of fiscal or foreign exchange reserve targets, which is the marker for restrictive fiscal policy, continues (IMF 2014).

50   Cross-country research shows that labor-intensive exports are associated with wider gender wage inequalities, underscoring the incentive for governments to maintain wage inequality (Busse and Spielmann 2006). In general, export sector wages are lower for both women and men compared to sectors that produce for the domestic economy. While in some countries women's wage rates in export sectors are above the country minimum wage or poverty line, in others they do not reach these levels. In some countries, over the long haul, the average real wage rate in the export sector has declined, while in the dynamic export sector of China they have increased. Even when gender wage gaps narrow on average, the gap between equally skilled women and men workers has widened, indicating rising wage discrimination against women. See Berik (2011) for a review of these studies.

51   For gender-aware overviews of the tax revenue effects of neoliberal policies see Çağatay (2003b), Berik (2011), and Williams (2007).

52   Ecological economics was defined by Costanza (1989: 1) as "including neoclassical environmental economics and ecological impact studies, as well as encouraging new ways of thinking." The subject has since evolved into an interdisciplinary field that examines the co-evolution and interdependence of human systems and ecosystems across time and space. See also Daly and Farley (2004).

53   See Perkins (2007) and Nelson (1997) for discussion of these principles.

54   See Perkins (1997) and Veuthey and Gerber (2010) for review of the various strands in feminist ecological economics.

55   According to Danby, if the post-Keynesian framework is to integrate gender, it needs to shed three institutional assumptions common to post-Keynesian analysis.

These are: (1) the capitalist entrepreneur who is assumed to behave much like the neoclassical rational economic man; (2) the concept of the economy that solely comprises monetized transactions where households are solely sites of consumption; (3) the notion of a neutral, all-powerful state, enforcing contracts freely entered by individuals, which reinforces a vision of society that is free of conflict, coercion, power differences, or inequality.

CHAPTER 3

Markets, Globalization, and Gender

The market when left to itself becomes an efficient distribution of resources. This logic, however, carries a big assumption in that everyone has the same set of capabilities needed to take advantage of market opportunities. Those of us who grew up in societies where there are deeply entrenched inequities based on class, ethnicity, religion, race and sex/gender systems, know fully well that this assumption does not hold water. It never did.

Josefa Francisco, DAWN

Introduction

Since the late 1970s, the process of global economic integration has become a most powerful source of change driving national economies and affecting all aspects of social, political, and cultural life. Globalization has become a widely used term, often with different meanings for different people. It has been associated with positive change such as economic growth and prosperity but also with negative outcomes such as increasing inequality, deterioration of labor market conditions, persistent deprivations in capabilities, and environmental degradation. However, proponents and critics of globalization agree on the nature of the process unfolding since the late 1970s: unprecedented expansion of markets beyond national borders and the shrinking of time and space enabled by technological advances in communications and transportation. The dramatic increase in economic interaction and interdependence across countries has taken place through the rapid growth of trade and capital flows, the formation of regional and multilateral institutions, and the transformation of the way production processes are organized.

In this chapter we provide an overview of the nature of contemporary globalization, the policies that have driven it, and the ways in which it has transformed economic relations and people's lives. Women as well as men have been affected by these processes—as workers, consumers, producers, investors, and borrowers in credit markets. The trends associated with contemporary globalization have been changing women's connection to the market, influencing gender roles and gender relations, and altering the meanings of gender across countries and cultures.

Global economic integration has brought about profound changes in human behavior. Market-oriented choices and personal gain have become the central goal of economic activity even in remote parts of the world. In low-income countries production is increasingly oriented towards the market, and market exchange is replacing other forms of exchange such as reciprocity, barter, and state provisioning. What is distinct about contemporary globalization is the extent of commercialization and the domination of financial capital in global production. Commercialization has brought new groups into the orbit of capitalist production. These processes are reminiscent of Karl Polanyi's remarks more than 70 years ago in his book *The Great Transformation* (Polanyi 1944). Based on his analysis of European societies in the late nineteenth and early twentieth centuries, Polanyi argued that gain and profit had never before played such an important role in human activity. His observation is even more valid in the early twenty-first century. Similarly, Karl Marx's analysis of the laws of motion governing profit and accumulation of capital, laid bare more than 160 years ago, is as relevant today as then. The works of these authors are key for understanding contemporary globalization and its consequences.

We first present an overview of the neoliberal policies, which, together with technological change, have been instrumental in the global expansion of commodity and financial markets. Neoliberal policies have accelerated capitalist development, with its characteristic processes of capital accumulation, commodification, and proletarianization. They have also reinforced the norms and values associated with the rational economic man model of mainstream economics and transformed individuals' values and goals. Against this background, we take up a number of consequences of contemporary globalization. First, commodification and financialization have proliferated the values, attitudes, and social practices associated with market behavior. Second, inequality within and across countries has increased and it has been accompanied by rising economic insecurity and vulnerability for most people. Combined with commodification, rising inequality has made it difficult to reach higher levels of human development for a large proportion of the population, and the precipitous growth of consumerism has had negative consequences for sustainable development. Third, since the early 1980s women have been rapidly integrated as workers in global production processes. We examine the "global feminization of labor" thesis, which refers to the increasing incorporation of women in paid work and the associated changes in working conditions. Feminization of labor has been uneven across regions and sectors and over time; and it has not necessarily been a force for raising absolute living standards. We also evaluate the extent to which gender inequalities in the household are reproduced, weakened, or reconstituted as women's participation in wage work has expanded.

The Rise and Consolidation of Neoliberalism

Key to contemporary globalization has been the spread of capitalist labor processes and expansion of markets worldwide, enabled by the rise of the neoliberal paradigm as expressed through the SAPs and Washington Consensus policies during the 1980s and 1990s in the global North and South. Neoliberalism became the dominant policy framework to spearhead changes in legal, political, and social institutions and to broaden the rights of owners of capital at the expense of the working population. Neoliberal policies encompass government budget cuts, privatization of social services, infrastructure, and production that was previously owned and operated by the public sector; deregulation of domestic economies; trade liberalization; orientation of production towards international markets, and the easing of controls on capital flows. In many low-income countries these policies were introduced in the form of structural adjustment programs (SAPs) under the auspices of the World Bank and the International Monetary Fund (IMF). Along with transnational corporations and the interventions of dominant countries' governments and commercial banks, the power of these international organizations has been crucial in determining the policy and direction of most economies.

Initially affecting primarily heavily indebted low-income countries, SAPs facilitated a profound shift from earlier development policies towards policies that integrated these economies with global markets. The neoliberal measures of economic restructuring and belt-tightening were based on agreements between national governments and the IMF and the World Bank, which imposed (and continue to impose) conditionalities for negotiating new loans and terms of payment. Eastern European economies transitioning from central planning were also guided by the World Bank and the European Development Bank and by teams of advisors from the capitalist world to implement similar policies (Kotz 1995; Sachs 1991; Woo et al. 1997; Haney 2000). Implemented during a short period of time, these transitions caused profound disruption of the social and economic order. By contrast, China's transition to capitalism has been much slower and on its own terms (Qian 2003). Neoliberal policies have become the new normal in several parts of the world including the global North, as seen in the government responses to the economic crisis of 2008. In Europe and the US, austerity programs have been added to the market liberalization policies that were in effect since the 1970s. The features of austerity programs since 2008 are substantially similar to the SAPs of the 1980s and 1990s, and they are driven by the same set of objectives: to remove fetters on markets and to protect the interests of creditors.

Contrary to the laissez-faire myths, the workings and global expansion of markets require a coherent set of government actions that reduce or eliminate legal and other institutional barriers to the movement of goods, services, and capital. As Polanyi (1944) argued forcefully, the market economy did not evolve naturally on its own.[1] Rather, historically the expansion of markets has relied on government policies that have increased the economic freedom of the actors involved in the functioning of markets and who benefitted from their growth. Deliberate state intervention—often carried out in the name of market freedom—has been imposed from the top and without a participatory process of decision-making among all affected parties. This was the case for the expansion of national markets in late nineteenth and early twentieth centuries—as Polanyi analyzed—as it is the case in contemporary globalization.[2]

One prominent reform of contemporary globalization has been the strengthening of private property rights. As argued by Polanyi, security of these rights is considered an important prerequisite for the expansion and functioning of markets as they facilitate the enforcement of contracts in market exchange. As shown by the policies associated with the IMF and World Bank-initiated SAPs, governments typically have responded to the interests of national and global elites, rather than to the wishes and votes of most citizens, both women and men (Sparr 1994; De Vogli and Birbeck 2011; Nwagbara 2011). In this way, economic policies under neoliberalism have become instruments to lock in the rules favoring the global expansion of markets and relentless capital accumulation (Gill 2000).

Governments have set in motion the privatization of state-owned enterprises everywhere and a new round of "enclosure of the commons," including privatization of public housing in Britain, public utilities in the Philippines, Argentina, and South Africa, and opening up of public lands for private profit-making opportunities in Turkey. In Eastern Europe and the former Soviet Union, overnight privatizations created massive transfers of public assets to a handful of individuals and corporations. In Africa, Asia, and Latin America, land grabs by global interests in the early twenty-first century have become commonplace (McMichael 2012). Government interventions have created the conditions enabling owners of capital to rapidly accumulate while dismantling the welfare state, changing the relative bargaining power of workers and owners of capital, and weakening national sovereignty. Rhetorically and in practice, the proclaimed sanctity and protection of private property and investors' rights increasingly trump human rights such as the universal right to work, to education, and to an adequate standard of living for those who lose out from these changes.

Under neoliberalism, governments have been required to eliminate budget deficits. Indeed, one rationale for privatization of public assets is to generate revenue (albeit a one-time revenue increase) for governments. In practice, the goal of balancing budgets has led to cutting government spending, rather than raising tax revenues. Tax policy has shifted away from relying on direct taxes (on income or wealth) to the regressive indirect (sales) taxes, thereby favoring the interests of the wealthy and the investors. Along with trade liberalization, which reduced tax revenues from imports, especially in low-income economies, these changes have reduced public resources available to finance social goals and development imperatives such as provision of education, health, and other basic services, or employment policies. Since the wealthy and foreign investors do not rely on government-provided services but rather purchase the services they consume (for example, education, healthcare) through the market, they have little incentive to pay taxes; and since they are globally mobile ("footloose"), governments have limited power to impose new taxes on them or enforce existing tax laws (Elson and Çağatay 2000).[3] The case of Chile in the early 2000s exemplifies the resistance to increase corporate and income taxes and thereby to finance spending to improve public education, health services, access to safe water, and sanitation management (López and Miller 2008).[4] The same kinds of policies have been adopted through the austerity programs in the case of Northern countries affected by the 2008 crisis (Peet 2011; Karanikolos et al. 2013; Greenglass et al. 2014).

Trade liberalization and export orientation of production have been instrumental in promoting the expansion of international trade and investment. As developing countries were pressured to orient production to the world market they were also required to reduce trade barriers to open up markets and in doing so, exposed domestic industries to global competition. Key instruments of trade liberalization have been transnational entities, such as the WTO, and free-trade agreements, such as the North America Free Trade Agreement (NAFTA), and the proposed Transatlantic Trade and Investment Partnership (TTIP) and Trans-Pacific Trade Partnership (TPP).[5] These organizations and agreements have imposed rules on national governments, such as the most favored nation treatment, making sure governments could not favor their domestic firms over others. For instance, the WTO, unlike its predecessor the GATT (General Agreement on Tariffs and Trade), has independent jurisdiction beyond national legislation and its rules on trade, patents, and intellectual property rights are binding for all members. The controversial agreements reached in WTO negotiations reflect the tensions and debates about the fairness of such agreements to small farmers, indigenous groups, and small business owners, in particular to women among them, in developing countries. Civil society groups question the extent to which the WTO is serving the interests of developing countries, in particular the vulnerable segments of the population (Carr and Williams 2010; Francisco 2012). The strengthening developing country opposition, mostly representing larger business interests, explains the impasse in the Doha Development Round of trade negotiations in the first decade of the new millennium, which has prevented the organization from moving further in its trade liberalization agenda in recent years.

Since the early 1980s, the internationalization of production has accelerated in response to neoliberal policies and technological change in communications and transportation. The promotion of foreign direct investment, the creation of export-processing zones (EPZs) and the encouragement of offshoring and global subcontracting (outsourcing) chains by government tax codes have led to the relocation of production—wholesale or at least the labor-intensive stages of production—to developing countries. As part of the neoliberal policy paradigm, host governments have further encouraged such relocation and foreign direct investment by offering incentives such as profit tax holidays, duty-free imports and exports, unrestricted repatriation of profits, and exemptions from selective domestic regulations.

In this way, production in the era of globalization has become an increasingly interdependent process involving the joint use of resources of many countries, which has also made it more difficult to identify who is producing what in a globalized, integrated system of production. One type of reorganization, indeed its earliest form, has involved a firm relocating its entire production process—for example, textile manufacturing—from a high-wage country to a lower-wage developing country, while maintaining certain tasks such as management, product design, and/or technology development in the former. Another type of relocation involves a partitioning of the various production stages, locating each in different parts of the world, then assembling them in yet another country, as in the case of electronic goods. In this type of reorganization what may be perceived as a trade of commodities across national boundaries and between business entities actually involves transfers between two departments of the same firm.

In addition to investing across countries and regions, a growing number of firms have become involved with labor outside the traditional workplace through the process of decentralization, outsourcing, and offshoring, thus extending the link between the formal and informal economy. Transnational companies often do not organize production directly, but rather become contractors (buyers) of products and services made according to order by companies in developing countries. Such is the case with garment manufactures, accounting or technical support services, or sporting goods. Accordingly, large companies with market power subcontract production of lower value-added activities to firms that operate in a highly competitive environment. To minimize costs, local companies use contingent labor and resort to casual or subcontracted work arrangements. In doing so, firms—domestic producers and buyers—have tapped into the seemingly abundant labor supply of women, who are employed in workplaces ranging from formal establishments to their own homes. Where feasible, subcontractors have created new forms of putting-out systems whereby workers produce goods or perform tasks in their homes or informal workshops (Roldán 1985; Castells and Portes 1989; Prügl 1999; Carr et al. 2000; Freeman 2000; Buechler 2002; 2013; Lund-Thomsen et al. 2012; De Ruyter et al. 2012). The result of this restructuring is an international production process that is carried out by multi-layered networks of parent firms, subsidiaries, contractors, subcontractors, and home-based workers—what Gereffi and others have called "commodity chains"—that make finished goods for buyers across the world (Gereffi 1998).

Foreign direct investment to expand production in developing countries has been highly concentrated—mostly going to a handful of emerging countries, primarily to China, India, and the East Asian and Latin American economies. Such was the case with South Korea, Taiwan, Singapore, Malaysia, Brazil, Mexico, and Chile during the earlier stages of globalization; in later stages, other regions have been added such as Bangladesh, Cambodia, Central America, Indonesia, Eastern Europe, and Turkey (Morrissey and Udomkerdmongkol 2012; UNCTAD 2013).[6] Underlying this unevenness are differences in not only the incentives provided by host governments to attract foreign companies, but also proximity to markets, the level of development of infrastructure, and trade facilities. Likewise, the growth in trade flows across countries is highly uneven. Much of the enormous growth in trade over the last 50 years has occurred in trade among high-income countries and a few emerging countries concentrated in East Asia and Latin America.

From the 1990s onward, financial flows to developing countries have also increased as a result of capital account liberalization. Massive amounts of capital have flowed into financial markets including those of stocks, property, bonds, hedge funds, derivatives, and other new financial instruments, which are prone to asset (price) bubble formation and bursts, and thus have endangered the stability of the global economy. These flows resulted in boom and bust cycles centered in a number of emerging economies (such as Brazil, Mexico, Hong Kong, Malaysia, South Korea, Indonesia, Thailand, Turkey, Russia, Argentina), where speculative funds stimulated economic booms that were followed by financial crises. By contrast, the 2007–08 financial crisis originated in the US and its effects were felt globally due to the high level of global integration of markets. The increasing frequency and scope of the crises underlines the risk-taking tendencies of finance capital and the dangers of unregulated financial markets.

The global expansion of markets has proceeded at an uneven pace; while some countries have experienced rapid economic growth, others have stagnated. And some resource-rich countries have experienced unbalanced, enclave-type growth. For instance, except for a small number of countries, the Middle East and Africa regions have lagged behind other areas in terms of their integration into the world market economy (Nassar 2007). On the other hand, some countries such as India, Vietnam, Bolivia, Brazil, Peru, South Africa, and Nigeria have experienced rapid economic growth though with uneven investment across their economic sectors. Others like Bhutan, Afghanistan, and Burma have yet to develop their basic market infrastructure, set legal institutions protecting private property rights, and experience massive inflows of capital. As a result, the economic divide between "developed" and "developing" countries continues to persist, with a small group of countries remaining at the top of the world income distribution; only a few countries in the developing world have joined that high-income group (Ortiz and Cummins 2011). Wade (2011) shows that, despite all the neoliberal celebrations of globalization, "catch up development" has not occurred; and inequalities among countries have continued to increase (UNDP 2010). That said, the first decade of the new millennium brought a major break from the stagnation or low-growth pattern of the 1990s to many countries in the global South, which was fueled by the commodities boom. Regional average growth rates per capita indicate stagnation in the global North in sharp contrast to those in Sub-Saharan Africa (Cypher 2014).

Economics and the Davos Man

In this section, we trace the connections between the above analysis of globalization processes and the more theoretical aspects behind them, including some of the critiques of orthodox economics made by feminist economists and analyzed in Chapter 2. The development of capitalism since its early stages could not have happened without deep changes in values and the ways people make decisions and relate to each other. Karl Polanyi (1944: 71) argued that "a market economy can only exist in a market society," that is, it can only exist if it is accompanied by the appropriate changes in norms and behavior that enable the market to function. The dominance of capitalist logic and the expansion of markets at the turn of the millennium have indeed transformed values and subjectivities in a manner that supports this expansion. The central character of mainstream economic models, the "rational economic man," has become a more familiar personality; the selfish individual seeking to satisfy his own desires through the market is more commonplace today than ever. The neoclassical concept of rationality, assumed to be the norm in human behavior, specifies a particular set of ends concerning individual self-interest; human beings are assumed to pursue maximum gains, with the entrepreneur seeking to maximize profit, the worker to maximize income, and the consumer his/her utility. Economic rationality, in turn, is argued to ensure the functioning of markets towards the most efficient allocation of resources and the maximization of production at the lowest possible costs.[7] Adam Smith, in his most influential work *The Wealth of Nations,* linked the selfish pursuit of individual gain to the well-being of society (resulting from economic growth) through the invisible hand of the market and, in so doing, he saw no contradiction between the two. Neoclassical economics has continued to rely on and emphasize this basic link without questioning the consequences of selfish pursuit of individual gain for institutions, human behavior, and society as a whole. Indeed, the assumption of rational economic man is embedded in the neoliberal policy framework, underlying all the efforts to make the individual solely responsible for his or her own livelihood. This is so whether policies dismantle the social safety net, relax labor market regulations that protect workers or financialization, which links individual retirement income to the performance of the stock market.

An important question in this regard is the extent to which women's behavior has become more like men's in the sense of being influenced by economic rationality à la "economic man" rather than by other motives associated with non-market behavior, such as love, empathy, and cooperation.[8] Neoclassical models generally assume that women as well as men behave in rational ways. Gary Becker's household model is a notable exception, whereby in the allocation of resources within the household he assumes that the male head of household acts in an altruistic manner and takes everyone's well-being to heart whereas other household members are selfish (Becker 1981). Feminist economists have much criticized both Becker's analysis of altruism in the family and the standard model's exclusion of other types of motivation such as altruism, empathy, love and compassion, cooperation, reciprocity, and care (see, for example, Ferber and Nelson (1993); Folbre (1994); Bergmann (1995)).

In many societies, on the other hand, women's behavior has been less connected to assumptions of economic rationality and driven by other motives. To be sure, the main reason for these perceptions is that women have historically concentrated their activities within the family and the domestic sphere, caring for others; as such, their behavior and the norms affecting it have not been subject to the dictates of the market, such as competition and the pursuit of private gain. A variety of studies have shown that women's choices and behavior, while they have elements of self-interest, tend to be more altruistic than men's, often guided by a variety of feelings such as love and empathy but also by traditions, norms, and other forms of socially prescribed behavior (Agarwal 1997; Kamas et al. 2008; England 1993). However, with the increase in women's participation in markets as workers, consumers, and borrowers, it is reasonable to expect their behavior to be affected by the norms of the market as well. Thus, while women's work on household maintenance and caregiving sustains the relational aspects of their behavior, the process of marketization and globalization is likely to accentuate their self-interest. At the same time, entry into the labour market helps them strive for individual autonomy and draws them into market participation and exchange.

Contemporary globalization has been accompanied by triumphalist affirmations of neoliberalism that continually emphasize the norms and behavior associated with economic rationality and the assumption that the invisible hand of the market is a form of organizing the economy and society superior to any form of state intervention. We have witnessed these affirmations in different forms of public discourse, ranging from the strong emphasis on productivity, efficiency, financial returns, individualism, competitive behavior, consumerism, and an apparent tolerance for, and even acceptance of, social inequalities and greed. Emblematic of these values were the representations of lives of the affluent urban professionals in the 1980s and the investment bankers of the 1990s and 2000s.[9] The celebration of these values has not been limited to affluent economies. The shift towards the predominance of pro-market discourses has been particularly dramatic in the transition countries of the former Soviet Union and in the People's Republic of China. The abuses associated with the search for individual economic gain and rapid accumulation of wealth, facilitated by the newly created markets, have been criticized even by those who have benefited from global expansion of markets (Soros 1998).

Back in 1997 the neoliberal weekly *The Economist* associated the emerging values and norms with the emergence of the "Davos Man," in reference to the annual meeting of the World Economic Forum (WEF) in Davos, Switzerland, of "people who run the world" (Benería 1999b). According to *The Economist*, Davos Man epitomizes the successful "rational economic man," and refers to businessmen, bankers, officials, and intellectuals who all share beliefs in individualism, laissez-faire markets, (Western-style) democracy, and "innovative capitalism" that incessantly maximizes profit through technological change. They control many of the world's governments and the bulk of its economic and military capabilities. The Davos men at the June 2007 meeting entitled "Global Asset Backed Securitization: Towards a New Dawn!" were described by the *Financial Times* journalist Gillian Tett (2007: 168) as:

> smooth-talking, white-toothed salesmen from large American Banks, eagerly selling repackaged mortgaged debt; self-deprecating British traders; and earnest, chain-smoking representatives from German insurance companies and banks. Their prey included asset managers from Italy, Spain, Germany and Greece, often decked in elegant pastel colors. A silent gaggle of Chinese and Singaporeans circulated . . . A few regulators could also be spotted, conspicuous in looking generally dowdier than the bankers. Some of the biggest delegations, though, came from the three credit rating agencies that were drawing fat profits from the CDO (collateralized debt obligations) boom.[10]

At the same time, social norms have evolved to strongly define people according to their consumption patterns. While consumerism provides the solution to periodic bottlenecks in markets by assuring the steady demand for commodities, higher consumption levels also have become the measure of economic prosperity, social standing, and even well-being. Belief in the high probability of upward mobility often accompanies the incessant demand for social-status commodities. And "the greater is the income and wealth inequality, the greater is the amount that must be consumed by everyone beneath the wealthiest to maintain or improve their relative status" (Wisman 2011). These beliefs were also the focus of Thorstein Veblen's critique of the behavior of the wealthy in the US in the late nineteenth century (Veblen [1899] 1973), but they have re-emerged in the era of contemporary globalization. Not surprisingly, consumption as a yardstick of individual worth has served as *raison d'etre* for working harder and earning more.[11]

Commercialization and Financialization of Everyday Life

Contested Commodities and Outsourced Lives

The long-run trend of capitalism to shift livelihood-related activities from the household to the market has accelerated since the 1980s. People are meeting a high proportion of their needs through the market, in a world where the market increasingly encroaches on many aspects of personal lives and creates wants for ever-new goods and services sold in the market. This development has occurred in tandem with increasing dependence of individuals on wages for provisioning their lives. In rich economies and among the relatively affluent middle and working classes in many countries, the high level of market dependence has become the counterpart of complete wage dependence. Women and men purchase commodities and services that expand their choices and provide help in their time-poor lives. While the extent of provisioning through the market depends on the degree to which the market has developed in a given society and to which people have the money or means to make market purchases, commodification has increasingly affected lives in many parts of the globe today.

Marketization has also brought many "contested commodities" to the market on an unprecedented scale, such as body parts, particularly organs, blood, and even children (Radin 1996; Stolcke 2012). These commodities go beyond the longstanding practice of commodification of women's bodies—men buying sex services (prostitution). The scope of these exchanges is global and the rhetoric of freedom of choice accompanies them, whereby "willing" buyers are presumed to purchase commodities from "willing" sellers. Yet, the enormous gap in income between the buyers and sellers raises ethical questions and moral concerns about the individual choices involved in these exchanges.

Reproductive work has also been rapidly commodified. As state support for families (for example, public provision of childcare) has declined or is inadequate, the market has stepped in to offer an expanding array of market substitutes for daily care activities, in the form of nannies, live-in maids, and eldercare providers. The crisis of care in the global North, which is due to increases in women's labor force participation rate combined with inadequate public support for childcare and eldercare, is creating a demand for paid care services. In many countries, an expanding immigrant workforce has been supplying these services (Benería 2008; Lyberaki 2008; Rosewarne 2012).

Likewise, reliance on the market for intergenerational reproduction has become increasingly common. Since the 1980s new reproductive technologies have created the option of leaving the work of child-conception and childbearing to someone else who gets paid for this work: there are sperm and/or eggs to buy, wombs to rent. New technologies have thus divided parenthood into various categories, such as intending mother/father, womb mother, gamete donor/mother/father, while at the same time making it possible for everyone to procreate. One of the latest developments is transnational surrogate motherhood whereby affluent women outsource the work of gestating the fetus to poor women in mostly low-income countries (Hewitson 2014). The legal framework of paid surrogacy also shapes the nature of these exchanges. Since the US is one of a handful of countries where commercial surrogacy is legal (along with a few others such as Thailand, India,

Mexico, Ukraine), it has attracted couples seeking surrogacy services from a wide range of countries. This additional dimension thus defies the characterization of the typical surrogate mother as a poor woman from the global South. While reproductive work is still women's work, motherhood is fragmented, and in the context of rising global wealth inequality, the expansion of this market has created racial/ethnic divides among women. Even though the contractual relationship is characterized as representing freedom of choice for both parties, "one woman helping another," or poor women supporting their own families by selling this service, the fundamental determinants of the exchange are class, race, ethnic, and gender inequalities. As a result, Hewitson (2014) observes, these inequalities undermine the promise of new reproductive technologies to proliferate forms of caring relationships outside of the heteronormative nuclear family or establishing transnational caring bonds.

The latest frontier for commodification is that of intimate lives. In the early twenty-first century, people increasingly live "outsourced" lives, as Arlie Hochschild (2012) has put it, whereby not only care services and reproductive services but also other intimate activities are sourced from the market: there are life coaches, love coaches, "wantologists" (to help one figure out what one wants), graveside mourners. The rhetoric of markets as well as the exchange relations associated with these new services is increasingly normalized in intimate daily lives, but at what price? While these services are predominantly consumed by those who can afford them, their availability reflects and fuels the cycle of commodification: to achieve a particular outcome in their lives—a well-behaved pet or child, appropriately mourned relatives, a thriving love life—individuals work longer hours to pay for them, becoming even more time-poor and dependent on the market. And as with the consumption of goods, there is a demonstration effect, with lower-income people also entering the market for such refined services as status symbols. Moreover, these exchange relations fragment the human experience; the emotional attachment is outsourced (that is, someone else does the emotional work, in part or in total, for pay). As with the purchase of contested commodities, the experience of outsourcing services chips away at the integrity of being human.

Financialization of Lives

A trend that has greatly affected poor women is the financialization of everyday life. Since financial liberalization from the late 1980s onward, not only has there been a dramatic increase in the power of the financial sector's growing dominance in the global economy, but also an increasing number of people have been drawn into the financial markets as borrowers and investors. Access to credit can help households cope with shocks, mobilize savings, and provide funds for investment; but the elevation of financial instruments as primary determinants of value in a society feeds into the growing influence of this sector over economic outcomes. As a result, the terms under which savings and credit services are accessed can be onerous, especially for vulnerable segments of the population. Those with very limited cash incomes, in particular poor women in the global South and women of color in the global North, have been targeted for loans with high interest and service charges by a wide range of commercial institutions and moneylenders.

An example is the predatory lending of home loans to low-income families and racial minorities in the US and in other high-income countries, particularly in the years leading up to the financial crisis of 2007–08. Historically excluded from borrowing, African-Americans have been targeted for predatory lending (Dymski et al. 2013). Cases of unregulated credit and subprime lending in the US show how an unregulated financial sector linked low-income citizens, especially African-Americans, to a profit-based logic, made for stressful lives ruled by concerns about returns and ability to repay, and wreaked financial and personal havoc in their lives (Shlay 2006; Rugh and Massey 2010). Multiple evictions as a result of the financial crisis have also provided many examples of the negative effects of financialization for those who could barely afford mortgages on their homes.

In recent years, financialization has also encompassed the lives of micro-credit borrowers. Microcredit has faced growing criticism, particularly with its increasing commercialization to broaden its reach to low-income households and small entrepreneurs (Coleman 2006; Mersland and Strøm 2010; Augsburg and Fouillet 2013; Esguerra 2011). Widely acknowledged as a critical tool for moving households out of poverty, microcredit used to be exclusively provided by non-governmental organizations (NGOs) to poor women, but is now a fast growing industry involving transnational investment companies, commercial banks, and financial companies. Women borrowers' high repayment rate on loans made microcredit a highly attractive target for investment by commercial banks and corporations. The for-profit trans-formation of microcredit schemes since the late 1990s has multiplied the funds available for lending and financialized poor people's lives in ways that heightened their vulnerability (Wichterich 2012). In this way, poor rural women have been integrated into the returns-based logic of global financial markets. As Roodman and Morduch (2009: 4) put it, "30 years into the microfinance movement, we have little solid evidence that it improves the lives of clients in meaningful ways." In fact, the rules of microfinance institutions (MFI) are "set up not to tolerate any failure, and this 'zero-default model' of microcredit has worked because the inability to pay loans would be a source of shame/dishonor for the borrower and her family" (Banerjee and Duflo 2011: 174). The result is sometimes tragic: in order to settle debts, group members would be involved in seizing assets from a defaulting member, sometimes dismantling her house to sell the pieces for scrap (Karim 2011). In extreme cases, as in the 2010 microcredit crisis in Andhra Pradesh, India, suicides by overly indebted borrowers were a symptom of their financial stress and frayed social relations (Taylor 2011; 2012). These borrowers who were on the verge of default committed suicide rather than face its shame.

Concentration of Wealth, Inequality, and Vulnerability

The twin engines of global economic integration—neoliberal policies and technological change—have been instrumental in accelerating two processes associated with capital accumulation: the concentration of ownership in the hands of a small group and proletarianization.

Concentration of Wealth

The neoliberal policy regime has accelerated capitalism's inherent tendency towards concentration of ownership in many industries—where a few large firms control production—and in the financial sector, which serves as the main engine of capital accumulation. Through the laws of competition, the most efficient firm eliminates the weaker firms, although oligopolistic strategies and political power also might be at work. As Harvey (2007) has argued forcefully, deregulation of markets has produced more avenues for the centralization of capital and has led to waves of takeovers, mergers, and consolidations in many sectors such as airlines, retail, automobiles, and petroleum. Rapid technological changes in communications and transport have also played a crucial role in reducing or eliminating spatial barriers, subjecting local businesses, both large and small, to competition from not only local companies but also firms elsewhere. In high-income economies, the owners of capital have benefitted from the productivity increases generated by new technologies including the digital revolution. At the same time, they have been awarded further protection through international commercial laws, patents, and intellectual property rights that allow monopoly (or oligopoly) powers to be asserted globally. The pharmaceutical industry, for example, has acquired extraordinary monopoly powers world-wide in part through massive centralization of capital and in part through the protection of patents and licensing agreements.

Monopoly power, in turn, allows firms to charge high prices and to further consolidate their economic power (Stiglitz 2012). And, as legal cases involving Monsanto and other biotech companies have shown, the legal playing field is not level. Stiglitz (2012: 273), for example, refers to an "arms race" in the

US justice system where the outcomes are stacked in favor of the economically powerful. When weaker firms or groups of workers and consumers take legal action against abuses of near-monopolies, their resources often do not allow them to fight the superior power of the larger firms.[12] Finally, unabashed promotion of the interests of capitalists and investors has taken place through government assistance including investment subsidies, infrastructural support, tax concessions, and the Federal Reserve or Central Bank rescue interventions during financial crises (Pollin 2003; Herszenhorn 2008; Krugman 2013a; 2013b). These processes, together with financial investments, speculation, and tax evasion, have resulted in rapid wealth accumulation at the top of the wealth distribution pyramid at both the national level and global level, leading commentators such as David Cay Johnston (2006: 12) to gush in the *New York Times* that, a "crashing wave of capital is minting new billionaires each year."

Proletarianization

The process of wealth concentration has been accompanied by the growth of a "reserve army of labor" in the Marxian sense or the formation of the *precariat* (Standing 2011a). As capitalism expands and draws non-capitalist production processes into its orbit, it creates pockets of marginally employed and unemployed workers, including discouraged workers, in both high-income and low-income countries. This surplus labor has been generated by both proletarianization in the classic sense and the enormous expansion of the global labor supply since the early 1980s. As Marx emphasized, the bargaining position of employed workers vis-à-vis employers weakens as the reserve army of labor grows, since the employed can be readily replaced by the members of this reserve labor pool. Moreover, deskilling through technological change enables the substitution of some workers with others willing to work for a lower wage.

One major route to expansion of the reserve army of labor is the growing landlessness in the countryside. Since the early 1980s an increasing proportion of rural populations have become dispossessed as they lost the ownership and control of the means of producing their livelihoods, so that their own labor has become the only means of survival available. Agricultural trade liberalization and elimination of state subsidies to small farmers have been key policies in fueling this process of proletarianization. Small farming has declined under pressures of both export agriculture and import competition. The inability to compete for the best land and water sources for export production and to compete with low-priced food imports in domestic markets have led to indebtedness, eviction of farmers, and abandonment of farming (Pérez et al. 2008; Koopman 2009). These processes have increased the supply of landless and near-landless workers; they have spurred rapid rural-urban migration and international migration and increased the concentration of land in the hands of large farmers. For example, the unraveling of the smallholder sector in Mexican agriculture since NAFTA went into effect in 1994 has kept strong both the migration streams to the US and the labor supply for border factories (*maquiladoras*). Similarly, the displacement of small commerce by larger enterprises (such as supermarkets and shopping centers) has contributed to this process.

The declining capacity of national governments to implement full-employment macroeconomic policies (under the neoliberal budget mandates) has further expanded the pool of unemployed, underemployed, and precariously employed workers. Moreover, governments have adopted labor laws—both in the global North and South—that tolerate, and even promote, labor market flexibility. These laws have weakened or withdrawn state support for collective bargaining, social safety nets, and unemployment compensation schemes. The decline in social protection and emphasis on individual responsibility for survival have led to the proliferation of nonstandard and insecure forms of livelihood, which weaken the capacity of the household and its members to mitigate or manage risk and deal with shocks (Chambers 2006; Standing 2011a). While the unemployed and underemployed rely on a variety of means for survival, they experience vulnerability in the form of heightened defenselessness and exposure to risk, shocks, and therefore the possibility of material, political or social deprivation.[13] In contrast to the Davos men, the vulnerable segments of global society are experiencing impoverishment, insecurity, illnesses, marginalization, and political voicelessness.

The internationalization of production has expanded the scope of the reserve army of labor beyond national borders. Investor and corporate buyer mobility enables tapping into an almost infinite supply of labor around the globe. The first tier comprises workers in firms operating in low-wage economies to produce goods and services for export. This group of workers expands the potential size of the reserve army in higher-wage economies such as the United States; on the basis of these workers, US firms can credibly claim that relatively high wages or labor costs would undermine their competitiveness in the global market. Especially in mobile industries in high-wage economies, a firm can make a credible threat to move to low-wage countries when their workers demand or expect higher wages (Bronfenbrenner 2000; Pollin 2003). A second tier of the reserve army takes the form of the informally employed workers in low-wage economies, and increasingly in crisis-affected high-income countries. A good proportion of these workers are women. Firms hire and lay off workers in order to adjust to market fluctuations while the informally employed provide the cushion that supplies much flexibility for capital, resulting in a shift of the burden of survival onto the individual worker (Benería and Floro 2006). When export manufacturing loses dynamism in a given country (due to loss of competitiveness or trade preference erosion) formal export sector workers tend to join the ranks of underemployed labor or the informally employed and keep wage growth in check in the local economy.

Widening Income Inequalities

The outcome of the growing power imbalance between workers and owners of capital has been the widening of social and economic disparities. The increase in wealth inequality since the late 1970s is manifested in the dramatic rise over the last few decades in the share of total income going to top income groups in most countries. The enormous rise in productivity enabled by technological change since the 1970s has brought few income gains for the working population in most countries (Reich 2012). Labor's share of output has shrunk globally (Palma 2011). In a large sample of OECD countries, the wage share declined between 1970 and 2012 and this was accompanied by a decline in economic activity (Kiefer and Rada 2014). In the case of the US, the income share of the richest 10 percent reached almost 50 percent by 2007, as shown in Figure 3.1. Most of the gains experienced by this income group have been due to the increase in the income share of the very top 1 percent of earners, and even more so in the top 0.1 percent, whose share has more than quadrupled from 2.6 percent to 12.3 percent

Figure 3.1 Top decile income share in the United States, 1917–2007

Source: Atkinson, Piketty and Saez 2011, Figure 1, p. 6.

Note: Income is defined as market income including realized capital gains (excludes government transfers). In 2007, the top decile included all families with annual income above $109,600.

between 1976 and 2007 (Atkinson et al. 2011: 6–7). These household (class) inequalities are exacerbated when they interact with other social stratifiers such as gender, race, ethnicity, to produce a far-reaching influence on daily lives. Arestis et al. (2013), for example, show that the financialization of the US in the twenty years leading up to the 2008 crisis has been associated with the rise of an occupational distribution that favored white men in the highly lucrative occupations.

The distributional imbalances are also manifested in the rise in income inequality worldwide. Using household survey data for 122 countries, Branko Milanovic (2012) provides updated estimates of inequality across world households using the Gini index, a main indicator of the degree of inequality, for the 1998–2005 period. Milanovic finds an upward trend in global inequality whereby, on a scale of 0–100, the global Gini index rose from 68.4 in 1998 to almost 71 in 2005 (Figure 3.2).[14] These are extremely high levels of inequality, higher than the Ginis for the world's most unequal countries. Moreover, as in the US, there is a concentration of global income in the hands of the richest households: in 2005 the richest 10 percent of the world's

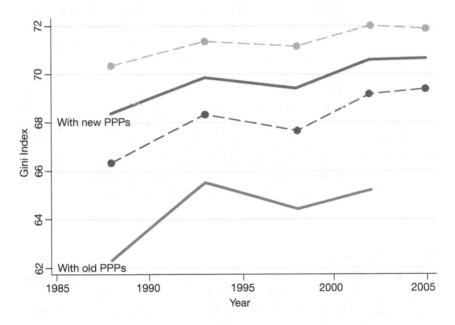

Figure 3.2 Global Gini estimates, 1988–2005

Source: Milanovic (2012), Figure 2, p. 14.

Note: The estimated Gini indices for 1998–2005 are calculated using the new (2005) purchasing power parity (PPP) and the old PPP exchange rates. The 2005 estimates of PPP exchange rates are considered to be more comprehensive and better than the old estimates since they cover 146 countries and for a number of countries, the estimates are obtained for the first time from direct price comparisons. The one-standard deviation confidence intervals around the new Gini estimates are displayed with dashed lines.

population took 55 percent of the global income, while the top 5 percent controlled over a third of the global income.

Another way of viewing global inequality is provided by the income gap between the richest 10 percent and the bottom 40 percent of households in each country. According to this measure, across countries, there has been a polarization of income between the richest and lowest-income groups in the 1985–2005 period (Palma 2011).[15] Using the same measure, dubbed as "the Palma," and focusing on developing countries only, Cobham and Sumner (2013) confirm that between 1990 and 2010 the rise in income share of the richest 10 percent came at the expense of the bottom 40 percent of households.[16] It is not surprising therefore that the widening inequalities within and across countries have generated tensions that have surfaced in rather dramatic ways since the 1990s and more so since 2008.[17]

Moreover, high levels of inequality create structural vulnerability, which predisposes the economy to financial crisis. Atkinson et al. (2011) provide time series data to show that the share of income going to the top 1 percent peaked in both 1928 and 2007, right before the Great Depression and the Great Recession. While neither Piketty (2014) nor Piketty and Saez (2014) consider the relationship of increasing concentration of household wealth to gender or race inequalities, either over time or in the period leading up to the financial crisis, others have shown race and gender inequality to be at the center of the distributional dynamics that predisposed the economy to financial crisis. The indebtedness was heavily concentrated among low-income women, particularly from African-American communities, who were targeted by financial institutions for subprime mortgage loans that put these households at high risk for default. These mortgages in turn were bundled into new financial assets and marketed by financial institutions, which spread the fragility far and wide, in a context of little regulatory oversight, and thereby prepared the ground for the crisis (Fukuda-Parr et al. 2013).

Global Feminization of Labor

A major feature of global economic integration has been the enormous increase in women's participation in paid work since the late 1970s. While women's integration in the labor force has varied by country, region, race/ethnicity, and class, for most women it has involved either first-time entry into wage labor or transition from intermittent to continuous participation in paid work. The rise in women's educational levels has been an important contributor to their entry into paid work.[18] Women's higher skill levels, along with the modest success of anti-discrimination policies, have opened up professional employment opportunities for educated women in many countries. This trend may be viewed as a vindication for feminist movements that have sought access to paid employment for women on equal terms with men since the nineteenth century. For less-educated women, on the other hand, the pressure to earn an income has often led to employment in precarious and unstable conditions.

The term feminization of labor refers to women's increased share of employment. In addition to opening up opportunities for professional women, this trend has been tied to the growth of activities such as export manufacturing, services, subcontracting, and commercial agriculture. Guy Standing (1989; 1999) referred to this trend as the "global feminization of labor," where labor is understood in the double sense of both those who fill the jobs and the deterioration of working conditions. Accordingly, in high-income and low-income countries alike, since the late 1970s the type of jobs held by women and men has often converged towards precariousness and insecurity, as women entered paid employment in increasing numbers. This global trend is the outcome of both increasing demand for women's labor in the expanding sectors and of pressures on women to secure the livelihoods of their families. Specifically, the labor market flexibility promoted by neoliberal policies has resulted in employment and income insecurity, pushing an increasing proportion of women into paid employment; export-oriented production has recruited a large number; and informalization of employment, in the form of casual, contract labor, and home-based work, has further facilitated the rising demand for women workers. Since highly educated women have benefitted from high paying labor market opportunities during the neoliberal era, one related feature of the feminization of the labor force has been the increasing economic and social differentiation among women. This inequality has fed into higher household income inequality as high-earning women tend to marry high-earning men. In the discussion that follows, we first examine the feminization of labor/ employment, followed by the patterns of employment in manufacturing, agriculture, and services where we review wages, working conditions, and stability of employment.

Feminization of labor is neither universal nor necessarily irreversible. There are prominent cases of stagnant female share of the labor force since the 1980s, such as in Turkey and urban India (Çağatay and Berik 1991; Moghadam 2001; İlkkaracan 2012; Klasen and Pieters 2013). There are also reversals of feminization of employment at sectoral levels, such as defeminization of manufacturing employment in East Asian economies (Berik 2000; Tejani and Milberg 2010; Kucera and Tejani 2014) or in a specific sector such as with the Mexican *maquiladoras* since the mid-1980s (De la O 2006).These trends in women's share of employment have been associated with slow change or persistence in gender segregation by industry or occupation.

As a trend, feminization describes the rising segment of the long-run U-shaped pattern of labor force participation in the course of economic development that is widely viewed as a stylized fact of capitalist development. The upturn has been explained by a variety of processes associated with capitalist development, such as rising education levels of women and expansion of service sector jobs, and structural adjustment programs in developing countries (Goldin 1995; Çağatay and Özler 1995). However, there are also questions as to whether the U-shaped pattern of women's participation is an artifact of gender biases in recording women's remunerative work. New evidence from European history suggests that there was either no declining portion of the U-pattern or only a shallow U-shaped curve, depending on country, legislation, and weight of informal sector (Humphries and Sarasúa 2012).[19] The same biases may have been at work in late twentieth-century statistical practices, showing a declining trend in women's share of employment. When these statistical biases are rectified, the result is a subsequent upturn in women's labor force participation—in manufacturing, agriculture, and service sectors—in the developing countries, as in South Africa (Elson 1999; Roncolato 2014).

Manufacturing

Notwithstanding these measurement questions, the increase in women's employment has represented a very significant contrast with earlier processes of inward-looking development in the global South. As argued by Ester Boserup (1970), industrialization in the early-mid twentieth century had mostly generated employment for men, while women had been relegated to subsistence production or to work in the household. Since the late 1970s, however, we have seen employer preference for women workers in a variety of activities, particularly those in export-oriented, labor-intensive industries that rely on low-cost production to maintain competitiveness.[20] Over time the composition of this workforce has changed from young, single workers towards a more diverse workforce, which includes older, married women, and mothers. Employers that produce for the world market have relied on women's labor as the most flexible and the lowest cost, thus most suitable for labor-intensive processes. Women are prominent in EPZs (export processing zones), export sectors in general, and the lower tiers of global commodity chains because they enable exporters to attain lower unit labor costs than are possible with male workers. Underlying these lower costs are both women's lower wage rates and their greater productivity compared to male workers.[21] Both these features are sustained by patriarchal gender norms and are reproduced in the workplace by the concerted efforts of employers and government policy.

First, employers are able to pay lower wages to women compared to men because of employment segmentation. Women are often segregated in unskilled jobs because employers perceive or classify them as unskilled workers. Employers and male-dominated unions would often invoke gender norms that designate women as secondary earners and dependent on men who are viewed as the breadwinners.[22] In addition, a variety of policies reinforce lower pay for women such as denial of training for women, application of two-tier wages, and suppression of union rights in EPZs (Seguino 1997; Doraisami 2008; Berik 2008).

Second, export sector employers attain higher labor productivity with women workers due to the temporary nature of their employment. Short tenure on the job is commonly the result of marriage or childbearing. While marriage bars—according to which women workers are dismissed upon marriage—are no longer legal, and the export sector workers are more diverse in terms of age and marital status than the 1970s' generation, the practice of leaving the job upon marriage is still prevalent, particularly when children are involved. Limited job tenure of women workers, in turn, allows employers to draw upon a highly productive workforce and yet pay relatively low wages that are held in check by high turnover. On the other hand, to the extent that women workers conform to gender norms—submissiveness, willingness to accept factory discipline—these are also likely to contribute to their high productivity (Salzinger 2003).

Institutional rules also can generate the high productivity of export factory workers. In China's export factories, where employment has been conditional on urban residency permits and short-term employment contracts, workers' willingness to work overtime and comply with factory discipline is high. In this case, the capitalist adaptation to the regulation of internal migration in the pre-reform period (the *Houkou* system) has produced a highly profitable arrangement for export factories. Housing workers in dormitories adjacent to the factory also ensures very long working days, control of young women workers, and quick mobilization of labor when needed to meet shipping deadlines (Ngai 2007). Elsewhere too, where export performance depends on increasing the export volume rather than the unit price, especially in apparel and footwear industries, excessive overtime and continuous work schedules are the norm (Berik and van der Meulen Rodgers 2010; Milberg and Amengual 2008). Moreover, excessive overtime is correlated with low wage levels and the gender wage gap, and explains the eagerness of workers to work overtime in order to earn as high an income as possible in the few years that they are on the job.[23]

Third, export sectors also achieve lower risk and flexibility by relying on women workers who are employed in informal jobs or home-based work in the lower tiers of global supply chains, which are characterized by intense competition among supplier firms. Women workers absorb the risks of shifting orders, falling unit prices, and lead times. They also save firms on fixed costs as well as enabling lower labor costs.

While women workers are preferred in labor-intensive export manufacturing, the trajectories of several export powerhouses indicate that feminization of manufacturing has been followed by a defeminization of the sector as production has moved towards more skill-intensive and capital-intensive methods. In manufacturing at least, there seems to be a strong relationship between upgrading of technology (rising capital intensity and value added per worker) and decline in the female share of employment (Tejani and Milberg 2010; Berik 2000). The *maquiladora* sector on the US–Mexican border has experienced such changes (Cravey 1997; Fussell 2000; Salzinger 2003; De la O 2006; Charles 2011). Decline in women's share of employment can be accompanied by change in the composition of women workers. Fussell's study for the case of Tijuana, Mexico, found that, in their drive to keep production costs low, transnational manufacturers tapped into the labor of mothers of young children who had no other options for employment and would make loyal workers.[24]

Agriculture

In rural areas too there is evidence of feminization of labor. In Latin America under the neoliberal policy regime, rural women's participation increased dramatically, albeit from a small base (on average, from 16.2 percent to 25.2 percent between 1980 and 2000) (Deere 2009). This increase was in response to the need to diversify livelihoods in the context of rising social and economic inequalities and persistent poverty associated with the neoliberal reforms. Peasant agriculture lost its profitability due to the cuts in farm support, agricultural trade liberalization, and growth of nontraditional agricultural exports. Deere (2009) argues that women are taking on increased responsibility for peasant (own account) production due to men's absence from the farm (as men either migrate or take on better paying off-farm jobs). Women's wage employment in non traditional agro-export production is rising, on the other hand, as the new export crops are more labor-intensive and require seasonal labor in the fields and packing houses. As in export manufacturing, women's gender socialization makes them the preferred workers: they possess the requisite gendered skills, yet can be paid lower wages and are less likely to organize. Given the ongoing undercounting of women's work in Latin American agriculture (as unpaid family workers, own-account workers, and temporary wage workers), Deere is cautious about calling these trends feminization of labor; rather, the form of participation may be changing, such that there is a feminization of *responsibility* or of *market* participation.

Similarly, in India as elsewhere in Asia, agricultural trade liberalization, privatization, decline in public investment in agriculture, and elimination of food subsidy programs have contributed to the integration of women in paid labor in agriculture (Wright and Wolford 2003; Garikipati and Pfaffenzeller 2012; Yokokawa et al. 2013). These processes have led to decline in farm earnings, increased indebtedness, and distress sale or pawning of land, bringing about the demise of smallholder farms and tenancy arrangements in rural areas. As a result, there has been a shift in women's labor market position from farmers and unpaid family workers to landless worker status. The majority of the absolutely or near landless belongs to scheduled castes, ethnic minority groups, and women, constituting one of the most exploited segments of the labor force, hired irregularly and earning very low wages (Padhi 2007; Breman 2010). Based on survey research, Garikipati and Pfaffenzeller (2012) show that, as the relative importance of agriculture declined in post-reform India, there was feminization of agricultural wage labor. As agricultural inputs became more expensive in the post-reform period, farmers who were looking to cut costs substituted women for men as wage workers; women were both more productive (and obedient) and cheaper to hire. This proletarianization of female agricultural labor contrasts with the stagnant trend in urban women's labor force participation in India during the same period (Klasen and Pieters 2013).[25]

Working conditions of wage labor in export agriculture have generally been poor. Samarasinghe (1998) shows that the promotion of tea production for export in Sri Lanka has further entrenched the subordinate role of women in this sector as it has led to the increased use of casual work, temporary work, and part-time contracts. In some agrarian societies, the commercialization of agriculture has marginalized women workers. These practices include piecework labor contracts for planting, tied planting, and harvesting contracts, and more exclusive pre-arranged harvesting contracts that weaken the bargaining position of women vis-à-vis employers, while, at the same time, facilitating greater exploitation by employers (Naylor 1994). Carney's study of Gambia demonstrates how market contracts between horticultural (male) contractors and women farmers are often regularly broken or abused by the former with the effect of shifting marketing risks onto the latter and so reducing women farmers' returns to labor (Carney 1992). There are also instances where technological change in agriculture brought about defeminization of employment. The study by Naylor (1994) demonstrates how the introduction of modern agricultural technology utilizing market inputs in Indonesia has resulted in increased men's participation in what were previously exclusively women's tasks. Similar observations were made by Hart (1992) with respect to tasks that used to be carried out by female wageworkers in Malaysia. More recent studies arrive at similar conclusions for Senegal and Uganda (Fisher et al. 2000; Kasante et al. 2001; Peterman et al. 2010).

The dispossession of land, together with very low wages and poor working conditions faced by rural landless workers, has led to the formation of rural workers' organizations and social movements especially in parts of Asia and Latin America. For instance, the *Movimento dos Trabalhadores Rurais Sem Terra* (MST) in Brazil, peasant-Indian *Confederación de Nacionalidades Indígenas del Ecuador* (CONAIE) in Ecuador, and Ekta Parishad in India have gained strength and support (Wright and Wolford 2003). Women have struggled to assert their voice in these social movements so that their rights are recognized and they are included as beneficiaries in any land reform proposal (Deere and León de Leal 2001b).[26] In the context of large-scale land acquisitions and land grabbing underway since the 1990s, these groups, such as the Movement of Babassu-Breaker Women (MIQCB) in Brazil, are critical in the defense of the traditional use rights of peasants whose livelihoods depend on using forest resources (Porro and Neto 2014).

Services

In the services sector, the global expansion of markets has resulted in the employment of an increasing number of women in "pink-collar" jobs. They include jobs for data entry and data processing, call centers, insurance and financial services such as credit card, banking and insurance services. Pink-collar jobs often mean higher wages (in relation to manufacturing or seasonal agriculture), higher social prestige, and more pleasant working conditions; but they also typically require working during odd hours such as "graveyard shifts" and for long periods with very short breaks. Women represent a high proportion of the workforce in these sectors in a variety of locations such as the Caribbean, Chile, India, China, Malaysia, and the Philippines (Ng and Mitter 2005; Howcroft and Richardson 2008). Women's employment has also expanded in the areas of health, health-related services, education, and tourism (Freeman 2000). However, the majority of the jobs in some service industries such as tourism tends to be seasonal and can be unstable, depending also on the ups and downs of international demand and the extent of market competition. Economic restructuring in the North has shifted the composition of the labor force to services. However, deindustrialization (followed by the economic crisis of 2008) has been associated with the growth of low-wage service jobs. As a result, women's rising share in services has slowed the narrowing of the gender wage gap in the US economy (Kongar 2008).

Migration

Globalization has also fostered the dispersion and relocation of female labor across the globe, through migration from low- to high-income countries.

A variety of economic and political factors have contributed to increased migration, including the search for a better life. The higher demand for low-skilled labor in the global North and emerging economies has contributed to increased migration flows, both for women (as caregivers) and for men (as construction workers) (UNFPA 2006; Benería et al. 2012). The high participation of women in the labor market, longer life expectancy rates and other demographic factors, and reduction in state services in the global North have resulted in the shortage of care labor and related services (Benería 2008). At the same time, the frenzied construction and real estate boom in emerging economies has raised the demand for workers in these sectors. Owing to the rise in labor demand, male immigrants in many countries are often employed in the informal parts of the construction sector while women immigrants can be found in a range of informal and formal service jobs. Of significance is the large number of domestic and day care workers from developing countries supplying their labor to elite or middle-class families in need of caring labor. Pushed by poverty and the search for a better life— imagined or real—migrant married and unmarried women from the Philippines, Sri Lanka, Pakistan, Mexico, Ecuador, Peru, and other Latin American countries have been working in destinations as diverse as the US, Canada, the European Union, East Asia, and the Middle East.

The numbers in the migration streams are not easy to estimate because of the informality and precariousness associated with this type of employment. Data from Spain shows that women accounted for over half (54.62 percent) of the migration flow from Latin America in 2006 while the proportion was higher for specific countries such as Nicaragua (70.09 percent) and Honduras (66.73 percent) (Benería 2008). In Italy, the estimated number of family-based care workers was between 700,000 and 1 million in the second half of the 2000s (Simonazzi 2009; Huber et al. 2009). In the Netherlands, the number of migrant workers in the health and care sector was estimated to be 875,000 in 2008, the majority of whom were women. In Germany, there are an estimated 100,000–150,000 households who usually employ two migrant carers (on two-week shifts) or about 200,000–300,000 workers (Da Roit and Weicht 2013: 485).

The recurring economic crises and the accompanying social tensions in the destination countries have led to new restrictions on the entry of migrants. The restrictions have been justified by the need to prioritize employment of native workers, particularly during the crisis since 2008. The anti-immigration sentiments, xenophobic attitudes, and support for proposed immigration reforms in the US and in parts of Europe illustrate how the problem of unemployment can be blamed on the presence of migrant workers, often leading to the growth of the political right as in the case of Europe in the past decade. Despite these restrictions on labor mobility, women continue to migrate as a strategy to cope with lack of employment opportunities and low wages in their own countries.[27] Often women take desperate measures which include illegal migration, which subjects them to human rights abuses and exploitation (Pérez 2012; Pearson and Kusakabe 2012; Rosewarne 2012).

Human Trafficking

Illegal migration and human trafficking are often difficult to distinguish, yet an inordinate amount of public attention has been paid to sex trafficking in particular, which is only a subset of undocumented migration flows (Rao and Parenti 2012). Sex trafficking itself is on the rise globally, since globalization has facilitated the formation of international networks linked to trafficking for prostitution and related services. Cross-country evidence indicates that attempts to regulate prostitution by legalizing it have produced a rise in trafficking, rather than keeping the numbers of women engaged in prostitution under check (Cho et al. 2013). Recent estimates provide an indication of the scale of this phenomenon for a selected number of countries, even though the figures vary widely by source. To illustrate, estimates for the period 1995–2004 put the number of cases of commercial and sexual exploitation worldwide at 12.3 million individuals (Akee et al. 2009). A large share of women in forced sex work, particularly in Europe, Asia, and the Pacific, are also victims of international and internal trafficking.[28] For instance, 63 percent of the forced commercial sex workers in high-income economies were brought in by traffickers. In Europe, the economic crisis seems to have increased trafficking; according to a Eurostat study (2013), the number of trafficked persons increased by 18 percent between 2008 and 2010. What is also striking is the magnitude of profits made from forced sex work as a result of trafficking. Belser (2005) reports that global profits made from trafficking into forced commercial sex work over the 1995–2004 period amounted to $27.8 billion, $13.3 billion of which was in the high-income countries, $9.5 billion in Asia, $3.2 billion in the transition economies, and $1.0 billion in the Middle East and North Africa. The in-depth analysis of sex work in Malaysia by Chin (2013) highlights the ways in which economic restructuring and labor market changes brought about by neoliberal policies and accelerated globalization have facilitated women's international migration for sex work. Women in particular, Chin argues, are negatively affected by the shift towards flexible labor, which results in heightened job insecurity, precariousness in employment, and gaps in the employment rates between men and women.

Discrimination and Patterns of Women's Integration in Paid Employment

Increasing labor force participation of women has been much celebrated and encouraged by organizations such as the World Bank, and more recently by the IMF, which have emphasized the importance of women's labor force participation and educational attainment for long-run economic growth (World Bank 2011; Elborgh-Woytek et al. 2013). Wage levels, gender wage inequality, and working conditions have largely been absent from this discourse. This may be in part because the evidence on gender wage gaps does not support mainstream economic theories, which predict gender-equitable effects of trade liberalization. Standard trade theory predicts that the right kind of specialization by low-income countries (that is, production of low-skill content, labor-intensive manufactured goods and services) will increase jobs for women and reduce gender wage inequality. Becker's theory of discrimination, on the other hand, predicts that rising (trade) competition will erode the higher wages paid to men, thereby eliminating wage discrimination against women.[29]

Given data constraints, much of the statistical analysis of gender wage gaps has focused on formal enterprises in manufacturing sectors of a relatively small set of countries.[30] Notwithstanding this limitation, research examining these two theories has failed to support the relationship between increase in women's employment and decline in gender wage inequality (and wage discrimination) in trade-related jobs. Major exporters that rely heavily on women workers in export sectors, such as Bangladesh and China, have experienced increases in discriminatory wage gaps (that is, the wage differences between equally skilled women and men workers have increased) (Paul-Majumder and Begum 2000; Khatun et al. 2008; Maurer-Fazio et al. 1999). And trade liberalization has either had no effect on wage discrimination in low-income countries (Oostendorp 2009) or it is associated with a rise in wage discrimination in Mexico (the *maquiladora* sector), Taiwan, and India (Hazarika and Otero 2004; Berik et al. 2004; Menon and van der Meulen Rodgers 2009).

Likewise, neither mainstream theorists nor the World Bank and IMF staff examine the possibility that gender inequality (in the form of wage gaps) could be instrumental for economic growth. One strand of feminist research has problematized this relationship. Seguino (2000c) and Busse and Spielmann (2006) have shown that gender wage inequality is associated with export competitiveness in labor-intensive manufactures. Seguino (2000c) showed that the Asian economies that grew the most rapidly in the 1975–90 period had the widest wage gaps. Similarly, Hsiung (1996) illustrated how Taiwan's high level of flexibility and market adaptability in export markets has been heavily based on low wages and poor working conditions of women home-based workers. More recently, Berik and van der Meulen Rodgers (2010) have provided evidence on how export competitiveness considerations create serious obstacles towards improving wages and working conditions in Bangladesh's female-intensive garment export sector. Thus, based on statistical evidence thus far, feminization of employment in export manufacturing does not appear to be associated with reduction in gender wage inequality. In fact, one reason for the persistence of gender wage inequality may be its instrumental role in country export competitiveness. When combined with rising education levels of women, the implication of persistent wage gaps is that women workers are cheated out of higher earnings by employers who benefit from rising productivity of women but do not give them a commensurate increase in wages (Berik et al. 2009).

Other contentious issues concern the wage levels in export sectors or EPZ jobs and their long-run trajectory. Lim (1990) and Kabeer (2004) have argued that EPZ jobs offer better wages for women than alternatives in the domestic economy. Lim predicted improvements in wages and working conditions over time. Moreover, Kabeer and Mahmud (2004) have argued that, in the case of Bangladesh, these wages are well above the domestic poverty level. To be sure, these assessments of wage levels do not take account of the excessive hours worked in export factories/EPZs, which may actually amount to lower hourly wages for EPZ workers. That said, since workers are concerned about the total earnings they generate in order to meet their needs, they are less likely to pay attention to the long hours worked as they try to increase their take-home pay by working overtime. Also, use of the local yardstick of either the poverty line or the minimum wage is inherently problematic, since these minimums tend to be set at very low levels that are insufficient to cover basic needs.[31]

Moreover, there is contrary evidence from *maquiladoras* in Mexico and Central America on wage levels, showing that women's earnings are not necessarily higher than the local alternatives for women, in particular, the self-employment option (Fussell 2000; Domínguez et al. 2010). Export sectors in Mexico (non-EPZ) and Taiwan pay lower wages to both women and men workers than the sectors that produce for the domestic market (Domínguez-Villalobos and Brown-Grossman 2010; Berik 2000).[32] Furthermore, evidence from Mexico and Mauritius indicates that the EPZ wages have not improved over time (Fussell 2000; Otobe 2008). This lack of improvement is likely related to the lower export competitiveness of these sectors compared to China after this country joined the WTO in 2001. It also underscores the instability and insecurity of this form of employment in the context of the enormous expansion of the global supply of labor. In the case of Mexico at least, Stagnant EPZ wages are also the result of the availability of a large supply of labor released from rural areas. In addition, there is the disruption brought about by economic crises; the resulting economic contraction interrupts or reverses improvements in working conditions, as these deteriorate following lay-offs and decline in demand for orders from EPZs (Domínguez et al. 2010).

The period since the 2008 global economic crisis provides evidence on the instability of jobs not only in the US where the crisis originated and other developed countries but also in developing countries. The crisis resulted in lay-offs in sectors where contraction in the high-income countries has been severe, such as construction and manufacturing and in export-oriented industries in developing countries. As exports declined rapidly in textiles, apparel and clothing, footwear, and electronics sectors in Asia, Central America, and the Caribbean, women were more susceptible to losing their jobs (Sirimanne 2009). In Cambodia, for example, thousands of women workers lost their jobs in the garment industry and had no other option but to engage in informal activities (Dasgupta and Williams 2010). In Vietnam, women workers from several export industries reported a larger fall in income compared to men (Hung 2009). In the textile *maquila* factories in Honduras, approximately 19,000 workers lost their jobs due to the crisis (as of April 2009); about 11,400 of these were women (Touza and Pineda 2010). In Mexico and Argentina, the contraction of the formal economy pushed the displaced workers, women as well as men, to undertake employment in the informal economy (Esquivel and Rodríguez Enríquez 2014).

Moreover, the increase in the ranks of the reserve army of labor during the crisis has strengthened the employers' ability to impose harsher working conditions and to squeeze workers further. A study of the effects of the recent global economic crisis on women workers in Peru's Ica Valley agribusiness area illustrates the employer strategies to increase labor exploitation (Arguello 2010). Some employers have used the crisis as an excuse to lay off workers who were about to gain permanent positions after a given number of years of work and replaced them with new workers hired under harsher labor contracts and at lower wages. Employers also have felt emboldened by the rise in the ranks of unemployed and underemployed to speed up work. The effect on workers is expressed in the following statement by an Ica Valley woman farm worker:

> Every day my quota of asparagus to pick is increased by my supervisor. I have to work longer hours to finish it otherwise they won't pay me. I am tired and I feel depressed. I can no longer cook or look after my children after work. I work more than 11 hours a day, but I cannot complain. (Arguello 2010: 245)

Feminization of Labor and the Dynamics of Gender Relations

The internationalization of production and the accompanying expansion of markets raise questions about their impact on gender relations at the household and community levels. Global supply chains, subcontracting, outsourcing, and factory employment encompass social relations that are imbued with gendered meanings. Gender hierarchies are embedded in the organization of production, such that, for example, on the factory floor the giving of orders and the making of payments are considered a male prerogative, while carrying out the orders is viewed appropriate for women (Elson and Pearson 1981; Benería and Roldán 1987; Carr and Chen 2008). Given the embeddedness of gender norms, a key question is the extent to which expansion of capitalist development transforms gender relations. In particular, how does participation in paid work weaken or perpetuate patriarchal forms of power and gender inequalities?

Women's entry into the paid labor force and the extent and nature of their participation have responded not only to the strength of demand for women's labor and the nature/history of the industries they work in but also to the nature of gender norms. These norms can vary by culture, class, caste, ethnicity, religious group, and life cycle stage, so that women's wage labor participation can lead to differential effects on women's bargaining power and gender relations in the household. The effects are marked by ambiguity, tensions, and contradictions. Even so, feminist authors have argued that women's employment in production for global markets has altered the terms of gender subordination for the better. Paid work has the potential to increase women's decision-making and self-esteem, and enhance the value of daughters.

Sen's conceptualization of the intra-household process has provided a useful framework for researchers to examine these effects (Sen 1990a). He identifies three variables through which engaging in paid work participation could affect women's bargaining power: women's sense of self, their perception of their economic contribution to the family, and their fallback position. Feminist researchers hold three distinct positions on the strength of these feedback effects from participation in paid work to women's relative bargaining power in the household. One position, argued by Benería and Roldán (1987) in the case of women engaged in subcontracting and domestic *maquila* in Mexico City, is that women can feel empowered by paid jobs even when their earnings might be low and their work unstable. Kabeer (2000; 2004) also argued that having a job that pays more than the available alternatives is a major step in enhancing women's decision-making power in the household. An example is the resulting increased decision-making by women over marriage and fertility decisions, as identified by export sector workers in Bangladesh (Fontana 2009).

Second, research shows that the life cycle stage of export sector workers is relevant in assessing whether paid work enhances women's self-esteem and autonomy. Young, unmarried women, in particular, report an increase in their self-esteem and ability to make a wider range of life choices. An early 1980s study of workers in Mexicali found that women, especially those with a higher education level, view themselves as choice-making individuals with some degree of control over their lives (Fiala and Tiano 1991). For older women with children, however, income from *maquiladora* work in Central America is argued to be no more than a means of economic survival which results in a double burden for women (Domínguez et al. 2010). It is, of course, possible that the differing interpretations of the effects of paid work in the two periods arise from the deterioration of conditions of employment in the *maquila* factories over time.[33]

A third position is that the type of jobs held by women matters in shaping women's fallback position in the household. Some researchers argue that the key ingredient for increasing women's bargaining power is for women to work in large factory settings where they are positioned as a group vis-á-vis the employer. For example, Sen (1990a) articulates the importance of "gainful work outside" (that is, wage work away from kinship relations) for improving women's bargaining power in the family. Indeed, this is the presumption underlying Engels's classic argument advocating wage work for women. However, this type of argument overlooks the extent to which patriarchal norms may be embedded in capitalist workplaces and reproduce the values and practices associated with traditional gender norms (Elson and Pearson 1981; Albelda and Drago 2013).[34] Moreover, others argue that, even if the work fits the characteristics of "gainful work outside," low-skill, low-wage jobs generated by labor-intensive export industries are likely to have a limited effect on women's chances for economic security, their well-being and decision-making power in the household (Koggel 2003; Domínguez et al. 2010).

These contradictory effects were articulated by Elson and Pearson (1981), who distinguished three tendencies in the relationship between factory employment and women's subordination. Participation in paid work in export-oriented factories, they argued, can "intensify" or "decompose" existing forms of women's subordination to men or "recompose" new forms of subordination. All three tendencies might be simultaneously operating in different degrees and combinations as well, such that one cannot make any general presupposition regarding the transformative effects of women's labor force participation on gender and other power relations. We frame our discussion of evidence by distinguishing among three types of effects of women's participation in paid work.

Liberating Effect

Globalization has created opportunities for women to enter the labor market and to earn higher wages than the no-wage scenario of unpaid family laborers in agriculture or working in domestic service jobs, which in turn can have positive effects for women. Earning their own income can lessen women's economic dependence on husbands and fathers, while giving them the ability to act and defend their interests and those of their family and community in the face of adverse circumstances. To the extent that women have control over their earnings, they can gain the leverage to negotiate and exercise greater decision-making power. This, in turn, not only may release women from the constraints of patriarchal traditions but also it can increase women's well-being and status through different avenues (Lim 1990; Tiano 1994; Friedemann-Sánchez 2006).

Kabeer (2000), for example, argues that Bangladeshi women's paid work has been associated with an increase in the "power to choose" and positive subjective evaluations, even if within the many still-existing constraints; in this sense, women have become what Kabeer calls "weak winners, powerful losers" (2000: 364). Berik (1989) has shown that women's earnings in rural Turkey enabled young couples to negotiate and achieve separation from the extended family compound and to set up independent households. Dedeoğlu (2010) argues that increasingly, young women are able to resist arranged marriage and marry a person of their choosing. Similarly, Wolf (1992) found that industrialization brought young Javanese women workers more control over economic resources, which also strengthened their position in family decision-making, particularly in marriage and fertility. Likewise, Friedemann-Sanchez (2006) argues that formal wage employment in Colombia's export-flower industry has given women new opportunities to oppose male domination. She points out that these jobs have provided them access to workshops on violence prevention, literacy, and self-esteem. As a result, a number of women workers are leaving unequal and abusive marriages, choosing to remain single, or using newly acquired leverage to bargain for more equality within their households.[35] Based on an overview of feminization of rural labor in Latin America, Deere (2009) points out that peasant women's wage work in nontraditional agricultural export production has given them the opportunity to become independent wage workers for the first time, to earn higher wages than in other rural alternatives, and to have an option besides the urban domestic service jobs. In some instances wage work has led to more equitable relations in the household. Thus, the feminization of employment can accelerate the diffusion of such liberating practices that break down or weaken prevailing gendered norms.

Intensifying Effect

Women's participation in paid work can also intensify the existing unequal gender relations. First, employers may deliberately preserve and utilize some traditional gender norms to maintain discipline and control, and these practices in turn may reinforce women's submission to patriarchal rules in the household. For example, at the height of the carpet export boom in

Turkey in the early 1980s, owners of carpet workshops in conservative rural areas built daily prayers into the work schedule; not only did the work start and end with the morning and evening prayers but also the women were required to participate in the noon and afternoon prayers organized in the workshop (Berik 1989). These practices infused the work routine with piety and reinforced the dutiful daughter and wife values. Here, and in other communities, where gender norms dictate that only men handle cash, when women become wage workers it is their male relatives who collect their wages (Samarasinghe 1998). There is also evidence that supervision of women's behavior becomes the business of everyone, transforming a private form of patriarchy involving the male household head into a broader and more public/social form (Dedeoğlu 2010). With the increased visibility of garment workers the supervision and control of young women in public spaces has increased to include distant male kin, supervisors, employers, and acquaintances. Further, in Taiwan and Japan the industrial work of women did not disrupt patriarchal norms (Takenoshita 2012). Working women maintained their role as dutiful and filial daughters, either in the family-owned businesses that are part of the global supply chain or as factory workers, sending their earnings to their parents.

Second, taking up paid work rarely accompanies a commensurate decline in women's unpaid work responsibilities, resulting in an increase in women's total workload. Engaging in paid work inevitably creates stresses and growing tensions for men and women trying to balance old roles—as dictated by gender norms—and the new roles brought about by the feminization of employment. While new employment opportunities for women may challenge existing gender roles, women continue to perform their socially ascribed roles as caregivers. There is evidence to suggest that norms regarding the household division of labor often evolve slowly, leaving women with a disproportionate share of the household and care work (World Bank 2011; Kan et al. 2011). Deere (2009) and Chang et al. (2011) provide evidence of a rise in total workload with participation in wage work in rural Latin America and rural China. In rural China, the daily total work hours increased in an absolute sense for both women and men, leaving the gender gap in hours unchanged. In transition economies, engaging in paid work meant increase in total workloads of women in low-paying jobs, as a result of erosion of the social safety nets and reduction or elimination of maternity leave and childcare facilities by employers (Pastore and Verashchagina 2011).

Third, increased paid work participation or economic opportunities can increase violence against women in its various forms—sexual harassment at the workplace, spousal violence, the so-called honor killings—even as these opportunities may increase women's bargaining power. During the past few decades, reports of rising or continuing violence against women have been common, and not solely the result of an increase in its reporting (World Bank 2011; 2014b). According to the 2013 World Health Organization (WHO) report, the estimated incidence of physical and/or sexual violence and intimate partner violence among ever-partnered women in their lifetime is estimated to be 30.2 percent globally. Using all available databases worldwide, the report shows that the problem is prevalent in both high-income and low-income countries, ranging from 36.6 percent in Africa to 29.8 percent in the Americas and 25.4 percent in Europe (WHO 2013).

There is evidence of increasing violence against wives, daughters, sisters, by relatives who perceive the women as somehow defying the patriarchal norms. This is the case with the so-called honor killings prevalent in the Middle East and parts of South and Central Asia. With migration, the practice has spread from the regions within national borders where particular ethnic groups predominate to large metropolitan areas or other countries that receive these groups as migrants (Appiah 2010). There is also evidence of a backlash against women who are improving their economic status. In the state of Veracruz, Mexico, between 1990 and 2000 rape and grievous crimes that cause bodily harm have increased along with improvement in women's wage distribution (Blanco and Villa 2008).

Domestic violence or threats of violence by men may also increase, at least in the short run, as women's economic opportunities increase and men perceive a relative loss of status and privilege (World Bank 2011; 2014b). For Bangladesh, early ethnographic evidence suggested a backlash against rural women who were gaining economic autonomy through microcredit (Schuler et al. 1998). However, empirical studies have shown that there may be a context-specific element in such violence (Koenig et al. 2003; Duvvury and Nayak 2003): only in the more culturally conservative areas were women's autonomy and membership in savings and credit groups associated with significantly high risks of domestic violence. More recent statistical evidence from both the south and north of India shows that women's labor force participation reduces the likelihood of women experiencing spousal violence (Panda and Agarwal 2005; Jeyaseelan et al. 2007; Krishnan et al. 2010; Bhattacharyya et al. 2011; Chin 2012). More recent evidence for India indicates a positive association of women's paid work participation with spousal violence, which suggests that women who experience violence are more likely to seek paid employment (Bhattacharya 2015). However, given the accompanying evidence that these women are also less likely to control their earnings, paid work does not appear to be a path to empowerment for them.

All together, these different forms of gender-related violence translate into the disturbing fact that, well into the twenty-first century and despite the progress reported in other indicators of gender equality, violence against women continues to be a serious and stubborn problem worldwide that is far from decreasing (WHO 2013; World Bank 2011; 2014b).When the target is school girls as in the case of kidnappings of school girls in Nigeria in 2014 or attacks on girls' schools in Pakistan, it is an assault on future independent women. The problem of violence against women is not only a question of fundamental human rights; it also raises many questions regarding the roots of violence and sexism and about ways of eradicating them.

Reconstitution of Gender Inequalities

Women's paid work can also contribute to new forms of gender inequality. The new relations may be a recomposition of unequal power into new forms that allow for continued subordination of women in the household. A common phenomenon is the income insecurity and vulnerability that young women export factory workers face, should they lose their jobs in an economic downturn: having become dependent on the cash nexus and achieved a degree of autonomy from their families, these women may find themselves destitute and accept jobs on arguably worse terms such as sex work. Second, in many low-income countries, among recent rural–urban migrants women's paid work participation in the urban setting may contribute to "housewifization," enabling them to achieve stay-at-home wife status—the urban middle-class ideal for women in some countries such as Turkey; if women's wage earnings allow their husbands/fathers to start a small business, then women become dependent wives and mothers (Dedeoğlu 2010; Berik 1989). Third, where commercialization of agriculture has marginalized women workers in terms of loss of jobs and earning power to men, then gender relations are re-constituted in ways that enable unequal power relations between women and men to persist. Fourth, in transition countries, the development of capitalism has brought reversals in government's commitment to gender equality, albeit this commitment was realized mostly in the form of high labor force participation of women. Transition also has brought a reassertion of gender norms that emphasize women's dependence on men, giving priority to men in job searches.[36]

To sum up, economic globalization has allowed gender biases and gender inequalities to persist in a variety of social and economic contexts. The effects of engaging in paid work on women's status and autonomy are not uniform and invariably positive. Participation in paid labor can have contradictory effects on gender inequality, depending on the gender norms in context, the dimensions of gender inequality under consideration, the conditions of employment, and worker characteristics. To counter the adverse outcomes requires a variety of complementary policies, ranging from strengthening women's fallback position via institutional changes to generating jobs under decent conditions with adequate wages, which offer greater prospects for personal autonomy and economic security.

Conclusion

We have discussed the far-reaching effects of contemporary globalization on shifting production sites, labor markets, feminization of employment, daily lives, and gender inequalities in the household. As women and men are integrated in globalized markets as workers, consumers, and borrowers, the cash nexus can undermine the gender norms and social constraints associated with traditional patriarchal relations. Women become economic agents, increasingly treated as individuals in their own right, and exercise newfound powers in the household decisions or in decisions over their lives. The degree of change varies by context but the tendency is towards individuation— individual choice, autonomy, responsibility. Many international institutions and women's advocacy organizations celebrate the trend towards greater participation of women in labor markets and the reduction in gender inequality as demonstrated by a variety of indicators (World Bank 2011; 2014b). However, neoliberal globalization also has encompassed deregulation and informalization of markets, affecting a large proportion of the working population. Although many women have been able to enter new spaces not open to them in the past, a large proportion of them are still relegated to the lowest echelons of labor market hierarchies and facing exploitative conditions. In addition, participation in paid work can reinforce existing gender inequalities or generate new ones, and almost invariably it increases the total work burden of women. We have shown that the unprecedented levels of commodification that have resulted from globalization have had contradictory effects through which increased choice and convenience can coexist with new burdens and continued poverty. Thus the agenda for gender equality is unfinished.

Notes

1 Polanyi's insight on the expansion of markets during the late nineteenth and early twentieth centuries is clearly applicable to contemporary globalization:

> The gearing of markets into a self-regulating system of tremendous power was not the result of any inherent tendency of markets towards excrescence, but rather the effect of highly artificial stimulants administered to the body social. (1944: 57)

2 For an elaboration of this point, see Benería (1999b) and Fraser (2010).

3 Likewise, these economically powerful groups insist on deflationary policies that keep inflation low and interest rates high, allowing them high returns on their financial assets.

4 Despite Chile's success in reducing poverty due to a combination of economic growth and anti-poverty programs, income inequality has remained at extremely

high levels, owing to successive governments' inability or unwillingness to tax the wealthy and the natural resource sector.

5   Entities such as the European Union (EU) have also been driven to a great extent by interests of financial and industrial capital, including transnational corporations and specific economic sectors, which expected to profit from expansion of a less regulated trade and foreign investment environment. However, the political objectives of European unification were prominent, from its early stages, as a way to overcome historical tensions and divisions in the continent. In addition, the EU's policies have been very important in promoting the welfare state—at least until the 2008 crisis—pushing for environmental regulations and promoting gender equality (often through massive financial transfers).

6   Sub-Saharan Africa has received very little foreign investment—with the exception of Nigeria (due to oil resources) and South Africa. Africa's share of FDI to developing countries was only 7.3 percent in 2012 (OECD 2013). These FDI flows to Africa are mainly concentrated in extractive industries of resource-rich countries, which represented about 70 percent of the total share of African FDI flows in 2012.

7   To be sure, there have been many efforts among economists to conceptualize individual behavior in the direction of what Nancy Folbre (1994) called "Imperfectly Rational Somewhat Economic Persons." These agents pursue their self-interest in ways that do not neatly fit the clear-cut definitions of economic rationality and "selfishness." These can be complex mixtures of behavior—from solidarity to competition or from altruism to selfishness—that are difficult to model even if they approximate reality better. As Folbre pointed out, these revisionist models undermine any strong claims about the inherent efficiency of a market economy.

8   For a more detailed discussion of this question, see the first edition of this book, Chapter 3, pp. 86–90.

9   While some people resist these values and attitudes, the evidence showing the shift has been overwhelming. As Jan Pronk (2012: 24) puts it:

    At the turn of the millennium, the prevailing character of globalization was not only lopsided and Western, but also capitalist. Companies and shareholders were aiming to maximize profit by means of fast and massive capital accumulation . . . Risk was shifted onto others and from there to others again, until a complete lack of transparency clouded economic and social cost-benefit relations. Social and environmental concerns were neglected. Inequalities widened. . . . An overriding drive to make money with money ousted feelings of social responsibility.

10   The CDOs are the opaque financial instruments that brought down the financial markets. The very next day (June 12, 2007), the news broke in New York that a big hedge fund linked to Bear Stearns was on the verge of default. This was followed by a series of shockwaves of financial turmoil in the months to come leading up to the 2007–08 financial crisis.

11   The imperative to consume has transformed individual goals. Working harder— rather than enjoying life or contributing to different forms of volunteer work—

has become central, putting society, as Polanyi pointed out, at the service of the economic system rather than the other way around. Moreover, the more affluent people become, the more rapid is the increase in resource use, especially fossil fuels and associated carbon emissions (Schandl and West 2010).

12 See, for example, Schneider (2011), Farm-to-Consumer Legal Defence Fund (2013).

13 González de la Rocha (2007), for example, shows that the survival strategies that vulnerable households use to cope with the mounting risks and shocks they face have deleterious welfare consequences for them. These include engaging in subsistence production, mortgaging and selling assets, the dispersal and migration of family members, eating less, deferring medical treatment, and replacing former market-purchased goods and services with home-produced ones, resulting in longer hours of unpaid labor in domestic work.

14 The value of the Gini index (also known as the Gini coefficient or Gini ratio) ranges between the hypothetical extremes of 0 (perfect equality) to 100 (perfect inequality). Most country Ginis fall in the 30 to 50 range.

15 The change in income inequalities within countries is more nuanced however. Palma (2011) points out that there was a remarkable deterioration in the relatively less unequal countries (mostly due to increase in inequality among the transition economies) between 1985 and 2005. This is in contrast to a relatively minor (but much heralded) improvement in the relatively more unequal economies such as Malaysia and Brazil.

16 The Palma measure is nearly perfectly correlated with the Gini coefficient, but has a more intuitive interpretation. For example, in 2010 Jamaica had the highest level of inequality, where the Gini index was 66 and the Palma was 14.67, that is, the national income share of the richest 10 percent was 14.67 times that of the bottom 40 percent of the population (Cobham and Sumner 2013).

17 These tensions have been part of the mass protests in different countries since the late 1990s, including anti-globalization demonstrations—from Seattle in 1999 to the different cities where the G-8 have been meeting. The recurrent financial crises and economic recessions in different parts of the world since the 1990s brought thousands of people to the streets, contributing to political crisis and government changes. In high-income countries, the economic crisis of 2008, fiscal pressures, unemployment, the weakening of the welfare state, and the austerity measures imposed to deal with the recession in the Eurozone have also generated strong protests. The Occupy Wall Street movement in the US and the M15 movement in Spain were examples of the many groups that voiced the indignation of a large proportion of the population with rising inequality.

18 Gender gaps in education have been decreasing across regions since the 1980s. The Arab countries have experienced some of the most dramatic increases in women's educational levels, with women's literacy rates doubling during the period, and the progress has also been impressive for Southeast Asia and the Pacific countries (UNDP 2010; 2011; World Bank 2011). Likewise, in many Latin American countries, educational indicators for women have surpassed those of men practically across the board.

19 Feminization of labor was probably less massive than it appears in official European records; women were working for pay in larger numbers before but they were unrecorded by official statistics.

20 The relationship between labor-intensive export-oriented production and the rise in female share of manufacturing employment is established by several studies (Özler 2007; Seguino 1997) and has become a stylized fact of economic development literature.

21 While it is difficult to document higher productivity of women as a group relative to men in the same sectors, there are pressures on women workers in particular that likely lead to higher productivity and there is evidence of higher labor productivity growth in female-dominated, export sectors (for example, Seguino (1997)).

22 While the role of unions in shaping occupational segregation and the gender wage gap is documented in the history of US and other high-income economies (for example, Hartmann (1979a)), there is more limited evidence for the global South. In major exporters, either there are no independent unions (China) or they are absent in the export sector (Bangladesh).

23 Some studies show that women garment workers in Bangladesh, who in 2006 earned an average of 72 to 80 percent of men's earnings for identical work, do not object to overtime and periodic continuous work schedules of up to 20 days (Khatun et al. 2008; Berik and van der Meulen Rodgers 2010).

24 The proportion of women in the *maquiladora* labor force, which originally reached levels above 60 percent, began to decrease after the mid-1980s (Pearson 1995). As pointed out by different authors, this was due to several causes, including technological shifts towards more flexible production systems requiring new skills, and increasing employment and availability of male labor (due to high levels of unemployment in the agricultural sector and migration), particularly of young men willing to work for low wages (De la O 2006). This example shows that both feminization and defeminization of the labor force may occur depending on the nature of technological change and labor market conditions.

25 Chang, MacPhail, and Dong (2011) also document feminization of rural labor in China in the post-1992 period when reforms accelerated. But they use a broader definition of labor, which includes unpaid labor (both farm labor and domestic work) and off-farm wage employment. Based on time-use data, the authors show that over the 1991–2006 period women's share of total household work time increased.

26 Deere and León de Leal (2001b) point out, for instance, that there was a relatively low share of female agrarian reform beneficiaries until the mid-1990s since women's land rights were not a top priority of any of the rural social movements in Brazil.

27 Women also migrate for other reasons, including the search for more freedom, better working conditions, and to escape discrimination (King and Sweetman 2010).

28 An international debate has emerged around the extent to which prostitutes/sex workers choose this profession (Juliano 2004; Kamler 2014; Samarasinghe 2009;

Chin 2013; Apne App 2014). One argument is that these women should not be viewed as victims, but in charge of their own circumstance. The other side of the debate focuses on the "contested commodity" argument, that women, girls, and boys are forced into prostitution by men and that this kind of work is an affront to human dignity. At the same time, the growing phenomenon of child prostitution, male and female, has also become a matter of increasing concern, and here too estimates vary widely according to the source (Gupta 2014). Child prostitution raises difficult questions in terms of how to prevent minors from being drawn into it. Sex tourism is one area where international migration and prostitution converge in Asian countries and Latin America, for example in the Dominican Republic (Brennan 2002).

29   Becker's thesis that markets erode discrimination has been applied to gender wage gaps in the context of an open economy by Black and Brainerd (2004) who argue that the theory holds for the US. Kongar (2007), however, shows that while wage gaps have indeed declined under import competition, the underlying story is quite different from one of harmonious elimination of discrimination against women.

30   See Berik (2011) for a survey of the theory and evidence on gender dimensions of international trade, covering employment, wages, and working conditions, mostly in manufacturing sectors.

31   Domínguez et al. (2010) present evidence for the first decade of the millennium that shows the *maquiladora* earnings in Mexico are below the minimum salary, which is inadequate for meeting basic needs.

32   Berik examines the 1984–93 period, which can be characterized as Taiwan's mature export-led growth period, when the country's productive structure moved away from labor-intensive, low-skill content exports. Domínguez-Villalobos and Brown-Grossman examine the 2001–05 period and find that not only are the wages lower for both women and men but also that the gender wage gap is wider in the more export-oriented sectors of Mexico's non-*maquiladora* manufacturing.

33   Domínguez et al. (2010) note that the more recently established garment *maquiladoras* in Central America have worse conditions than their counterparts in Mexico which have a longer history.

34   Specifically, Elson and Pearson argue that gender is not only a characteristic of kinship-based (gender-ascriptive) relations, but extends to non-gender-ascriptive relations in labour markets as well.

35   This conclusion may be specific to the floriculture in Colombia that Greta Friedemann-Sanchez (2006) has studied, particularly given that the industry provides long-term job security, which differs from the temporary character of employment in global assembly factories in other countries or seasonal wage employment in non-traditional agricultural export farms.

36   Liu (2007) shows that state-owned enterprise reforms in China have disadvantaged women in both lay-offs and rehiring prospects due to the patterns of pre-reform occupational and industrial segregation by gender.

CHAPTER 4

Labor Markets under Globalization

If only I could take a day off when I am sick, without risking my family's livelihood; if only we could have one day off at Eid and not have to come in for work . . .

Shahana[1]

The central plank of the 'neo-liberal' model was that growth and development depended on market competitiveness; everything should be done to maximize competition and competitiveness, and to allow market principles to permeate all aspects of life.

Guy Standing, *The Precariat*, p. 1

Introduction

Since the 1970s, labor markets in both high-income and low-income countries have experienced profound changes. Deindustrialization, particularly in the global North, has accompanied continued industrialization of emerging economies and the rapid growth of the service sector. These changes have altered employment patterns, skill requirements, skill and gender composition of the workforce, wage hierarchies in firms, and wage structures within and across countries. The process has had uneven consequences, creating new sources of livelihoods in some places while increasing insecurity of livelihoods elsewhere. In this chapter we examine the changing nature of the employment landscape, the contributing factors, the labor market trends under way, and the strategies to address the adverse consequences of labor market transformations.

At the onset of the third millennium, and despite the existence of professional and high-end jobs in the most privileged economic sectors, labor market outcomes are characterized by informalization and growing precariousness of employment, the erosion of labor rights, unemployment, persistent poverty, and the increasing vulnerability of a large proportion of the working population. These trends have differential impacts on men and women workers. As discussed in Chapter 3, feminization of the labor force and decline in men's labor force participation in many countries have been integral to the labor market transformations. Although a variety of high-skill and professional jobs have been generated, bringing prosperity for this group of workers and to the dynamic sectors they work in, the race to the bottom has made many jobs traditionally held by men more similar to those held by women: insecure and with low pay. Multitudes of workers and their families have joined the ranks of informal workers earning livelihoods as self-employed; others are compelled to accept any job offered, even under harsh terms. That said, in the altered employment landscape women workers tend to predominate in the bottom tiers, occupying the lowest-paying jobs, piece-rate sub-contracted work, and other insecure forms of self-employment.

In high-income countries in particular, the old social contract of the 1950s and 1960s between employers and workers has been shredded and reconstituted in new forms that involve varying degrees of recognition of workers' rights. The male breadwinner-worker notion of the post-World War II period—based on a predominantly male labor force, with stable employment and attachment to a specific firm—has been replaced by a less stable labor contract still in the process of transformation. These changes have contributed to the weakening of bargaining power of labor vis-à-vis capital, to the decline in real wages and the proportion of total income going to labor in many countries, and to rising income inequality. The frequent crises experienced by many countries during the neoliberal era, especially the economic crisis of 2008, have exacerbated these general trends, with joblessness further undermining the bargaining power of workers. Of particular concern are the trends towards declining employment security and other types of worker protection, the increasing risks that labor in general must bear in the context of decline in workers' voice, labor union membership, and collective bargaining.

Labor market restructuring has been brought about by the interplay of technological change, reorganization of production, and global integration, driven by neoliberal policies. New production regimes and firm restructuring have generated new opportunities for firms, particularly as globalization and increased market competition induce firms to continually search for lower production costs. As a result, offshoring and outsourcing have become the order of the day for most firms, particularly large corporations. The use of casual labor and a contingent labor force have become "the new normal" practice when it comes to hiring.

The neoliberal policies pursued since the early 1980s have reinforced the competitive pressures from global markets while increasing flexibility and opening new channels for the accumulation of capital. Capital account liberalization has fueled the movement of capital worldwide, further enabling the reorganization of production processes and the shifting of jobs across sectors, countries, and regions. Trade liberalization has had significant effects as well, bringing about growth in employment in export sectors while causing loss of workers' livelihoods in sectors that are unable to compete with lower-priced imports or to cope with heightened market fluctuation and volatility.

In this chapter, we first examine the specific labor market features of contemporary globalization—changes in technology, organization of production and firm restructuring, and the neoliberal policies that have shaped labor markets. This overview is followed by discussion of the interrelated consequences of economic restructuring: employment and income insecurity; deterioration of working conditions; widening income inequality and social polarization; rising informality; persistent poverty and expansion of pockets of vulnerable workers among whom women are overrepresented. In the last section, we focus on the responses of multilateral institutions, labor unions, and grassroots organizations, particularly women's advocacy groups, to promote workers' rights, to increase women's voice, and to address the challenges brought about by the changes in the labor market.

Firm Restructuring and Labor Flexibility

Since the 1970s the development of new technologies has revolutionized production in many sectors, enabling firms to increase productivity while saving on labor. The electronic and digital revolution generated lightning-speed communications, new transportation, and information technologies. These technologies have made possible the development of labor-saving production methods and systems of decentralized or modular production and distribution networks. Thus, the traditional Fordist model of firm organization and assembly line approach that was developed in the 1920s for mass production has been increasingly replaced by the lean production/supply chain model along with a variety of flexible production and labor arrangements (Rubery and Grimshaw 2003; Hinrichs and Jessoula 2012).

The macroeconomic conditions created by the neoliberal policies discussed in Chapter 3 further intensified the process of decentralization of production, both geographically and vertically within firms. Market liberalization policies strengthened the power of capital, exercised through corporations' negotiations with countries over conditions for new investment and their collective influence over international, regional, and bilateral trade agreements. The same can be said for arrangements regarding property rights, environmental and labor standards. The accelerated mobility of capital, along with trade liberalization, since the 1980s has meant that firms confront both new investment opportunities and heightened market uncertainty; they are thus driven to constantly seek ways to reduce their costs and to expand their market niches.

These pressures have brought about a frenzy of offshoring and outsourcing activities.[2] Firms have moved either their entire operation or a stage of production across borders in search of cheaper labor, and/or developed global value chains (GVCs) (also known as global supply chains) by splintering of production stages in which value is added through production across different locations and countries (Gereffi and Korzeniewicz 1994; Chen et al. 2005; Flecker and Meil 2010). This process began with labor-intensive manufacturing sectors like garments, footwear, and parts of electronics, particularly with the relocation of transnational corporations to East Asia (Lim 1983; Elson and Pearson 1989; Herrigel and Zeitilin 2010).[3] As discussed in Chapter 3, due to employer preferences for hiring women workers in export sectors, this process contributed to the expansion of women's employment in many countries. By the 1990s, the increasing flexibility of production and dispersion of functions and activities had also taken place in more technologically complex, capital-intensive sectors such as cars, industrial construction, agricultural machinery, pharmaceuticals, steel, electrical equipment (Arndt and Kierzkowski 2001; Herrigel and Zeitilin 2010). In addition, in the 1980s and early 1990s, as average wages increased in the "Asian Tigers," capital and plant sites moved to the next tier of lower-wage countries, for example to Indonesia, Pakistan, Bangladesh, and the transition economies. In the 1990s and early 2000s, China and India, the two economies with the largest domestic markets, also joined the process as both destination sites and sources of investment.

Firm restructuring has been very dynamic, responding and adapting to the intensity of market competition and changes in production costs, market prices, investment incentives, labor laws, and relative wages across countries. Thus, more recently, in order to tap into labor markets where labor productivity is rising faster than wages, factories have been shifting from China to Vietnam, Indonesia, and Cambodia where labor costs are roughly a third of those in China (Jacob 2013). This pattern is replicated elsewhere as well. European companies, for example, have moved to North African countries and to neighboring transition economies like Hungary where the working conditions are less regulated, thereby enabling firms to demand from their employees longer working hours, weekend work, and long-distance assignments with long absences from home (Flecker and Meil 2010). As chains lengthen and more outsourcing takes place, competition between sites and suppliers intensifies. Hence, Hungarian subsidiaries pass on lower-level tasks to their offshore sites in Romania as the labor market in Hungary gets tight and wages rise.

The practice of multi-layered outsourcing, or subcontracting, for example involving factory- as well as home-based women workers, has become widespread in a broad range of sectors, from garments, toys, shea-butter, artificial flowers to sportswear, computers, electronics, medical equipment, and pharmaceuticals. It involves different arrangements of production networks and types of suppliers or subcontractors. For instance, in the case of the artificial flower industry in Thailand, suppliers often involve individual agents like Sanit, a homeworker in a Chiangmai slum area, as well as small cooperatives who sign the agreement and then distribute the work among women group members (HomeNet Thailand 2002). Subcontractors may be large factories employing hundreds of workers as in the case of sportswear such as Nike's subcontractor, PT NikomasGemilang IY in Indonesia or Apple's subcontractor, FoxConn in China (Bellman 2012; Zielenziger 2012). The offshoring of production can also provide firms with better access to large and growing consumer markets such as China, India, and Brazil (Buckley and Ghauri 2004; Ghemawat 2007). For example, Volkswagen and Sony can serve the local markets in China and Brazil more easily by means of offshoring and adapting designs to suit local consumers' tastes. This is also true for the toy company Mattel Inc. that opened facilities in China and developed toy designs for the Chinese and Asian markets.

Offshoring has been associated with deindustrialization in high-income countries and with industrial expansion in the emerging economies such as India, Korea, Thailand, Malaysia, China, Mexico, Brazil, and Chile, followed by other countries like Peru, Colombia, Vietnam, and Cambodia. Greater reliance on outsourcing and supply chains resulted in downsizing of large firms, not only affecting low-skilled workers but also reaching professional and management ranks and middle-skilled jobs (World Bank 2012). Ongoing advances in communications and information technologies and global competition have facilitated further reduction of firm size and created continuous pressures to lower production costs. These advances paved the way for not only the use of labor-saving methods but also the steady expansion of the core activities in new outsourcing sites in other countries. Further, climate change is producing, among other things, greater market uncertainty as natural disasters and unusual weather patterns affect plant sites, supply of raw materials, production, and consumer demand (Raunikar et al. 2010; Lamers et al. 2014; Halls and Johns 2013). Firms tend to address such uncertainties and unexpected disruptions by adjusting and reorganizing production in a manner that minimizes the costs borne by them (Hugo and Pistikopoulos 2005; Halls and Johns 2013).

Some low-income economies, on the other hand, have seen their economies transformed by the inflow of capital and new factories or service centers as investors have taken advantage of the growing educated and young workforce (Hampson and Junor 2005; Muturi 2006; Kuruvilla and Ranganathan 2010; Beerepoot and Hendriks 2013). Although for the world as a whole the employment share of manufacturing has remained at 21.5 percent on average, the Southeast Asia region experienced an employment share increase from 12.7 to 19.4 percent between 1991 and 2008 while South Asia's share rose from 15.4 percent to 22.4 percent (Van der Hoeven 2010).

Since the early 1990s, most economies also have experienced rapid growth in their service sector, particularly finance, information technologies, retail trade, communications, and e-commerce. Globally, the employment share of the service sector increased from 33.6 percent in 1991 to 43.8 percent in 2008 (Van der Hoeven 2010). The service sector has become the largest contributor to employment growth in high-income countries while increasing sharply its employment share among the emerging economies. East Asia, for example, saw a rapid increase of employment in services from 19.5 percent in 1991 to 35.7 percent in 2008. As with manufacturing, the service sector engages in outsourcing and offshoring, with firms such as United Airlines or Dell Computers Inc. splintering and dispersing various services and service-related functions worldwide to take advantage of lower costs. These activities include accounting, call centers, customer service, data entry and coding, insurance claims processing, medical/legal transcription services, all of which were once considered "non-tradables"—services that did not enter international trade (Rajan and Srivastava 2007).

The push towards trade liberalization in services and the extension by the WTO of the General Agreement on Trade in Services (GATS) to the service sector have further accelerated the expansion of call centers and support service operations to transition economies—such as Russia, Hungary, and Poland—and to countries such as India, China, Chile, Jamaica, Ireland, South Africa, and the Philippines (Williams 2001; 2004; Ng and Mitter 2005; Muturi 2006; Beerepoot and Hendriks 2013). According to the *World Development Report 2013*, the share of developing countries in exports of services rose from 11 to 21 percent between 1990 and 2008 (World Bank 2012: 54). This shift in composition of trade as well as the relative growth of services has contributed enormously to the feminization of the labor force in many countries, as we discussed in Chapter 3.

Neoliberal policies adopted by many governments from the 1980s onward played an important role in creating the labor market flexibility that enabled outsourcing and offshoring. For example, as a result of structural adjustment programs (SAPs) imposed upon them during the 1980s and 1990s, in many parts of Latin America labor markets became *de facto* very flexible. High inflation combined with wage freezes resulted in a dramatic decline in real wages (Egaña and Micco 2011). On average, real wages fell by 28 percent during the 1980s, underscoring the deterioration of living standards of labor. As countries undertook fiscal austerity, privatization, trade and financial liberalization, informal jobs grew dramatically. While growth of informal jobs kept unemployment rates in check, it also signified a substantial change in the employment structure (Egaña and Micco 2011).

In addition, labor market deregulation became the centerpiece of neoliberal reforms. Labor reforms were implemented based on the belief that labor market flexibility and competitive wages will promote economic growth and improvement in living standards. In neoliberal policy circles, until the Asian financial crisis, the performance of the Asian Tigers was touted as evidence for this argument.[4] Several Latin American countries adopted substantial labor reforms between the mid-1980s and 1999: Chile (1979 and 1991), Argentina (1991), Colombia (1991), Guatemala (1990), Panama (1995), Peru (1991), and Venezuela (1998) (Lora 2001).[5] The reforms included the reduction of costs of firing workers; decrease in employer contributions to social security and other non-salary benefits; facilitation of hiring temporary or contingent workers; and the dismantling or weakening of labor law enforcement institutions, which relieved the pressure on firm compliance.

In Europe, policymakers promoted labor market flexibility by relaxing the rules for dismissing employees in both temporary and permanent jobs, while promoting various nonstandard contracts. These changes have led to the expansion of atypical employment, including temporary and part-time jobs or the now notorious German "mini jobs" (Rubery and Grimshaw 2003; Crompton et al. 1996; Poch-de-Felieu et al. 2013).[6] Belgium and Italy introduced labor policy reforms during the 1990s that lowered employers' cost of firing workers from temporary jobs and made it easier for firms to create temporary jobs (OECD 2004; Boeri and Garibaldi 2007; Kahn 2010). The same can be said for the 2012 labor reform in Spain (Benería and Martinez-Iglesias 2014).[7] Labor reforms allowed firms greater latitude in setting wages, thus resulting in a larger spread of earnings among workers and the growth of the so-called working poor. Within these general trends however, the level and pace of labor market reforms have varied greatly from country to country and from one political regime to another (Hinrichs and Jessoula 2012). Among high-income countries, the United States has the most deregulated labor market with feeble employment protections and heavily restricted collective bargaining rights for workers (Chor and Freeman 2005).

Another factor that contributed to labor flexibility was the erosion of the social safety net in most countries of the global North and the weakening of already limited safety nets in the global South. In Europe, the comprehensive welfare systems that evolved during the post-World War II period up to the 1970s have been gradually dismantled. They were organized around the male-breadwinner model of the family and the notion of a "standard employment relationship" that defined a specific form of gainful employment (Hinrichs and Jessoula 2012). Although with differences between countries (Esping-Andersen 1990), the standard employment relationship usually entailed coverage of a range of worker rights, including collective bargaining, working-time standards, full entitlement to job benefits and procedures, longer periods of employment, internal labor market wage setting practices, a family wage deemed sufficient to maintain the needs of a nuclear family, and generous health insurance. These long-established labor market arrangements were altered in the context of high unemployment rates brought by increased market competition, the adoption of neoliberal economic policies, and prolonged periods of stagnant or low economic growth, particularly after the 2008 crisis.

The safety nets were undermined by budget cuts under the neoliberal macroeconomic policy regime. Economic restructuring in Latin America and the Caribbean during the period of market liberalization was accompanied by a general decline in tax rates on personal income and enterprises and an increase in indirect taxes such as the value added tax. For example, Brazil's average personal income tax declined from 60 to 27.5 percent between 1986 and 2001 and its average enterprise tax rates declined from 35 to 15 percent for the same period. These trends were also observed in Bolivia, Chile, Costa Rica, Dominican Republic, El Salvador, Guatemala, Honduras, Mexico, and Peru (Egaña and Micco 2011). In turn, government budget cuts resulted in the disappearance or erosion of public services, which amounted to regressive redistribution, hurting the lower-income groups in particular. The absence of social safety nets, such as unemployment compensation schemes, put much of the labor market adjustment burden on workers and added more unpaid work burden to women in these households.

The effects of firm restructuring, global relocation of production, and institutional changes have been deep and oftentimes tumultuous. In the next section, we examine labor market outcomes and broader consequences of these changes for workers.

Consequences of Labor Market Restructuring

Decline of Unions

Historically, unions have served as the main instrument in improving the living standards and working conditions of workers through their role in contract negotiations and collective bargaining. They have also sought the public provision of worker protections against labor market risks, such as unemployment benefits, and the adoption of social security systems. As such, they have played a substantial role in democratizing economies, in promoting the spread of wealth and incomes, and in protecting workers' rights. However, the transformations in the organization of production and labor processes described in the previous section have undermined the traditional bases of workers' collective action and labor organizing in many industries, especially in the global North. The result has been the decline of workers' rights and labor unions (Tilly 1995; Broad 2002; Dannin 2006). For instance, the study of labor practices around the world by Chor and Freeman (2005) shows that the United States is virtually indistinguishable from China when it comes to the latitude and bargaining power of employers in the negotiation of work contracts.[8]

Of the 58 countries for which the ILO publishes data, union density fell in 42 countries from the mid-1980s to the mid-1990s. In numerous cases, the decline exceeded 20 percent (ILO 2009; Floro and Meurs 2009). Not surprisingly, the decline in union membership has been accompanied by falling average wages and shrinking pension benefit coverage among workers as well as lower bargaining power of workers to resist poor working conditions in factories.

The bargaining power of labor was undermined by the loss of jobs and the development and mobilization of multi-tiered reserve armies of labor on a global scale that include home-based workers and those in the informal economy. In the global North, unions have been unable to resist the dismantling of safety nets, nor turn the tide against rising employment and income insecurity for workers. Likewise, the collective bargaining rights of workers embedded in labor laws and legal frameworks of nation states have been weakened through diminishing state sovereignty. Governments that insist in maintaining their role of protecting their citizens' livelihoods and labor rights risk being abandoned by investors who want to attain the maximum possible profits. At the same time, the individualization of labor contracts has served as a means for detaching workers from their class identity and collective interest, further contributing to the decline in unions.

Employment and Income Insecurity

The enormous shifts in the organization of production and the associated labor market restructuring have resulted in rising labor market insecurity

(Standing 2011a). First, as jobs have disappeared in some sectors, while being relocated or created in another sector/country, there has been a sharp increase in unemployment and underemployment. In the US, for example, female and male underemployment rates hover around 12.8 and 12.4 percent as of April 2014 (compared to the unemployment rate of 6.2 percent among women and 6.4 percent among men) with variations by race and ethnicity (US BLS 2014).[9] However, employment statistics and labor force data do not adequately capture all effects. Standard labor force surveys tend to miss or underestimate many atypical, nonstandard, casual, and informal forms of employment that have proliferated across countries (Floro and Komatsu 2011; Hirway and Jose 2011). In fact, policy impact assessments that rely on conventional labor force data take into account, in large part, only the changes in formal employment.

Second, employment instability has increased, initially at the bottom of the value chains and wage scales, but more recently affecting also jobs held by highly skilled, educated professionals. Internal labor market structures of firms have been opened up to competition from the external labor market. This has led to dismantling or altering labor hierarchies and the extension of inter-firm networks.[10] The new practices have reversed many features of the old labor contract in the global North, leading to individualized contracts and shorter-term agreements. Jobs that used to pay family wages to workers with low education levels—for example, assembly line work in manufacturing—gave way to jobs with individual wages, pressuring other family members to enter the labor force. Rising employment and income insecurity has been one contributor to the rise in women's share of the labor force discussed in Chapter 3.

At the same time, individual workers are increasingly confronting the need to shift regularly from one contract or job to another and to adjust to the highly fluid labor market conditions. The new labor contract means that the risks of job or income loss are privatized, given the weak or nonexistent social safety net regimes. The risks associated with market volatility and changes in demand are often pushed down to the lower tiers of the value or supply chain where employment is often insecure, particularly among those at the bottom of the supply chain. When lead firms move the location of production or contracts from one site to another, they precipitate upheaval in livelihoods of workers. For instance, when the EU firms shifted from Turkey to rural Bulgaria for garment work, and from Italy to the Balkans for leather footwear work, these shifts resulted in massive lay-offs in one sector in a country and the creation of short-term jobs in another (Esim 2002). In such labor-intensive sectors, women bear heavily the costs of instability and poor labor conditions, particularly some specific groups such as immigrant women (Rio and Alonso-Villar 2012; Pearson and Kusakabe 2012).[11]

The evolving labor market landscape is increasingly characterized by heightened competition among workers whose work can be outsourced or offshored. For example, telecommunication firms have used the threat of outsourcing in order to win labor concessions (Doellgast and Greer 2007; Flecker and Meil 2010). Even the core workforce may be reduced as companies lengthen the supply chain by farming out more functions and spinning off more subsidiaries. The effects of automation and robotization also add to the threats of job losses and instability in the longer term (Ritzen and Zimmermann 2014; Breman and Linden 2014).

Third, the number of part-time and temporary workers (also referred to as nonstandard employees) has risen significantly, making it a fast growing segment of the labor force in both high-income and low-income countries (Leigh 1995; Standing 2011a). For example, the proportion of employed people who are working part-time in Australia rose from 22 percent in 1990–91 to 30 percent in 2010–11 (Australian Bureau of Statistics 2012). The low cost of dismissal and instability in market demand are mainly responsible for the increased use of casual contracts in industries such as retail trade (42 percent of employees are casual), and accommodation and food services (65 percent), even though these workers generally receive a higher hourly rate of pay compared to regular workers (Australian Bureau of Statistics 2008).[12]

Increase in part-time work has been the source of the so-called Dutch "employment miracle" whereby since 1983 three-quarters of the two million jobs have been part-time, the majority held by women (ILO 2010; OECD 2014).[13] Part-time employment among women is also high in several countries of the global North, exceeding 35 percent in Germany, Ireland, Switzerland, Italy, United Kingdom, Australia, and New Zealand (OECD 2014). In some of these countries, the high share reflects the lack of paid parental leave and affordable childcare services. In Japan, over a third of the labor force held temporary or nonstandard jobs in 2010, but the proportion is highest in South Korea where more than half of all workers have temporary work contracts (UN Department of Economic and Social Affairs 2010). For the OECD countries as a whole, the incidence of part-time employment rates has increased by an average of 5 percentage points between 2000 and 2010, with Austria, Ireland, Mexico, the Netherlands, and Chile experiencing larger increases (OECD 2011). Another example is from the state of California, US, where a rapidly growing part of the economy has been the "temp" business. One of the companies called Express Employment Professionals prides itself for being "one of the fastest growing recruiting and staffing companies in the US. Company sales totaled more than $2 billion in 2011" (Express Employment Professionals 2013).

Fourth, many production processes that were "invisible," "undocumented," and/or once viewed illegal three or four decades ago are now parts of regular labor markets and of global value chains that squeeze labor costs at every step of the way. As typically represented by the way large transnational clothing retail firms like Gap, Zara, and others function, outsourcing has shifted many processes to the informal part of the economy, often blurring the lines between formality and informality and between legal and illegal. Labor conditions that would have been unacceptable under the old employment contracts are normalized and have adjusted to the changing needs of the lead firms in the value chains. In the new employment landscape, as Marchington et al. (2005) and Flecker and Miel (2010) have argued, the old "irregularities" have been accepted as normal.

Deterioration of Working Conditions

In the global South, labor laws that promote workers' rights, at least on paper, were the product of intense labor struggles, workers' mobilization, and the accompanying efforts of grassroots organizations and international organizations. However, the adoption of neoliberal policies and intense competition in export markets, especially after the 1980s, has led to low enforcement of workers' rights and easing of labor laws, undermined democratic institutions, and weakened the voice of vulnerable segments of the population. The competition fueled by globalization has encouraged or enabled domestic-market-oriented firms to adopt such labor practices as well.

Studies that examine the effect of the main indicators of globalization, such as international trade (or trade openness) and FDI flows, on union rights and working conditions have produced mixed evidence. Many cross-country regression analyses focus on the existence of child labor, forced labor, employment discrimination, and weak union rights as indicators of working conditions problems. These are "the core labor standards" delineated by the ILO in 1998.[14] Some of these studies find that trade expansion and inward FDI reduce the incidence of child labor (Neumayer and Soysa 2006); and trade expansion is also negatively associated with forced labor and slavery and gender discrimination (Neumayer and Soysa 2007). A historical perspective on Asian development shows that there has been a widespread decline in child labor in the region, albeit it continues to be prevalent in South Asia (Kucera and Chataignier 2005). Other studies show that trade expansion erodes trade union rights enshrined in labor laws (Mosley 2011). However, working condition problems are often sector-specific—such as clothing, electronics—and involve problems beyond the core standards spotlighted in these cross-country studies, such as wages and hours violations.

While working conditions violations are not limited to export factories, these factories are the focus of most analyses that assess these conditions because they are most directly linked to the processes of globalization. In export factories that supply corporate brands, working conditions often do not comply with one or more of the core labor standards. Export factories, some of which are located in Export Processing Zones and employ hundreds of workers, are granted exemptions from labor laws, most notably, union rights. While some research suggests that transnational firms or their subcontractors provide better facilities and higher than average pay compared to firms that produce for the domestic market (Bhagwati 2004; Kabeer 2004; Kabeer and Mahmud 2004), as discussed in Chapter 3, these comparisons tend to not consider the long and arduous work hours.

Typical violations of labor rights in export factories (often foreign-owned) involve wages and hours legislation—forced or excessive overtime, non-payment of overtime wage rates, and withholding of wages (Liu et al. 2004; Berik and van der Meulen Rodgers 2010). For example, workers in one of Nike's contractors in Indonesia have complained that they were regularly shortchanged on their pay by being forced to work overtime without pay to meet production targets (Bellman 2012). The dispute was resolved in 2012 when in response to union negotiations and consumers' protests, the contractor agreed to pay workers for past overtime.

There are also persistent safety violations. In 2012, 112 Bangladeshi factory workers lost their lives in an export garment factory fire that broke out due to the owners' refusal to adopt occupational safety and hazard measures.[15] This was followed by one of the biggest industrial disasters in 2013, which killed over 1,100 workers, when a garment factory in Bangladesh collapsed because of substandard construction (Allchin 2013). These stories are consistent with evidence from studies that have examined the labor practices worldwide ranging from agribusinesses to domestic firms and retail store chains (Chor and Freeman 2005; ILO 2008; Yu 2008; Gross 2010).

While it is common to hear the retort that the poor conditions are the product of low levels of capitalist development, it is important to keep in mind that these conditions in export factories are not indigenous to low-income countries. Rather, they are modern creations to extract as much labor as possible from workers at the lowest possible cost. In other words, they are the product of internationalization of production itself, which transplants production processes and degrades labor conditions in low-income countries (Piore 2004).

Rising Inequality and Social Polarization

Policies adopted by many governments during the neoliberal period have generally favored the massive redistribution of growth benefits from labor to capital and resulted in growing income polarization in most countries. Statistics on income distribution are unambiguous on these growing inequalities, as shown in Chapter 3. Despite the capacity of the global economy to generate unprecedented levels of output and increases in productivity during the post-1980 period, inequality has grown across the board and unacceptable levels of poverty have remained in many countries. In both global North and South countries not only has the economic and social divide between owners of capital and labor increased but also disparities have grown among workers in terms of pay, access to benefits, and working conditions.

Widening inequality trends have been accompanied by a worsening distribution of earnings among workers in many countries (Stiglitz 2012; Reich 2012; World Bank 2012). The ratio of the average wage in the top decile of the wage distribution to that of the bottom 10 percent has increased in 70 percent of the countries between 1995 and 2007 (Van der Hoeven 2010). Significant changes in the labor hierarchy within firms associated with down-sizing and outsourcing have widened the difference in average earnings among workers. In some cases, rapidly changing technologies tend to remunerate young new hires better than experienced workers, producing inequities that have negative repercussions on the morale of older workers (Cappelli 1999). Decline in union membership is also an important contributor to rising wage inequality. In the US, between one-fifth and one-third of the growth in inequality among hourly-wage workers in the 1973–2007 period was attributable to the decline in unionization (Western and Rosenfeld 2011).

In the United States, rapid wage growth among executives and those in the financial sector is deemed as the main reason why incomes of the top 1 percent have exploded since 1979 (Mishel et al. 2013). In 2013, CEO pay in the US was 331 times that of an average worker, up from more than 50 times that of a typical worker in the late 1970s, while the CEO-to-minimum-wage-worker pay ratio was estimated to be 774:1 (AFL-CIO 2014). This high wage inequality cannot be attributed to technological change alone (EPI 2014).[16] Rather, the divergence of productivity and median real wage growth characterizing the post-1979 period has been due to shifts in power in the labor market hierarchy driven by policy changes. The most pronounced divide between top executives and the rest of the employees has evolved due to the power of top executives, who not only negotiate highly remunerative compensation packages but also endorse compensation raises for other executives when they serve on boards of corporations.

By contrast, in the United States, the hourly wage of the median worker (the worker who earns more than half of workers but less than the other half) rose just 10 percent between 2000 and 2011 even though productivity has increased nearly 23 percent during the same period (Mishel 2012). In 2011, the federal minimum wage was only half the real wage earned by non-supervisory workers in the late 1960s; and in spite of the three-step increase, the minimum wage in 2011was 37 percent of the wage earned by non-supervisory workers. American workers in the bottom tenth percentile of the wage distribution actually earned less in 2011 than the lowest 10 percent of wage earners in 1979. Over 1979–2011, the wages of the median worker grew only 6 percent, with all the growth occurring in the late 1990s. On the other hand, the wages of high earners (those in the top fifth percentile) rose by more than 37 percent, and those in the very top 1 percent of the wage distribution saw their wages rise by 131 percent in the same period (Mishel et al. 2013).

Rising wage inequality bodes ill for women, especially for the workers on the bottom rung of the labor market who receive the lowest pay and hardly any benefits (Chen et al. 2005). By contrast, the gender wage gap narrowed among non-agricultural, formal sector workers between 1980 and early 2000 in parts of the developing world, some OECD countries, and post-Soviet countries where women earn more than 70 percent of what men do (Floro and Meurs 2009; Ñopo 2012; Piras 2004; Brainerd 2000; Hegewisch et al. 2013).[17] Between the 1990–92 and 2006–08 periods, women made gains in earnings relative to men in the manufacturing sectors of many countries, as shown in Table 4.1. Some of the increases in the gender earnings ratio were impressive, on the order of 20 percentage points or more in Mexico, Japan, and UK. Only a small number of countries experienced declines in the manufacturing earnings ratio (Egypt, Hong Kong, Sri Lanka among the low-income countries). It is notable, however, that in the rapidly growing economies of East Asia (Hong Kong, Singapore, Korea) women manufacturing workers still made about 60 percent of what men earn. Some studies have found that gender wage gaps are greater in the informal than the formal sector. This is the case in countries as diverse as Egypt, India, and South Africa (Bivens and Gammage 2005).

One of the consequences of the rising income inequality is the decrease in the labor share of total income. As the 2008 ILO report points out,

> [i]n 51 out of 73 countries for which data are available, the share of wages in total income declined over the two decades that preceded the report. The largest decline in the share of wages in GDP took place in Latin America and the Caribbean (−13 percentage points), followed by Asia and the Pacific (−10 points) and the Advanced Economies (−9 points). (ILO 2008: 20)

Likewise, a recent study of 13 OECD countries by Kiefer and Rada (2014) also shows a downward harmonization of the wage share of total income over the 1970–2013 period. The wage share index for nine of these countries declined by 12 percentage points between 1976 and 2012. This study further documents adverse long-run shifts in economic activity. Although more episodic and linked to the 2008 crisis, the loss of economic activity in OECD countries appears to be associated with worsening income inequality.

Table 4.1 Ratio of female to male monthly earnings in manufacturing, 1990–92 and 2006–08 (latest available in each interval), %

	1990–92	*2006–08*
Egypt[a,b]	68	66
China, Hong Kong SAR[b,c]	69	60[d]
Cyprus[a,b]	58	56
Jordan	57	63
Republic of Korea	50	57
Singapore	55	65
Sri Lanka[b,e]	88	77
Thailand[f]	64	75
Costa Rica	74	81[g]
Mexico	50	72
Paraguay	66	108
Czech Republic	68	65[b]
Denmark[g]	85	87[h]
France[b,g]	79	85
Hungary[i]	70	73
Ireland[b,g]	69	80
Latvia	84	81
Luxembourg[b,g]	62	73
Netherlands	74[a]	83
Sweden[b,g]	89	91
Switzerland	71	79
United Kingdom[i]	61	82
Australia[g,i]	82	90
Japan[h]	41	61
New Zealand[g,i]	75	81

Notes: **a** Earnings per week; **b** Wage earners; **c** Wage rates per day; **d** Including outworkers; **e** Earnings per day; **f** Wage rates per month; **g** Earnings per hour; **h** Data are for the private sector only; **i** Full time or full-time equivalent employees.

Source: Computed based on ILO Laborstat Table 5b (Accessed on April 19, 2013) and UN Department of Economic and Social Affairs (2010), Table 4.10, p. 97.

Rising Informality

The growth of self-employment and part-time as well as temporary employment in high-income economies is an indication of informalization globally. Informal forms of employment are no longer the feature of labor markets in low-income countries, as emphasized in early studies on the informal sector during the 1970s and early 1980s. The received wisdom in international development circles at the time was that the informal "sector" provided a transitory and precarious form of employment, especially for rural migrants arriving at urban areas in search of jobs (Hart 1972). The economy was conceptualized in dualistic terms, whereby the informal sector was characterized as "backward" and of low productivity, in contrast with the formal or "modern," higher productivity sector. The two were also considered to be operating separately and independently of each other. It was assumed that, with modernization and industrialization, the formal sector would expand and absorb most informal activities and the associated working population.

These predictions did not materialize. By the mid-1990s it had become clear that the informal "sector" had not withered away with economic growth, nor had it been absorbed by the "modern" sector. Moreover, job informality was growing in formal sector employment as well, including temporary, short-term, and other types of casual labor, and in high-income economies.

The concept of the informal sector was defined and redefined a number of times by the ILO International Conference of Labour Statisticians (ICLS) in an attempt to gauge its size and the size of the labor force involved and to keep up with the rising trends in various forms of non-standard employment. In its formal definition of 1993, the 15th ICLS put emphasis on the characteristics of the production units (enterprises) in which the activities took place, rather than the characteristics of the persons involved or their jobs.[18] This definition implied that a person is considered as being employed in the informal sector if she or he worked in an enterprise with characteristics corresponding to this sector. In 2002, the International Labour Conference updated the definition and allowed the following criteria: (a) the non-registration of the enterprise; and/or (b) small employment size of the unincorporated household or firm enterprise.[19] Also, it introduced the term "informal economy," which refers to "all economic activities by workers and economic units that are – in law or in practice – not covered or insufficiently covered by formal arrangements" (ILO 2002a). Employment in the informal economy thus comprised two components: (a) work in the informal sector as defined by the 15th ICLS resolution; and (b) informal work outside the informal sector (ILO 2002b). In 2003 the 17th ICLS introduced the term "informal employment."[20] Rather than focusing simply on the legality of bureaucratic registration, regulation, and taxation of the enterprise as the defining feature, the ICLS defined informal employment as a specific employment relation or labor contract that does not include basic protection or employment benefits.

Available statistics indicate that informal employment is an integral part of many economies, making a substantial contribution to GDP. Given the lack of reliable statistical information about the extent of informality, we can only rely on estimates, which show that between the 1970s/80s and 2005/10, the relative importance of informal employment increased across regions (Charmes 2012). Major increases in the informal share of nonagricultural employment are estimated for North Africa, and South and Southeast Asia over this long period, with a decline for a few countries in 2005–10. The highest levels of the informal share in 2005–10 are estimated for Sub-Saharan Africa and South and Southeast Asia, where this share reached nearly 70 percent of nonagricultural employment. In countries such as Mozambique, Bolivia, Bangladesh, and India, the share of informal employment in total nonagricultural employment reached as high as 87.2 percent, 75.1 percent, 76.9 percent, and 84.2 percent respectively during this period (Charmes 2012). These estimates seem rather high but they give us some idea of the importance of the informal economy.

For low-income and some transition countries, informality has clearly become the rule rather than the exception in employment. Marginality and precarious jobs are an integral part of the labor market experience for a large proportion of (male and female) labor. For workers and their households in low-income countries, it is clear that informal employment has been the main, if not the sole, source of livelihood. However, in some emerging economies that experienced rapid industrialization since the 1980s, informalization seems to have slowed down. For instance, the share of informal employment in nonagricultural employment has decreased for Brazil and Thailand, even though in the Latin American and Southeast Asian regions as a whole it reached 57.7 percent and 69.7 percent respectively in the 2000s (OECD 2009).

High-income countries, on the other hand, have experienced a rise in the share of self-employment, part-time work, and temporary work in total employment.[21] Large firms and even multilateral organizations and the public sector have increased their recruitment of temporary, contractual, and short-term workers. Nonetheless, the deterioration of labor market conditions in high-income countries since the early 2000s has placed many of these workers in unstable working conditions and among the underemployed or unemployed. Altogether, these workers form what Standing (2011a) has called the "precariat," which he defined as those who work in and out of temporary, insecure, and sometimes shadow-economy jobs and thus do not have both security of employment and income.

The precariat are excluded from the old forms of government protection and employer-based benefits. They are not involved in the type of social contract that regular salaried and wage workers have, whereby job security is provided in exchange for subordination and contingent loyalty. As Standing (2011b: 10) puts it: "a feature of the precariat is not the (low) level of money wages or income . . . but (rather), the lack of community support in times of need, lack of assured enterprise or state benefits, and lack of private benefits to supplement money incomes." This vulnerability is heightened with the erosion of traditional community networks and informal support mechanisms under pressure of expanding market relations. As in the case of informal employment, the number of people included in this labor category is likely to be underestimated in standard labor force statistics. The underestimation is due to the general difficulty in identifying workers with short-term contracts and/or with no employment benefits, and the fact that a person's position in the labor market is fluid. The precariat's occupational breakdown also is difficult to pin down, given that its members are engaged in multiple jobs with multiple employment conditions. The precariat bear the brunt of economic restructuring and market adjustments, reinforcing their mistrust in and sense of disillusionment with society.

The informal economy is heterogeneous and often dynamic. The nonstandard forms of employment have multiplied since the 1980s, thereby introducing a greater diversity in working life patterns of both men and women. There is wide variation in the range of activities, skill, and capital requirements, and in the working conditions of informal work. Research on the informal economy shows the interconnectedness of formal activities to informal ones (Ranis and Stewart 1999; Benería and Floro 2006). In their pursuit of lean production, large firms in the formal sector have increased their involvement with temporary and short-term jobs and informal production through outsourcing and subcontracting. These interconnections point to the dependence of the capitalist economy on informality as a way of lowering costs, indicating that there is no incentive for the former to absorb informal activities. Firm reorganization and decentralization of production and supply chains have extended these links in such a way that the distinction between the two economies has become increasingly blurred. Market deregulation has also made it difficult to identify where the formal sector ends and the informal sector begins.

In addition, the informal economy responds quickly to evolving patterns of work organization and fluctuations in the formal economy. Figures 4.1a and 4.1b depict the typical fluidity of labor that shifts between formal and informal jobs and illustrate the extent to which individual workers (and their households) are responsible for their own survival and for managing risks as economic conditions change and social protection weakens. Figure 4.1b shows how, during economic crises and downturns, the informal economy expands to pick up the slack of the formal economy and of the public sector.

Although the traditional association of informal employment with low skills and low productivity still holds, the last few decades have increased the diversity of working patterns and led to a dichotomous pattern of economic growth. This can involve a "high road to development" among highly skilled, technical and managerial, full-time workers and a "low road to development" associated with precarious and insecure types of employment.[22] Additionally, technology transfer involving the use of modern equipment, computers, and/or technical know-how has occurred along the value chains, thus the production associated with these processes is no longer connected with either marginality or low productivity.

Nevertheless, many forms of informal work remain disconnected from formal sector production, particularly those related to survival activities organized at the household and community level. These are precarious forms of self-employment with weak or no links to the more formal production and value-chain processes and without possibilities for capital accumulation. They include street vending, vegetable gardening, mechanic shop repair, food stalls/eateries, dressmaking/tailoring, laundry service, water selling, car cleaning, and many forms of artisan production. These are, in fact, the most visible activities in the rural and urban landscapes of many low-income countries.

The informalization of employment observed in high-income countries has mostly taken place within the context of legality, with exceptions located in the underground economy. Short-term consultancies and the temp agencies that facilitate nonstandard work or the above-mentioned mini jobs for example, are legal operations—the product of labor market deregulation—though they do not offer the benefits and stability associated with regular employment. This is less the case in low-income countries where, despite their importance, informal activities typically lack legal status and work takes place under precarious conditions and threats of police harassment. The recent growth of informal work contracts in agriculture, service, and construction sectors in high-income countries, however, indicates that informal work is increasingly occurring outside the purview of labor laws and regulations. The workers in these sectors are predominantly immigrants whose temporary work arrangements do not provide regular sources of income (Rosewarne 2012).

Women comprise a significant proportion of workers engaged in the informal economy, including part-time and temporary work, and subsistence activities. The proportion of women in informal employment varies across countries, Mali and India leading with 89.2 percent and 86 percent as share

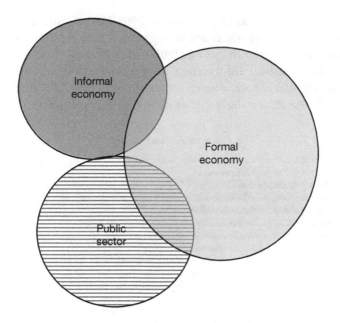

Figure 4.1a Areas of economic activity and labor use during economic growth

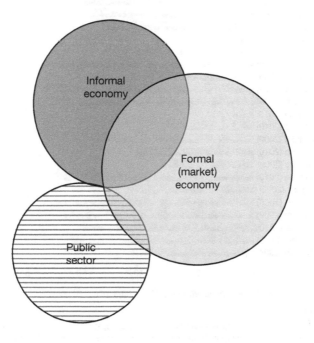

Figure 4.1b Areas of economic activity and labor use during economic crisis

of female nonagricultural employment in 2004/2005 (Figure 4.2).[23] In over half of the 44 countries where sex-disaggregated data are available, women tend to outnumber men in these activities (ILO 2011a).

Although statistical information regarding the nature and scope of informal activities where women concentrate is generally inadequate, a number of case studies have shown that they range from subcontracting

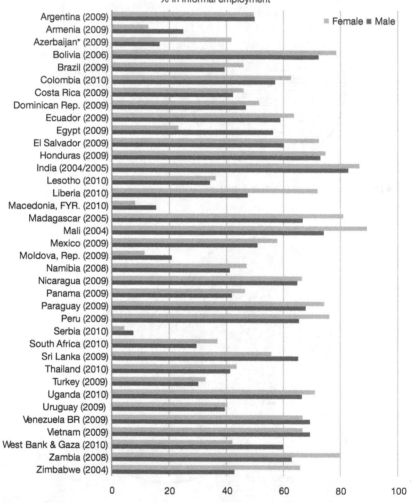

Figure 4.2 Employment in the informal economy (% in non-agricultural activities)

Source: ILO (2011a).

Notes: The above are based on country responses to ILO data request, special tabulations of labour force survey data, and extracts from survey reports. For Latin American countries, data are based on household survey micro-database.
* Employment refers to employees only.

processes linked to export-oriented industrialization—including home-based work—to street vending and service activities that evolve around survival strategies such as laundry work and housekeeping (Portes et al. 1989; Carr et al. 2000; Chen et al. 2005; Mitra 2005; Benería and Floro 2006). Domestic service continues to be a major source of informal employment for women in many countries, particularly in those with high levels of income inequality.[24] To the extent that vulnerable employment, which comprises own-account and contributing family workers, suggests the informalization of employment trends, the estimates in Figures 4.3a and 4.3b indicate that the share of female workers classified as vulnerably employed is higher than those of male workers in nearly all regions, with the exception of post-Soviet and developed countries. Over the 2000–11 period, however, the proportion of the vulnerable employed in the female, non-agricultural labor force has decreased in all regions, except for North Africa.

For the most part, the vulnerable employed in developing countries face conditions common to many informal workers; they are subject to a high level of job insecurity and do not have access to safety nets during times when they are unemployed or unable to work. Own-account workers typically receive very low labor remuneration and their work situation is generally precarious, being prone to high levels of competition and sensitive to economic fluctuations and cycles, while contributing family workers receive no cash returns. Women tend to predominate among both groups in most of the regions, except for high-income countries. With few marketable skills or hampered by other constraints such as lack of mobility, discriminatory practices, and gender norms, and/or the need to combine paid work with childcare and domestic chores, many women from poor households go into informal activities to generate whatever income they possibly can. Even when participating in home-based work and microenterprises, their jobs often serve primarily as means of subsistence rather than as a form of dynamic entrepreneurship (Messier 2005; Floro and Messier 2010; Floro and Bali Swain 2013).

Firm restructuring has expanded the linkages between core firms, sweatshops, and decentralized stages of production through subcontracting in a manner that replicates the gender hierarchy observed in formal employment. For instance, the lower levels of decentralized production are increasingly based on informal labor contracts that have many features which border on illegality. As Figure 4.4 shows, women are concentrated at the bottom of the value chains, where labor regulations are rarely implemented. In this tier women constitute the majority of home-based workers, reaching over 80 percent level in some countries (Chen et al. 2005). Home-based workers comprise two groups: independent, own-account producers and "dependent subcontract workers," who are also referred to as "homeworkers"

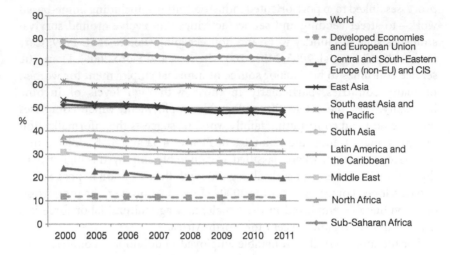

Figure 4.3a Vulnerable employment shares among men by world and regions
Source: ILO (2013a) Table A12, p. 142.

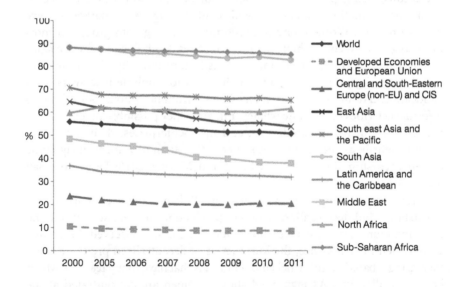

Figure 4.3b Vulnerable employment shares among women by world and regions
Source: ILO (2013a) Table A12, p. 142.

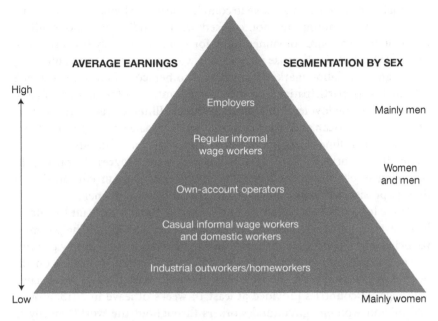

AVERAGE EARNINGS

SEGMENTATION BY SEX

High

Employers

Mainly men

Regular informal
wage workers

Women
and men

Own-account operators

Casual informal wage workers
and domestic workers

Industrial outworkers/homeworkers

Low

Mainly women

Figure 4.4 Segmentation of informal employment, by average earnings by sex

Source: UNIFEM (United Nations Development Fund for Women, now UN Women). 2005. Progress of the World's Women 2005: Women, Work and Poverty, UNIFEM (now UN Women): New York.

(Carr et al. 2000). Several studies conducted by WIEGO on subcontracted work show that earnings lower than in formal jobs prevail along with no consistency in work contracts, difficult working conditions, and very long hours of work (Chen 2005; Chen and Carr 2004). Home-based work in the service sector has also been expanding in high-income countries such as Australia, the UK, and the United States, for example in telemarketing and childcare (Quinlan 2012).

Some subcontracting firms show a strong preference for married women with children as home-based workers, as in the cases of Thailand, the Philippines, Bangladesh, and other Asian countries, and Turkey (Balakrishnan 2002; Chen et al. 2005; Dedeoğlu 2010; Floro and Pichetpongsa 2010). Due to their limited mobility and narrower range of options in the labor market, married women in particular offer greater labor force security for firms. Firms raise productivity through piece-rate payment and quota systems, in addition to relying on the self-discipline that women impose on themselves by their need to remain at home to care for children and other domestic activities while they earn an income.

In general, women's primary involvement in domestic work and childcare responsibilities is a major contributor to their choice of certain forms of informal work where they are able to combine earning a living with care work, such as street trading and home-based work. And care responsibilities continue to be a source of vulnerability for women, not only because this is unpaid labor but also because it constrains women's mobility and autonomy to design their labor market strategies. Another contributor to women's informal work participation and their concentration at the bottom of labor hierarchies is the low level of women's literacy. Illiteracy rates are still very high in some African and Asian countries while female primary and secondary school enrollment has not achieved parity with men in others (UNDP 2010; 2011; World Bank 2012). Despite important progress in raising the schooling levels of girls and reducing the gender gaps in education, low literacy persists and constrains labor market choices of women.

At the legal level, rising informality has made it more difficult to enforce labor laws. In most countries, maternity protection, which could help women participate in more formal jobs and earn higher wages, is given low priority. There are relatively few countries that have maternity protection on the books, notwithstanding the question of implementation of these laws. Although 98 countries provided at least 14 weeks of leave in 2013, around 830 million women agircultural workers throughout the world, mostly in Africa and Asia, do not have adequate protection in case of maternity (ILO 2014a: xiv). And the likelihood of both new ratifications and their national-level implementation is even more remote in the context of deteriorating labor market conditions.[25]

To be sure, during the late 1990s and early 2000s, there were attempts to regulate informal labor that falls outside the coverage of most labor laws, such as the ILO initiatives to prevent the use of contingent workers and to extend protections to marginalized workers (ILO 2000a). These are the Convention Concerning Home Work, No. 177 (of 1996) and the expert meeting on Workers in Situations Needing Protection (ILO 2000b), which call for registration of homeworkers and employers and the creation of special programs to facilitate workers' associations and collective bargaining. They also address issues regarding minimum age, collective representation, minimum wages, comparable treatment in remuneration, benefits and statutory entitlements, and protections for homeworkers, including provisions on social security, hours of work, weekly rest and sick leave and maternity protection. However, as of August 2014, very few countries (only ten) had ratified the Home Work convention.

Whether in formal jobs or informal activities, we observe that women's rising labor force participation is accompanied by unequal division of household labor between women and men, with the predominant share of unpaid work being shouldered by women (Pearson and Kusakabe 2012). This burden has inevitably created tensions for women in trying to balance their dual roles of caring for their households while searching for jobs or participating in the labor market. Even in countries where policies to reconcile family and labor market work had been introduced, the 2008 economic crisis has been used as an excuse to return to lower standards (Benería and Martinez-Iglesias 2014). These constant tensions between performing paid and unpaid work leave many women disenfranchised and disempowered. While women might benefit from labor market opportunities, they also tend to suffer from increased burdens and stress.

Poverty and Vulnerability

The spread of precarious jobs and economic insecurity in both high-income and low-income countries translates into poverty and vulnerability, which can become permanent features of the lives of large proportions of the population. This is of course not a new phenomenon but, with labor market deregulation, increased flexibility in production, and global competition, it has taken on new dimensions. In particular, the inability of many economies in the global North to generate jobs that provide at least minimum wages and to provide support during transitions and structural changes are key to understanding the persistence of poverty and increasing economic insecurity even in high-income countries. Moreover, in the case of informal, self-employed labor where there is no labor contract, as in the case of microenterprises, labor's weakness results from the insecurity and high levels of competition in the product markets where the self-employed operate.

As discussed earlier, neoliberal policies have de emphasized not only socialized forms of protection but also the distributive aspects of macro-economic policies. Reforms in social policy and a weak fiscal state have led to fragmented forms of social protection at best, which are the result of sporadic efforts to cope with the most urgent problems rather than any systematic way of dealing with universal provisioning. It is in this climate that we increasingly observe a process of privatization of family survival and risks (Foley and Michl 1999). In the end, households and families are left to pick up the slack and often engage in heroic efforts for daily survival, particularly when also facing unemployment (Molyneux 2006; Razavi et al. 2012). Even those households that are above the poverty line are not immune from the process of impoverishment. Shocks such as job loss, droughts, flooding, serious health problems, increase in food prices and education expenditures can quickly shift their relative income and asset position and move them to poverty.

A question of interest is how labor market restructuring, discussed in this chapter, affected gendered poverty outcomes. This question is linked to the intense debate since the mid-1990s on whether women are disproportionately poor and whether their share among the poor is rising. The notion of the "feminization of poverty" has received much attention since the 1995 Beijing

Platform for Action declared the eradication of the "persistent and increasing burden of poverty on women" as one of its key goals (UN 1996). A number of international organizations and women's groups have taken the UN challenge seriously and have explored the connections between poverty reduction and improvement in the status of women. For example, the Asian Development Bank views the goal of poverty reduction to be closely linked to gender, considering that gender equity is an essential factor in transforming growth into development and reducing poverty (ADB 2001). Likewise, the Economic Commission for Latin America and the Caribbean has given priority to the analysis of women's poverty (CEPAL 2004). The notion of the feminization of poverty has thus been used widely in international policy circles as it raised the prospect of realizing gender equality goals while reducing poverty. It has quickly acquired slogan value and caught on in poverty analyses, to the point that its popularization has led to "a feminization of anti-poverty programs" (Chant 2008).

Despite its value in focusing the international development agenda on the disadvantages women face in making a living and supporting their families, the notion of feminization of poverty is problematic in several ways (Chant 2008). On the measurement front, the evidence for it—in the sense of a trend of rising share of women among the poor—has been missing (Fukuda-Parr 1999). The claim has not been empirically substantiated for the simple reason that there is a paucity of comprehensive, sex-disaggregated data that would allow us to provide evidence on the gender differences in poverty rates. For the most part, data in developing countries are collected on the assumption of a unitary household, without giving enough information by gender. In the absence of sex-differentiated income data, researchers have long used female-headed households as a proxy measure to assess the incidence of women's poverty and to determine whether women's share of the poor is rising. While some early studies found support for the claim that these households are poorer than male-headed ones (Buvinić and Gupta 1997) this pattern is not universal (Fukuda-Parr 1999; Chant 2008).

A simplistic female household headship approach to measuring women's poverty has been contested on several grounds. First, female-headed households are quite heterogeneous; they range from elderly widows to lone mothers, and include both *de jure* and *de facto* female heads, thus reflecting the varied ways in which they are formed (Deere et al. 2010).[26] Moreover, female headship of a household does not necessarily connote hardship or desperation (Chant 2008). For some women household heads, a separation, divorce, and even widowhood may be liberating in the sense that such change in marital status can bring about greater personal autonomy, freedom from conflict or violence, and from the uncertainty of erratic economic support from the spouse. Lone motherhood can thus be "a preferable kind of poverty"

(Chant 2008: 175). Importantly, the focus on female heads of households obscures the inequality within male-headed households that can lead to the deprivation of its female members, even if a household is considered non-poor in income terms.

Also problematic is the use of income poverty to connote the feminization of poverty trend. As Sen (1999: 87) argues, "[p]overty must be seen as the deprivation of basic capabilities rather than merely as lowness of incomes." Such arguments have led to a growing acceptance of the multi-dimensional nature of poverty. Multi-dimensionality of poverty raises the question as to which particular aspects of poverty make women poorer than men, and to what extent their relative deprivation is based on measures such as income, consumption, available time, education, or women's and men's own perceptions of wellbeing (UNDP 2011). Finally, the term feminization of poverty tends to overlook the class, race, ethnicity, and generational differences among women.

Regardless of these problems, the debate around the feminization of poverty has propelled academics, policymakers, and advocacy groups to scrutinize the conceptualization and meaning of poverty. As Chant (2007) has pointed out, this debate has brought feminist research into the forefront of poverty analysis and poverty-alleviation policy evaluation. In the process of challenging a popular term, feminist research has demonstrated the centrality and crucial significance of gender, alongside other factors, in understanding and monitoring poverty dynamics.[27]

Recent evidence supports the case for moving away from both income and household headship in the characterization of the gendered nature of poverty. Moreover, Chant (2008) argues that, if the term feminization of poverty is to be useful in gender analysis of poverty, it has to be broadened to incorporate the trend towards what she calls "feminization of responsibility and/or obligation." Specifically, evidence for 2003–05 from Costa Rica, the Gambia, and the Philippines indicates that women are providing more diverse and increasing amounts of labor for household survival compared to men, yet they are unable to negotiate their obligations or the rewards within the household. In such a context, the introduction of poverty reduction strategies that increase women's workload and responsibilities, such as the conditional cash transfer schemes, are particularly problematic. Instead, policy design must aim to reduce the work burden of women and promote more equality of responsibility in the household.

In sum, while we cannot confirm whether there has been a feminization of income poverty during recent decades of labor market restructuring, there are indications that in non-income (time poverty and capabilities) terms, the majority of women in low-income groups are experiencing increased workloads and responsibilities to support their families.

Paths to Improving Working Conditions

Since its creation in 1919, the ILO has provided international regulation of labor standards. Over the years, it has done so through the adoption of conventions and recommendations on labor standards, which has led to the introduction of national statutes, laws, measures, and guidelines regarding working conditions and labor rights, from health and safety standards to rights such as maternity leave and those applicable to domestic work. In this way, international labor standards have grown into a comprehensive system of measures addressed to regulating work and social policy at the national level. To be sure, the ILO conventions have to be ratified by country members and even ratification does not guarantee implementation. During the post-World War II period, ILO conventions on labor standards such as those that guarantee freedom of association (No. 87, 1948) and the right to organize and collective bargaining (No. 98, 1949), were adopted by many governments of the global South. However, as we discussed, with the international race to the bottom to achieve the lowest possible unit labor costs, labor market regulation has weakened and working conditions in many sectors have deteriorated. Moreover, informal activities that are beyond reach of regulation have grown. These key challenges have led to new initiatives and channels to explore ways in which labor might regain its bargaining power to uphold its rights. The strategies and mechanisms that we discuss below include attempts to link labor standards to rights to trade; ILO's Declaration of Fundamental Principles and Rights at Work; the Decent Work Agenda of the ILO; social responsibility schemes, such as corporate codes of conduct; and initiatives to organize the informal labor force as well as traditional unionization drives.

International Labor Standards: The Social Clause

After its inception in 1995, particularly in the late 1990s, the World Trade Organization (WTO) ministerial meetings have served as an arena for debate on enforceable global labor standards. This, in part, was due to the instrumental role of trade liberalization policies in the race-to-the-bottom competition and in the spread of unacceptable forms of work and labor contracts. The alarming rate at which workers' rights were being eroded and labor conditions deteriorated worldwide has resulted in pressures from labor unions, women's organizations, and other non-governmental organizations (NGOs) on international bodies to find ways to protect labor rights and improve working conditions.

One proposal, pushed forward by a broad coalition of labor groups, feminists, academics, and governments, mainly from the global North, was a trade rule that would link a country's right to trade internationally to its upholding of a common set of labor standards. These groups argued that certain minimum international labor standards should be observed in the production of all goods and services including those that are outsourced, subcontracted, or imported. The minimum standards were usually interpreted as the "core labor standards," articulated in ILO's Declaration of Fundamental Principles and Rights at Work (ILO 1998). If exporting countries failed to comply with these standards, then they could be subject to trade sanctions. This form of linkage of trade and working conditions, commonly referred to as the "social clause," would thus ensure that goods and services that enter international trade are produced under conditions that comply with ILO conventions. The WTO and the ILO were to jointly administer the workings of this rule.

The social clause idea was met with strong opposition from a coalition of advocates for the global South (in favor of these countries' right to economic growth through trade), mainstream economists, trade theorists, and some feminist scholars. These groups labeled the social clause as a protectionist measure, a scheme by high-income countries to undermine the exports of low-income countries in goods where the latter have comparative advantage, hence their prospects for industrialization. Some of the arguments against the social clause had libertarian undertones (emphasizing the freedom to trade and to determine one's own labor standards). Others, including some feminists and development economists, pointed to the danger of exacerbating the gap between formal and informal workers as there are no mechanisms to implement them in the informal economy. Opponents also dismissed the concerns of workers in the North whose jobs were undermined by imported goods and services made under much weaker labor standards.[28]

The effect of global enforcement of standards on women workers was front and center in the debate. Several feminists argued that international labor standards are urgently needed in the context of the current trade and financial regimes that have privileged capital vis-à-vis labor and have allowed the rights of investors to take precedence over the human rights of the large majority of citizens, especially those in low-income countries (Çağatay 1996; 2001; Hale 1996). Although there are limits to what global labor standards can do by way of addressing the concerns of women workers, they are necessary in setting the boundaries and in restraining the race-to-the-bottom competition. Having internationally enforceable labor standards is also a means for raising the issue of labor rights in macroeconomic policy discourses, where it is often ignored or neglected. Moreover, if all countries raised labor standards, as envisioned in the social clause proposal, a specific country's fear of losing investment as a result of higher labor standards would have little basis.

Others objected to the social clause approach arguing that any global enforcement of labor standards will inevitably result in job losses for women workers and that keeping export jobs should be a priority concern (Razavi 1999; Kabeer 2001; 2004). Kabeer (2004) argued that such standards, for example workers' rights to collective bargaining, would drive up labor costs and drive investment away from the country. Even poorly paid women workers, Kabeer argued, see their export sector jobs as providing them material and personal benefits; their ability to earn an income gives them a sense of self-reliance and self-esteem. Women also value their access to new social networks and the greater voice they can exercise in household decision-making. Singh and Zammit (2001; 2004), along with Kabeer, predicted an increase in informality as another consequence of a social clause: higher wages in the formal economy can slow down growth of jobs covered by these rules, and encourage informal job growth instead. Not only would low-income countries' development prospects be stifled but also women workers would end up disproportionately in these lower-paying informal jobs.

Others have emphasized the ineffectiveness of international labor standards to cover informal and nonstandard employment where women predominate (Ghosh 2000). In the context of informalization, improvements in working conditions that can be monitored in formal enterprises, at best, would be limited. Moreover, some pointed out that some of the worst labor conditions are found not in export-oriented and transnational firms but in a range of traditional and service sector activities. Kabeer and Mahmud (2004), for example, provide evidence that export sector jobs in Bangladesh paid higher wages than available alternatives for women workers.

The downside of these arguments is that they can be used as an excuse to not improve labor standards. While Kabeer (2004) has proposed an alternative to the social clause in the form of a basic income program (a "social floor") so as to strengthen the fallback position of workers vis-à-vis employers, the opposition to the social clause has generally amounted to a "do-nothing" position. Many social clause opponents have promoted workers' rights, but in the context of weak unions and governments hostile to unions, this approach has not provided an effective alternative. Moreover, the opponents have tended to overlook the benefits of improvements not only in working conditions for women workers but also to the overall prospects for raising the levels of well-being in low-income countries. Specifically, many have argued that higher labor standards promote social stability and help develop democratic government and are instrumental in raising economic welfare—a "race to the top"—and that the fear by some academics and governments that higher wages will discourage foreign direct investment (FDI) is misplaced. Rodrik (1996) provided empirical evidence indicating that countries with stronger civil liberties and political rights experience greater stability in economic performance and adjust better to adverse shocks.

Further, Kucera (2002) showed that FDI does not avoid countries with stronger labor rights, and Galli and Kucera (2004) provided evidence that, in Latin America in the 1990s, higher labor standards—union rights—did not lead to informalization of employment.[29] Finally, evidence from Indonesia suggests that the fear of job losses owing to increased wages in export firms may also be misplaced (Harrison and Scorse 2010). The anti-sweatshop campaigns in Indonesia in the 1990s resulted in large increases in real wages in foreign-owned and export companies but did not have adverse employment effects, albeit there was some loss of investment.

Despite this evidence, the do-nothing position won the day; the objective of incorporating global labor standards in the multilateral trade agreements was abandoned, as it proved to be difficult to pass at the WTO meetings. Notwithstanding this outcome, the social clause debate has focused public attention on working conditions in labor-intensive production in lower-wage countries and helped mobilize various constituencies. It has also propelled the need to develop new strategies for addressing the working conditions in which many of the goods and services being traded are produced. Since the demise of the social clause, one unexpected approach to addressing poor working conditions has been the inclusion of labor clauses or provisions in a growing number of preferential trade agreements (ILO 2009; 2013b).[30] Whether these labor clauses are having an effect on government compliance and actually improving working conditions has yet to be examined.[31] Otherwise, the predominant, international response to poor working conditions has morphed into schemes of a voluntary or nonbinding nature.

ILO's Decent Work Agenda

One outcome of the social clause debates, indeed a concurrent development, has been the ILO's platform of action referred to as the *Decent Work Agenda*. As noted on the ILO website, "decent work sums up the aspirations of people in their working lives" (ILO 2014b). *Decent Work*'s mandate includes all workers, especially those "beyond the formal labor market – unregulated wage workers, the self-employed, and homeworkers and its immediate objective is to put in place a social floor for the global economy" (ILO 2002b: 2 and 4). Implementation of the *Decent Work Agenda* has four strategic objectives, with gender equality as a crosscutting goal: creating jobs; guaranteeing rights at work; extending social protection; and promoting social dialogue (ILO 2002b; 2014b). The rights at work component promotes the core labor standards mentioned earlier: union rights; equal pay and non-discrimination in employment; and the elimination of both forced labor and child labor. However, this is a minimum labor rights agenda in comparison to the list of labor rights accumulated through the ILO conventions over time. While union rights may be viewed as instrumental to promoting all other rights at work, delineation of the core itself implies other international conventions are not as relevant or worthy of emphasis.

The responses to the *Decent Work Agenda* illustrate the tensions that have underpinned its creation from the beginning. For one, there are varying interpretations of the concept of decent work and different views or approaches to its implementation. Those in support of the Agenda view *Decent Work*'s focus on workers at the periphery of the regulated economy as demonstrating its new commitment to bring these workers—once considered to be outside its constituency—into its standard and norm-setting activities (Vosko 2002). Supporters also view the agenda as a feasible alternative to having a social clause mechanism for enforcing global labor standards. In this sense, *Decent Work* is perceived as a way of mediating the tensions and conflicts between global capital, member states, labor unions, and NGOs. Some governments such as the US have given their support because of the use of moral suasion, rather than sanctions, as a tool. Similarly, several G-77 countries have accepted the Agenda because of its non-binding nature and absence of a trade linkage, which implies that it cannot be used for protectionist purposes by high-income countries.

Yet others have emphasized what is missing in the *Decent Work Agenda*. Several women's groups and labor unions gave it a weak endorsement as a step "in the right direction," which brings attention to the struggle for labor rights for all workers (Baccaro 2001). However, critics argue that *Decent Work* remains inadequate since it does not address these groups' central concern in the global labor standards debate, namely, the predominance of the rights of capital alongside the erosion of basic labor rights: it does not include measures and mechanisms to control the actions of employers and does not provide sufficient protection for workers. In particular, the Agenda does not include any countervailing force to the race to the bottom that has been devastating for labor. Similarly, it does not include any measures to counter capital's incessant demand for a flexible workforce. Also, since the Agenda is nonbinding, its effectiveness in promoting decent work is questionable.

The core labor standards central to the *Decent Work Agenda* are often ignored in practice (World Bank 2012). To be sure, references to these principles are made in several national legislations and regional procedures of international organizations, and increasingly in some bilateral free trade agreements. And there are substantial declines in violations of some of the principles of rights at work, for example child labor (ILO 2013c). However, the persistence of forced labor, discrimination, and the weakening of collective bargaining and labor unions worldwide is testimony to the ineffectiveness of the Agenda (ILO 2013a). Many labor policies continue to cover only formal sector workers. In addition, many governments have exempted the application of certain labor regulations in export processing zones and other sectors in order to attract investment.

Corporate Codes of Conduct and Ethical Trading Initiatives

In recent years, as a result of consumer boycotts or even mere threats, a number of transnational corporations have devised social responsibility programs and adopted voluntary codes of conduct, replacing the notion of designing and implementing internationally sanctioned codes. The voluntary codes are intended to be implemented in the overseas suppliers who source a specific company and to protect the corporate brand from the perception of poor working conditions. However, these codes are rather piecemeal; their implementation is far from being automatic, making it critical for unions and other workers' rights organizations to monitor their compliance by employers. In addition, many grassroots organizations have gone further by setting up alternative trading organizations and fair-trade labeling movements (Raynolds et al. 2007; Rice 2001; LeClair 2002). Often companies become part of multi-stakeholder initiatives, such as the Fair Labor Association (FLA), which bring together corporate brands, their overseas suppliers, and consumer groups (such as universities, student advocacy groups). In such cases, the FLA sets up an inspection system in supplier factories to monitor working conditions and releases periodic inspection reports to the public.

One problem concerning the implementation of labor standards has to do with the setting up of systems of inspection to enforce regulation. This is expensive and it requires some level of organization often not available in many developing countries, especially in the context of budget cuts in the post-1980 period. Moreover, the complex organization of global value chains and the use of many subcontractors have challenged the monitoring of labor conditions of firms, which has yielded limited results (Locke et al. 2006). An interesting program that both addressed the inspection issue and provided incentives for improvement of labor standards was the *Better Factories Cambodia* (BFC) Program, which grew out of a partnership between the ILO and the Cambodian and US governments in the mid-1990s (Polaski 2006). The program relied on market incentives to monitor and improve working conditions in factories that produced for the US market. The ILO served in the capacity of monitoring working conditions and, if the factories were deemed compliant, Cambodia received preferential treatment in the US market (lower tariffs on its exports of apparel to the US). The cost of monitoring the factories was shared between the US government, the Cambodian government, and the ILO.

The *Better Factories* Program was promising in that it demonstrated that it is possible to use trade incentives (rather than punitive trade sanctions) to improve working conditions, while at the same time expanding exports and employment (Berik and van der Meulen Rodgers 2010). However, there were also several important limitations: the scope of the working conditions that were monitored was limited;[32] and, as a factory-based program, it was not attentive to the state of union rights in Cambodia. Indeed, some have argued that the program functioned to undercut unions in Cambodia. Thus, the positive outcomes in the ILO reports were in sharp contrast with the violence against union members in Cambodia (Miller et al. 2008).

The overall decline in tariffs under trade liberalization has reduced the attractiveness of using tariffs as an incentive and limited the potential for replicating the BFC design. Indeed, the *Better Work* programs that have emerged after 2008 in several countries (for example, in Jordan, Lesotho, Nicaragua, Vietnam) function as ILO monitoring programs in the garment industry that are financed by the International Finance Corporation (IFC) and that deliver goods (certified as clean) to brand manufacturers (Better Work 2014). *Better Work* has thus evolved into a corporate social responsibility program that provides reputation insurance.

Worker Organizations

Workers' ability to collectively organize is critical in improving working conditions. Countries that recognize and enforce labor standards have done so only as a result of long struggles. However, as we discussed earlier, since the early 1980s the power of labor has diminished across countries, particularly in parts of the global North where jobs were lost to lower-wage areas. Nonetheless, new working-class formations have emerged in the sites/areas of relocation. Globalization of production has created a labor force that increasingly shares convergent working conditions and can even face the same employer. This is the case for example of the automobile industry with multiple factories in different continents or—more relevant for women workers—the large supply chains that operate worldwide, such as Benetton, Nike, Walmart, Zara. Thus, decentralization of production opens up the possibility of new national and international labor alliances and broad coalitions.

Moreover, where jobs are growing in export sectors mass production factories provide opportunities for organizing. Labor unrest and trade union activity has persisted in several countries, for example in the case of garment export firms in the Dominican Republic, Bangladesh, and other countries (Werner 2012; Hossain et al. 2013). The sub-human working conditions and low pay among women factory workers have led to their rise in leadership roles, thus challenging the assumption of docile, female labor. Weeks of protests by women workers erupted, for example, in the Dhaka garment factory area after the widely publicized 2012 fire and the factory collapse of 2013, both the result of lapses in safety provision and monitoring. Against all odds, these workers are striving to build union strength, for example in the Bangladesh Garment and Industrial Workers Federation (BGIWF), which is helping to create adequate working conditions to the garment sector in Bangladesh. In the Dominican Republic nine collective agreements were reached in export garment firms where women workers predominated in the bargaining process (Werner 2012).

In many countries of the global North, unions have responded to declining membership by organizing previously under-organized groups (women, ethnic minorities) and sectors, including the services where women predominate. As a result, union membership rates for women have either been stable (or their decline has slowed) in the last few decades. In a number of countries—Australia, US, UK—the gender gap in union density has narrowed in the context of a decline in overall unionization (ILO 2014c). In Canada, on the other hand, union density among women increased slightly between 2000 and 2011, and reversed the gender union gap in favor of women.[33] These trends in women's union density partially reflect the general rise in women's labor force participation and their longer tenure on the job as well as the increase in women's representation in the service sector and public sector unions. It also reflects a shift in union coverage—at least for many European unions—to include part-time workers: predominantly women, the self-employed, and their spouses (Visser 2006).

To be sure, increases in women's membership do not always translate into increased voice and bargaining power for women workers. In most countries, union leadership remains male-dominated and focuses on the interests of male, full-time workers. In response, in several sectors, some union leaders have argued for separate women's structures within unions to give women a stronger voice and bring them to the attention of central leadership. As the two case studies of UK unions by Colgan and Ledwith (2002) show, this strategy has successfully increased women's influence in a public service union where women are a large majority of workers, while it has not enhanced participatory social processes in a private union with minority female representation. Other unions, such as the Coalition of Latin American Banana Unions (COLSIBA), which represents about 40,000 male and female banana workers in seven countries, have begun to address sexism and chauvinistic attitudes in order to strengthen their unions. They integrate gender equity in their mode of organizing and other union activities. As Frank (2005) observes, the banana workers of Latin America provided a new model for integrating gender issues in labor organizing and building labor solidarity across countries. In this model, the global struggle against transnational corporations is intrinsically linked with the struggle at home for women's equality and respect. Their experience has been a source of inspiration to those who envision a global labor movement that places women's issues at its core.

In yet other cases, it is possible to organize women workers into unions with sponsorship and activism initiated and sustained by a civil society organization. A recent success story in organizing Indian garment workers in Karnataka indicates that success depends on flexible, tailored approaches to mobilization at the micro level that are supported by a network of macro-level NGOs (Jenkins 2013). In this case, the women workers were deemed impossible to organize by established national unions; yet grassroots activists were able to establish networks with workers away from the workplace through micro-savings groups, which then grew into a social movement that in turn led to the formation of a garment workers' union.

Labor organizing among women workers in the informal economy and nonstandard employment is also crucial in bringing about transformative change in the legal and policy environments. Unless women workers become members of labor unions and organizations and regularly elect their own representatives and leaders, their interests will remain neglected in the labor movement and in national policy interventions. The lack of association and formal representation of the informally employed feeds into the division within labor and deepens labor market inequalities.

A hopeful sign is the increase in membership in a variety of organizations focusing on women in informal work. They include the Self-Employed Workers Association (SEWA) in India; Self-Employed Women's Union (SEWU) in Durban, South Africa; PATAMABA in the Philippines; StreetNet, Bangladesh Garment and Industrial Workers Federation (BGIWF), Movimiento de Mujeres Trabajadores y Desempleadas Maria Elena Cudara (MEC) in Nicaragua; General Agricultural Workers Union in Ghana; Hong Kong Domestic Workers' Union; Workers Solidarity Association (WSA) in Chiang Mai, Thailand and Yaung Chi Oo Worker's Association in Mae Sot, Thailand. Their strategies are wide ranging, from getting legal recognition to lobbying for policy reforms to collective bargaining, strikes, and protests. For example, SEWA has developed a very sophisticated organization, which includes its own bank, social protection, employment training, and housing. Likewise, domestic workers in India have organized in order to obtain legal recognition as workers and to access some protection accorded by labor law, leading to the enactment of the 2008 Unorganized Workers Social Security Act (Carr and Chen 2008). Moreover, workers in forestry and fishing have lobbied for laws to protect their traditional and community rights of access to resources, which led to the 2005 Forest Rights Act and the 2009 Traditional

Coastal and Marine Fisherfolk (Protection of Rights) Act (India Ministry of Environment and Forests 2011). Such legal reforms provide a basis for further action and demands, but enforcement of legal gains tends to be weak unless continued pressure and monitoring occur.

Women's organizations have also made an effort to address the problems associated with home-based work. Recent ILO initiatives have provided space for coordination among women's groups, trade unions, and informal workers' organizations. An interesting example was the key role of women's organizations in getting the ILO Convention on Home Work (No. 177) approved in June of 1996. It was considered a victory for women, with some women's organizations and international networks such as HomeNet and SEWA providing extensive information for the formulation of the Convention (Prügl 1999). Although the Convention's ratification at the country level remains low, it provides concrete goals and a regulatory tool around which to organize further action. As Elisabeth Prügl (1999) has pointed out, these conventions are significant not because they have made substantial legal reforms; rather they have brought about a global discourse on regulating flexible labor.

There is also need for building solidarity across labor groups and grassroots organizations in the form of alliances and networks, both domestically and globally. It should be noted that alliance formations, especially across political and social boundaries, often emerge around specific sets of issues with transcultural resonance and high stakes (Keck and Sikkink 1998). For instance, during the 1990s, the International Ladies Garment Workers Union and the Amalgamated Clothing and Textile Workers Union joined forces to carry out union programs in Mexico and Canada (Cook 2002). Similarly, the international alliance of homeworkers' and other home-based workers' organizations, and that of street vendor organizations, such as StreetNet, have been vital in increasing the voice and visibility of these workers as well as in negotiating with contractors, municipal authorities, governments, and international bodies.[34]

An important recent example of transnational labor-activist alliance is the Bangladesh Accord ("Accord on Building and Fire Safety in Bangladesh") that was adopted in the aftermath of the factory collapse of April 2013. The Accord represents a new model for improving working conditions in global supply chains, as it holds apparel brands and their local subcontractors jointly responsible for working conditions (in this case, building safety) (Anner et al. 2013). Another promising initiative is the agreement between the Spanish TNC INDITEX (the largest global clothing distributor) and the IndustriALL Global Union of garment and textile workers, renewed in July 2014. This agreement aims to implement decent work and other ILO conventions throughout the production chain (IndustriALL Global Union 2014).

Conclusion

In this chapter we discussed the ways in which global economic integration has shaped labor markets and has altered the environment in which labor rights are exercised and defended. We have discussed changes in employment patterns and shifts globally, particularly in terms of their connection to the informal economy and the ways in which work has become more unstable and precarious for a large proportion of the population. In particular, we have argued that, although the proportion of the population in the informal economy might have decreased in some emerging economies with relatively high levels of growth during the past decade, informality and marginality have increased in other parts, including in high-income countries. The global economic crisis has reinforced the tendency for these economies to generate increasing problems of unemployment, underemployment, and the creation of precarious jobs feeding the ranks of the precariat. These tendencies have also reinforced labor's loss of power vis-à-vis capital in many countries, illustrated by the decreasing proportion of workers who are unionized.

Women workers represent an important proportion of the informal economy. Their traditional presence at the lower echelons of the labor market hierarchy and concentration in activities such as home-based work requires non-traditional forms of organizing. While the ILO's *Decent Work Agenda* is relevant as a frame of reference, for this group of workers it is organizations such as SEWA, WIEGO, and StreetNet that have been and will be instrumental in the struggle to self-organize, improve working conditions, and provide different forms of social protection. For workers employed in factories it will be important to pursue a range of strategies to achieve union representation and collective bargaining. Social movement pressures everywhere need to support this process so that governments are held accountable for upholding national laws and their international commitments to both rights to work and rights at work.

Overall, however, it is not easy to be optimistic about global labor market conditions in this second decade of the new century. The pressure to adopt the lowest common denominator in a globalized economy, the retrogressive policies followed under the neoliberal regime, and the economic crisis since 2008 have led to high levels of unemployment, employment and income insecurity, rising informality, and deterioration of working conditions. These labor market trends, together with rapid accumulation of capital and concentration of wealth and economic power, contribute to growing income inequality and social polarization. Social tensions and discontent are fueled further by the contradiction between an international climate that has been emphasizing human rights, individual agency, and empowerment on the one hand and the daily adverse labor market conditions that confront the working poor and marginal populations on the other. Growing inequality is a threat to the construction of democratic societies and needs to be confronted by every possible means.

Notes

1   This was one worker's response to the question "What would make (the garment factory job) a better job?" in a focus group discussion of Günseli Berik with garment workers in Rayerbazar Basti, Dhaka, Bangladesh in 2006.

2   Offshoring refers to the shifting of a part of a firm's operation abroad, either to be undertaken by the same company or a different one. Outsourcing (or subcontracting) occurs when a firm hires another, whether locally or elsewhere, to carry out a production task that it no longer wants to perform in-house. The latter may be a different firm or a spinoff of the original company created specifically to carry out that task.

3   For a detailed case study based on the relocation of the Smith-Corona corporation from Cortland, New York, to Tijuana, Mexico, see the 2003 edition of this book.

4   The devastation brought by the Asian financial crisis showed the shortcomings of an approach that combined labor market flexibility with lack of social protection, and led the East Asian and Southeast Asian economies to introduce social safety net provisions.

5   Some of these labor market reforms have subsequently been reversed in the early 2000s.

6   The "mini jobs"—part time, precarious and often below minimum wages— emerged especially since the late 1990s in an otherwise prosperous country with a dynamic economy that has become a leader within the European Union. Mini jobs barely provide a living wage, are often of short duration, and have resulted in a two-tier labor system (Connolly and Osborne 2013).

7   The European Central Bank was instrumental in pushing the agenda for creating low-wage jobs. On December 7, 2011, it was reported that the European Central Bank sent a letter in August to José Luis Rodriguez Zapatero's government, suggesting that Spain implement a mini-jobs job category with salaries of 400 euros, a value considerably lower than Spain's minimum wage of 641 euros. This suggestion was presented as a condition for the European Central Bank to continue purchasing Spain's debt (http://economico.sapo.pt/noticias/bce-pediu-salarios-inferiores-a-400-euros-em-espanha_133239.html)

8   This finding is based on a scoring index that they developed using global labor survey (GLS) data for ranking countries on the basis of the extent of employment regulations. Low scores indicate a higher propensity towards employer discretion while high scores indicate greater use of labor laws or collective bargaining. The United States ranked second lowest, alongside China.

9   In the US, the underemployment rate includes workers who meet the official definition of unemployment as well as those who are working part-time but want

to and are available to work full-time plus those who want to work but have given up actively looking. In April 2014, underemployment rates were higher for certain groups: 16.3 percent among Hispanic workers and 20.3 percent among black workers (EPI Bulletin, August 2014).

10   The diminishing importance of internal labor markets has brought many advantages to firms, such as the ability to respond quickly to market changes, lower long-term liabilities, increased flexibility in production, and reduced costs, at least in the short run. To be sure, it has also created problems for them, particularly the inability to retain the best workers when labor markets become tight.

11   The claims of rising employment instability are not always shared. The *World Development Report 2013* notes that such claims may be true only in the short run for "the demand for labor should increase in the longer run as specialization generates efficiency gains . . . (*and*) lower prices for goods and services and a growing consumption demand from emerging countries as they prosper, can only reinforce the upward trend in the global demand for labor." (World Bank 2012: 243). As evidence, the Report shows the EU data for average job tenure, a proxy for employment stability, as remaining roughly the same during the 1992–2005 period, although younger workers face shorter employment spells and flexible employment.

12   There is no standard definition of a casual worker across countries. According to the Australian Council of Trade Unions (ACTU), the term in Australia refers to a worker for whom a full week's work is not provided in the award or agreement. Hence s/he works in temporary jobs that have irregular hours. Casual workers are entitled to some, but not all, of the benefits given to permanent workers. Casual employees do not get paid holiday leave or sick leave but they are entitled to a higher rate of pay (casual loading), parental leave and, under the new Fair Work laws, casuals are protected from being sacked unfairly (ACTU 2014).

13   There is no universally accepted definition of part-time work/employment. A definition proposed by the ILO defined part-time work as "regular employment in which working time is substantially less than normal" (OECD 2014).

14   According to the *ILO Declaration on Fundamental Principles and Rights at Work and its Follow-Up*, member countries are encouraged to adhere to four fundamental principles and rights at work, which are spelled out in eight ILO Conventions and jointly referred to as "core labor standards": (a) freedom of association and effective recognition of the right to collective bargaining; (b) the elimination of all forms of forced or compulsory labor; (c) the effective abolition of child labor; and (d) the elimination of discrimination in respect of employment and occupation (ILO 1998).

15   See "Factory in Bangladesh Lost Fire Clearance Before Blaze," *New York Times*, December 8, 2012, p. A9.

16   Occupational upgrading—in terms of the decline of middle-wage occupations and a corresponding expansion of high-wage occupations—has been taking place at

least in the last six decades, including periods of declining wage inequality and growth in median real wages (EPI 2014).

17   In Latin America for example, the average gender wage gap decreased from 25 percent to 17 percent between 1992 and 2007 (Ñopo 2012). Information for African countries is very limited (Floro and Meurs 2009).

18   The informal sector may be broadly characterized as consisting of units engaged in the production of goods or services with the primary objective of generating employment and incomes to the persons concerned. These units typically operate at a low level of organization, with little or no division between labour and capital as factors of production and on a small scale. Labour relations—where they exist— are based mostly on casual employment, kinship or personal and social relations rather than contractual arrangements with formal guarantees (ILO 2013e: 13).

19   The employment size adopted in this definition varies from country to country. It ranges from five workers (Panama) to ten (India and Turkey), and eleven (Ethiopia).

20   The 17th ICLS defined "informal employment" as comprising: "(a) own-account workers and employers employed in their own informal sector enterprises (household unincorporated enterprises with at least some market production that are unregistered or small in terms of the number of employed persons (e.g., fewer than five employees)); (b) all contributing family workers; (c) employees holding informal jobs, i.e., employees not covered by legal protection or social security as employed persons, or not entitled to other employment benefits such as paid annual or sick leave; (d) members of informal producers' cooperatives (not established as legal entities); and (e) own-account workers producing goods exclusively for own final use by their household (if considered employed)" (ILO 2013d: 42).

21   Several types of informal employment—self-employment, casual, daily or seasonal contracts, and many jobs in the construction industry—are typically not covered by employment protection, nor are they covered by hiring and firing regulations. Where employment protection for regular contracts is very strict, employers may resort to hiring workers on nonstandard contracts to avoid regulation (Venn 2009).

22   For an elaboration of this point, see Benería (2003), Chapter 4.

23   These statistics are based on what is called a "residual estimation method." Until recently, only a few countries directly measured informal employment and employment in informal enterprises, so an indirect approach based on existing published statistical data from different surveys in developing countries was used.

24   In the case of Brazil, estimates of the proportion of employed women in domestic service ranged between 16 and 20 percent in the late 1990s (Benería and Rosenberg 1999).

25   The Maternity Protection Convention (ILO Convention No. 183) has been formulated to enable women to successfully combine their reproductive and productive roles and prevent unequal treatment in employment due to their reproductive role. About 29 (30 percent) UN member countries nominally meet the paid maternity leave requirement of Convention No. 183, namely provision

of at least 14 weeks of leave at a rate of at least two-thirds of previous earnings. The regions with the highest proportion of countries in conformity with the Convention are Central Asia and Europe, while conformity is particularly low in Asia and the Pacific and the Middle East.

26   A *de facto* female-headed household refers to one whereby the male head is temporarily away.

27   In addition, the debate has challenged the notion of poverty as a static problem that is detached from agency and power relations. It has also questioned the persistent assumption of unitary households behaving as consensual or harmonious agents that underlies most macro- and micro-economic models and poverty reduction policies, together with data collection and household survey designs.

28   See Berik (2008) for the ethical underpinnings of the arguments in the global labor standards debate.

29   More recent work that examines the US FDI outflows at the industry level confirms that strengthening democracy is compatible with attracting FDI. The exception is mining and oil and gas extraction, which raises the specter of a race-to-the-bottom in resource-rich countries, and suggests the need for a two-pronged strategy in strengthening democracy (Kucera and Principi 2014). More disaggregated industry analysis may also indicate a race to the bottom in subsectors of manufacturing such as apparel.

30   While the nature of these labor provisions and the forces that shape them are not yet well studied, there is a clear uptick in preferential trade agreements that have such clauses, up from 4 percent in 1995–1999 to 31 percent in the 2005–09 period (ILO 2009).

31   There is some evidence to suggest that certain conditions, such as pressure from transnational advocates, are key to ensuring the enforcement of the labor clause (Nolan Garcia 2011).

32   The standards that were monitored were important but narrow, covering wages and hours and health and safety standards (Berik and van der Meulen Rodgers 2010). Not surprisingly, in 2006 and 2007, the monitored factories were in near full compliance with the wage standards (such as correct payment of overtime wages), but performed poorly on other standards, and fared worst on excessive overtime (defined as more than two hours per day).

33   In the US, the union membership rate among women declined from 14.6 to 10.5 percent between 1983 and 2013, while the rate for men shrunk from 24.7 to 11.9 percent. In the UK the decline between 2000 and 2011 was from 29.4 to 28.5 percent for women and from 30.2 to 23.0 percent for men. During the same period, women in Canada increased their unionization rate from 29.9 to 31.1 percent, while the rate for men declined from 29.5 to 28.2 percent. In Australia where a sharp decline in unionization took place, women's and men's union density gap not only narrowed but women's unionization rate overtook that of men (18.9 percent vs. 17.5 percent in 2012) (ILO 2014c).

34   See www.streetnet.org.za and www.homenetseasia.org for more information.

CHAPTER 5

Paid and Unpaid Work: Meanings and Debates

Women make a great contribution to the welfare of the family and to the development of society, which is still not recognized or considered in its full importance . . . The upbringing of children requires shared responsibility of parents, women and men and society as a whole . . . Recognition should also be given to the important role played by women in many countries in caring for other members of their family.

United Nations, Beijing Declaration and
Platform for Action, 1996, p. 27

Introduction

Our day-to-day living depends on doing varied forms of work. We meet our daily needs by earning a living as wage or salaried workers, farmers, self-employed, or by depending on others who do. We also carry out a range of daily activities such as cooking, washing clothes, making beds, housecleaning, shopping, washing dishes, throwing out the garbage, caring for children, the sick, disabled, and elderly, and we depend on others who do similar tasks. In many communities, the labor provided by volunteers is vital in meeting basic services such as cultural celebration, immunization, adult literacy, school maintenance, irrigation, canal repairs, and forest conservation. This is also the case in the restoration of homes, businesses, and schools, including those damaged by floods, fires, and earthquakes. Although the performance of these tasks ensures our daily survival and well-being, until the 1990s they did not receive the attention of policymakers. Given that most of this household and volunteer labor is typically not paid, it has been largely invisible in economic terms and, until very recently, not included in conventional national income accounts, labor statistics, and other economic indicators.

To be sure, middle- and upper-income households tend to source a majority of their care and domestic needs through the market. The ongoing shift of activities from the household to the market has affected many aspects of people's lives especially in urban areas and high-income countries, where tasks ranging from childcare, laundry services, and cooked meals to grocery delivery have increasingly become commodified. However, a large proportion of the population, particularly in the lower income groups, largely depends on the unpaid domestic and care labor that they and others perform for their day-to-day sustenance and well-being. The lack of attention to these forms of labor in economic policy debates and development plans seriously inhibits advancement towards gender equality.

The historical invisibility of unpaid work in economic analysis is not surprising, given that traditionally it focused on the market. Viewed from a male and upper-class perspective and at a time when societies were perceived to have separate public and private spheres, the economists who pioneered the discipline sought to understand the motives, behavior, and decisions of individuals in market activities that took place in the public sphere. The private sphere, that of household work and other non-market activities generally carried out by women, was not of interest.[1] This perspective became institutionalized in economic analysis. As markets developed and livelihoods became increasingly linked with wage labor, individuals were categorized either as "breadwinners" (male household head) or "their dependents" (women and children).

In the dominant neoclassical approach in economics the economy is viewed as a vast terrain of optimizing behaviors by self-interested individuals with exogenous tastes and budget constraints, who interact primarily through markets in their quest to obtain the highest utility or satisfaction and to secure the biggest profit. Within the heterodox economics tradition, the economy has been similarly viewed as the domain for productive activities that center on wage labor–capitalist relations; the preoccupation with wage labor and capitalist production left out the reproductive work of (mostly) women.[2] This perspective is a departure from Friedrich Engels's emphasis on the dual character of production activities (unpaid and paid) that he deemed were essential for the reproduction of society.[3] The labor involved in taking care of people, through a myriad of unpaid tasks undertaken within households and communities, was thus rendered invisible in economic analysis. And the concept of work became synonymous with paid or market work.[4]

The conceptual neglect of unpaid work is reflected in the measurement efforts of the 1930s and 1940s that produced the System of National Accounts (SNA). These accounts compute the annual value of marketed goods and services in order to estimate a country's national output, for example the gross domestic product (GDP) or the gross national product (GNP). Even though Simon Kuznets, who is credited for his contributions to establishing the US SNA in 1947, cautioned against the use of GDP as a measure of well-being, such interpretation has become commonplace in political and economic discourses as well as in the media.[5] Parallel efforts were made to define the concept of labor as "work for pay or profit," and to measure it with the use of labor force survey statistics. The important 1954 International Conference of Labor Force Statisticians solidified this notion of work. These concepts eventually became the norm for labor market analysts, economists, and policymakers; what mattered was the size of marketed final output and the labor expended in its production.

In this chapter, we shift our attention from the wider issues of development, globalization, and labor markets to examine the cumulative efforts to bring attention to the importance of unpaid work and to bring it out of the statistical shadows. These efforts by feminists, women's groups, development scholars, time-use researchers, and the United Nations culminated in the landmark 2013 resolution for measuring work passed during the 19th International Conference of Labour Statisticians (ICLS), which includes unpaid work (International Labour Organization (ILO) 2013e). The resolution delineates work as "any activity performed by persons of any sex and age to produce goods or to provide services for use by others or for own use" (ILO 2013e: 2) and provides a new framework for measuring all forms of work done by persons over 15 years of age, including various unpaid categories of work, such as subsistence work, household work, unpaid training, and volunteer work.[6] Although the framework has yet to be implemented in terms of changes in the way labor statistics, economic models, and policy discourses conceptualize work, the resolution is an important step towards broadening the notion of the economy to include all forms of work. It is also illustrative of the broader relevance of the issues and concerns raised by feminists and of the serious challenges posed by their questions regarding the basic tenets in conventional economic thinking.

First, we review the historical statistical practices and debates around unpaid work. Second, we examine the "Accounting for Women's Work Project" (hereafter the "Accounting Project") construed as a means of making women's work and all forms of unpaid work more visible (Benería 1992; Waring 1988). Underlying the argument for statistical visibility of women's work is the basic question of what is valuable to society. Our review of the Accounting Project addresses three basic questions: Why account? How to account? What do we see when we account? Thus, we start with the argument for accounting and a defense against critics of the effort; move on to evaluate the conceptual, theoretical, and methodological contributions that culminated in systematic collection and use of time-use data; and then examine the development of new measures of well-being such as time poverty and work intensity. We conclude the chapter by highlighting the ways in which information regarding unpaid work can be used to support policies to balance family life and paid work and equitable distribution of care provisioning between men and women. Although these concerns are not new, globalization processes and feminization of the labor force have exacerbated these tensions, thereby pushing them to the forefront of the development policy agendas and debates.

Unpaid Work: Statistical Issues and Challenges

Feminists and women's advocacy groups have long decried the undercounting and undervaluation of women's contributions in national output and labor force statistics, particularly since the late 1970s. Until the major revisions recommended by the 19th International Conference of Labour Statisticians in 2013, the statistical convention of the SNA was that women's (and men's) hours of work would be counted in labor force statistics only when they are looking for or are employed in paid work.[7] Some unpaid work performed in gathering fuel and water, subsistence production and assistance of family members on the family farm or enterprise was officially acknowledged and added to the SNA in 1993. However, when women cook meals, clean the house, bathe the sick, feed the elderly, and care for their children or do volunteer work, these activities are not considered work for the purposes of identifying the economically active population. Thus, unpaid household work (domestic labor and care labor) and volunteer work are considered non-SNA economic activities.[8]

It is no wonder that, for a long time, we discerned a large disconnect between the official statistics on economic activity rates among women and the material processes and realities that we, for example, have observed in our field visits in countries like Bolivia, Ecuador, Mexico, Morocco, the Philippines, and Turkey. Women are constantly moving about the busy streets of Manila, Guayaquil, Marrakesh, and Mexico City or working in the fields in Turkey, as part of their chores done at home or in their communities. Yet the latest statistics (for 2009) on activity rates for the female population were 26 percent (vs. 80 percent for men) in Morocco and 24 percent (vs. 70 percent for men) in Turkey (Population Reference Bureau 2011).[9] In the case of Mexico, the corresponding figure is 43 percent (vs. 81 percent for men), 47 percent (vs. 78 percent for men) in Ecuador, and 49 percent (vs. 79 percent for men) in the Philippines.

The information embedded in the labor force and output data is powerful, for it provides the foundation for measuring the level of economic activity and its changes over time, and for economic policy and development planning. If so, what has determined the conventions regarding what is included and excluded in the statistical information that is collected? The statistical undercounting of women's contributions derives, first and foremost, from the theoretical bias of the economics discipline to focus on the market economy. Since a substantial part of women's work performed within their households and communities has traditionally been unpaid, it was excluded from labor force statistics and national income accounts.

Historically, statistics on the labor force were gathered through population censuses, but the persistent and high unemployment during the Great Depression of the 1930s generated a growing interest in the collection of reliable and more accurate labor force statistics. In 1938, the Committee of Statistical Experts of the League of Nations recommended a definition of the concepts "gainfully occupied" and "unemployed," and drew up proposals to standardize census data with the purpose of facilitating international comparisons (League of Nations, 1938; ILO, 1976). In 1966, the UN Statistical Commission adopted the recommendation of the International Conference of Labour Statisticians to define the "economically active population" as comprising all persons above a specified age who furnish the supply of labor (employed and unemployed) for the production of goods and services during a specified time reference period.[10]

Subsistence Production

While the basic concepts and conventions defining the labor force and national accounting statistics did not change between the 1930s and the 1990s, one important exception were the efforts to include estimates of subsistence production in GNP accounts. As early as 1947, Simon Kuznets, the economist who developed the first comprehensive SNA for the US, called attention to the need to improve the SNA and argued for the inclusion of subsistence production on the grounds that its output is potentially marketable. The methods to estimate and assign value to this type of production activity and the proportion of the population engaged in it were recommended in the UN SNA guidelines during the 1950s, particularly for countries such as Nepal, Papua New Guinea, and Tanzania where the sector was perceived to be relatively important.[11] This recommendation, however, was not followed by efforts to implement it, until the recommendation by the International Conference of Labour Statisticians in 1966, which broadened the labor force to include those who engage in subsistence production, including unpaid family labor.[12] Despite the practical difficulties in estimating the market value of subsistence production and thus the labor engaged in it, its inclusion in national output and labor force estimates became an accepted practice. In 1993, the SNA boundary was further expanded to include the production of specific types of goods and services within the household for own consumption (ILO 1993).[13]

In practice however, the participation of women in subsistence production remained not fully accounted for. To the extent that women's subsistence activities are woven seamlessly in their domestic chores—milling flour, weaving, food cultivation, care of animals, and many others—the line between the conventional classifications of subsistence production, which is considered part of SNA, and household work which is considered non-SNA, has been difficult to draw. Underreporting problems continued due to the relative irregularity of women's work in subsistence production and the persistence in some cultures of the deeply ingrained view that women's place is in the home. In some cases, the boundary between production for sale and that for own consumption is blurred since what women produce or make is consumed as well as sold in the local market. Thus, even the 1993 revision of some statistical conventions has not prevented the tendency to underestimate women's and men's contribution in subsistence production (Heston 1994; Charmes 1998).

Informal Labor

A different type of underestimation problem exists for women's work in various types of informal employment. They range from self-employment to working as employers, employees, or contributing family workers in small or unregistered enterprises and family farms, or as members of informal producers' cooperatives—all of them generally difficult to record (UN Statistical Commission 2004). The measurement problem in this case is not necessarily one of conceptualization, since unpaid family workers in these enterprises fall within conventional definitions of work. Rather, the problem has to do with the persistence of gender role perceptions in survey and data collection methods, as well as methodological difficulties in obtaining reliable statistics.

The propensity to underreport both men and women unpaid family workers and casual, temporary, or seasonal (wage) labor in informal enterprises, small businesses, and agriculture is widespread across countries. This underestimation issue became particularly apparent to feminist researchers in cases where censuses classified workers according to their "main occupation," which would often result in women being recorded as housewives and therefore not in the labor force.[14] In these cases, the unpaid labor performed by women in the family farm or enterprise can easily be perceived by both survey interviewers and respondents to be part of their role in assisting their husbands or fathers. Until this practice was gradually remedied, it resulted in the underestimation and unreliability of national statistics regarding women's agricultural work (less so in the case of men), not to mention the difficulties in making meaningful comparisons across countries.[15]

Until recently, the general absence of appropriate and systematic data collection on these activities was a serious problem, given that they employ a large proportion of the workforce in many countries. Although the 1993 International Conference of Labour Statisticians introduced the concept of the informal sector for improving SNA estimates, a comprehensive methodological guideline was not developed until the early 2000s so that the task of collecting information tended to be haphazard and inadequate (United Nations Statistical Commission 2004; Husmanns 2004).[16] As mentioned in Chapter 4, the tendency for women to engage in informal employment and to work as casual, seasonal agricultural laborers or unpaid family workers is likely to have increased with the adoption of neoliberal policies and promotion of labor market deregulation, making the need to obtain more accurate estimates of informal employment more urgent.

Household Work

By far the most serious challenge confronting the Accounting Project has been the longstanding exclusion of unpaid labor spent on household work, which is treated as outside of the SNA boundary. Unlike subsistence producers or informal workers, in this case the exclusion is based on conceptual grounds. With few exceptions such as Margaret Reid, this practice was not seriously questioned and challenged until the 1970s. The issue of unpaid work was taken up by feminists including Sue Himmelweit and Maxine Molyneux who brought attention to the importance of domestic work in their examination of the relationship between capitalist accumulation and its requirement involving unpaid work performed by wives and mothers of workers. Later on, the term "reproductive work" was used by Lourdes Benería (1979) and Benería and Sen (1981) to highlight the necessary and vital role of this form of unpaid work for reproducing the workforce, present and future.[17] The demands of women's groups and feminist scholars to make household work visible continued throughout the 1980s and 1990s at various international conferences, and in policy dialogues and academic discourses.

Since the 1990s, the terms "household work" and "care work" have been used in feminist discourses to emphasize the nature of the work performed for the maintenance and care of children, the sick and disabled, the elderly, and other able-bodied members in the household. In this conceptualization, household and care work is defined as set of activities and relations involved in meeting the physical and emotional requirements of dependent adults and children (Daly and Lewis, 2000; Elson 2005; Razavi 2007). In the last 15 years, further development of the notion of care work has led to varied conceptualizations. Some adopt a strict definition, referring only to the "direct" care activities of people and distinguishing these from domestic work activities such as cooking, cleaning, washing clothes, etc. However feminist scholars such as Diane Elson, Nancy Folbre, and Shahra Razavi point out that domestic work can be thought of as "indirect care." In fact, in developing countries the distinction between care and domestic work is often blurred, for the work schedules of many women involve switching from one to the other and even performing them simultaneously. Care work can also be conceptualized in terms of who benefits (Folbre 2012). While typically care work is perceived to involve meeting the needs of dependents that is, children, the sick and disabled, and the elderly, much care is also involved in meeting the needs of healthy adults in the form of domestic work activities. To be sure, many domestic and care activities have progressively been shifted to the sphere of market production while men's share in these activities has grown in some countries. Yet, by and large, women are still performing most of them (Benería and Martinez-Iglesias 2014; Craig et al. 2010; Fisher et al. 2007; Gershuny and Sullivan 2003).

The measurement and valuation of goods and services produced within the household domain faced several criticisms and met strong resistance from policymakers and statistical agencies. This is illustrated by the justification made in the System of National Accounts 2008 Report for maintaining the exclusion of household production from the SNA:

> It is clear that the economic significance of these flows is very different from that of monetary flows. For example, the incomes generated are automatically tied to the consumption of the goods and services produced; they have little relevance for the analysis of inflation or deflation or other disequilibria within the economy. The inclusion of large non-monetary flows of this kind in the accounts together with monetary flows can obscure what is happening on markets and reduce the analytic usefulness of the data. (UN et al. 2009: 6)

Volunteer Work

Another type of unpaid work that has remained in the statistical shadows is volunteer work, which refers to "work without monetary pay, or legal obligation provided for persons living outside the volunteer's own household" (UN 2003: 4). Even though volunteer work has long been a part of the established customs and norms of sharing as well as mutual support mechanisms in most societies and is deeply embedded in many cultures throughout the world, it was conceptualized as outside the SNA boundary as with household and care work. Volunteer work can be performed in public and in non-profit organizations such as Habitat for Humanity, Meals on Wheels, hospitals, humanitarian aid and social programs, done informally in one's neighborhood or it can be in the private sector. In all these cases, documenting and analyzing such work is important, particularly if it provides free substitutes for what otherwise would be paid market work. Indeed, in Canada, the growing use of volunteer labor in hospitals has been linked to the reduction and casualization of registered nursing jobs throughout the country (Valiani 2011).

The definition of volunteer work remains unsettled, in part because the term carries different meanings in diverse cultures and settings (Rochester et al. 2009; Salamon et al. 2011). This difficulty undoubtedly fuels the lack of interest among economists and statistical agencies in measuring volunteer work. Also, certain types of volunteer work are difficult to categorize. For example, activities associated with charitable or church-related organizations and assisting in community activities are sometimes viewed as "socializing" or "participation in religious activities," even though they provide service benefits to members of the community. Second, the close connections between household chores and some volunteer work—as when volunteer work takes place in one's neighborhood—can make the boundaries difficult to draw. For example, the communal soup kitchens in the Andean countries during the debt crisis of the 1980s and 1990s provide an example of collective voluntary work among the poor that sprung up to deal with the economic crisis. Organized and run mostly by women, these communal kitchens functioned as survival strategies to cope with the drastic deterioration of living standards that resulted from structural adjustment policies and increasing urban poverty. In Lima these communal kitchens were estimated to be run by 40,000 low-income women in 2,000 sites in poor neighborhoods who pooled their resources to feed about 200,000 people as much as five times a week (Barrig 1996; Lind 1997).

Volunteer work tends to vary by gender and educational status. A number of studies indicates that women volunteer in greater numbers than do men. For instance, in the United States, a recent study of over 60,000 Americans showed that in all age groups more women, particularly those who are well-educated and married, reported volunteering compared to men (US Bureau of Labor Statistics 2010). In another study conducted in Ethiopia, more than 80 percent of community health AIDS care volunteers during the 2008 food crisis were women (Maes et al. 2010).

There are also gender differences with respect to the nature of the volunteer work and in the preferences for the type of organization chosen (Mesch et al. 2006; Wymer and Samu 2002; Heymann et al. 2007). For example, a study by Wymer (2011) on US volunteering found that women have a stronger preference than men for serving in organizations dedicated to helping needy people or people in distress. Men, on the other hand, are

188 • Gender, Development, and Globalization

more willing to volunteer in risky or dangerous situations, or those involving confrontation and conflict with others. Wymer's study also suggests that women tend to volunteer in organizations characterized by consensus building and participatory decision-making while men tend to prefer volunteering in roles, which place them in positions of authority. However, these differences cannot be generalized since much remains to be done to document systematically the amount of volunteer work worldwide.

That said, the nature of volunteer work is distinct from unpaid household work in terms of its effect on the worker's well-being. Volunteer work is typically done out of choice; its performance provides women and men with a sense of belonging and fulfillment by serving others; it also gives them opportunity to socialize and to be active in the community. Unpaid domestic and care work on the other hand, is often done out of necessity and a sense of obligation as dictated by socialized roles. It can increase one's sense of fulfillment but can also bring stress, fatigue, feelings of isolation, and even boredom, depending on norms, social class, and other factors. For many household workers, the fact that their labor is unpaid makes them economically dependent on the "breadwinners"; and since their contributions are invisible and not valued, they have a low or subordinate status in society.

To date, efforts to measure volunteer work at the country level have been sporadic, partly due to the paucity of reliable and comparable data. With the exception of a few high-income countries, volunteering is not tracked in official surveys.[18] Available data usually come from privately sponsored surveys that use relatively small samples and are based on varied definitions and methodologies, which results in a wide range of estimates (Rochester et al. 2009; Salamon et al. 2011).[19] This picture is expected to change with the increased awareness of the contributions of volunteer workers in various sectors of the economy. Recently, the United Nations Statistics Division, the ILO, and Johns Hopkins University produced documentation on methodologies for systematic data gathering on volunteer work (ILO 2008; 2011a; Salamon et al. 2011). The first global estimates using these methodologies indicate that about one billion people perform volunteer work in public, non-profit, or for-profit organizations, or directly for friends or neighbors in a given year (Salamon et al. 2011).

The Accounting Project: Making Women's Contributions More Visible

The "Accounting for Women's Work" Project refers to the collective efforts that have sought to remedy society's undervaluation of women's unpaid contributions by addressing the conceptual, theoretical, and statistical biases that are at the root of the undervaluation. The Project has posed far-reaching challenges to the basic tenets of economic thinking and statistical methods by revealing the embedded bias in conventional wisdom that identifies work as paid labor and productive activities for the market. The invisibility of unpaid work has left unnoticed, and perpetuated, the serious imbalances in the distribution of work burden across individuals.

At the most basic level, the Accounting Project entails documenting the unpaid work performed by women by estimating the amount of time spent in each activity and providing a monetary valuation to its labor or outputs. The Project has represented the combined efforts of women's advocacy groups, feminist scholars, international organizations, and policymakers that were energized by the UN World Conferences on Women and the landmark 1995 Beijing Platform for Action. Initially envisioned to obtain a full accounting of women's contributions to human welfare and to integrate the totality of women's work in economic analysis and policy discussions, the Accounting Project has led to the broader objectives of improving labor force statistics on informal work and measuring all unpaid activities. It has also helped generate new measures of well-being, such as time poverty and work intensity, which can be used for policy formulation and evaluation. Moreover, the statistical visibility of unpaid care work has contributed to the discussions around the care economy and its crucial linkages with the market economy.

Why is it Important to Count?

Feminist economists have articulated a number of arguments in favor of undertaking the project of measuring and documenting unpaid work (Delphy 1984; Delphy and Leonard 1992; Benería 1999c; Folbre 2006; Esquivel et al. 2008). First, unpaid work is an important contributor to building human capabilities, and measuring would make its contribution more visible and socially appreciated. Second, unpaid work, especially unpaid care work, creates disadvantages (costs) for the worker; hence its measurement is crucial to analyze the extent to which total work (paid and unpaid) is equitably shared in the household.[20] Third, its measurement is crucial if there is a case to be made for policy to reconcile paid and unpaid work and address equitable distribution of work. Fourth, it is a crucial input for the project of engendering macroeconomic policies and budgets in order to make explicit their gender-differentiated effects on unpaid work. Such analysis can then help governments in designing gender-aware, macroeconomic, and social policies. Fifth, the Project generates statistics for creating satellite accounts on aggregate household production and for improving labor force statistics. Sixth, even if productivity levels are not easy to compare, time-use indicators can be used to analyze trends in the share of paid/unpaid work over time, enabling us to understand shortfalls of well-being due to time poverty and intensification of work. In addition, the measurement of unpaid work has other practical uses such as in litigation and in estimating monetary compensation in divorce cases (Cassels 1993; Collins 1993; Çağatay et al. 1995; Bakker and Elson 1998).

To be sure, there were efforts to include unpaid household work in the 1930s when the national income accounts were being developed in the United States. We have mentioned the work of Margaret Reid who designed a method to estimate the value of housework in her 1934 book *Economics of Household Production*. Later on, Ester Boserup (1970: 163) pointed out that "the subsistence activities usually omitted in the statistics of production and income are largely women's work." She was a pioneer in emphasizing the time-consuming character of these activities, which, in rural economies, included physically demanding tasks such as fetching wood and carrying water as well as food production and processing. She saw clearly that these activities underlie the sustenance of human life and maintain the satisfaction of bodily needs, standard of living, and the fabric of affective relations within families and communities. Although Boserup mentioned the omission of "domestic services of housewives" from national accounts, she failed to acknowledge the exclusion of caring for children, the sick, disabled, and elderly.

Feminist economists have contributed to the intellectual explorations of the relationship between gender inequality and unpaid work, and the body of work dealing with the Accounting Project has grown considerably from its early explorations and efforts to conceptualize it (Benería 1981; Folbre and Pujol 1996) to the empirical and technical effort of measurement that followed. Marilyn Waring's book *If Women Counted*, published in 1988, helped make the case for the underestimation of women's economic activities and to contributions of unpaid work to human well-being as it reached a wider audience beyond academics and researchers. Thus, it became clear that valuing unpaid work, particularly care work, is indispensable to any overall assessment of gendered responsibility for human maintenance and the production of human capabilities. Folbre (2006) argued that, given that men overall tend to devote more money for consumption needs while women give more of their labor (care) time, only by some common denominator between these two, can comparisons of their overall contributions be made.

Another important body of work involved time-use data collection and analysis. Time-use data were first produced in the early 1920s as part of social surveys on the living conditions of working-class families. One of the first estimates of unpaid household work was done by Statistics Norway in 1912 (Aslaksen and Koren 1996). In 1924, the USSR undertook the first systematic collection of this data with the objective of obtaining information about variables such as leisure time and community-oriented work (Juster and

Stafford 1991). The Bureau of Home Economics of the US Department of Agriculture (USDA) also collected time-use data in the 1920s, for the purpose of understanding the impact of new technology on the time use of farm homemakers (Frazis and Stewart 2007). Sweden followed the example of Norway in the 1930s in depicting and measuring the size of the economy as constituted by the household and the market (Aslaksen and Koren 1996).[21]

By the 1980s, the usefulness of time-use survey data as a key source for estimating women's unpaid work had become evident (Goldschmidt-Clermont 1983; Chadeau 1992). At the time, time-use survey data were not necessarily linked to feminist analysis that questioned workload disparities and gendered well-being, but this changed as feminist economists and other social scientists joined the effort (Bittman 1991; Juster and Stafford 1985; Gershuny and Robinson 1988; Ironmonger 1996; Floro and Miles 2003; Antonopoulos and Hirway 2010; Budlender 2010). Researchers have advanced the collection, methods, and analysis of time-use data in both developed and developing countries, particularly through the activities of the International Association for Time Use Research (IATUR) and its flagship academic journal, the *electronic international journal of time use research* or *e-ijtur.*

The work of the United Nations, leading to the four UN World Conferences on Women in the 1975–95 period and the follow-up mechanisms and related conventions, has been instrumental in putting the question of accounting for women's work on the agendas of meetings and subsequent plans of action. Since 1986, the International Training and Research Institute for the Advancement of Women (INSTRAW) and the Statistical Office of the UN Secretariat took the lead in the initial reviews of national accounts and other statistical information on women's work and called for their revision. Unpaid work was also a key focus of discussion at the UN Social Summit in Copenhagen in March 1995. These various meetings provided opportunities for government representatives of member countries to discuss the issues pertaining to its measurement and valuation with NGOs, feminist academics, researchers, and women's groups. The process unfolded gradually over two decades, despite initial skepticism and even hostile reactions to the overall project. A significant consensus was then built on the need to measure unpaid household work on the basis that it makes an important contribution to welfare.

The Accounting Project's objective was officially sanctioned and summarized in the Platform of Action adopted in 1995 at the Fourth World Conference on Women in Beijing, which called for the design and implementation of:

> suitable statistical means to recognize and make visible the full extent
> of the work of women and all their contributions to the national econ-

omy including their contribution in the unremunerated and domestic sectors, and to examine the relationship of women's unremunerated work to the incidence of vulnerability to poverty. (UN 1996: 119)

The United Nations Development Programme (UNDP), the UN Statistics Division, and regional agencies of the UN in the Asia-Pacific Region, Latin America and the Caribbean, and Africa promoted this strategic objective of the Beijing Platform. In a pioneering effort, UNDP reported the estimated shares of paid and unpaid work for a small number of countries in its 1995 *Human Development Report* (HDR). These efforts helped encourage governments in developing and developed countries, researchers, and women's groups to collect and use gender-disaggregated data and information, including on unpaid work, for planning and evaluation (UN 1996). As a result, by 2011 there was a substantial body of research and evidence on time use, which the World Bank reported in the 2012 *World Development Report* (World Bank 2011).

Objections to the Accounting Project

The methodological concerns and practical difficulties in accounting for women's total contribution, not to mention the institutional resources and efforts that it requires, have cast doubts on the merits of the Project. From the outset, criticisms and debates accompanied the concerted efforts to promote the Project. A number of scholars, feminists, and policymakers have voiced their concerns and serious objections. The objections fall into different categories:

Theoretically Misguided

Despite criticisms emanating from economists' circles in fora and meetings, very few have expressed their objections in writing. An early comment by Charlotte Phelps in the *American Economic Review* tended to dismiss the idea altogether, on the basis that "many women regard their household activities primarily as acts of love; i.e., leisure activities by my definition. In that case, the money income they receive is not conditional on earning approval. They suffer no loss of self-respect for the way they choose to occupy their time" (Phelps 1972: 167). Hence, the household division of labor is as much a matter of individual choice as it is a rational one based on comparative advantage; women are maximizing their utility by doing this work without pay and that it is a reward in itself to do this work.

Sujai Shivakumar (1996) further captured several of the unwritten criticisms. He pointed out that any imputation of monetary value to unpaid work is not consistent with modern economics, so it is merely a "rhetorical effort" without theoretical foundation; just a "dubious game of statistical football" (p. 374). He claimed that the Accounting Project is associated with theories that are debunked or alien to mainstream economics, such as the Ricardian-Marxian labor theory of value and socialist-feminist rhetorical effort that presents gender as the central "tool of analysis" and economic processes in terms of "provisioning of human life." Contrary to these theories in modern economics, he argued, price is established in markets. Thus, it is not possible to assign prices to a service that is not exchanged on the market. Moreover, price is not solely a reflection of value of labor, but also of other production costs. Finally, because mainstream theory offers no theoretical guide to valuation, the selection of the "valuation method" (which wage per hour or price per unit to assign to obtain the total value of an activity) will be arbitrary.

This position is contrary to the longstanding mainstream economic practice of using "shadow prices" and assigning market value to household production in New Household Economics. It is also contrary to the statistical practice of imputing value to subsistence production for national income account estimation. Shivakumar, however, does not make any reference to this body of work. He also ignores the fact that the literature regarding the measurement of unpaid work includes scholars and researchers with diverse theoretical approaches and practical politics. His misplaced arguments and reasoning likely reflects the irritation felt, to say the least, in the economics profession for spoiling a well-defined, presumably "objective" economic paradigm that focuses on markets and their price-based, allocative mechanism—a point also made in the 2008 SNA Report's justification for excluding household production.

While an increasing number of economists have since recognized the importance of non-market (household) production, the resistance to measuring it or to incorporating the information obtained into their research or examination of economic issues remains.[22] The resistance to the accounting of unpaid work may also have to do with the methodological individualism in mainstream economics. As Julie Nelson (2010) argues, this approach reinforces the notion that the autonomous individual is rational and self-sufficient and that dependence on others or any faltering of self-reliance is a weakness. Hence, an acknowledgement of care work is anathema to the "separative selves," who simply don't need care.

A Waste of Time

This objection is based on two different arguments. The first stems from the concern that the Project is fraught with serious methodological and practical problems and any attempt to address them would either yield data of poor quality or require a substantial amount of resources, which can be scarce, particularly in the least developed countries. The second argument is based on the fear that, once measured, the ensuing statistics generated might not improve women's lives. Can the information be of use in reducing the burden of poor women who have to toil many hours a day or in empowering the urban housewife with no income of her own? For example, Bergmann has been skeptical about the possibility that better information on unpaid work "can help a single woman," in the same way that "the inclusion in the GNP of food produced in the subsistence sector does not make any difference to farmers."[23] On the contrary, this argument goes, greater social recognition of the importance of household work might in fact reinforce a division of labor that relegates women to activities that are socially valued but do not provide financial autonomy and offer little control over the resources they need. Bergmann fears that statistics on housework are likely to be used by those who want "to glorify the housewife," as in the case of some conservative groups who view women's primary role as that of homemaker, on the grounds that housework is irreplaceable because it performs crucial services to society. This would therefore not contribute to gender equality; rather, it would help perpetuate women's dependence on men. Bergmann concludes that "there is an anti-feminist implication in valorizing housework." Instead, she argued, feminists should emphasize the need for women to engage in paid work in order to reduce their dependence on men and to increase their bargaining power in and outside of the home. Resources and effort are better used in the advocacy for and implementation of policies that facilitate the participation of women in the labor force, such as affordable childcare provision and paid maternity leave, and that enforce gender equality in the labor market, such as pay equity, affirmative action, and comparable worth.

The first argument does raise valid points, which feminists and women's groups have also acknowledged. Nevertheless, there has been significant progress over the last two decades on the conceptual and methodological issues, which has made it feasible to produce reliable statistics. The establishment of international guidelines and manuals by various UN agencies, the development of training workshops for government officials and statisticians, and the support of donor agencies have fostered attention on data quality issues, and have helped enhance the data collection efforts of many developing countries whose governments, facing strong pressure, have the political will to collect such information. Although this, by itself, does not guarantee an improvement in women's condition, it does generate valuable information that can be used towards this end.

The second argument does raise caution over what changes can be expected in terms of policy design and implementation. Still, it is important to point out that women's engagement in paid and unpaid work requires systematic information on both. As the Indian feminist Devaki Jain once pointed out, "One of the greatest difficulties in assisting women has been the absence of any reliable data regarding their number, problems and achievements" (Jain 1975, personal communication). Data on the amount of unpaid work can be important, for example, in demonstrating the substantial time spent in fetching water, without which authorities may give low priority to deep-well and safe-water provisioning. Likewise, time-use information on hours spent in caregiving for HIV/AIDS patients can provide vital information for developing a comprehensive health policy. As illustrated by the papers in the special issues of *Feminist Economics*, "Time Use, Unpaid Work, Poverty and Public Policy" (2010 and 2011), time-use research shows the impact of economic and social policies on the quality of life and progress in human development (Grown et al. 2010; Floro and Pichetpongsa 2010).

Moreover, time-use statistics are playing an increasingly important role in the critique of government budgets and macroeconomic policies for their gender biases and building arguments for gender-aware policies. For example, in Spain the Personal Autonomy and Dependent Care Law (39/2006), which guaranteed public support for care of dependents, was approved and implemented in 2007, after empirical studies showed the large amount of hours women devoted to caring as part of their unpaid domestic labor (Eurofound 2014). Similarly, in South Korea, the realization of the serious demographic, social, and economic consequences brought about by the neglect of the unpaid care work burden of women as shown in time-use studies, has led to social policy to provide childcare subsidies and eldercare services (Park 2010; Yoon 2014). As Yoon (2014) shows, however, time-use studies continue to be important after the implementation of such policies in order to document the extent to which they transformed gender relations in care provision and redistributed care costs between the family, market, and the state.

The Accounting Project must be viewed not as an end in itself but as a means to understand who contributes to human well-being, and to what extent. While it may be the case that the data can be used for promoting "women's place in the home," this is a matter of political and ideological debate and not a question of whether such information should be collected. The concern that some groups might use the information for their own political agenda must be weighed against its use for a variety of positive outcomes, including the more effective design of gender-aware social, labor, and economic policies.

Care Work is Qualitatively Different

Another objection, focused on the care component of unpaid work, springs from the notion that this type of activity involves personal and relational aspects that make it qualitatively different from market work and other types of unpaid work. Himmelweit (1995) raised questions about the merits of the

Accounting Project itself, particularly "whether the best way for women's contribution to be appreciated [is] to force it into a pre-existing category of 'work'" (p. 2). In the first place, caring, or caregiving, encompasses both physical and emotional aspects; while physical care "might to some extent be independent of the relation between the carer and the person cared for," the emotional component requires that "the person doing the caring is inseparable from the care given" (Himmelweit 1995: 8). Moreover, caring contains its own reward in the fulfillment the caregiver derives. These two features make caregiving qualitatively different from wage work and therefore very difficult to quantify and value. Himmelweit concludes that not everything needs to be seen as "work."[24]

This objection also highlights the shift in feminist work on unpaid work away from the economic reductionist formulations of unpaid work that focused on its function for social reproduction, particularly of the labor force. The discursive shift from "unpaid (domestic) work" to "care work" was partly due to dissatisfaction with these formulations but partly due to the transformation of households in the course of market expansion and capitalist development (Esquivel 2011). The decline in the amount of housework required by middle- and upper-class families due to reliance on market substitutes, especially in high-income countries, has meant that "home life is becoming more and more concentrated in sharing meals or telling bedtime stories for which substitutes cannot be purchased" (Folbre and Nelson 2000: 129).[25]

Along similar lines, other feminist economists have argued that something essential is lost in the process of attaching monetary value to unpaid care work in the quest for making it visible. There are fears that imputing monetary value to unpaid care work opens up caregiving to being subjected to the norms of the market, i.e. the price reflects the opportunity cost in terms of foregone earnings. Another issue is that the quality of care can differ substantially, for example in the case of childcare, meals, nurturing services, when provided through the market as opposed to the unpaid caregiver. Folbre argues that when caring work is paid it will likely "corrode ties of affection and obligation" (Dorman et al. 1996: 83). Similarly, Peter Dorman warned about how the "greased chute" of the spread of market ideals leads to the "marketization of just about everything" (Dorman et al. 1996: 75), while Deirdre McCloskey wrote that if childcare, friendly listening, and similar care activities "were paid labor the love would disappear. Love is, in this regard, the opposite of market exchange" (McCloskey 1996: 138). More recently, Julie Nelson (2010) argued that marketization brings with it norms of individualism and self-interest, which are incompatible with the generous, close, emotionally satisfying characteristics that we want in authentic care relationships.

To be sure, some paid care services are not likely to provide the same quality of care and emotional support that a loving family member can offer. However, it is not difficult to find exceptions to these cases. Indeed, there can be market-based care that provides selfless emotional support beyond the exchange contract. For example, motives associated with solidarity, altruism, and caring can be found in the performance of paid caregiving provided by nurses, nursing aides, elderly care assistants, nannies, and daycare center workers. As Braunstein et al. (2011) point out, there can be variety of motives underlying the performance of care work: altruism, self-interest, and the desire/compulsion to fulfill social norms or be useful to others.[26] Hence, it is difficult to argue that there are no personal and relational aspects in services offered in exchange for a monetary reward. Moreover, one cannot assume or idealize families to be sites of mutual caring and love and respect, given the problem of domestic violence (Duvvury et al. 2012). Second, many unpaid activities performed by primary caregivers at home are not necessarily self-fulfilling, nor do they incorporate feelings of care. There can be family care based on selfish expectations (an inheritance) or on some form of social coercion (as in the case of a wife having to take care of her in-laws even when there may not be much affection between them). Third, there are virtually no skills that are intrinsic to unpaid care work. To some degree the skills used in the household can be used in market work and vice versa. Thus, a paid nanny or nurse might provide a high quality of personal care with skills learned at home; and managerial skills learned in the labor market might be used as a way to reduce unpaid work time in the household, without reducing the quality of the service.

To sum up, while some feminists who make this argument against the Accounting Project provide important insights into the nature of caregiving, paid or unpaid, their arguments need to be seen in the broader context of what its measurement can achieve. It may be that something gets lost in the process of measuring the time input and estimating the monetary value of unpaid caring work, but a deeper understanding of the material and time dimensions of care work is crucial in demonstrating its importance for human welfare; it brings attention to the economic costs of care that are ignored in economic analysis and policymaking. These dimensions are just as important as the relational aspects of care and the social norms that determine who provides them.

Another incommensurability argument has centered around one of the main challenges to measuring unpaid work, particularly household work, namely, the difficulty of comparing it with market production. The presumption typically made is that unpaid household work requires lower skills and has lower productivity compared to that of wage labor.[27] As a result, some researchers and practitioners argue that monetary valuation of non-market work is forced and misleading; and in fact, it can lead to the incorrect conclusion that the market provides perfect substitutes for non-market-produced services.

However, the main reasons for measuring and documenting unpaid work have more to do with making it visible and socially appreciated and for identifying its contribution to social well-being and the reproduction of human resources, than simply for making comparison with paid work. Issues of comparability should not deter us from acknowledging and understanding the crucial linkages between paid and unpaid work, in particular on how total work is shared in the household, and how one's time is allocated between paid and unpaid work, along with leisure and rest.

Progress Towards Measurement and Valuation of Unpaid Work

Although questions on whether unpaid household work time should be measured continue to be raised, the last decades have witnessed significant progress in addressing conceptual and practical issues pertaining to the Accounting Project. This progress has been mainly on three fronts: conceptual, theoretical, and methodological.

Conceptualizing Work and the Economy

The task of implementing the agenda of measuring unpaid work required two crucial steps: delineating work from non-work and redefining economic activity.

First, given the numerous and varied activities that are performed in the household, the question of which tasks to include as work has been an important topic of discussion. Margaret Reid's "third person" principle was adopted as the operational criterion. Accordingly, household production should refer to unpaid activities that can also be performed by another person for pay. Tasks such as shopping, cleaning, food preparation, and childcare are included as work under this criterion, while watching television, sleeping, reading, and getting dressed are not. While there are still some ambiguities, for example, the very rich or the ill might have a paid person to help them dress, the adoption of the third person principle represents an important step in setting a standard of definition that allows for comparisons between countries.[28]

Second, as discussed in Chapter 2, a significant shift has recently taken place in the conceptualization of economic activity by feminist economists and scholars since the late 1970s to include social reproduction and human maintenance tasks that are not directly connected with the market. This redefinition demands that any measure of aggregate output include the production of all final goods and services that human beings need in order to survive and flourish, whether produced for and exchanged through the market, or produced in the home, communities, and social organizations without pay. This expanded concept of the economy has brought into question the conventional use of the SNA in the estimation of production and consumption and has led to the development of "satellite accounts" of aggregate household production, as discussed below.

Theoretical Contributions

On the theoretical front, major developments in economic modeling preceded or ran parallel to the Accounting Project. As discussed in Chapter 2, since the 1960s a variety of economic models have been developed to examine household production and the gender division of labor within the household, from the New Household Economics to mainstream bargaining models (Manser and Brown 1980; Thomas 1990; Bourguignon and Chiappori 1992). Critical of these approaches, feminist economists have suggested analytical frameworks that place greater emphasis on the social construction of gender roles that result in unequal division of labor and other asymmetric outcomes among household members (McCrate 1987; Sen 1990b; Agarwal 1997; Katz 1995; Braunstein and Folbre 2001; Doss 2013).

At the macroeconomic level, since the 1990s, feminist economists have developed gender-aware macroeconomic models that introduced unpaid work and gender differences in a variety of ways (Braunstein 2000; Fontana and Wood 2000; Ertürk and Çağatay 1995; Braunstein et al. 2011; Walters 1995). These models reveal the hidden costs and adverse consequences of economic policies in terms of unpaid work, women's well-being, feedback loops on future economic growth, and the nurturing and development of both present and future generations. Hence, they have provided a deeper understanding of how non-market production is necessary for the functioning of other economic sectors that conventionally have served as the domain for macroeconomic analysis.

Measurement and Valuation Methods

In practical terms, the Accounting Project faces two challenges: (a) where to obtain information on labor time spent on these activities; and (b) how to estimate the value of labor time. Efforts to address these concerns have resulted in several developments. First, there have been improvements in data-gathering methods to capture with greater accuracy the various types and amounts of unpaid work performed by men and women. In particular, efforts by national statistical agencies, the United Nations, and time-use researchers have led to the construction of time-use surveys (TUS) that are suited to developing countries' conditions, leading to their implementation in nearly 100 developed and developing countries.[29] Second, approaches have evolved to measure the value of unpaid work and to produce a parallel "satellite account" that estimates the aggregate value of household production and can accompany a country's SNA (Ahmad and Koh 2011).

Role of Time-use Surveys

As recognized by the 19th ICLS of 2013, time-use surveys (TUS) have been invaluable in estimating the labor time contributed by household members and in measuring all forms of work (ILO 2013d). The detailed accounting provided by this type of survey allows for a comprehensive coverage of all activities and enables the documentation of tasks of short duration.[30] Whether by self-administered diary, recall interview or short-task list method, TUS typically asks a household member respondent to record the different activities and tasks that she/he undertakes during a given reference period—usually in the past 24 hours or in the past week.

In addition to providing information on unpaid labor time, TUS has also led to the improvement of data collection in the areas of SNA work that are missed in standard labor force surveys such as in India and South Africa, including subsistence production and informal jobs, for example, casual, contingent, and home-based work (Hirway and Jose 2011; Floro and Komatsu 2011). Comparing the National Sample Survey Organisation's 1999–2000 employment–unemployment survey in India with the findings of the 1998–99 pilot Indian Time Use Survey, Hirway and Jose (2011) show that the size of the workforce in India is much larger than estimated by the labor force survey. The widest gap between the labor-force and time-use survey estimates holds for urban women, whose workforce participation increases from an average of 12.8 percent to 30.9 percent, while urban men's participation increases from 51 to 59 percent. For rural women, the estimates more than double, rising from 25 percent to 58 percent.[31] In the case of South Africa, the 2000 national time-use survey was used by Floro and Komatsu (2011) to identify individuals who would have been classified as either not in the labor force (NLF) or unemployed by standard labor force surveys but who had actually performed subsistence production and casual and short-term jobs. Their study findings indicate that 11.1 percent of women and 15.8 percent of men who were classified as NLF spent an average of 2.6 hours and 3.6 hours per day respectively, in labor market activities. In addition, about 12 percent of unemployed women and 26.7 percent of unemployed men spent about 2.9 hours and 4.6 hours respectively in the labor market working in very short-term jobs and in subsistence production (Floro and Komatsu 2011).

Admittedly, time-use surveys are costly to conduct and resource constraints have prompted some developing countries to adopt the least expensive approach, which utilizes stylized questions on specific tasks, referred to as "short-tasks list" method (Esquivel et al. 2008). For example, the 2001 Bolivian time-use survey listed only seven tasks, namely, taking care of children, cooking and cleaning, food shopping, laundering and ironing, minor repairing, production for self-consumption, and fuel and water collection. The respondent was then asked a yes/no question for each task and the "average time per day" as well as daily frequency. Similarly, in their 2003 time-use surveys Guinea and Nigeria used the recall interview method with a pre-listing of 9 and 14 activities respectively.

Unlike the systematized data collection of the SNA, the frequency and method of TUS data collection varies across countries. While countries such as Australia, Canada, France, the Netherlands, Norway, Sweden, and the UK have collected them on a regular basis over a few decades, others have only collected the data once or twice.[32] Moreover, the sampling and survey designs tend to vary. This has made the development of international standardization and harmonization of time-use data quite challenging. Proponents of standardization have argued in favor of adopting the International Classification of Activities for Time Use Statistics (ICATUS) developed by the United Nations Statistics Division in 1997 and harmonizing time-use data across countries.[33]

However, standardization is difficult for developing countries, which face other practical difficulties that high-income countries, for the most part, do not. One serious concern, especially for the least developed countries, is the low literacy rate, making it difficult to use the time diary method, which is deemed to be more reliable (Juster and Stafford 1991). Second, many poor households do not commonly use a clock or watch to tell the time, casting doubt on the reliability of responses to short-tasks lists survey or time-use recall questions such as: "How long or how many minutes did you spend in (given) activity?"[34]

Many developing countries have approached time-use data collection in a pragmatic manner. They design their time-use surveys to suit local needs and budgets, aware that there are methodological trade-offs involved (Esquivel et al. 2008). Table 5.1 shows the differing objectives for conducting time-use surveys in a selected group of countries. Similarly, the type of activity classification is selected on the basis of the country's interest and political conditions. For example, South Africa conducted its national TUS in 2000 primarily to assist in the conceptualization and measurement of all types of work and in making more gender-responsive policies (Budlender 2008). Other countries, such as Bhutan and Laos, have other objectives for collecting time-use survey data including the estimation of Gross National Happiness index, measuring productivity in farming, and calculating labor input in small businesses. Time-use surveys in high-income countries, on the other hand, are mostly used for measuring time spent on interactive and mobile technologies, leisure time, quality of life, and travel or commuting time.[35]

Countries also differ in the mode of collecting time-use data. South Africa has implemented a stand-alone TUS with supplementary demographic and other household and community-level information. Other developing countries collected TUS information by attaching time-use modules to other national surveys including household surveys (Thailand, Oman, Laos, Bolivia, Mexico, Tunisia), labor force surveys (China, Costa Rica, Bangladesh, Ecuador, Nepal), health and nutrition surveys (China), or the Living Standards Measurement Survey (Ghana, Guatemala, Madagascar, Malawi, Sierra Leone) (Esquivel et al. 2008). Collecting time-use information using modules to ongoing surveys has proved to be a viable strategy for meeting limited budgets and it is a less costly method for developing longitudinal data that can be valuable as monitoring tools.

Another difficulty that arises in both rich and low-income economies has to do with the prevailing gender norms and patterns of socialization that can lead to underreporting of certain activities, typically childcare. Time-use research has shown that childcare frequently shows up as a secondary activity (Ironmonger 2004; Bittman et al. 2004). Supervision and child-minding as well as care of sick and disabled persons often takes the form of a background activity, which the respondents may not report. For example, childcare may be done in a collective manner by mothers who gather for a chat in the afternoon. The social nature of the activity may be perceived as socializing, and hence reported by women as "leisure." Likewise, women are often socialized to take on certain tasks such as childcare without being aware that they are performing a task and therefore do not report it. Hence, when a woman carries her baby on her back while tending to her vegetables she may report only vegetable gardening as her activity.

Researchers have shown that "multitasking," that is, the performance of overlapping or simultaneous tasks, especially by women and involving care work, is not an isolated phenomenon, nor is it limited to developing countries.[36] To address the problem of underreporting of simultaneous activities, time-use researchers have developed a number of methods. One approach is to ask about primary and secondary activities in the same time segment. Second, in high-income countries where time diaries are used,

Table 5.1 Objectives of national time-use surveys, selected countries, various years

COUNTRY	SURVEY YEAR	SURVEY OBJECTIVES
Bhutan	2007–08	To use time-use studies to measure Gross National Happiness index.
		To understand how people spend their time on different activities to determine their happiness.
		To study time spent on unpaid work (household work, care and so on) linked with socio-economic characteristics of respondents.
Cuba	2001	To gain information on changes in and the status of performing unpaid work, observing the time distribution by activity.
Ecuador	2003–04, 2005	To collect information on the time spent on unpaid care by men and women in informal/subsistence work.
Ghana	1991[a]	To collect information on the time spent by men and women in Ghana.
		To collect information on living standards of people in Ghana.
India	1998–99	To collect and analyze time-use patterns of men and women.
		To generate a more reliable estimate of workforce.
		To estimate and value unpaid work.
		To develop a conceptual framework and a suitable methodology for designing and conducting time-use studies in India.
Laos	1997–98[b]	To measure productivity in farming, mainly rice cultivation.
		To measure labor input work in small-scale business and informal sector.
Madagascar	2001[a]	To understand sharing of paid and unpaid work by men and women.
		To estimate time spent on subsistence and informal work by men and women.
Malawi	2003–04[a] 2004[c]	To collect information on the time spent by men and women on household work, collection of fuel, agricultural activities, fishing, and so on.

continued . . .

Table 5.1 Continued

COUNTRY	SURVEY YEAR	SURVEY OBJECTIVES
		To estimate unpaid domestic work performed by men and women.
Palestine	1999–2000	To provide data on the time spent by people on different activities for policymaking and decision-making.
South Africa	2000, 2009–10	To measure and analyze time spent by men and women.
		To provide information on division of paid and unpaid work by men and women.
		To incorporate unpaid work in satellite accounts.
		To gain more insight on productive activities such as subsistence work, casual work, and work in the informal sector.
Tanzania	2004, 2006[c]	To estimate workforce employed in paid work, including informal work.
		To collect data on time spent by men and women in unpaid work.
Thailand	2000–01	To get comprehensive knowledge on how people over ten years of age spend their time on different paid and unpaid work.
		To understand gender differences in paid and unpaid work.
		To provide data to markedly improve the estimates of labor contribution to GDP.
		To provide internationally comparable time use data for the country.

Notes: [a] Part of the Living Standards Measurement Survey (LSMS).

[b] Part of the Household Income and Expenditure and Consumption Survey.

[c] Part of Labor Force Survey.

Source: Adapted from Antonopoulos and Hirway (2010); Centre for Time Use Research- information gateway, http://www-2009.timeuse.org/information/studies/Accessed May 7, 2013.

researchers have incorporated context information in parents' diaries (for example by asking "who else was with you during this activity?") or have combined time-use information of parents and children to obtain better estimates of the care provided (Mullan 2010).[37] These innovations in time-use data collection have provided more accurate measures of unpaid care work especially by women (for example, Bittman and Pixley 1997;

Ironmonger 1996; Floro and Miles 2003; Floro and Pichetpongsa 2010). In turn, more fine-grain time-use data have promoted their use for framing public policy and guiding social policies (Budlender 2010; Grown et al. 2010).

Development of Valuation Methods

Parallel to the progress in data collection, there have been methodological developments in the valuation of unpaid work. One method is based on the imputation of a shadow value to labor time, referred to as *input-related method*, and the second method is based on the imputation of market prices to goods and services produced by unpaid labor, referred to as *output-related method*. For the input-related method, the key question focuses on how to impute the market value of unpaid labor time. Three valuation techniques have been identified in response to this question:[38]

- The *global substitute* method, which uses the cost of a hired domestic worker who carries out various household tasks.

- The *specialized substitute* method, which applies the average wage of each "specialist," such as gardener, cook, or nanny, to each specific household task.

- The *opportunity cost* method, which applies the market wage that could be earned by the person performing unpaid work.[39]

The first two methods are also referred to as *replacement cost* method. Each method has some advantages and disadvantages. The global substitute method tends to give low estimates, given that domestic workers are at the lower end of the wage scale, thus reinforcing the tendency to assume that any type of unpaid work requires little or no skill and hence is of low productivity. On the other hand, the specialized substitute method would be more indicative of the market value of the different household tasks, assuming that such specialized markets exist. Its use raises the practical problems of disaggregating unpaid work time according to specific tasks and of obtaining a specific market wage for each.

The opportunity cost method produces a wide range of estimates, depending on the skills and earnings level of the individual involved. Hence, this method can result in rather absurd estimates; for example, a meal produced by a doctor will be imputed a higher value than an identical meal prepared by a market vendor even if the latter might be a better cook. It also reproduces any gender bias embedded in labor market operations and reflected in the gender wage gap, resulting in greater imputed value for unpaid work performed by male household members, compared to that of female household members.

In practice, the replacement cost approach, and the global substitute version, are most commonly used, given the relative ease of obtaining data on domestic workers' wages. Some researchers use two different wage rates to generate lower-bound and high-variant estimates of the value of an activity. For example, Folbre (2008) uses the average hourly wage of a childcare worker and the median wage for all workers to generate two estimates of the value of parental time devoted to childcare for two family types in the US.[40] This exercise leads Folbre to conclude that the conventional estimates of the cost of children (based solely on monetary expenditures on children by parents) overstate parental standards of living and understate the contribution parents make to the economy.

The output-related method involves estimating the value of output produced by unpaid labor, net of the input costs. This approach has the general advantage of being comparable to the accounting method used in the SNA, which uses the market prices for goods and services, rather than time-use data for its calculation. For practical reasons, however, the input methods are more commonly used especially in developing countries, since the labor time spent doing unpaid work can be obtained in time-use surveys.

It is important to note that the estimated value of household production is likely to vary, depending on the method used.[41] The input and output approaches tend to produce different valuation estimates especially in a labor-intensive chore such as childcare (Bittman et al. 2004).[42] Not surprisingly, estimates of aggregate household production using replacement cost approach tend to be lower compared to the opportunity cost valuation method, as shown in Table 5.2. The replacement cost estimates ranged from 53.3 percent in Turkey to 11 percent in Norway, while the opportunity cost estimates varied between 83 percent and 30 percent of GDP for these countries.

In recent years, more nuanced methods of valuing household production and unpaid work have been adopted, such as combining or simply juxtaposing replacement and opportunity cost measures. They put emphasis on what is termed "quality-adjusted" replacement cost as a method of input valuation (Abraham and Mackie 2005). Accordingly, time-use survey data are linked with other survey information to factor in the level of household technology that might be in use in particular households. Overall, the establishment of guidelines by international organizations such as the United Nations Statistics Division, and the accumulation of experience in measuring and valuing unpaid work have laid a foundation from which to proceed in accounting for women's unpaid work and their contributions.[43]

Development of Satellite Accounts on Household Production

An important outcome of the efforts to measure household production is the development of supplementary accounts that would permit the generation

Table 5.2 Estimates of household production for 2008, selected countries

	REPLACEMENT COST APPROACH		OPPORTUNITY COST APPROACH	
	USD PER CAPITA[A]	% OF GDP	USD PER CAPITA[A]	% OF GDP
Australia	9,682	24.73	26,144	53.54
Austria	8,708	21.85	23,833	49.08
Belgium	8,577	23.26	22,928	50.44
Canada	8,882	22.84	22,902	47.95
Denmark	8,731	22.11	23,839	49.43
Estonia	8,999	41.59	21,861	71.35
Finland	8,425	22.29	22,741	49.20
France	8,119	23.72	21,666	51.16
Germany	9,488	25.53	24,726	52.99
Hungary	8,384	40.50	19,524	67.13
Ireland	8,142	19.09	23,248	45.78
Italy	9,429	28.34	24,255	56.81
Japan	6,546	19.31	19,310	47.74
Korea	6,031	22.44	15,605	47.42
Mexico	7,576	49.55	18,064	79.00
Netherlands	9,397	21.91	24,875	47.58
New Zealand	9,182	31.58	23,008	60.14
Norway	6,690	11.04	20,206	30.02
Poland	8,484	46.97	20,340	76.62
Portugal	9,668	38.73	22,854	65.99
Slovenia	9,808	33.54	24,058	61.61
Spain	8,478	25.56	22,594	54.25
Sweden	9,024	22.86	23,936	49.35
Turkey	7,971	53.27	18,934	82.56
United Kingdom	8,861	24.07	23,028	50.41
United States	8,497	18.12	22,720	41.01

Notes: [A] The USD per capita values are expressed in purchasing power parity adjusted terms. The estimates are obtained by taking the difference between GDP per capita and extended GDP (=GDP + Household Production) per capita estimates in Ahmad and Koh (2011), Table 10.

Source: Ahmad and Koh (2011), Tables 9 and 10 (pp. 30 and 31).

of "extended" estimates of GNP (UN 1989). In a pioneering effort to provide a comprehensive picture of economic activity in the late 1980s, Statistics Norway created a satellite account and estimated the value of unpaid household work using national time-use surveys. This value amounted to almost 40 percent of GDP (Aslaksen and Koren 1996: 67). Another example is the development of satellite accounts for household production in Australia. Duncan Ironmonger (1996) provided estimates of the economic value added by the unpaid work and own capital of households, which he termed "Gross Household Product." He showed that the unpaid labor inputs (in hours, whether used in a main or secondary work activity) in Australian households are approximately the same magnitude as the labor inputs provided in the market (estimated on the basis of SNA data). The satellite accounts of household production now accompany official national accounts for several countries, as shown in Table 5.3.

Table 5.3 Selected countries with satellite household production accounts to SNA

COUNTRY	YEAR	METHOD USED	ESTIMATED VALUE OF HOUSEHOLD PRODUCTION (BILLIONS)	CURRENCY	% OF GDP*
Finland	2001	Input method	62.80	€	33.10
Germany	2001	Input method	820.00	€	29.40
Finland	2001	Wage concept	57.27	€	31.00
Germany	2001	Wage concept	1008.00	€	34.00
Australia	2000	Opportunity cost approach	471.00	2002 AUS$	43.80
Canada	1998	Replacement cost approach	297.30	CAN$	33.00
United Kingdom	2000	Output method	877.30	£	37.40
Colombia	2012–13	Specialized substitute wage method	135.87	Colombian Peso	20.40

Notes: * All percentages are calculated using extended GDP (GDP + SNA household production + non-SNA household production), except for Canada.

Sources: Ahmad and Koh (2011); Departamento Administrativo Nacional de Estadistica (DANE) (2014).

What Difference Does Accounting Make?

Monitoring the Gendered Trends and Patterns of Unpaid Work

As the number of countries that have implemented time-use surveys has increased the availability of statistics on the amount of time women spend in unpaid work and the unequal distribution of the work burden between women and men has expanded. The estimates as shown in Table 5.2 indicate that the economic value of unpaid work can be large. However, as Table 5.4 illustrates, the daily unpaid work hours of women varies widely across countries, ranging from an average of three hours (Benin and South Africa) to over six hours per person per day (Turkey and Italy). Men, on the other hand, spend an average of less than half an hour per day on unpaid work in some countries, including Madagascar, Cambodia, Pakistan, and Republic of Korea, while they spend a little over three hours per day in Bulgaria, Estonia, France, Poland, Slovenia, and Sweden.

A significant proportion of women's work involves the performance of unpaid care and household work. Strikingly, Figure 5.1 shows that women perform anywhere from 59 percent (in Sweden) to 89 percent (in India) of the total time devoted to these activities. Figure 5.2, reproduced from the 2012 *World Development Report*, reveals that women do most of the housework and care work, even when they perform most of the market work hours done by the couple (World Bank 2011).[47] In Ghana for instance, wives tend to do more than 80 percent of housework even when they earn all of the household income. And in France, women provide half of care work time even if they are the sole earner in the family.

It must be noted however that the unpaid work data used in Table 5.4 and Figures 5.1 and 5.2 are based on time-use surveys that have different sampling designs and data collection methods.[45] Recognizing the need for caution in making comparisons, these estimates nonetheless provide a valuable glimpse of the general pattern of unpaid labor contributed by women and men across countries.

The level of unpaid domestic and care work and the gender division of labor are not static. They change in response to labor market conditions, number and age of household members, policy reforms, and a host of other demographic and social factors such as urbanization, migration, and divorce rates. Changes in technology, earnings, and access to social services can cause households and individuals to shift time between activities. Studies in high-income countries have shown that while large differences persist in men's and women's time in paid and unpaid work, these converged between the 1960s and 1990s (World Bank 2011).[46] The change is primarily due to the reduction in mothers' unpaid work and an increase in the case of fathers' as mothers' labor force participation has continued to rise.

Table 5.4 Time women and men spent in unpaid work (in hours and minutes per day)

REGION	COUNTRY	YEAR OF SURVEY	WOMEN'S MEAN TIME	MEN'S MEAN TIME	MEAN DIFFERENCE (W-M)
Africa	Benin (urban)	1998	3:15	1:00	2:15
	Benin (rural)	1998	3:15	1:05	2:10
	Madagascar (urban)	2001	3:45	0:55	2:50
	Madagascar (rural)	2001	3:30	0:40	2:50
	Mauritius	2003	4:37	1:13	3:24
	South Africa	200	3:36	1:23	2:13
	United Republic of Tanzania	2006	4:13	1:15	2:58
Asia	Armenia	2004	5:46	1:06	4:40
	Cambodia	2004	3:54	0:56	2:58
	China	2008	3:54	1:31	2:23
	Iraq	2007	5:47	1:00	4:47
	Kyrgyzstan	2005	5:42	2:19	3:23
	Lao People's Democratic Republic	2002/03	2:30	0:36	1:54
	Mongolia	2000	4:36	2:10	2:26
	Occupied Palestinian Territory	1999/2000	5:01	1:16	3:45
	Oman	1999/2000	4:56	1:46	3:10
	Pakistan	2007	4:47	0:28	4:19
	Republic of Korea	2004	3:31	0:44	2:47
	Turkey	2006	6:11	1:28	4:43
More developed countries	Australia	2006	5:13	2:52	2:21
	Belgium	2005	4:38	2:57	1:41
	Bulgaria	2001/02	5:29	3:06	2:23

continued . . .

Table 5.4 Continued

REGION	COUNTRY	YEAR OF SURVEY	WOMEN'S MEAN TIME	MEN'S MEAN TIME	MEAN DIFFER-ENCE (W-M)
	Canada	2005	4:12	2:42	1:30
	Denmark	2001	3:30	2:26	1:04
	Estonia	1999/2000	5:29	3:11	2:18
	Finland	1999/2000	4:34	2:51	1:43
	France	1998/99	4:54	2:45	2:09
	Germany	2001/02	5:01	3:07	1:54
	Hungary	2000	4:57	2:39	2:18
	Ireland*	2005	5:07	1:42	3:25
	Italy	2002/03	6:06	2:06	4:00
	Japan	2006	4:18	1:08	3:10
	Latvia	2003	4:39	2:24	2:15
	Lithuania	2003	5:08	2:46	2:22
	Netherlands	2005	4:01	2:06	1:55
	New Zealand	1999	4:46	2:46	2:00
	Norway	2000/01	4:19	2:53	1:26
	Poland	2003/04	5:38	3:08	2:30
	Portugal	1999	5:02	1:17	3:45
	Romania	2000	5:12	2:42	2:30
	Slovenia	2000/01	5:26	3:10	2:16
	Spain	2002/03	5:32	2:00	3:32
	Sweden	2000/01	4:21	3:07	1:14
	The former Yugoslav Republic of Macedonia	2004	5:42	1:57	3:45
	United Kingdom	2000/01	5:06	2:55	2:11
	United States of America	2006	4:19	2:40	1:39

Note: * Data refer to weekly average. Paid work refers to employment and study.

Source: UN Department of Economic and Social Affairs (2010), Table 4c, p. 211.

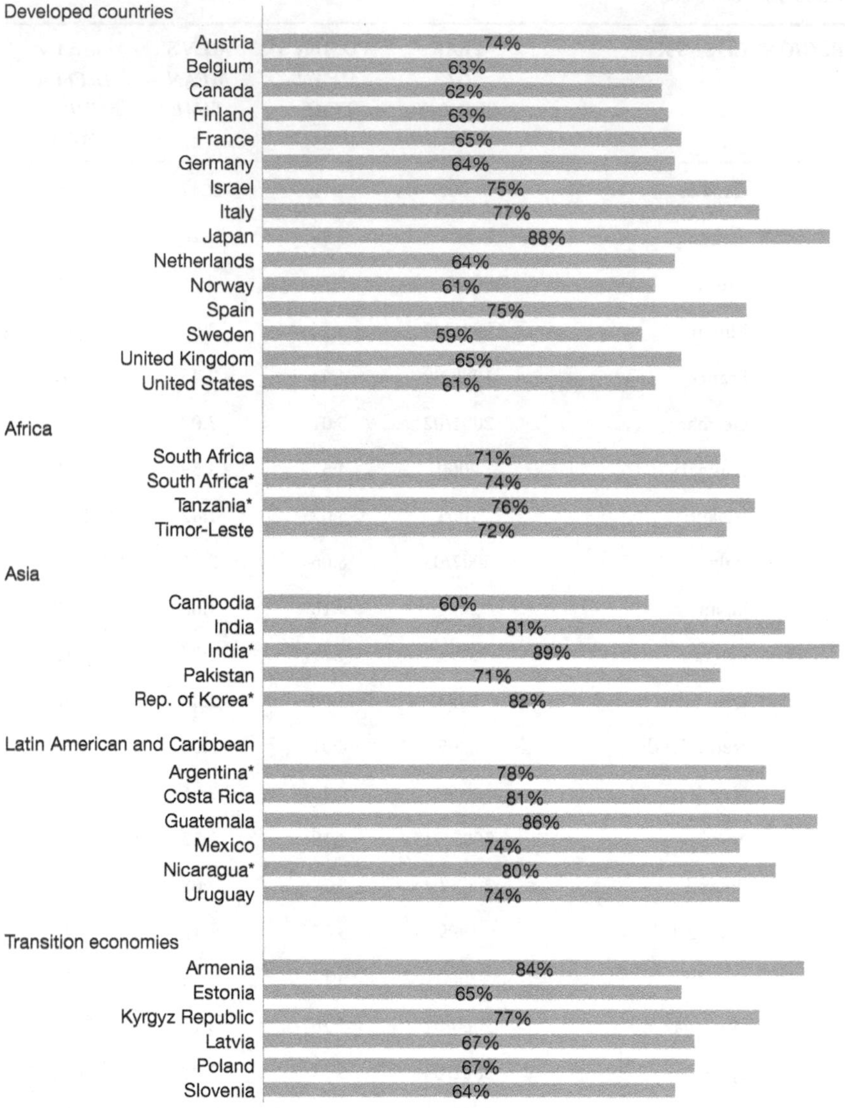

Developed countries

Country	Percentage
Austria	74%
Belgium	63%
Canada	62%
Finland	63%
France	65%
Germany	64%
Israel	75%
Italy	77%
Japan	88%
Netherlands	64%
Norway	61%
Spain	75%
Sweden	59%
United Kingdom	65%
United States	61%

Africa

Country	Percentage
South Africa	71%
South Africa*	74%
Tanzania*	76%
Timor-Leste	72%

Asia

Country	Percentage
Cambodia	60%
India	81%
India*	89%
Pakistan	71%
Rep. of Korea*	82%

Latin American and Caribbean

Country	Percentage
Argentina*	78%
Costa Rica	81%
Guatemala	86%
Mexico	74%
Nicaragua*	80%
Uruguay	74%

Transition economies

Country	Percentage
Armenia	84%
Estonia	65%
Kyrgyz Republic	77%
Latvia	67%
Poland	67%
Slovenia	64%

Figure 5.1 Percentage of unpaid care and household work performed by women, by country and region

Sources: World Bank (2011), Figure 5.9, p. 219; Budlender (2007)

Note: * From Budlender (2007), Figure 4, p. 14.

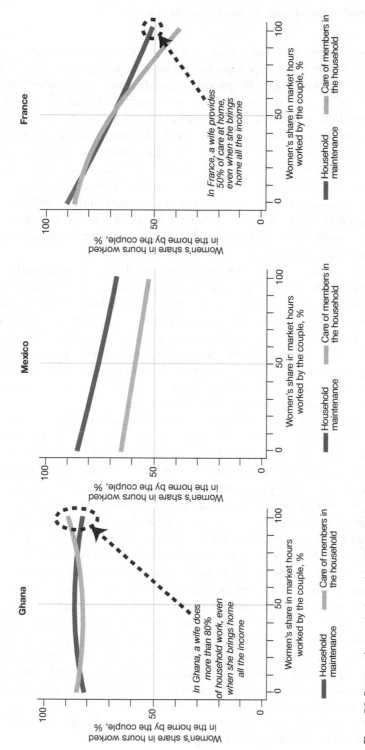

Figure 5.2 Patterns of women's share of total household work, by women's share of total market work (at household level), selected countries.

Source: World Bank: 2012 World Development Report: Gender Equality and Development. 2011, Figure 5.10. under CC BY 3.0 IGO license.
http://siteresources.worldbank.org/INTWDR2012/Resources/7778105-1299699968583/7786210-1315936222006/Complete-Report.pdf

However, these trends can easily reverse. For example, convergence in Australia seems to have stopped and taken a reversal between 1997 and 2006 in the context of increasing labor market deregulation and the spread of "long-hours culture," beyond the 40-hour work week norm (Craig et al. 2010). As a result, the 2006 division of unpaid work in households with children was not substantially different from that in 1992. The return to greater gender disparity in paid and unpaid work took place during the government's adoption of neoliberal and socially conservative policies. Berik and Kongar (2013) show a similar reversal after a small narrowing of the unpaid work gap between mothers and fathers during the US recession of 2007–09.[47] These examples show the strong influence of social policies and macro-economic conditions on the gender distribution of time being spent in housework and care work.

It should be pointed out that the convergence trend (or its reversal) has been identified on the basis of primary activities, without taking into consideration the extent to which secondary work activities (or multiple tasks) are performed simultaneously. As noted earlier, women accommodate the increase in labor market participation by reducing leisure time and by performing overlapping work activities. The work intensification resulting from overlapping activities could require a revision of the convergence thesis; the gender gap in unpaid work time might not have declined if women had increased their multi-tasking in household chores and care work more than men.

Cross-country studies have found a strong relationship between types of welfare regimes and the total workload of spouses and the distribution of housework between them (Fuwa 2004; Goodin et al. 2008; Gálvez-Muñoz et al. 2011; Kan et al. 2011). The comparison of total work time of women and men across 15 European countries by Gálvez-Muñoz et al. (2011) for example, reveals that those with considerably high state provisioning in social services and benefits such as Sweden and Norway show gender parity or near gender parity. This outcome contrasts with the longer work time (at least one hour per day) experienced by women in Southern and Eastern European countries such as Lithuania, Slovenia, Estonia, Hungary, Italy, and Spain, which have relatively low social expenditures per capita and weaker family policies. These findings are consistent with those based on the longitudinal Multinational Time Use Study (MTUS) data for 1961–2004 (Kan et al. 2011; Fisher and Gershuny 2013). Figure 5.3 shows that women's proportion of total unpaid work has reached much lower levels over time in countries with extensive welfare policies, extended parental leaves, and subsidized childcare, such as the Nordic countries, compared to those with weaker welfare regimes as in Southern Europe. The variation in the rates of decline in women's share of domestic work across the different policy regimes is indicative of the effect of social and other public policies on gender equality.

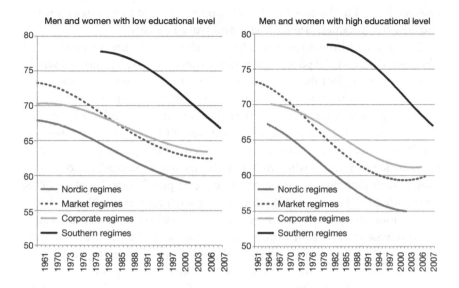

Figure 5.3 Trends in women's share of total unpaid work (%), 1961–2007, by type of welfare regime

Source: Gershuny and Fisher (2013), Figure 3.

Note: Total unpaid work time of women and men, both aged 40, in couple households with children.

Enhancing Our Understanding of Poverty, Inequality, and Well-being

Time Poverty and Work Intensity

The Accounting Project, along with the early work of scholars like Claire Vickery on time poverty and the development of the capabilities approach, has brought attention to less recognized forms of deprivation such as the intensification of working time and lack of time to develop a person's capabilities. According to the capabilities approach, any inquiry into people's well-being must involve asking not only how much people earn but also how they use their time in order to acquire the goods and services to meet their livelihoods. Time poverty is a serious constraint on individual well-being as it prevents having adequate rest and sleep, enjoying leisure, and/or taking part in community/social life. The amount of unpaid work performed particularly by women—as shown in Table 5.4—in addition to paid work that many do, can lead to stress and overwork. In recent decades, a growing body of social science research has shown that chronic and severe time pressures put on balancing family and work life have serious implications for the worker's health and other functionings (Hyder et al. 2005). This research has led to the construction of two time-related measures of poverty and well-being namely, time poverty and work intensity.

The notion of time poverty was first developed by Claire Vickery (1977) who argued that official poverty measures do not correctly measure household needs for they neglect the importance of labor time necessary to meet them. She introduced the concept of "time poverty" and developed a method for identifying households whose combined money income and available time are deemed insufficient to provide a standard of living above the poverty line.[48] More recently, researchers constructed a time-poverty threshold in order to identify those who work long hours out of necessity, not out of choice, such that they are deemed to be "time poor" (Goodin et al. 2008; Burchardt 2008; Bardasi and Wodon 2010; Zacharias et al. 2012). According to a 12-hour time poverty threshold, Gammage (2010) estimates that in 2000 in Guatemala an average of 33 percent of women and 14 percent of men were time poor. When examined by income quintile, women experienced between two and three times more time poverty than men across quintiles.

Studies have shown that persons who are time poor are likely to cope by multi-tasking, that is performing secondary work activities in conjunction with another (primary) work activity such as child-minding and cooking, or childcare and market work (Roldan 1985; Baruch et al. 1987; Benton 1989; Floro and Miles 2003; Floro and Pichetpongsa 2010). The multiplicity of roles that women perform, as income earners, principal housework and care providers has led to the construction of a "work intensity" measure.[49] Work intensity refers to the length of an average (paid and unpaid) working day and the incidence of "likely to be stressful" overlapping work activities. Consonant with the concept of poverty as capability deprivation, work intensity measures the time spent in doing two or more tasks at the same time or through frequent switching within a given slot. The longer the time an individual performs two or more simultaneous tasks, the greater is the amount of stress generated from the work process, especially when the activities at hand require continued concentration or energy. While time poverty is usually measured on the basis of time use on primary activities, if data on secondary activities are also compiled the time poverty rate of women increases more than men's rate because women are the ones who typically engage in overlapping tasks. For example, Diksha Arora's research in northern Mozambique shows that when time spent on simultaneous care work while enjoying leisure is accounted for, daily work hours of women go up from 11.70 hours to 12.42 hours while men's total work day is virtually unchanged (increases from 6.42 to 6.46 hours) (Arora 2014). This gender gap reflects women's experience of carrying out care work during their leisure time and not reporting care as work, unless asked about simultaneous activities.

Paid and Unpaid Work: The Continuing Debate

As an increasing number of countries implement time-use surveys, time-use data can be used to examine new research questions that emerged or became prominent in the new millennium for the design of policies to support care provision or alleviate workloads. In particular, it is important to keep track of what is happening to unpaid work, along with paid work hours, as a result of a number of developments that suggest care needs are growing.

The major developments that signal growth of care needs have to do with women's increasing labor force participation since the 1980s in a context of aging populations and rising healthcare needs and inadequate or declining government provisioning of social services. These trends have in fact developed into the so-called "care crisis" affecting high-income countries but also beginning to be felt in some developing countries. As a result, the debate on the importance of unpaid work to policymaking continues.

First, in most countries the increased participation of women in the labor market has brought to the forefront of social and employment policy debates the tensions around the distribution of family work. Women have increasingly been taking on the dual responsibilities of income earners and caregivers. Moreover, urbanization, migration, and the nuclearization of households, especially in urban areas, have undermined the traditional caregiving support provided by kinship networks so that families are further stressed to find their own solutions to meet their care needs. Thus, attempts to meet the demands of both paid and unpaid work have been shown to lead to long hours of work and stress, especially for low-income workers, as shown in the study among home-based workers in Thailand (Floro and Pichetpongsa 2010).

Second, the demographic changes witnessed over the last few decades in many countries, such as lower fertility rates, longer life expectancy, and urbanization have intensified the need for care of the elderly. In many countries, fertility rates have reached levels below replacement, such as in Spain, Italy, Japan, and South Korea (Benería 2009; Floro 2012). In developing countries, major health concerns such as HIV/AIDS, dengue, and malaria have contributed to the increased time spent on caregiving. Hence, the crisis of care is already being felt in many countries, intensified by the fact that, as Mary Daly (2001: 6) has argued, "care work tends to be squeezed to the margins of many people's lives."

In turn, the rise in unpaid caregiving hours can adversely affect labor force participation and earnings (Lilly et al. 2007; Friedemann-Sánchez and Griffin 2011). Market liberalization policies reinforce the notion that workers and their families should find their own solutions to deal with family and care responsibilities, albeit these solutions are conditioned by social class. Historically and in the present, hiring domestic workers, typically women, is a common solution for middle-income and upper-class families in both developing and high-income countries—Spain, South Africa, Kenya and the Philippines (ILO 2007; Carrasco and Domínguez 2011). This is not an option for many low-income workers, who have to find a way to combine employment and unpaid care work. The study by Vo et al. (2007) among working parents in Vietnam found that 63 percent of one or both parents (the majority of whom are mothers) lost income or promotions or had difficulty retaining jobs due to their caregiving responsibilities.

Studies show that household and care responsibilities are one of the reasons why women often turn to informal employment. For example, 40 percent of mothers in the slums of Guatemala City cited lack of childcare as a key reason for not taking formal economy jobs where children could not accompany them (Quisumbing et al. 2003). Survey evidence also shows that many women in Costa Rica have opted to take on informal employment that involves low wages and no benefits because of the need for flexible work hours (Ramírez and Rosés 2005). Time-use data are needed to document the amount and gender distribution of the changing workload in households as they face increasing care needs or cope by taking on informal jobs.

Third, the general deterioration of labor market conditions worldwide, brought about by the interplay of technological change, firm restructuring, and neoliberal policies, amplifies the need to monitor the level and distribution of unpaid work. Those who are unemployed, underemployed, and face unstable and low incomes in labor markets are likely to develop coping mechanisms that involve greater reliance on unpaid work for meeting their needs. These private solutions may involve an increase in unpaid domestic and care work, volunteer work, and subsistence work and unpaid family labor on farms and enterprises in an effort to substitute for market purchases that are no longer affordable. Under the current conventions these changes in time use are not captured in labor force statistics, but can be captured in time-use surveys. The pressures to substitute home-produced goods and services using unpaid labor are particularly acute in countries with weak or non-existent unemployment compensation and social protection schemes. The increase in unpaid work however is not necessarily shouldered equally among household members; gender norms tend to put much of the additional work burden on female members (Berik and Kongar 2013; Benería and Martinez-Iglesias 2014).

Related to these trends, market reforms associated with contemporary globalization have resulted in shrinking resources for social services, and inadequate government provisioning can increase the unpaid labor in housework and volunteer work. To be sure, until the 2008 crisis the majority of the OECD countries had made important strides in extending paid parental leave and expanding public and subsidized childcare (Benería and Martinez-Iglesias 2010; 2014). While there are a variety of social policies in OECD countries, which affect affordability and access to care, the level of publicly financed care is inadequate in most countries (Gornick and Meyers 2003; Floro and Meurs 2009; İlkkaracan 2013a).

Post-Soviet countries had achieved high rates of preschool participation (ages 3–6) in the 1980s, ranging from around 70 percent or more in the European areas to about 20–50 percent in Central Asia and the Caucasus. But these rates have fallen in Central Asia and the Caucasus since 1990, as state subsidies, household incomes, and access to education have decreased (UNICEF 2008; Giddings et al. 2007). The trend towards the shrinking of social welfare schemes, in high-income and post-Soviet countries alike, has made it increasingly difficult for women and men to balance the time demands of their jobs and family life. In China, for example, recent reforms that reduced public care services have increased the time women devoted to caring for elder kin, particularly parents-in-law, resulting in their reduced participation in paid labor and earnings (Liu et al. 2010).

In developing countries, government support for care provisioning remains limited or declining. In some developing countries there are efforts to address childcare needs by providing child support grants to all low-income people (in South Africa) and developing childcare policies and establishing publicly provided or subsidized daycare (in Colombia, Mexico, Argentina, and Brazil) (Niño-Zarazúa et al. 2012; Patel 2012).[50] An evaluation of the effects of these policies in terms of the changes in workload, its distribution in the household, and the effects on time poverty requires systematic statistical information on unpaid work. In Colombia, a 2012 national law mandates the government to collect time-use data and to monitor trends in unpaid work (Rey de Marulanda 2012; López-Montaño 2013). This has led to the collection of the country's first national time-use survey data in 2012 and the production of Colombia's satellite accounts of household production in 2014 (DANE 2013; 2014).

On the policy front, time-use data also can help address the unintended adverse effects of policies and program initiatives on the total workloads of women. Research on conditional cash transfer schemes (CCTSs), a millennial strategy for poverty reduction, suggests that participation in the program can increase the unpaid workload of women in beneficiary households in addition to taking time away from paid work (Molyneux and Thomson 2011; Escobar and González de la Rocha 2008). In Guatemala, using time-use data Gammage (2010) shows that women's time poverty can intensify as they substitute for their children's labor when the children maintain regular school attendance as a condition of the cash transfer. In households that are already time and income poor the additional unpaid work burden may reduce well-being. Time-use data can help monitor the impact of these cash transfers and help design programs to adjust for time poverty (by increasing the cash transfer and reducing the implicit costs).

In sum, the Accounting Project has helped push the development and social policy agenda forward to address the critical issue of care by bringing visibility and recognition to the significant amount of unpaid work that is performed by women. And time-use data can help make the case for and design care policies that promote work–family balance and gender equitable distribution of workloads.

Conclusion

This chapter has evaluated the Accounting Project, which has sought to make unpaid work visible. Since the 1980s the Project has addressed the conceptual underpinnings of the statistical biases that led to the under-estimation of women's contributions. It has also promoted the development of methodologies to make unpaid work visible, and an increasing number of governments, statistical agencies, and researchers throughout the world have taken up the Project and have included the collection of time-use data in their agendas. The Accounting Project also illuminates the connections between paid and unpaid work and how gender inequalities are replicated in the allocation of the unpaid workload and the distribution of care. In turn, the unequal sharing of unpaid workload between men and women has a profound impact on their access to decent paid work, mediated by class, ethnic, and racial divisions among women: affluent households can purchase market substitutes such as cooked meals and laundry service or employ other women for household chores and care work, while those in poorer households have to produce these goods and services at home and without paid help. Finally, the Accounting Project also helps make the case for the design and implementation of policies that seek to balance family life with paid work, to achieve gender-equitable distribution of unpaid work, and to promote shared responsibility of care provision among families, governments, and employers.

At a more general level, the Accounting Project can be characterized as transformative in Elizabeth Minnich's terms, since it calls for "transforming knowledge" or moving beyond the boundaries of conventional paradigms. This includes the rethinking of "mystified concepts" or "ideas, notions, categories, and the like that are so deeply familiar they are rarely questioned" and which result in "partial knowledge" (Minnich 1990). Although the information regarding unpaid work has sometimes been used in conservative agendas so as to emphasize the importance of having women stay at home, these instances do not detract from its significant impact. The Project has led us to question the ways in which we measure well-being and to understand who contributes to life sustenance in our communities and in society as a whole. Further, it leads us to question the assumptions behind received knowledge, in this case those that identify "work" with paid labor and market-oriented work. By deepening our understanding of unpaid work, particularly the centrality of care in our daily lives and its economic/financial and time dimensions, the Project underscores women's fundamental contribution to life's sustenance and reproduction as well as an important dimension of gender inequality: namely, the unequal division of household labor.

Notes

1 A rare exception is John Stuart Mill, a classical economist who made some reference to domestic labor in his discussion of productive consumption and the potential advantages of women's employment in his *Principles of Political Economy* (John Stuart Mill 1848 [1965]) and *The Subjection of Women* (John Stuart Mill 1869 [1970]).

2 By the heterodox tradition we refer to Marxian, institutionalist, and Keynesian perspectives, albeit institutionalist economists use a broader focus on provisioning activities and have been attentive to gender norms. We consider feminist economics to be a part of heterodox economics at this point in time, although it has emerged after the earlier heterodox perspectives.

3 Preface to *The Origin of the Family, Private Property and the State* ([1884] 1981).

4 As typified by the expression "my mother does not work" even if she may work very hard in domestic, unpaid activities. An exception is the New Household Economics discussed in Chapter 2.

5 First adopted in 1953 as an official accounting system of the United Nations member-states, the SNA defines what is considered market production of goods and services. The SNA has since undergone several revisions. The last major set of revisions was done in 1993. Pressures from women's organizations, feminist scholars, and some women parliamentarians led to substantive changes in the SNA during the 27th Session of the United Nations Statistical Commission, such as the inclusion of subsistence production and the gathering of fuel and water activities in a harmonized and systematic way. The 1993 revision of the system was coordinated by the Inter-Secretariat Working Group on National Accounts (ISWGNA), which comprised the United Nations Statistics Division (UNSD), the International Monetary Fund (IMF), the World Bank (WB), the Organization for Economic Cooperation and Development (OECD), the Statistical Office of the European Communities (Eurostat), and the United Nations regional commissions.

6   Using a "main purpose" test, it identifies five categories of work:

> a) *own-use production work* comprising production of goods and services for own final use; b) *unpaid trainee work* comprising work performed for others without pay to acquire workplace experience or skills; c) *volunteer work* comprising non-compulsory work performed for others without pay; d) *employment work* comprising work performed for others in exchange for pay or profit; and e) *other work activities* such as unpaid community service and unpaid work by prisoners, as well as unpaid military or alternative civilian service. (ILO 2013d: 3)

7   When women work in small enterprises, especially based at home, or as unpaid family workers, their labor tends to be underestimated in labor force statistics, even though it is supposed to be counted. This is also the case for contractual, temporary, and very short-term jobs performed by both women and men. Labor in subsistence production (tending to animals or work on a garden plot to grow food for the household), is also underestimated in labor force statistics, even though their output is considered part of the system of national accounts.

8   The SNA makes a clear distinction between SNA production activities and non-SNA production activities. Accordingly, the work performed is referred to as SNA work and non-SNA work, respectively. The former includes paid market work in formal and informal enterprises, work in subsistence production, and unpaid work in family farms and enterprises. Non-SNA work, on the other hand, refers to productive work outside the SNA production boundary such as unpaid household chores related to its upkeep and management, care of family dependents, and voluntary services (United Nations Statistical Commission 1993).

9   Turkey's low rate for women partly reflects the dramatic decline of family farming and women's unpaid family work in the new millennium.

10   UN Statistical Commission (1983). For a more detailed account, see Benería (1981).

11   By 1960, a working group of African statisticians recommended the estimation and incorporation of rural household activities such as the backyard vegetable cultivation as part of subsistence production in agriculture, forestry, and fishing (Waring 1988).

12   Unpaid family workers, also known as contributing family workers, are those who work in a market-oriented establishment or farm operated by a related person living in the same household who is designated as self-employed or own-account worker (downloaded from http://www.ilo.org/trends, accessed on March 10, 2013).

13   Household production of goods for own use that are included in the System of National Accounts includes: agricultural products; collection of firewood; hunting and fishing; other primary products, e.g. the supply of water; processing of agricultural products, e.g. grain threshing, milling of flour, the preservation of meat and fish products; the production of beer, wine or spirits; the production

of baskets and mats; weaving cloth, dressmaking and tailoring, production of footwear, pottery, furniture etc. It also includes the production of goods for own capital formation such as machines, equipment, construction of roads, dams, etc. Household production of services for own final use only includes paid domestic services and production of housing services for own final consumption by owner-occupants, e.g. imputed rent (ILO 1993).

14   Recognizing the practical difficulties associated in collecting such information, several UN agencies in the early 1990s developed a series of conceptual and methodological guidelines for the measurement of women's work in the informal sector including unpaid family work. These agencies have carried out useful pilot studies, such as in Burkina Faso, Congo, the Gambia, and Zambia (UN Statistical Office/ECA/INSTRAW 1991a; 1991b; INSTRAW 1991). These efforts have resulted in the refinement of labor force definitions to include unpaid family workers, and in the incorporation of their contribution to output as a component of income in the SNA and in GDP estimations (Charmes 1998; 2004).

15   For further detail, see Benería (1981).

16   See United Nations Statistical Commission 2004 for more discussion of the treatment of the informal sector in the 1993 SNA.

17   Ester Boserup (1970) argued strongly for the inclusion in national accounts "of food items obtained by collecting and hunting, of output of home crafts such as clothing, footwear, sleeping and sitting mats, baskets, clay pots, calabashes, fuel collected by women, funeral services, haircuts, entertainment and traditional administrative and medical services," together with "pounding, husking and grinding of foodstuffs and the slaughtering of animals" (pp. 162–63). However, she considered these activities mostly as subsistence production, i.e. as "marketable goods," not as household work. Although Boserup mentioned the omission of "domestic services of housewives" from national accounts, she was less concerned about it than in the case of subsistence production. Moreover, she failed to acknowledge the exclusion of an important household activity, that of caring for children, the sick, disabled, and elderly.

18   Regular surveys of volunteering are currently conducted by the statistical offices of Australia, Canada, the UK, Switzerland, Norway, and the United States.

19   For instance, a comparison of different survey results shows that participation in volunteer work in the United Kingdom varies wildly from 48 percent of the population in 1997, to 2 percent in 2009, and then back to 29 percent in 2010 (Salamon et al. 2011).

20   Unpaid (non-market) work includes both unpaid care work and unpaid family work on farms or enterprises.

21   Time-use surveys were also carried out in other developed countries later on but they addressed issues not necessarily related to feminist goals, such as commuting to work, use of mass media, and leisure time (Hirway 2010: 3). In the developing countries, the earliest time-use surveys were conducted by research scholars in Gambia (1952), Burkina Faso (1967), and Peru (1966) to name a few.

22 Others, such as Nordhaus (2006), advise against adding major non-market activities into the main National Income and Product Accounts and argue in favor of developing satellite non-market and environmental accounts first.

23 Based on Lourdes Benería's conversations with Barbara Bergmann on the topic, March 14, 1998. Bergmann has been a staunch, vocal advocate of labor market solutions to gender inequality.

24 "[B]y insisting that domestic activities gain recognition by conforming to an unchallenged category of work, the significance of caring and self-fulfilling activities remains unrecognized" (p. 14).

25 These claims are supported by time-use data. See, for example, Bittman (1999); Bianchi et al. (2000); Sayer (2005); Gershuny and Sullivan (2003); Gershuny and Fisher (2013).

26 Defined in this way, there is no reason to exclude from care relationships those situations in which the caregiver receives a payment or monetary reward. This newer concept of care departs from the Beijing Platform for Action framework and is defined "more specifically, [as] focusing on the labour process rather than the relationship to the site of production (home vs. market) or the production boundary (in the SNA or not)" (Folbre 2006: 186). This new conceptualization moves beyond unpaid work to include care work performed in the paid economy—the work of teachers, nurses, doctors, paid domestic workers, etc.

27 One could argue that the competitive pressures of the market spill over to the household and increase the efficiency of each hour of housework, at least for individuals who engage in both unpaid household work and paid work.

28 The third party (or third person) principle has been criticized for assuming the market as the yardstick of economic activity (Wood 1997), even though it could include a domestic activity performed by a third person outside of market exchange, for example, through non-monetary labor exchange.

29 See http://www.timeuse.org/mtus/access for list of time-use survey data available for research.

30 The main categories are: (a) work activities such as labor market work, housework, childcare, shopping, and volunteer work; (b) leisure time, including socializing, active and passive leisure; and (c) other non-productive activities, including sleep, personal hygiene, and education.

31 Even when the time-use survey specifies higher benchmark paid work hours to capture stable workers with a certain work status, the estimates for urban women are higher than the NSSO survey-based estimated (at 22.7 percent for those who work for at least four hours per week and 18.8 percent for those who work at least eight hours per week). Without context questions, however, the time-use survey cannot distinguish between participation in informal and subsistence activities.

32 For example, Spain carried out two national surveys (2002–03 and 2009–10) and Turkey only one (in 2006).

33 See the UN Trial International Classification of Activities for Time-use Statistics (ICATUS) website: http://unstats.un.org/unsd/cr/registry/regcst.asp?Cl=231&Lg=1. Subsequently, John Gershuny and Kimberly Fisher of Oxford University Center

for Time Use Research (CTUR), in collaboration with other time-use scholars, produced a Multinational Time Use Survey (MTUS) dataset that contained harmonized activity episode and context information and that encompassed over 60 datasets from 25 countries. But the integration of other time-use surveys, especially from developing countries has stalled, given the political exigencies and methodological challenges in conducting time-use surveys.

34   Responses become even more problematic when the reference period is longer say, "in the past week."

35   Differences in activity focus as well as data collection objectives can affect the way activities are classified and the level of disaggregation. Unpaid household work can be coded as a single activity combining cooking, feeding the sick, playing with children, helping them in their schoolwork, cleaning the house, etc., or it can be disaggregated.

36   Improvements in the design of time-use surveys (TUS) have enabled the instrument to better capture the supervisory aspect of unpaid care work. These improvements range from an inclusion in the TUS of categories such as "minding children" or "passive childcare," which refer to caring for children without active involvement shown in the other care activity codes, to giving interviewers a clear set of instructions regarding secondary activities with "child-minding" as an example. These methods were adopted in the collection of national Australian TUS and in the 2002 TUS sample among Thailand urban homeworkers and provided better, estimates of childcare activities. By contrast, the 1999 South Africa TUS and the 2000 United Kingdom TUS, which lacked both these features, registered much lower levels of childcare (Folbre and Yoon 2007).

37   Mullan (2010) makes use of children's time-use information in order to calculate a measure of supervisory childcare, which includes the time when parents and children are not in the same room, but at the same location.

38   For more detail, see for example Goldschmidt-Clermont (1983; 1993); Benería (1992); Chadeau (1992); Allard et al. (2007); Craig and Bittman (2008); Fraumeni (1998).

39   A variation of the opportunity cost method is the lifetime-income approach (Fraumeni 1998).

40   Folbre's time-cost estimates of parental care for 2000 are for time spent in a two-child, two-parent family and in a two-child, single-parent family. The high-variant estimate also includes a broader accounting of parental time as well as using a higher wage rate. Combined with monetary expenditures per child, Folbre's lower-bound time costs amount to 62 percent of total expenditures per child per year in a two-parent family (and 65 percent in a single-parent family).

41   In Mullan's valuation of childcare in the UK, the input method using a broad measure of childcare time resulted in a value that ranged between 12 percent and 23 percent of GDP while the output method provided estimates that ranged between 7.8 percent and 13.8 percent (Mullan 2010).

42   The input method tends to yield a higher imputed value of childcare in two-parent households, compared to single-parent (mostly mothers) households since the

input value sums the time both parents are caring for children regardless of the number. On the other hand, the estimates of the output method are sensitive to the number of children being cared for. However, when adequate attention is given to the context and institutional aspects of the activity, the imputed value using the input method tends to approximate the imputed value of childcare using output method. This is illustrated in Mullan's study on the valuation of childcare in the United Kingdom.

43   The UN Statistical Division has constructed a guide to producing statistics on time-use: *Measuring Paid and Unpaid Work*, in 2005. Its website on time-use statistics contains methods, publications, and meeting documents as well as experiences of countries that have recently conducted time-use surveys. See: http://unstats.un.org/unsd/demographic/sconcerns/tuse/

44   There is some evidence of change in the division of household labor in some countries over time, which indicate that men's share of unpaid labor is increasing, although still lower than women's hours of unpaid work (Benería and Martinez-Iglesias 2014).

45   For example, the data used in creating Figure 5.1 is based on the Multinational Time Use Study (MTUS) that includes time-use survey data from 11 countries as well as 12 country-level surveys, which used different methodologies.

46   In the United States, the household division of labor has changed between the 1960s and 1990s as men doubled their housework hours, while women cut their housework hours almost in half (Bianchi et al. 2000). Nonetheless, women in 1995 spent nearly twice as much time on housework as men. Similarly, time-use studies in Australia show that there seems to be a narrowing of the gender gaps in time use in households with children during the 1990s as a result of women's increased labor force participation (Craig et al. 2010). This trend is consistent with that observed in other high-income countries which shows modest convergence in the work composition among men and women (Allard et al. 2007; Fisher et al. 2007; Sayer 2005; Kan et al. 2011; Fisher and Gershuny 2013).

47   In this case, the narrowing of the unpaid work gap occurred because women substituted paid work hours for unpaid work hours during the recession, while men did not pick up additional unpaid work. This recession effect came in the context of stagnant trends in both unpaid and paid work gaps after the convergence ended by the 1990s.

48   She calculated the trade-off between money and time (a threshold curve) representing a composite (time and income) poverty line, so that households are defined as poor if they have less than a certain combination of time and money.

49   Overlapping work activities involve the simultaneous performance of two or more work activities that either require attention and/or energy or that are monotonous and repetitive.

50   The evidence from these countries as well as from European countries with similar schemes suggests that the availability of these programs tends to increase the number of hours worked by women as well as leading them to work in formal employment (Folbre and Yoon 2007; Razavi and Staab 2012; World Bank 2011).

CHAPTER 6

Development as if All People Mattered

What ought to be central to the post 2015 development agenda is attention to the kind of growth generated, and its overall contributions toward well-being and sustainability for all. This requires addressing the structural conditions that make economic inequality prevalent among and within countries and social groups.

DAWN, 2013

Introduction

In this book we have presented a gender-aware analysis of contemporary globalization and we have highlighted the ways in which neoliberalism has transformed economic landscapes affecting women and men across the globe. These transformations have had contradictory effects on different groups, both exacerbating problems that emerged in the 1980s and originating new problems that represent enormous challenges for human development. We have discussed many of these challenges from a feminist perspective; in this chapter we turn to questions of policy and action.

The end of the twentieth century and the first decade of the new millennium were marked by multiple crises of capitalism. Continued adherence to neoliberal policies and the global expansion of markets have failed to bring about improvements in living and working conditions for a large majority of people across the globe. While capitalist development has generated unprecedented economic growth in some sectors, countries, and regions, inequality of income and wealth has risen in most countries and across countries. The paths to decent work and livelihoods are blocked by capital's unprecedented geographic mobility and the increasing power of owners of capital, including those in the corridors of political institutions. With few exceptions, neoliberal policies continue to be the norm for macroeconomic management. Their influence has broadened and deepened across the globe, preparing the ground for greater economic instability in livelihoods of most people. Neoliberalism has resurged in the high-income countries hit by the 2007–08 financial crisis in the form of austerity measures, and the unprecedented integration of global economies has transmitted the crisis to low-income economies through a variety of mechanisms, such as a decline in exports, foreign direct investment, and remittances.

The financial crisis of 2007–08 has brought greater attention to the basic questions about the nature of capitalism and its ability to uphold human rights, promote sustainable and people-centered development, and construct just societies. To be sure, developing countries that went through the debt crisis and structural adjustment policies of the 1980s and 1990s were pioneers in asking these fundamental questions, at least in recent history, but the latest crisis has revived them in high-income countries as well. Moreover, the rise of economic and social inequalities across the globe is contributing to social unrest and weakening social stability even in affluent regions. Indeed, inequality is a threat to democracies, which cannot exist without equitable distribution of power. The survival of democracy is seriously compromised by persistent inequalities, as Drèze and Sen (2013) point out for the case of India, where the spectacular growth of recent decades has only benefitted a relatively small proportion of its population.

While rising class inequality and greater concentration of economic and political power are consistent with the logic of capitalism, the current state of the economic system subjugates democratic institutions to the interests of capital, creates periodic crisis in the economic system, and threatens the planet's capacity to support human life. The neoliberal era has deepened existing crises (climate, financial) and resuscitated past crises (food, fuel); it also has led to a growing crisis of legitimacy of the current international economic order; and awareness of the grave consequences of environmental problems is rising amidst the persistent neoliberal preoccupation with promoting economic growth. There has also been intensification of conflict and instability everywhere since the 1990s—ranging from civil wars to invasions, which devastate large swathes of countries, uproot millions from their homes, and multiply the existing refugee crises. Capitalism's tendencies to fuel conflicts and maximize short-term profit (hence its aversion to addressing problems with long-term horizons, such as the climate crisis) puts life on the planet at risk and leaves many groups and species teetering on the edge of survival, and paradoxically, can lead to its own demise.

In this chapter we first highlight three problems that prevent movement towards achieving equitable human development, focusing on what we identify below as *plus ça change* phenomena concerning policy. One is that the more poverty reduction is acknowledged as a development objective on the international agenda, the more it is viewed as a program separate from issues of distribution and inequality and from sustainable development strategy. Similarly, the more frequent and devastating the financial crises become, the stronger the power of capital and the more entrenched the neoliberal solutions become. Finally, the more gender is mainstreamed in the development policy agendas, the more women appear to be used as "instruments" that serve the neoliberal goal of economic growth. Despite many reasons for pessimism, we also believe that this is an opportune moment for breaking these patterns, which reinforce the status quo in the global economic order and in development policy. Thus we turn our attention to what can be done. We discuss the potential intellectual alliances among feminist economists, other heterodox economists, and ecological economists that could be forged to push a new development agenda. We argue for the need to work out governance reforms at both the national and international levels in order to implement alternative policies that reduce inequality, promote well-being, and address environmental degradation and climate change. However, we believe that none of these reforms and associated policies is likely to get off the ground, unless there is mobilization of civil society and growth of social movements.

Plus ça change . . .

In this section, we problematize the continuing inability of "development as we know it" to generate people-centered development. We focus on three main issues: (a) the extent to which the international development agenda has fallen short of redefining development so as to address urgent problems in today's world; (b) the ways in which the policy responses to the 2007–08 financial crisis represent a continuation of neoliberalism, which has been unable to meet the needs of a large proportion of the population; and (c) the remaining tasks in the integration of gender in development, despite the progress that has been made in closing some gender gaps as shown by socio-economic indicators in recent decades.

The Development Agenda

For the most part, the official development agenda of the early twenty-first century has focused on three core initiatives—Millennium Development Goals (MDGs), the Doha Round, and microfinance programs—promoted through multilateral organizations and various donor agencies. Chang (2011) argues that the development concept encapsulated in these initiatives illustrates how non-developmental, even anti-developmental, economic development strategies have become in recent decades. These initiatives, prone to sly maneuvering and cooptation, have been used to complement the neoliberal policy framework. Indeed, we can argue that all three have served to avoid the needed social change and transformation. The goals inherent in these contemporary development agendas are limited to the alleviation of extreme poverty and improving the health and education levels of populations through the tools of debt cancellation, expanded foreign aid, greater trade access to rich country markets, and microcredit. But such tools only work in enabling environments and economic systems that uphold human rights and where the gains translate to improved well-being of the bottom segments of the population, women as well as men.

While MDGs represent laudable goals and have brought worldwide attention to the persistent problems of poverty and gender inequality at the onset of the third millennium, they leave many questions about economic development strategy unanswered. Chang (2011) characterizes this impoverished development agenda as a case of "*Hamlet* without the Prince of Denmark," in that the production side that will generate the resources to fund the education and health spending for the population and create an economically sustainable path to well-being, especially in low-income countries, is missing.

This development agenda is a far cry from the notion that development involves transforming production structures, so as to create higher value-added industries where upgraded skills and new technologies can be utilized, decent employment is generated, and public goods and social services are adequately provided. The idea that developing countries can and should create dynamic comparative advantage through coordinated activities has all but disappeared in the current development policy framework shaped by decades of neoliberal economic policies. Indeed, developing country exports are expected to be driven by static comparative advantage, often based on colonial-era primary product exports, and at best, a limited range of labor-intensive manufacturing exports under outsourcing arrangements.

Meanwhile, there is little concern about creation of enterprises beyond the micro ones and the generation of decent jobs for the healthier, more educated labor force; it is as if the improved labor supply will magically create its demand (Amsden 2010). In fact, the MDGs do not include any objective regarding work and the labor market, hence they are not dealing with some of today's critical problems of unemployment, underemployment, and deterioration of labor market conditions for millions of people worldwide. Another component missing from the contemporary development priorities is a redistributive agenda to be financed by means of progressive taxation.

Without redistributive schemes to address inequality, protection of labor rights, social protection, agrarian reform, and regulation of global finance, the scope for improving women's opportunities remains limited.

Beyond the "missing Prince of Denmark" problems, evaluations of the MDGs' process also show its limitations on its own terms (Nayyar 2013; UN Women 2013). There are many problems associated with the conceptualization and measurement of their progress. In an attempt to make them simple and widely acceptable, the MDGs were stipulated without taking into account the initial conditions of countries nor are there references to the distributional outcomes. There is an implicit assumption that one-size-fits-all, making it difficult to identify whether there is little or substantial progress. Targets and indicators are not fully aligned with the broader principles in the Millennium Declaration, which originated from the human development framework. For example, the gender equality goal (MDG 3) is primarily measured in terms of eliminating gender disparity in education; crucial dimensions of gender equality—such as the distribution of care work and the balance between family and labor market work, and women's empowerment—are missing from consideration.[1] Furthermore, the MDG agenda's silence on the means for attaining the stated goals has meant that "orthodox economics occupied that vacant space" with its emphasis on growth (Nayyar 2013: 375). Above all, the MDGs do not imply a new vision of development to respond to many of today's pressing problems around inequality and increasing concentration of wealth and power, the urgent environmental crisis and sustainability objectives, consumerism and waste, and the need to build democratic governance. The siloed and narrow approach to development, as reflected in the United Nations High-Level Panel report on the Post-2015 Development Agenda, was also questioned by the women's coalition, Development Alternatives for Women in a New Era (DAWN) (DAWN 2013).

The Financial Crisis of 2007–08

The policy responses to the crisis that started in 2007 provide an example of the resilience of neoliberalism and its adverse effects on livelihoods. The financial crisis and its serious consequences reflect the crisis of orthodox economics as a discipline. As Robert Wade (2011: 23) states, "the economics profession for the most part slept into the crisis." Mainstream economics has fostered market fundamentalism: it has emphasized that "governments hamper economic growth [while] . . . markets create the wealth, and therefore, . . . markets should be 'master' rather than 'means'" (ibid. p. 23).Thus, the profession shares the blame for the hardship experienced by millions of people. Seven years beyond its unfolding, the crisis continues to raise questions about the ability of capitalism in general and of neoliberalism in particular to provide decent livelihoods for all and to meet the new challenges that have emerged, such as the environmental crisis and climate change. As the crisis quickly spread from the US to Europe and the rest of the world, the predominant response in most countries was to rely on more of the same medicine: continuation of neoliberal policies. In what follows we provide a quick review of the contours of the crisis, some of its most salient consequences, and the policy responses.

The main causes of the 2007–08 financial crisis were deregulation of financial markets and extensive indebtedness in the US.[2] As regulations were removed in the 1990s, banks in the US took on excessive debt and they sought to circumvent regulations by creating risky financial assets. The increasing fragility of the financial sector was accompanied by rapid increase in wealth and income inequality, as the enormous increase in productivity generated by technological innovations in the decade preceding the crisis accrued to asset owners while wages remained flat. Rising inequality, in turn, fueled household debt of wide segments of the population who attempted to keep up consumption as their incomes stagnated. Over time, deregulation resulted in the deterioration in the quality of debt and added to financial fragility, which erupted into the financial crisis once borrowers began to default.

Defaults and the failure of large financial institutions brought the rescue of the financial sector to the forefront of the US policy agenda. Public funds were quickly devoted to prop up banks, thereby building up public debt. As the US and European economies moved into a recession, the shrinking tax base and increase in public spending to address the impact of the crisis further increased the fiscal deficits as a share of GDP. In European countries where banks carried large debt burdens (government debt, real estate, mortgage-related security debt from the US), governments became pre-occupied with bailing them out. As the economic crisis unfolded, the policy priority moved from financial sector rescue operations to deficit reduction, and most governments became more concerned about deficits than job creation or the well-being of their citizens.

While the US government discontinued its countercyclical fiscal policy response in 2010 before economic recovery took hold, many European countries implemented austerity programs. These programs were a variant of the standard structural adjustment programs (SAPs) that developing countries were forced to implement in the 1980s and 1990s as a solution to their debt crises. They included cuts in public services such as health and education, reductions in social protection programs, privatizations and, in several countries, the implementation of labor reforms to increase labor market flexibility and lower labor costs. Altogether, these measures represented different forms and degrees of dismantling the welfare state, a process that had begun before the crisis, particularly in the US but also in European countries; the crisis, however, was used to accelerate it.

These policy choices were formulated and developed by a variety of interests, actors, and institutions. The pressure from investors and financial institutions—the IMF, the European Central Bank, and the European Commission—played an important role in pressing for fiscal discipline and austerity policies at the country level, even though the IMF eventually warned against the depressive effects of austerity. This approach was reinforced by the major creditor countries, such as Germany, with the objective that creditors were paid first and that economies did not experience an uptick in inflation, which would have undermined the value of assets of the wealth holders. The outcome of austerity in Europe was high unemployment, increase in poverty, decline in consumption, overall lowering of expectations about the future, and the return migration of immigrant workers, together with the outmigration of the young educated workforce from countries stuck in stagnation (Krugman 2009; European Commission 2012; Ezquerra 2012; Gálvez 2013; Martinez-Tablas 2012; Young et al. 2010; Krugman 2012).

The financial crisis itself has also contributed to the concentration of banks and to growing inequalities. These bailouts brought some stability to the financial sector but have also led to the rise in dividends and higher executive salaries in financial institutions (Schuberth and Young 2011). The rescue packages are part of a broader trend under neoliberal governance whereby the consequences of private risks undertaken by investors and financial institutions are socialized, while the costs are borne by taxpayers for years to come. There is increased privatized risk for the majority of the population: the poor and middle class experienced job losses, foreclosures, welfare cuts, and other austerity measures, while most banks that engaged in high-risk activities, and were only timidly regulated after the crisis, quickly became profitable. This reallocation of risks and resources—as a consequence of the crisis and the responses of governments and multilateral institutions—shows how market citizenship (i.e. one dollar, one vote) disproportionately puts the crisis burden on the shoulders of the poor and those providing unpaid work. Although parts of Europe and the US are showing some signs of economic recovery as of late 2014 it appears that it will be difficult to avoid a repetition of the "lost decade" experienced by Latin America and Africa in the 1980s, particularly in Southern Europe.

Meanwhile, the crisis was transmitted from the US and Europe to the rest of the world via crisis of confidence, volatility in capital flows, and declines in exports and remittances. Most developing country governments undertook expansionary monetary policies and some form of fiscal stimulus in 2008–09, mainly in the form of large-scale infrastructure investments, to address the impacts of the crisis. But the majority of responses were short-lived (Kyrili and Martin 2010; Floro et al. 2010; Ortiz and Cummins 2013).[3] A sizable group of developing countries cut public expenditures in 2010, despite the broad claims by the IMF of easing the budget reduction conditions on new IMF loans (Elson and Warnecke 2011). Countries had to do austerity when faced with shortfall of revenue, and the so-called "independent" central banks (those committed to inflation targets) would not allow for expansionary monetary policy to fund public spending. Their weak countercyclical responses also suggest the seeming inability of countries to shake off the neoliberal mindset.[4] As Ortiz and Cummins (2013) show, in their 2010–12 budget plans developing country governments considered expenditure cuts in subsidies, health and education budgets, wages, and pensions, each of which would have disproportionate adverse effects on women, children, and poor groups.[5] Thus, while there was greater variability in the developing country responses to the crisis compared to Europe and the US, the neoliberal policy stance was predominant.

There are alternative courses of action, to be sure. While austerity has proceeded relentlessly in some countries, critical voices in the economics discipline have emphasized, equally relentlessly, the counterproductive nature of austerity in dealing with the economic stagnation in the post-2008 period (Krugman 2009; 2012; Reich 2012; Stiglitz 2012). The immediate alternative path out of economic stagnation proposed by heterodox macroeconomists is a New Deal-type of package built around Keynesianism, but it has to go further than that in light of the current challenges and with feminist visions, as we discuss below. In a nutshell, a new regulatory framework has to be created to reduce excessive risk-taking by the financial sector and structural imbalances (high levels of inequality) have to be reduced (Wray 2008; Young et al. 2011; Arestis and Singh 2010; Fukuda-Parr et al. 2013; Bilginsoy 2015). If not, the increasing power and hegemony of capital and its crisis-prone tendencies are not effectively confronted.

Gender Integration in Development

Since the 1990s, a variety of socio-economic indicators for many countries indicate that there has been major progress in reducing some gender inequalities such as in education, health, employment, and access to credit. These improvements can be attributed to the progress in integrating feminist ideas and goals in the international policy agenda together with other related factors such as the increase in women's participation in the labor force and improved health and educational services in many countries. Yet, as discussed in Chapter 1, the process of gender mainstreaming witnessed since the 1980s has not led to a systematic elimination of patriarchal power and the deep-seated structural causes of gender inequalities. Gender machineries, for example, government ministries or bureaus, commissions, and institutions, have proliferated in response to demands for government action and leadership to promote gender equality and improve the status and rights of women, but they have been insufficient to deal with basic problems such as poverty and violence against women.

Given the power of market solutions in neoliberal agendas, gender issues have tended to be subsumed to them. The ensuing programs and policy reforms have often neglected the macroeconomic forces and their interplay with the social and institutional structures that allow unequal gender relations to prevail in markets, households, and societies. The neglect is especially problematic when these silences are manifest in programs of the same institutions that endorse and adopt the neoliberal framework. The active women's employment and enterprise agenda, which aims to get women into the labor market, gives scant attention to household arrangements and division of labor regarding care and domestic duties, including the problems of balancing family and labor market work for women and men. The neoliberal emphasis is on the shedding of government responsibilities to protect human rights, provide social services, and intervene or regulate when markets do fail or lead to social and economic exclusion and marginalization. This shedding has shifted even further the burden of human provisioning to the unpaid caregivers in households and communities.

The continued uncritical endorsement of trade openness and market liberalization and the persistent belief that macroeconomic policies are gender-neutral fail to consider the adverse welfare consequences and social costs brought about by such policies in the last few decades. For example, the promotion of women's employment in factories, commercial agriculture, and micro-enterprises may bring about increased earnings and even greater freedom and mobility. Yet, as discussed in Chapters 4 and 5, unless policies are designed with awareness of connections between the nature of labor force participation and the unequal burden of unpaid work shouldered by women, and between macroeconomic policies and working conditions, women workers' choices can involve difficult trade-offs and their human rights can easily be compromised and violated.

Likewise, despite their positive contributions, gender issues are still marginalized in many key poverty reduction initiatives, notwithstanding some policies targeted to women entrepreneurs, female heads of households, and mothers in low-income households (Grown 2014). Apart from the intrinsic contradiction and underlying tensions between neoliberal policies and poverty alleviation, the lack of a gender lens in many poverty discourses has produced policy interventions that can add to the work burden of women.

Even the gender-aware and successful conditional cash transfer (CCT) schemes of *Bolsa Família* in Brazil and PROGRESA/*Oportunidades* in Mexico and other similar programs in Chile, Colombia, and Ecuador have used women as a "conduit for policy" and tended to underline women's traditional roles associated with caring (Reynolds 2008; Molyneux 2006; Sen 2010). To be sure, CCTs have been helpful especially in situations where economic opportunities remain scarce or where people are confronted with income shortfalls or consumption shocks during crises. Cash transfers can give people the necessary means to survive and thus help avoid resorting to unsustainable coping strategies—such as the use of child labor or selling and pawning their assets (González de la Rocha 2012; Slater et al. 2010; Grown 2014). Indeed, evaluations of these programs have shown that they have reduced extreme poverty and improved educational outcomes (Veras et al. 2010). They have been less successful in the area of health and nutrition. And jobs that are commensurate with the education level achieved by the youth from the CCT-recipient households have been hard to come by.[6]

CCTs have also had some success in increasing women's decision-making power in the household, in durable goods expenditures, and the program-related areas of children's health expenses and school attendance. A recent longitudinal study of *Bolsa Família* indicates that women's decision-making power and voice have risen in several dimensions, including contraception decisions, though the impact is limited to urban areas (De Brauw et al. 2014). However, these programs have had unintended consequences in the form of increased unpaid work for women, since their formulation and designs fail to recognize the time demands such programs impose on women (Escobar and González de la Rocha 2008; Gammage 2010). The track record of these programs points to the need for adjustments in their design and for complementary policies that systematically address care issues and reduce women's unpaid care burden.

The practice of directing poverty alleviation programs to and through women is also evident in the microfinance schemes promoted by donors and multilateral organizations, especially since the mid-1990s. These programs are promoted as a key strategy for empowering women and addressing gender inequality while at the same time reducing poverty. There is no question that access to microcredit has helped many women and their households in some enabling environments, securing consumption smoothing or a modicum of income security, but there is mixed evidence to justify the strong belief in the positive impacts of microcredit (Armendariz and Morduch 2010; Chant 2010). In particular, the odds of business success are extremely low for borrowers with no other resources, yet microcredit is promoted as if these odds are identical and high for all. In some cases, as with rural poor women in Ethiopia, making women use time they do not have and take risks they cannot afford in order to pursue enterprise activities that have little chance of growth, is at best a waste of time (Sweetman 2010). On the other hand, there has been little effort in gender mainstreaming to systematically address the low earnings and poor working conditions faced by women wage or piece-rate workers, despite evidence that women's access to decent wage employment can make a difference to their wellbeing (Sender et al. 2006). Crucial mechanisms to support women's empowerment, such as improved access to affordable health and childcare services, have yet to be given adequate attention and funding.

An additional problem with the current gender mainstreaming model is that it ignores the fact that gender relations are intrinsically linked with social relations of class, race, ethnicity, and sexual orientation and permeate economic and social institutions, as pointed out in Chapter 2. Addressing gender inequality therefore requires an emphasis on reducing all forms of inequality and thus making concerns about distribution—in the areas of assets, incomes, risk burden, and work burden—central issues. As Kathleen Geier et al. (2014) point out, the persistent rise in inequality between the owners of capital and the owners of labor power demonstrated by Thomas Piketty's *Capital in the 21st Century* "bodes ill for women" (p. 1) as it creates a disabling environment for promoting gender equality and women's empowerment. Yet, reducing class inequality is not a priority concern in national and international policy agendas, which is the major obstacle in the path of people-centered development.[7] Nor is there recognition of the connection between rising class inequality and neoliberal policies. Thus, while there may be impressive progress towards gender equality, as highlighted by the World Bank's latest report on gender inequality, these discussions are disconnected from the orthodox macroeconomic policies advised by the Bank (World Bank 2014).

Another troubling development, which shows the shallow mainstreaming of gender in many national bureaucracies, is the general absence of gender-aware policy responses to the 2007–08 financial crisis. As Esquivel and Rodríguez Enríquez (2014) argue there was no gender awareness embedded in the countercyclical macroeconomic policy responses that Argentina, Mexico, and Ecuador undertook. For example, shaped by its neoliberal policy stance, the Mexican government's response to the crisis was weak and late.[8] Many women's organizations (and feminist NGOs) tend to focus on immediate gender concerns such as violence against women and promotion of social and care policy; they have yet to fully engage in activism for gender-aware macroeconomic policies, which are relevant for the generation of decent livelihoods. Indeed, while some pro-poor measures (such as expanding CCT schemes to weather the crisis) helped Mexican women, other measures such as investment in the care sector, which could have both benefitted the macroeconomic recovery and created more gender balance in employment growth, were not adopted.[9]

Looking Forward: There Are Alternatives

The above discussion illustrated three areas in which development policy agendas continue to be set within the neoliberal framework and to be trapped in narrow, often siloized approaches, thus holding back the movement towards equitable human development. The problems concerning policy that we have highlighted explain the frustrations of many involved in the task of promoting sustainable development. Yet, the global financial crisis of 2007–08 and the 2015 deadline for MDGs also have created the opportunity for re-evaluating the efficacy of reigning economic policies and development strategies of the post-1980 period. Given the ongoing social discontent across countries, there are many opportunities to build on the disparate but over-lapping critiques of neoliberalism and to unite around a vision and strategy of development that can move progressive agendas for change. Feminist economic ideas along with other heterodox economic proposals can contrib-ute to alternative visions. Critical evaluations of the consequences of MDGs also offer important insights for rethinking and revising the policy goals in the post-2015 agenda of international development. In order to break the stranglehold of neoliberalism, which is harmful to the well-being of the majority of people on Earth and to human life on the planet, we need to identify alternative visions and build movements around these visions.

Based on the problems we identified in this book and in the previous section we focus on three priorities: to pursue development strategies that transform the productive structures of economies so as to support livelihoods in a sustainable manner and systematically address issues of distribution; to address the urgent crises facing the world, including climate change; and to integrate gender in development policies in a comprehensive and transforma-tive manner. We believe that the policies needed to pursue each of these goals can synergistically support each other.

Building Bridges, Shaping Agendas for Change

As we discussed in Chapter 2, feminist economics seeks to expand people's livelihoods and capabilities in an equitable manner—attentive to not only gender but also class, racial, and ethnic inequalities. These goals are premised on, and indeed require, the expansion of goods and services and the redistribution of resources, which can be utilized to promote well-being in a manner that recognizes the importance of the sustainability of ecosystems. In addition to a development path that generates the needed means for sustenance and well-being for all, complementary institutional changes are also required to enable promotion of capabilities, such as the building of democratic freedoms, affordable educational and healthcare systems, transparency guarantees, social safety nets, and inclusive financial and economic governance. Without these institutional changes, the needs, rights, and demands of vulnerable groups are unmet and ignored in public discourses and policymaking. This agenda for change requires greater dialogue among heterodox economists not only to strengthen the critique of neoliberalism but also to flesh out coherent alternative agendas. It also requires broadening our development framework to address the crucial interconnections between human activities and the state of our ecosystem. Working together with ecological economists and environmental groups to better address the needs of the current generation and that of the next in this regard is vital as well.

In the last decade, feminist economists have made calls for greater engagement among heterodox economists and with ecological economists to build richer analytical frameworks (Danby, 2004; Brody et al. 2008; Van Staveren 2010; Fukuda-Parr et al. 2013; Power 2009; Perkins et al. 2005; Nelson 2013; Floro 2012).[10] Focusing on the goal of economic, social, and environmentally sustainable development, we argue that a similar cross-fertilization of ideas among various strands of thought would enable a stronger push for implementing alternative policies and contributing to alternative models of social change. Discussions among heterodox economists about alternative visions have been abundant; they range from the design of basic income schemes to work sharing and the transformation of productive institutions towards more cooperative forms of production. These alternative ideas, along with gender-aware restructuring of financial governance, promise a more sustainable economic system that offers the possibility of supporting decent livelihoods and promoting gender equality.

The feminist conceptual engagement with other heterodox economists and ecological economists has to start with the concept of development. This means going beyond the concept of human development embraced by most feminist economists, which seeks expansion of people's capabilities and values unpaid activities as important inputs to well-being. First, the new concept has to acknowledge the benefits for human well-being that societies derive from ecosystem services (or the deprivation that the environment's degradation generates).[11] This means valuing the environment's contributions in economic analysis, policy formulation, and assessments. The imperative to address pressing environmental concerns including climate change is upon us. This means that the notion of development should take into account the interdependence of not only the overall economy and the reproductive sector but also the ecosystem. Such interdependence operates at multiple levels and involves dynamic feedback loops, compelling us to avoid myopia and to take a broader perspective of the consequences and outcomes of policies and human actions.

Second, in order to expand people's livelihoods and capabilities the productive capacity and structures of developing countries need to be transformed, moving them away from enclave structures that are platforms for assembling standard export items with limited or no backward linkages towards structures that generate sustainable production of goods and services and decent employment. The expansion of capabilities of this generation and the next also requires transforming our economic activities and processes so as to reduce the stresses put upon the Earth's resource base and on care labor capacity, which are wrongly perceived to be in infinite supply.

Third, the concept of development should recognize a "common humanity and substantive responsibilities for care" (Nelson 2013: 150)—care of people and the environment—and it needs to incorporate a redistributive agenda. This ethic of care calls for policies that reallocate resources to support adequate care provision and enable equal sharing of responsibilities by women and men. It also requires the integration of the costs of raising the next generation along with the costs of maintaining the resilience and carrying capacity of the environment in development planning, gender mainstreaming, and economic policy formulation.

While no one will deny the importance of incorporating sustainability in development visions, there is much debate and even denial about the need to substantially change our way of thinking and decision-making, production techniques and methods, and consumption patterns and behavior. A commitment to sustainability requires recognition of the connections between rising income inequality, conspicuous consumption, and the accelerated fossil fuel and natural resource extraction. As Wisman points out, the "greater is the income and wealth inequality, the greater is the amount that must be consumed by everyone beneath the wealthiest to maintain and or improve their relative status" (Wisman 2011: 10).[12] Ultimately, the perspective of sustainability recognizes the limits to the organization of economic processes that are driven by competition and incessant pursuit of material prosperity. A sustainable, equitable development framework requires making decisions and undertaking economic activities where a more social rather than individualistic perspective is taken and effort towards building collective action and cooperation at the community, national, and global levels becomes paramount (Agarwal 2007; Baland et al. 2007; Nelson 2008).

We believe that as a vision for change, feminist, ecological, new developmentalist perspectives, and more radical transformations such as those intended through the solidarity economy can be complementary, building on the strengths of each perspective while recognizing each perspective's weaknesses. New developmentalism is one promising body of heterodox thought that could be integrated with feminist economics ideas in order to expand the scope of the conversation to include strategies for changing productive structures.[13] This strand of thought seeks to reclaim the ground of early economic development theorists of the 1940s to 1960s and to reassess the production processes being promoted by the contemporary international development agenda (Chang 2002; Khan and Christiansen 2011).[14] The new developmentalist agenda emphasizes the imperative of low-income country governments to use industrial policy to transform the productive structures of the economy so as to move up from low-skill, low-value added activities. This goal requires countries to have adequate policy space to pursue industrial policy and to generate the resources to improve human well-being.

New developmentalist research offers valuable insights on design of industrial policy, which could incorporate principles of ecological and social sustainability. Indeed, feminist economists have argued in favor of industrial policy as a tool for creating decent jobs for women as well as men (Seguino and Grown 2006). However, thus far questions of sustainability have not been of much concern in new developmentalist thought (Zarsky 2011). Two problems that may seem incongruent with the intellectual partnership we propose are the lack of gender awareness and the pro-growth position of new developmentalists (Berik 2014). New developmentalist writings do not take into account social sustainability—the maintenance of social relations in the community and unpaid care work that are at the core of provisioning for human and societal well-being. Moreover, while growth is necessary for low-income countries to raise the standards of living of the poor, incessant pursuit of growth is untenable from an ecological perspective. In a world that is in increasing peril from extreme climate events, where growth undermines decent livelihoods and the well-being of the most vulnerable while promoting overconsumption, this pro-growth position has to be revisited and articulated in light of a vision of sustainability in high-income and low-income countries alike (Zarsky 2011; Broad and Cavanagh 2013). Policies that are attentive to environmental, social, and economic sustainability are necessary so that the economy does not undermine the environment for future generations and does not fray social bonds by social exclusion or marginalization of groups or weaken the ability of families to care for their members.

Feminist economists and ecological economists would also benefit from further intellectual engagement. Feminist economists have favored capabilities expansion as the yardstick of economic success over income growth. As such, we share the appropriate time horizon with ecological economists who think in longer time scales that are relevant for achieving sustainability intergenerationally. This time horizon is consistent with the feminist emphasis on caring for the current and the next generation, thus contributing to social reproduction, imparting skills to children, building personal relationships and communities; and it is in stark contrast with the short-term horizons characteristic of financial markets, which have come to dominate all other markets and non-market aspects of our lives. Moreover, in the large body of feminist writing that has focused on how gender inequality adversely affects economic growth (or gender equality promotes growth), studies have tended to problematize the composition of growth, by arguing in favor of expansion of economic activities that support social sustainability (Seguino 2012; İlkkaracan 2013b).

However, feminist economists' scope of inquiry often fails to recognize that care and social reproduction encompass relationships and commitments between the current and future generations, which inevitably involves maintenance of the ecosystems. Further study is needed to explore the interconnection between gender inequality and the heightened demand for and unequal access to natural resources. The latter have created social tensions between groups, communities, and countries especially in access to water, arable land, and fossil fuels such as oil and shale gas. Conflicts over resources exist among and within units of every scale. Even within households, men and women may have different and occasionally conflicting, rather than complementary, resource use. The health of the Earth's ecosystem is therefore a significant factor that shapes households', communities', countries', and regions' vulnerability to shocks and risks as well as their capacity to respond. The poor are more vulnerable than other segments of the population; they are more likely to have limited or no access to safe water, be exposed to polluted environments, subjected to landgrabbing, and they have fewer resources and means to cope. At the same time, research shows that women are more vulnerable to climate risks, specifically natural disasters, than men (Neumayer and Plümper 2007). There is a need to examine in greater depth the gendered dimensions of climate change effects, environmental sustainability initiatives, and collective action building; this too requires further dialogue and collaboration between feminists and ecological economists.

The "social and solidarity economy" (SSE) movement that has been unfolding from the grassroots for some time provides additional visions of the types of institutions that can respond to the concerns about environmental, social, and economic sustainability. Although not easy to define, the SSE represents a "multiplicity of practices" linked to achieving economic democracy and participatory economics—as a way of building alternatives to neoliberalism (Dash 2014; Marques 2014). Historically, the SSE has its conceptual and practical origins in the social opposition to individualism and competition of the industrial economy that emerged in Europe in the nineteenth century. However, more recently it has often been connected to the emergence of the World Social Forum (WSF) formed in response to the World Economic Forum (WEF), which gathers global economic elites in Davos, Switzerland annually. The first meeting of the WSF took place in Porto Alegre, Brazil, in 2001 under the well-known slogan "another world is possible," symbolizing a global push for alternative economics and alternative institutions. Discourses and practices around the solidarity economy have developed from the grassroots and through a great variety of alternative organizations concerned about different but related goals.

Central to the SSE movement is building forms of social provisioning based on need, reciprocity, community, and sustainability, rather than profit and accumulation objectives. In many countries around the world, the establishment of cooperatives, community networks, ethical banking, fair trade organizations, sustainable farming, ecologically conscious firms and, in general, socially responsible business practices have contributed to this movement (Allard et al. 2007; Broad and Cavanagh 2013; Felber 2012). The cooperative model is fast becoming an important means for promoting not only decent livelihoods, working conditions, and access to services for its members but also goals of economic, environmental, and social sustainability (Wanyama 2014). In particular, by harnessing the collective power of women, cooperatives increase women's access to resources and economic opportunities and advance goals of gender equality. These efforts are part of what Evans (2008) has called "counter-hegemonic globalization," representing a variety of objectives, highly compatible with those of feminist economics, such as provisioning and sustainable production and reproduction. It is no surprise therefore that many feminist organizations and women's groups have become involved with the SSE (Marques 2014). Although these alternative routes have barely been taken seriously in conventional economic circles, the growing discontent and exclusionary trends of neoliberalism provide a fertile ground for the growing interest in the SSE in many places. Interest in envisioning the SSE is growing beyond the grassroots level, as illustrated by new research from multilateral institutions such as UNRISD and by scholarly conferences on the topic.[15]

Policies for Sustainable Economies

As emphasized in our conceptual overview, creating a sustainable economy requires attention to environmental, social, and economic sustainability.[16] Our discussion of the policies necessary to reorient economies towards sustainability in this section will show that these dimensions of sustainability can synergistically support each other.

While it is clear that human activities have contributed to climate change, the question of how to alter the scale, methods, and patterns of production and consumption have become important areas of debate. One debate focuses on whether trade-offs between economic growth and environmental protection can be overcome, and whether quality of life can be improved without incessant pursuit of economic growth. There is increasing recognition that the threats posed by climate change cannot be tackled without curbing economic growth. However, this raises questions of equity between the global North and the global South. Since poor countries need to expand production and provide basic livelihoods for their citizens, as emphasized by new developmentalists, some have argued that in order to tackle the climate crisis affluent economies have to slow down or stop growing in order to allow poor economies to grow.

From a broader perspective however, there are different entry points in tackling the stresses placed by human demand on the ecosystem for both high- and low-income countries. They include not only reducing the scale of global production and consumption but also changing the composition of what we produce and consume and the technologies and methods used. The latter approach suggests that the trade-offs between raising the level of living of the poor and curbing environmental degradation are not as stark as often assumed and can be resolved. Working towards this goal entails cooperation among feminist economists, heterodox macroeconomists, and ecological economists to promote sustainable livelihoods, ranging from agriculture to manufacturing and other economic activities. Their collective vision can lead to a development agenda and clear plan of action for transition to renewable energy, promoting agroecology, organic farming, and care provisioning. The plan also includes measures to prevent or mitigate ecological damage, to adapt to climate change, and a "new Industrial Revolution" that Stern (2011) speaks of.

The practical steps of creating a sustainable economy involve shifting resources away from environmentally harmful economic activities, generating resources for raising the quality of life sustainably especially for the low-income majority, and orienting away from consumerism. Thus, public policies for sustainability have to aim at creating productive and reproductive structures and services that support well-being—via education and healthcare policies, household and family policies, and the environment via renewable energy policy. These policies will expand the sectors and jobs that promote sustainability and address the jobs crisis, the ecological crisis, and the care crisis.[17]

Social sustainability also requires reorienting economies so that there is adequate care provision to support well-being for all. This goal will require the design of a new social contract, together with public policies that socialize the benefits as well as costs of raising children and caring for the elderly. Any employment policies must be accompanied by a comprehensive care policy that includes entitlements to the providers of unpaid caring labor—treating them as producers and active workers in their own right—and facilitates work-life balance that provides adequate leisure time, fosters social relations, and sustains communities.

In addition, policies must be implemented to phase out environmentally damaging activities. Stiglitz (2012), among others, has provided an outline of these policies, such as making polluters pay, giving subsidies (selective tax credits) to companies that save resources and jobs, government support for innovation to preserve the environment and jobs. Finally, curbing status consumption and modifying what might be defined as "excessive" lifestyles will have a positive environmental impact in terms of limiting the growth of energy and resource use, waste, and emissions (Melber 2012).[18] From both equity and environmental perspectives, such limits should first apply to the rich in both the global North and South. The means towards these goals can be, for example, progressive income taxation and higher tax rates on luxury items.

In order to achieve economic sustainability, it is necessary to reduce income inequality, which was a major contributor to the 2007–08 financial crisis as well as to many of the problems raised in this book, such as poverty and labor market instability. The economic policies needed for redistribution include reforms to curb accumulation at the top of the income (wealth) distribution, such as financial sector reform, implementing competition policies to break up near monopoly power in many industries, ending corporate welfare, and creating an effective progressive tax system. Boosting incomes of those in the middle or bottom of the income distribution entails policies to strengthen the bargaining position of workers vis-à-vis capital, such as improving access to healthcare and education, strengthening social protection, use of fiscal and monetary policies to achieve full employment, and tempering globalization, for example, via controls on crossborder short-term capital flows. Active labor market policies to create jobs are an additional key component of policies to promote equitable well-being but other more innovative measures also can be introduced, such as job sharing and the reduction of working hours/week. The latter policies are particularly important, given robotization and other labor-saving trends.

The human rights framework provides an important instrument for addressing income inequality and, more generally, reorienting economies away from neoliberal policies (Balakrishnan and Elson 2011). As discussed in Chapter 1, as signatory to international human rights covenants, governments can be held accountable by their citizens for failure to abide by their obligations to uphold economic and social rights.[19] According to this framework, austerity policies represent a violation of government commitments to safeguard these rights. For example, budget cuts, especially those that disproportionately affect women and racial minorities, violate a number of human rights principles, particularly when they curtail the provision of basic needs such as food, housing, and universal education for all. Similarly, absence of a regulatory framework, which allows risky behavior by the financial sector and endangers livelihoods of citizens, represents government's failure to protect citizens' economic and social rights. Thus, the human rights framework provides an important tool to evaluate and implement economic policy and to engage in activism to hold governments accountable. To be sure, the effectiveness of this tool depends on a well-functioning system of governance to ensure that governments implement the human rights obligations that they have signed onto. This ingredient, in turn, points to the importance of global governance reform, a project that includes many levels—from revamping the Bretton Woods institutions to a UN reform adapted to current needs.

Global Governance Reforms

In order to implement the policies outlined in the previous section, the international rules have to provide an enabling environment. Many of the problems highlighted in this book stem from the inability of most governments to regulate their economies in a manner that will support the livelihoods of the majority of their populations. Unfettered mobility of capital, enabled by liberalization policies that are endorsed and supported by multilateral financial organizations, has kept government regulation at bay, undermining governments' ability to tax capital and regulate the activities of capital within their national borders. Yet, a global economy requires global regulation. As Wade (2011: 23) points out, "[r]egulation will have to be much more multilateral than it has been, on the principle that the domain of regulation must coincide with the domain of the market." In order to create societies less prone to periodic financial crises, there needs to be international coordination to institute greater financial regulation and to implement macro management attentive to distributional effects. Chang and Grabel (2014) are optimistic about changes in global governance in the near future. Specifically, they see a weakening of the power of the IMF, starting with the Asian financial crisis, when the IMF's policy recommendations were discredited. Since then, several Asian and other emerging economies, particularly the BRICS, have created new institutions and sought to strengthen their policy autonomy in an economic crisis.[20] These responses are also due to the failure of the efforts to develop a new financial architecture to replace the Bretton Woods institutions and deal with the dominance of the US and Europe within the system.

Importantly, there is a need for regulation of capital flows—not only the destabilizing financial flows, but also mobility of capital engaged in outsourcing production, which undermines the creation of decent jobs and reduces government revenues by seeking tax havens. Curbing capital flows can be achieved in a number of ways, including capital controls and tax policy. Institutionalization of a financial transactions tax (FTT, also known as the Tobin tax or "Robin Hood" tax) also needs global governance. FTT has been much debated in the US, Europe, and in the global South as a policy tool to reduce the destabilizing effects of financial transactions on economies and to raise funds for development purposes. While the European Parliament approved such a tax in 2012, it has yet to be implemented in member countries due to continued attempts to water down the tax.[21] As of August 2014, its implementation by EU countries is scheduled to begin on January 1, 2016. The process has been slowed down due to the strong opposition of some member countries such as the UK. Each of these policies to regulate capital requires global coordination; it is difficult for one country to adopt such policies alone, as the economic cost of doing so is high.

The multilateral framework to support poverty reduction goals also needs to be strengthened, based on recognition that the root causes of the persistence of poverty lie in the workings of the international rules governing trade and finance and neoliberal macroeconomic policies. While MDGs represented a focused set of goals, the work involved in addressing even these narrow goals is incomplete. Gender inequality is very much at the center of this unfinished agenda and discussions of the contours of the post-2015 development goals. Many evaluations of MDGs emphasize the importance of gender equality for achieving development goals as well as being intrinsically important. Given the shortcomings of MDG3 however, there are calls for more transformative goals after 2015 in the Sustainable Development Goals (SDG) framework adopted in 2012. For example, UN Women (2013) calls for "a transformative stand-alone" gender equality goal that addresses the causes of gender equality by focusing on three priority areas: ending violence against women; expanding women's capabilities and resources; and ensuring their participation in decision-making in the household and in public institutions.

Achieving environmental sustainability also requires global governance. Insofar as environmental quality is a public good, along with health, education, sanitation, etc., its provision requires not a series of individual actions coordinated by the market but building collective action that addresses externalities and free-rider problems.[22] However, to date, there is no global governance body that effectively oversees and regulates various stakeholders whose actions impact the environment and put stresses on ecosystems that cut across national boundaries and political borders.[23] The principles and values of the 1992 Rio Declaration on Environment and Development have been overshadowed by the exigencies of jump-starting economic growth and meeting the ever growing demand for goods and services that in turn generate high demand for natural resource and energy use. For the most part, these principles have yet to be translated into policies and development agendas. The lack of democratic and inclusive global governance on environmental issues prevents the translation of the core values and principles in the agreed international commitments into enforceable rules and policies promoting sustainable, equitable development.[24] In the meantime, capital intervenes in multiple ways to try to subvert international bodies and fora away from their stated goals. For example, transnational corporations have sued governments at international fora in order to remove or challenge rules such as health or trade regulations that affect their profits. By contrast, communities and local groups are hindered from suing companies for the pollution and other harmful effects they inflict upon them (Melber 2012). Thus, reforming global governance requires addressing inequality between capital and labor head on; only then can there be a rebalancing of rights by "rolling back the rights of capital" (Melber 2012: 30) and upholding human rights.

Change Requires Social Movements

How transformative these policies and governance reforms are ultimately depends on the actions and demands of the public. Specifically, any real solutions to economic and ecological crises and persistence of inequalities depend on social movements, political activism, and collective action. While Piketty (2014) is pessimistic about the prospects for social change in the face of the corrupting influence of the rising economic and political power of capital on domestic democratic institutions, we believe that social movements are the only way to get progressive agendas off the ground. As witnessed in recent decades, cooperation and collective action among women, civil society, farmers, workers, and environmental groups have challenged powerful inter-ests. Through multiple tools—including scholarly debates, statistical conven-tions, activism at many levels, and the media—these groups have pressed for government action, and worked for social change. As discussed in other chapters, the feminist movement has been a tremendous source for social change locally and globally and with regards to gender and development issues since the 1970s. It has shaped gender-aware agendas for action at the national and international levels and made important contributions to some policy changes around health, education, domestic work, family laws and legal rights, peace and conflict, leadership and governance. One striking example that underscores the power of social movements is the evidence that the presence of an autonomous and strong feminist movement was the most important and consistent driving force of progressive state action to combat violence against women over the 1975–2005 period (Htun and Weldon 2012).[25] While many feminist struggles are still being waged, particularly the one against violence against women as highlighted by the World Bank (2014), this evidence underscores the general message that governments are responsive to organized, persistent, and strong social movements.

More generally, a large number of women's groups have joined regional and international networks and coalitions, such as DAWN, *Articulación Feminista Marcosur* (AFM), International Domestic Workers' Network,

Women's International Coalition for Economic Justice (WICEJ), Network Women in Development Europe (WIDE), African Women's Development and Communication Network (FEMNET), and India National Network of Autonomous Women's Groups (INNAWAG), which have engaged in activism for gender justice, gender-aware macroeconomic policies and have promoted new thinking to transform societies. Feminist networks working alongside the new Latin American development models such as Bolivia and Ecuador have contributed to the discussions about the crises of social reproduction and of the environment, calling for return to indigenous knowledge and ancestral practices. Such is the notion of "buen vivir" or "living well," referring to the community as a whole and arrived at communally, a concept highly compatible with the feminist economics notion of an economy addressing well-being as its central goal rather than capital accumulation or maximizing behavior, as discussed in Chapter 2.

Women's organizations such as the Self-Employed Women's Association (SEWA) of India, and regional and transnational networks such as DAWN and the Association for Women's Rights in Development (AWID), are not static; they continually re-examine and redefine themselves as they create space and mechanisms for dialogues and mobilization in order both to address standard gender issues as well as pursuing new possibilities for deep economic and social transformations. Other organizations such as WIEGO (Women in Informal Employment: Globalizing and Organizing) focus their activities on informal work conditions. The growth of regional and international networks is a result of the commonality of issues faced by women in the global North and South. Certain discourses—such as the recognition that violation of women's rights constitutes human rights abuse—have acquired greater importance among women in both the North and the South. Feminist networks and women's organizations have also participated in broader movements and fora on economic justice and social change, for example, in the World Social Forum and have sought alliances with labor movements, farmers' organizations, environmental groups, and other grassroots organizations. This is not to say that building coalitions and social movements is a smooth process. Far from it; there are tensions around political agendas, framing of issues, and there are many, often heated, debates around which solutions to work on and which policies to promote. But only in the articulation of diverse views and experiences, participation in intense debates, and in the implementation of alternative programs and initiatives on the ground can ideas for better development strategies and policies be nurtured and developed.

In sum, pursuit of progressive agendas for change will require coalition work among activists—feminists, environmentalists, marginalized and other socio-political groups—who work on goals towards creating more equitable, sustainable societies as well as building intellectual alliances that help develop the strategies needed to deal with the multiple tasks ahead and underlined in this book.

Majorities everywhere have to engage in activism to bring about political and long-term economic reforms, to tackle inequality in its various forms, and launch economies on sustainable paths. Feminists in general and feminist economists in particular will agree with Stiglitz (2013) and Sen and Drèze (2013), that high levels of income inequality and insecurity are the product of political choices, not the inexorable workings of economic forces over which we have no control. Without political change there can be no change in the economic policies pursued. While the intellectual alliances we identified as necessary for articulating designs of an equitable future are important, collective action is the force that is urgently needed to move forward the progressive and feminist agendas. To borrow from Weldon and Htun (2013: 246), only social movements will ensure that "words become deeds."

Notes

1 The goals and principles expressed in the Millennium Declaration, adopted by the UN General Assembly in September 2000, highlight gender more than the MDGs do, and the Declaration specifically mentions the UN Convention on the Elimination of All Forms of Discrimination against Women (CEDAW) (Johnsson-Latham 2010).

2 See Bilginsoy (2015) for an overview of the debates on the causes of the crisis.

3 Unlike the response made to the Asian crisis in the late 1990s, many developing country governments either maintained or increased their spending, despite the decline in revenues, which has led to a substantial increase in their fiscal deficits. In several countries, governments also provided tax cuts and subsidies to stimulate household and business demand. Kyrili and Martin (2010) show that the deficit in the 56 low-income countries they surveyed increased by $43.2bn in 2009. However, expenditures on infrastructure, health, and agriculture, which rose in 2009, fell in 2010. Spending on social protection steadily declined and by 2010, it was lower than its 2008 level.

4 As Esquivel and Rodríguez Enríquez (2014) point out, strong adherence to a neoliberal macroeconomic approach made Mexico both more vulnerable to the crisis and ill prepared to respond to it.

5 Based on IMF fiscal projections and IMF country reports, Isabel Ortiz and Michael Cummins (2013) show that in 2010, 70 of 128 developing countries reduced public expenditure by 3 percent of GDP and nearly a quarter of them reduced it below the pre-crisis (2005–07) levels.

6 A study of life histories in a balanced sample shows that 12 years after the inception of the program in Mexico, children from grant-recipient families, especially among indigenous and mestizo youth, are not successful in finding better jobs

than their parents (Sánchez López and Jiménez Rodríguez 2012). Work opportunities are scarce and jobs are temporary both locally and if they migrate.

7   An interesting exception is a recent IMF report, which suggests rising inequality is an obstacle to economic growth (Ostry et al. 2014). This report is in line with recent IMF reports that soften the longstanding IMF positions, such as its opposition to capital controls. Ostry et al. (2014) report that lower inequality is associated with faster economic growth, which confirms what heterodox economists have long argued. The true test of change in the IMF's stance, however, is whether this confirmation is followed by recommendations to countries to pursue redistribution and investments in public goods (health, education, and infrastructure).

8   According to the authors, Mexico's women's bureau, INMUJERES, did not seek to shape these macroeconomic policy responses.

9   Investment in the care sector would have created jobs, mostly for women, and provided much-needed services. Instead, in Mexico and elsewhere in Latin America, the focus was on investment in physical infrastructure (Esquivel and Rodríguez Enríquez 2014; Espino 2013).

10 Colin Danby and Irene Van Staveren articulated the overlaps and potential synergies between post-Keynesian and feminist economic analyses, while Fukuda-Parr et al. argued for the value of bringing together various heterodox strands of thought on economic crises to produce a richer analysis of the 2007–08 financial crisis. Similarly, Power highlights the overlaps between ecological and social provisioning perspectives. Floro (2012) discusses the overlaps and complementarities between feminist economics and ecological economics, while Perkins et al. and Nelson use the feminist lens to explore the urgency of addressing environmental issues.

11 In the documentary *Who's Counting: Marilyn Waring on Sex, Lies, and Global Economics* (1995), Waring urged attention to the contributions of ecosystem services—for example, clean air, clean water, forests—that, along with unpaid care work, have traditionally been neglected in standard economic frameworks. Since the 1990s the methods for measuring the value of ecosystem services have been developed, both as individual indicators and as part of composite indicators, such as the Genuine Progress Indicator (GPI), which also includes unpaid housework as a component (see Bagstad et al. 2014). To be sure, the notion of giving a monetary value to ecosystems services (as in the case of unpaid care work) is an important and ongoing subject of debate.

12 Similar observations were made by Thorstein Veblen in the *Theory of the Leisure Class* ([1889] 1973) in the late nineteenth century.

13 See Berik (2014) who makes the case for complementarity of new developmentalist, feminist, and ecological economists' perspectives on ends and means.

14 Prominent among the early developmentalist theorists are Raul Prebisch, Hans Singer, Paul Rosenstein-Rodan, Ragnar Nurkse, and Albert Hirschman, who emphasized the importance of low-income countries establishing the productive structures to facilitate paths out of low levels of living. In the contemporary era

the research of South Centre is premised on this vision. See for example, South Centre (2014) lays out the policies that are necessary for low-income countries to pursue sustainable development from the perspective of the economies of the South.

15 Examples include some of the UNRISD Occasional Papers (Dash 2014; Marques 2014) or the conference "Can a solidary economy be feminist?", organized by the Graduate Institute of International and Development Studies, Geneva, Switzerland, October 2014.

16 This includes the sustainability of life itself.

17 The complementarity between heterodox macroeconomics, ecological, and feminist ends and means is evident in the arguments of Harris (2013), İlkkaracan (2013b), and Antonopoulos et al. (2014). While Harris argues for fiscal policy to promote job creation that supports ecological goals, Antonopoulos et al. argue for fiscal policy to promote job creation in the care sector. İlkkaracan further argues that promoting the care sector would support both gender-equitable well-being and ecological goals: job creation in the care sector would expand women's employment, alleviate care burdens, and raise human well-being, while being less energy intensive and less ecologically damaging.

18 How to define "excessive" can of course be a difficult question but an abundant literature already exists dealing with theoretical and practical questions regarding "how much is enough" or "what is the high road" shaping human wants and objectives (Skidelsky and Skidelsky 2012; Frank 2004).

19 According to the Universal Declaration of Human Rights, economic and social rights encompass the right to work, the right to health, the right to food, the right to an adequate standard of living, the right to housing among others. The International Covenant on Economic, Social, and Cultural Rights (ICESCR) provides the principles that governments that are signatory to the covenant must abide by in order to safeguard economic and social rights.

20 BRICS includes Brazil, Russia, India, China, and South Africa. An example of their efforts is the creation of the New Development Bank in July 2014, representing the power that these countries have been acquiring without being given sufficient recognition in the Bretton Woods institutions.

21 For more details, see "Brussels proposes 30 billion euros Tobin tax," *Financial Times*, February 14, 2013 and EUbusiness (2014).

22 CO_2 emissions by rapidly industrializing countries, notably China, would be an example of a negative externality for small island nations that face an existential threat from rising sea levels caused by climate change, but one to which they did not contribute. Benefitting from investments in clean energy by a company, without having to pay for the cost of developing it, would be an example of a free rider problem.

23 The Intergovernmental Panel on Climate Change (IPCC) is the leading international body for the assessment of climate change. It provides the world with its scientific view of the current state of knowledge on climate change and its potential environmental and socio-economic impacts.

24   Lack of transparency and exclusion also characterize the decision-making processes of many international bodies that make economic and financial decisions. Improving global governance requires increasing transparency, accountability, and guaranteeing citizen (via civil society groups) participation in key economic, financial, and environmental decision-making processes.

25   In a study of 70 countries Htun and Weldon (2012) show that countries with the strongest feminist movements have more comprehensive government policies to address violence against women, all else being equal. Other factors, such as numbers of women legislators, national wealth, and left-wing parties are only weakly associated with the adoption of such policies. Feminist movements have worked at both the domestic and international levels, pushing for international measures to put greater pressure on governments. State machineries that focus on gender equality issues are formed in response to demands of women's movements and in turn these entities can help feminist movements put violence against women on the policy agenda.

References

Abraham, Katharine G., and Christopher D. Mackie. 2005. *Beyond the Market: Designing Nonmarket Accounts for the United States.* Washington DC: National Academies Press.

Abu-Lughod, Lila. 2002. "Do Muslim Women Really Need Saving? Anthropological Reflections on Cultural Relativism and Its Others." *American Anthropologist* 104 (3): 783–90.

ACTU (Australian Council of Trade Unions). 2014. Available at www.actu.org.au/actu_media/media_releases/2014/new_push_to_give_casual_workers_the_right_to_permanent_work. p. 259.

Adams, Dale, and Linda Mayoux. 2001. "Crossfire." *Small Enterprise Development* 12 (1): 4–6.

AFL-CIO (American Federation of Labor and Congress of Industrial Organization). 2014. "Executive Pay Watch." Available at, www.aflcio.org/Corporate-Watch/Paywatch-2014.

Agarwal, Bina. 1992a. "Gender Relations and Food Security: Coping with Seasonality, Drought and Famine in South Asia." In *Unequal Burden, Economic Crises, Household Strategies and Women's Work*, edited by Lourdes Benería and Shelly Feldman, 181–218. Boulder, CO: Westview Press.

———. 1992b. "The Gender and Environment Debate: Lessons from India." *Feminist Studies* 18 (1): 119–58.

———. 1994. *A Field of One's Own: Gender and Land Rights in South Asia.* Cambridge, UK: Cambridge University Press.

———. 1997. "Bargaining and Gender Relations: Within and Beyond the Household." *Feminist Economics* 3 (1): 1–51.

———. 2007. "Gender Equality, Cooperation and Environmental Sustainability." In *Inequality, Cooperation and Environmental Sustainability*, edited by Jean-Marie Baland, Pranab Bardhan, and Samuel Bowles, 274–313. Russell Sage Foundation and Princeton University.

Ahmad, Nadim, and Seung-Hee Koh. 2011. *Incorporating Estimates of Household Production of Non-Market Services into International Comparisons of Material Well-Being.* Paris: Organization for Economic Cooperation and Development.

Ahmed, Leila. 1992. *Women and Gender in Islam: Historical Roots of a Modern Debate.* New Haven, CT: Yale University Press.

Akee, Randall, Arnab K. Basu, Arjun Bedi, and Nancy H. Chau. 2009. "Combating Trafficking in Women and Children: A Review of International and National Legislation, Co-ordination Failures and Perverse Economic Incentives." *Journal of Human Rights and Civil Society* 2: 1–24.

Albelda, Randy P. 1997. *Economics & Feminism: Disturbances in the Field.* New York: Twayne Publishers.

———. 1999. "Marxist Political Economics." In *The Elgar Companion to Feminist Economics*, edited by Janice Peterson and Margaret Lewis, 536–43. Cheltenham, UK: Edward Elgar.

———. 2013. "Gender Impacts of the 'Great Recession' in the United States." In *Women and Austerity: The Economic Crisis and the Future of Gender Equality*, edited by Maria Karamessini and Jill Rubery. New York: Routledge.

Albelda, Randy and Robert Drago. 2013. *Unlevel Playing Fields: Understanding Wage Inequality and Discrimination.* 4th ed. Boston: Dollars and Sense.

Allard, Mary Dorinda, Suzanne Bianchi, Jay Stewart, and Vanessa R. Wright. 2007. "Comparing Childcare Measures in the ATUS and Earlier Time-Diary Studies." *Monthly Labor Review* 130 (27).

Allchin, Joseph. 2013. "Death Mill: How the Ready-Made Garment Industry Captured the Bangladeshi State." *Foreign Policy*, May 9. Available at, http://www.foreign policy.com/articles/2013/05/09/bangladesh_factory_collapse.

Allendorf, Keera. 2007. "Do Women's Land Rights Promote Empowerment and Child Health in Nepal?" *World Development* 35 (11): 1975–88.

Amsden, Alice. 2010. "Say's Law, Poverty Persistence, and Employment Neglect." *Journal of Human Development and Capabilities* 11 (1): 57–66.

Anker, Richard. 1998. *Gender and Jobs: Sex Segregation of Occupations in the World.* Geneva: International Labour Organization.

Anner, Mark, Jennifer Bair, and Jeremy Blasi. 2013. "Toward Joint Liability in Global Supply Chains: Addressing the Root Causes of Labor Violations in International Subcontracting Networks." *Comparative Labor Law and Policy Journal* 35 (1): 1–43.

Antonopoulos, Rania, ed. 2014. *Gender Perspectives and the Gender Impacts of the Global Economic Crisis.* New York: Routledge.

Antonopoulos, Rania, and Indira Hirway. 2010. *Unpaid Work and the Economy: Gender, Time Use and Poverty in Developing Countries.* London: Palgrave Macmillan.

Antonopoulos, Rania, Kijong Kim, Tom Masterson, and Ajit Zacharias. 2014. "Investing in Care in the Midst of a Crisis: A Strategy for Effective and Equitable Job Creation in the United States." In *Gender Perspectives and the Gender Impacts of the Global Economic Crisis*, edited by Rania Antonopoulos, 49–72. New York: Routledge.

Apne App. 2014. "Prostitution Is Commercial Rape; Don't Term Prostitutes as Sex Workers." Available at, http://apneaap.org/prostitution-is-commercial-rape-dont-term-prostitutes-as-sex-workers/.

Appiah, Kwame Anthony. 2010. "Wars Against Women." In *The Honor Code: How Moral Revolutions Happen*, 137–72. New York: W.W. Norton and Co.

Arestis, Philip, and Ajit Singh. 2010. "Financial Globalisation and Crisis, Institutional Transformation and Equity." *Cambridge Journal of Economics* 34 (2): 225–38.

Arestis, Philip, Aurelie Charles, and Giuseppe Fontana. 2013. "Financialization, the Great Recession, and the Stratification of the US Labor Market." *Feminist Economics* 19 (3): 152–80.

Arguello, Reineira. 2010. "Securing the Fruits of Their Labours: The Effect of the Crisis on Women Farm Workers in Peru's Ica Valley." *Gender & Development* 18 (2): 241–47.

Armendariz, Beatriz, and Jonathan Morduch. 2010. *The Economics of Microfinance.* Cambridge, MA: MIT Press.

Arndt, Sven W., and Henryk Kierzkowski, eds. 2001. *Fragmentation: New Production Patterns in the World Economy.* Oxford University Press.

Arora, Diksha. 2014. "Gender Differences in Time Poverty in Rural Mozambique." Salt Lake City: Department of Economics, University of Utah, Working Paper No. 2014–5.

Asian Development Bank (ADB). 2001. *Gender Action Plan 2000–03.* Manila. Available at, http://www.adb.org/documents/gender-action-plan-2000-2003.

Aslaksen, Iulie, and Charlotte Koren. 1996. "Unpaid Household Work and the Distribution of Extended Income: The Norwegian Experience." *Feminist Economics* 2 (3): 65–80.

Atkinson, Anthony B., Thomas Piketty, and Saez Emmanuel. 2011. "Top Incomes in the Long Run of History." *Journal of Economic Literature* 49 (1): 3–71.

Augsburg, Britta, and Cyril Fouillet. 2013. "Profit Empowerment: The Microfinance Institution's Mission Drift." In *The Credibility of Microcredit: Studies of Impact and Performance*, edited by Dwight Haase, 199–227. Leiden: Koninklijke Brill NV Publishers.

Austen, Siobhan, Monica Costa, Rhonda Sharp, and Diane Elson. 2013. "Expenditure Incidence Analysis: A Gender-Responsive Budgeting Tool for Educational Expenditure in Timor-Leste?" *Feminist Economics* 19 (4): 1–24.

Australian Bureau of Statistics. 2008. *Forms of Employment, Australia, November 2007.* Catalogue No. 6359.0. Canberra.: Australian Bureau of Statistics.

———. 2012. *Yearbook Australia 2012.* Canberra: Australian Bureau of Statistics. Available at, http://www.abs.gov.au/ausstats/abs@.nsf/.

Baccaro, Lucio. 2001. *Civil Society, NGOs, and Decent Work Policies: Sorting out the Issues.* Geneva: International Institute for Labour Studies, ILO.

Badgett, M.V. Lee. 1995a. "The Wage Effects of Sexual Orientation Discrimination." *Industrial and Labor Relations Review* 48 (4): 726–39.

———. 1995b. "Gender, Sexuality, and Sexual Orientation: All in the Feminist Family?" *Feminist Economics* 1 (1): 121–39.

Bagstad, Kenneth J., Günseli Berik, and Erica J. Brown Gaddis. 2014. "Methodological Developments in US State-Level Genuine Progress Indicators: Toward GPI 2.0." *Ecological Indicators* 45: 474–85.

Bakker, Isabella, and Diane Elson. 1998. *Towards Engendering Budgets*. Alternative Federal Budget Papers No. 297. Ottawa: Canadian Center for Policy Alternatives.

Balakrishnan, Radhika, ed. 2002. *The Hidden Assembly Line: Gender Dynamics of Subcontracted Work in a Global Economy*. Bloomfield, CT: Kumarian Press.

Balakrishnan, Radhika, and Diane Elson. 2011. "Introduction: Economic Policies and Human Rights Obligations." In *Economic Policy and Human Rights*, edited by Radhika Balakrishnan and Diane Elson, 1–27. London and New York: Zed Books.

Baland, J. M., Pranab Bardhan, and Samuel Bowles. 2007. *Inequality, Cooperation, and Environmental Sustainability*. Princeton, NJ: Princeton University Press.

Banerjee, Abhijit, and Esther Duflo. 2011. *Poor Economics: A Radical Rethinking of the Way to Fight Global Poverty*. New York, NY: Public Affairs.

Bardasi, Elena, and Quentin Wodon. 2010. "Working Long Hours and Having No Choice: Time Poverty in Guinea." *Feminist Economics* 16 (3): 45–78.

Bardhan, Pranab. 1989. "The New Institutional Economics and Development Theory: A Brief Critical Assessment." *World Development* 17 (9): 1389–95.

Barker, Drucilla K. 1999. "Neoclassical Economics." In *Elgar Companion for Feminist Economics*, edited by Janice Peterson and Margaret Lewis, 570–77. Cheltenham, UK: Edward Elgar.

Barker, Drucilla K., and Susan F. Feiner. 2004. *Liberating Economics: Feminist Perspectives on Families, Work, and Globalization*. Ann Arbor, MI: University of Michigan Press.

Barrett, Michele. 1999. *Imagination in Theory: Culture, Writing, Words, and Things*. New York: New York University Press.

Barrig, Maruja. 1996. "Women, Collective Kitchens, and the Crisis of the State in Peru." *UCLA Latin American Studies* 82: 59–77.

Baruch, Grace K., Lois Biener, and Rosalind C. Barnett. 1987. "Women and Gender in Research on Work and Family Stress." *American Psychologist* 42 (2): 130–36.

Basu, Kaushik. 2013. *The Method of Randomization and the Role of Reasoned Intuition*. Washington DC: The World Bank, World Bank Policy Research Working Paper, No. WPS 6722.

Baxter, Janeen, and Belinda Hewitt. 2013. "Negotiating Domestic Labor: Women's Earnings and Housework Time in Australia." *Feminist Economics* 19 (1): 29–53.

Becker, Gary. 1965. "A Theory of Allocation of Time." *Economic Journal* 75: 493–517.
———. 1981. *A Treatise on the Family*. Cambridge, MA: Harvard University Press.

Beerepoot, Niels, and Mitch Hendriks. 2013. "Employability of Offshore Service Sector Workers in the Philippines: Opportunities for Upward Labour Mobility or Dead-End Jobs?" *Work Employment Society* 27 (5): 823–41.

Behrman, Julia, Ruth Meinzen-Dick, and Agnes Quisumbing. 2012. "The Gender Implications of Large-Scale Land Deals." *Journal of Peasant Studies* 39 (1): 49–79.

Beller, Andrea H. 1979. "The Impact of Equal Employment Opportunity Laws on the Male-Female Earnings Differential." In *Women in the Labour Market*, edited by Emily Andrews, Cynthia Lloyd, and Curtis Gilroy. New York: Columbia University Press.

Bellman, Eric. 2012. "Nike Contractor Pays Indonesians in Settlement." *The Wall Street Journal*, January 13. Available at, http://blogs.wsj.com/searealtime/2012/01/13/nike?s-latest-sponsorship-deal-222-for-indonesian-factory-workers/.

Belser, Patrick. 2005. *Forced Labour and Human Trafficking: Estimating the Profits.* Geneva: International Labour Organization.

Bería, Lourdes. 1979. "Reproduction, Production and the Sexual Division of Labour." *Cambridge Journal of Economics* 3 (3): 203–25.

———. 1981. "Conceptualizing the Labor Force: The Underestimation of Women's Economic Activities." *The Journal of Development Studies* 17 (3): 10–28.

———. 1987. "Gender and the Dynamics of Subcontracting in Mexico City." In *Gender in the Workplace*, edited by Clair Brown and Joseph Pechman, 159–88. Washington DC: Brookings Institution.

———. 1992. "Accounting for Women's Work: The Progress of Two Decades." *World Development* 20 (11): 1547–60.

———. 1999a. "Structural Adjustment Policies." In *The Elgar Companion to Feminist Economics*, edited by Janice Peterson and Margaret Lewis, 687–95. Cheltenham, UK: Edward Elgar.

———. 1999b. "Globalization, Gender and the Davos Man." *Feminist Economics* 5 (3): 61–83.

———. 1999c. "The Enduring Debate over Unpaid Labour." *International Labour Review* 138 (3): 287–309.

———. 2003. *Gender, Development, and Globalization: Economics as If All People Mattered.* New York: Routledge.

———. 2008. "The Crisis of Care, International Migration, and Public Policy." *Feminist Economics* 14 (3): 1–21.

———. 2009. "Globalization, Women's Work, and Care Needs: The Urgency of Reconciliation Policies." *North Carolina Law Review* 88 (5). HeinOnline: 1501–26.

Bería, Lourdes, and Shelly Feldman. 1992. *Unequal Burden, Economic Crises, Persistent Poverty, and Women's Work.* Boulder, CO: Westview Press.

Bería, Lourdes, and Maria Sagrario Floro. 2006. "Labour Market Informalization, Gender and Social Protection: Reflections on Poor Urban Households in Bolivia and Ecuador." In *Gender and Social Policy in a Global Context*, edited by Shahrashoub Razavi and hireen Hassim, 193–217. Hampshire and New York: Palgrave Macmillan.

Bería, Lourdes, and M. Martinez-Iglesias. 2010. "The New Gender Order and Reconciliation Policies: The Case of Spain." In *Work–Family Life Reconciliation in Comparative Perspective: Towards Gender Equality in the Labor Market*, edited by İpek Ilkkaracan. Istanbul Technical University Center for Women's Studies in Science, Technology and Engineering.

———. 2014. *Taking Advantage of Austerity: The Economic Crisis and Care in Spain.* Working Paper, Istanbul Technical University Women's Studies Center and WWHR-New Way. Available at, http://www.kaum.itu.edu.tr/index.php?islem=sayfa&id=2&sid=100.

Benería, Lourdes, and Breny Mendoza. 1995. "Structural Adjustment and Social Emergency Funds: The Cases of Honduras, Mexico and Nicaragua." *The European Journal of Development Research* 7 (1): 53–76.

Benería, Lourdes, and Iñaki Permanyer. 2010. "The Measurement of Socioeconomic Gender Inequality Revisited." *Development and Change* 41 (3): 375–99.

Benería, Lourdes, and Martha Roldán. 1987. *The Crossroads of Class and Gender: Homework, Subcontracting and Household Dynamics in Mexico City*. Chicago: University of Chicago Press.

Benería, Lourdes and Fulvia Rosenberg, 1999. *Brazil Gender Review*, report/evaluation of World Bank projects in Brazil.

Benería, Lourdes, and Gita Sen. 1981. "Accumulation, Reproduction, and 'Woman's Role in Economic Development': Boserup Revisited." *Signs*, 279–98.

———. 1982. "Class and Gender Inequalities and Woman's Role in Economic Development – Theoretical and Practical Implications." *Feminist Studies* 8 (1): 157–78.

Benería, Lourdes, Carmen Diana Deere, and Naila Kabeer. 2012. "Gender and International Migration: Globalization, Development and Governance." *Feminist Economics* 18 (2): 1–34.

Benham, Lee. 1974. "Benefits of Women's Education within Marriage." In *Economics of the Family: Marriage, Children, and Human Capital*, edited by Theodore W. Schultz, 375–94. University of Chicago Press.

Benton, Lauren A. 1989. "Homework and Industrial Development: Gender Roles and Restructuring in the Spanish Shoe Industry." *World Development* 17 (2): 255–66.

Berger, Silvia. 1995. "Mujeres En Suspuestos: Clases Sociales Y Oferta de Trabajo En La Reestructuracion Del Capitalismo Argentino." *Estudios Sobre Reestructuración Socioeconómic Y Subordinación de Género En Argentina* 3.

Bergmann, Barbara. 1974. "Occupational Segregation, Wages and Profit When Employers Discriminate by Race and Sex." *Eastern Economic Journal* 1 (2): 103–10.

———. 1981. "The Economic Risks of Being a Housewife." *American Economic Review* 71 (2): 81–86.

———. 1995. "Becker's Theory of the Family: Preposterous Conclusions." *Feminist Economics* 1 (1): 141–50.

Berik, Günseli. 1989. *Born Factories: Women's Labor in Carpet Workshops in Rural Turkey*. Women and International Development Working Paper No. 177. Michigan State University.

———. 1997. "The Need for Crossing the Method Boundaries in Economics Research." *Feminist Economics* 3 (2): 121–25.

———. 2000. "Mature Export-Led Growth and Gender Wage Inequality in Taiwan." *Feminist Economics* 6 (3): 1–26.

———. 2008. "Growth with Gender Inequity: Another Look at East Asian Development." In *Social Justice and Gender Equality: Rethinking Development Strategies and Macroeconomic Policies*, edited by Günseli Berik, Yana van der Meulen Rodgers, and Ann Zammit, 154–86. New York and Abingdon, UK: Routledge.

————. 2011. "Gender Aspects of Trade." In *Trade and Employment: From Myths to Facts*, edited by Marion Jansen, Ralph Peters, and Jose Manuel Salazar-Xirinachs. Geneva: ILO.

————. 2014. "Towards Feminist, Ecological, New Developmentalism: A Conversation on Ends and Means." Paper presented at the URPE/IAFFE joint panel at ASSA Meeting, Philadelphia, PA, January 5, 2014.

Berik, Günseli, and Cihan Bilginsoy. 2000. "Type of Work Matters: Women's Labor Force Participation and the Child Sex Ratio in Turkey." *World Development* 28 (5): 861–78.

Berik, Günseli, and Ebru Kongar. 2013. "Time Allocation of Married Mothers and Fathers in Hard Times: The 2007–09 US Recession." *Feminist Economics* 19 (3): 208–23.

Berik, Günseli, and Yana van der Meulen Rodgers. 2010. "Options for Enforcing Labour Standards: Lessons from Bangladesh and Cambodia." *Journal of International Development* 22 (1): 56–85.

————. 2012. "What's Macroeconomic Policy Got to Do with Gender Inequality? Evidence from Asia." *Global Social Policy* 12: 183–89.

Berik, Günseli, Yana van der Meulen Rodgers, and Stephanie Seguino. 2009. "Feminist Economics of Inequality, Development, and Growth." *Feminist Economics* 15 (3): 1–33.

Berik, Günseli, Yana van der Meulen Rodgers, and Ann Zammit, eds. 2008. *Social Justice and Gender Equality: Rethinking Development Strategies and Macroeconomic Policies*. New York: Routledge.

Berik, Günseli, Yana van der Meulen Rodgers, and Joseph E. Zveglich. 2004. "International Trade and Gender Wage Discrimination: Evidence from East Asia." *Review of Development Economics* 8 (2): 237–54.

Bernstein, Jared, Heidi Hartmann, and John Schmitt. 1999. *The Minimum Wage Increase: A Working Woman's Issue*. Washington DC: Economic Policy Institute.

Better Work. 2014. http://betterwork.org/global/

Bhagwati, Jagdish. 2004. *In Defense of Globalization*. New York: Oxford University Press.

Bhatla, Nandita, Swati Chakraborty, and Nata Duvvury. 2006. *Property Ownership and Inheritance Rights of Women as Social Protection from Domestic Violence: Cross-Site Analysis*. Washington DC: International Center for Research on Women.

Bhattacharya, Haimanti. 2015. "Spousal Violence and Women's Employment in India." *Feminist Economics* 21 (2).

Bhattacharya, Sudhir. 1985. "On the Issue of Underenumeration of Women's Work in the Indian Data Collection System." In *Women in Poverty. Tyranny of the Household: Investigative Essays on Women's Work*, edited by D. Jain and N. Banerjee, 195–214. New Delhi: Shakti Books.

Bhattacharyya, Manasi, Arjun S. Bedi, and Amrita Chhachhi. 2011. "Marital Violence and Women's Employment and Property Status: Evidence from North Indian Villages." *World Development* 39 (9): 1676–89.

Bianchi, Suzanne M., Melissa A. Milkie, Liana C. Sayer, and John P. Robinson. 2000. "Is Anyone Doing the Housework? Trends in the Gender Division of Household Labor." *Social Forces* 79 (1): 191–228.

Bilginsoy, Cihan. 2015. *A History of Financial Crises: Dreams and Follies of Expectations*. New York: Routledge.

Bittman, Michael. 1991. *Juggling Time: How Australian Women Use Time*. Canberra, Australian Capital Territory: Office of the Status of Women, Department of the Prime Minister and Cabinet.

———. 1999. "Parenthood Without Penalty: Time Use and Public Policy in Australia and Finland." *Feminist Economics*, 5(3): 27–42.

Bittman, Michael, and Jocelyn Pixley. 1997. *The Double Life of the Family*. Sydney: Allen & Unwin.

Bittman, Michael, Lyn Craig, and Nancy Folbre. 2004. "Packaging Care: What Happens When Parents Utilize Non-Parental Child Care." In *Family Time: The Social Organization of Care*, edited by Michael Bittman and Nancy Folbre, 133–51. London: Routledge.

Bittman, Michael, Paula England, Liana Sayer, Nancy Folbre, and George Matheson. 2003. "When Does Gender Trump Money? Bargaining and Time in Household Work." *American Journal of Sociology* 109 (1): 186–214.

Bivens, Josh, and Sarah Gammage. 2005. "Will Better Workers Lead to Better Jobs in the Developing World?" In *Good Jobs, Bad Jobs, No Jobs: Labor Markets and Informal Work in Egypt, El Salvador, India, Russia, and South Africa* edited by Tony Avirgan, Josh Bivens, and Sarah Gammage, 1–30. Washington, DC: Economic Policy Institute.

Black, Sandra, and Elizabeth Brainerd. 2004. "Importing Equality? The Impact of Globalization on Gender Discrimination." *Industrial and Labor Relations Review* 57 (4): 540–59.

Blackden, Mark, and Elizabeth Morris-Hughes. 1993. *Paradigm Postponed: Gender and Economic Adjustment in Sub-Saharan Africa*. Technical Department, African Region, The World Bank.

Blanco, Lorenzo, and Sandra M. Villa. 2008. "Sources of Crime in the State of Veracruz: The Role of Female Labor Force Participation and Wage Inequality." *Feminist Economics* 14 (3): 51–75.

Blank, Rebecca. 1993. "What Should Mainstream Economists Learn from Feminist Theory?" In *Beyond Economic Man: Feminist Theory and Economics*, edited by Julie A. Nelson and Marianne Ferber, 133–43. Chicago: University of Chicago Press.

Blau, Francine. 1976. "Longitudinal Patterns of Female Labor Force Participation." *Dual Careers* 4. Washington DC.

Blau, Francine, Marianne Ferber, and Anne Winkler. 2014. *The Economics of Women, Men, and Work*. 7th ed. Boston: Pearson.

Boeri, Tito, and Pietro Garibaldi. 2007. "Two Tier Reforms of Employment Protection: A Honeymoon Effect?" *The Economic Journal* 117 (521): F357–F385.

Boserup, Ester. 1970. *Woman's Role in Economic Development*. New York: St. Martin's Press.

Bourguignon, François, and Pierre-Andre Chiappori. 1992. "Collective Models of Household Behavior: An Introduction." *European Economic Review* 36 (2): 355–64.

Brainerd, Elizabeth. 2000. "Women in Transition: Changes in Gender Wage Differential in Eastern Europe and the Former Soviet Union." *Industrial and Labor Relations Review* 54 (1): 138–62.

Branisa, Boris, Stephan Klasen, Maria Ziegler, Denis Drechsler, and Johannes Jütting. 2014. "The Institutional Basis of Gender Inequality: The Social Institutions and Gender Index (SIGI)." *Feminist Economics* 20 (2): 29–64.

Braunstein, Elissa. 2000. "Engendering Foreign Direct Investment: Family structure, labor markets and international capital mobility." *World Development* 28 (7): 1157–72.

Braunstein, Elissa, and Nancy Folbre. 2001. "To Honor and Obey: Efficiency, Inequality and Patriarchal Property Rights." *Feminist Economics* 7 (1): 25–44.

Braunstein, Elissa, Irene van Staveren, and Daniele Tavani. 2011. "Embedding Care and Unpaid Work in Macroeconomic Modeling: A Structuralist Approach." *Feminist Economics* 17 (4): 5–31.

Breman, Jan. 2010. *Outcast Labour in Asia—Circulation and Informalization of the Workforce at the Bottom of the Economy*. New Delhi: Oxford University Press.

Breman, Jan, and Marcel van der Linden. 2014. "Informalizing the Economy: The Return of the Social Question at a Global Level." *Development and Change* 45 (5): 920–40.

Brennan, Denise. 2002. "Selling Sex for Visas: Sex Tourism as a Stepping-Stone to International Migration." In *Global Woman Nannies, Maids and Sex Workers in the New Economy*, 154–68. London: Granta.

Broad, Robin. 1988. *Unequal Alliance: The World Bank, the International Monetary Fund, and the Philippines*. Berkeley: University of California Press.

———. 2002. *Global Backlash: Citizen Initiatives for a Just World Economy*. New York and Oxford: Rowman & Littlefield.

Broad, Robin, and John Cavanagh. 2013. "Reframing Development in the Age of Vulnerability: From Case Studies of the Philippines and Trinidad to New Measures of Rootedness." *Third World Quarterly* 32 (6): 1127–45.

Brody, Alyson, Justin Demetriades, and Emily Esplen. 2008. *Gender and Climate Change: Mapping the Linkages*. Brighton, UK: BRIDGE-Institute for Development Studies, University of Sussex.

Bronfenbrenner, Kate. 2000. *Uneasy Terrain: The Impact of Capital Mobility on Workers, Wages, and Union Organizing*. U.S Trade Deficit Review Commission.

Bruegel, Irene, and Diane Perrons. 1998. "Deregulation and Women's Employment: The Diverse Experiences of Women in Britain." *Feminist Economics* 4 (1): 103–25.

Buckley, Peter J., and Pervez N. Ghauri. 2004. "Globalisation, Economic Geography and the Strategy of Multinational Enterprises." *Journal of International Business Studies* 35 (2): 81–98.

Budlender, Debbie. 2000. "The Political Economy of Women's Budgets in the South." *World Development* 28 (7): 1365–78.

———. 2007. "A Critical Review of Selected Time Use Surveys." Paper N°2. Geneva: Unites Nations Research institute for Social Development.

————. 2008. *The Statistical Evidence on Care and Non-Care Work across Six Countries.* Geneva: United Nations Research Institute for Social Development.

————. 2010. *Time Use Studies and Unpaid Care Work.* New York: Routledge.

Buechler, Simone Judith. 2002. "Enacting the Global Economy in São Paulo, Brazil: The Impact of Labor Market Restructuring on Low-Income Women." PhD. Dissertation. Columbia University.

————. 2013. *Labor in a Globalizing City: Economic Restructuring in São Paulo, Brazil.* New York: Springer Interational Publishing.

Burchardt, Tania. 2008. *Time and Income Poverty.* London: Centre for Analysis of Social Exclusion, London School of Economics.

Busse, Matthias, and Christian Spielmann. 2006. "Gender Inequality and Trade." *Review of International Economics* 14 (3): 362–70.

Buvinić, Mayra. 1986. "Projects for Women in the Third World: Explaining Their Misbehavior." *World Development* 14 (5): 653–64.

Buvinić, Mayra, and Geeta Rao Gupta. 1997. "Female-Headed Households and Female-Maintained Families: Are They Worth Targeting to Reduce Poverty in Developing Countries?" *Economic Development and Cultural Change* 45 (2): 259–80.

Byrnes, Andrew, and Marsha Freeman. 2012. *The Impact of the CEDAW Convention: Paths to Equality.* Research Series No. 7. University of New South Wales Faculty of Law.

Çağatay, Nilüfer. 1996. "Gender and International Labor Standards." *Review of Radical Political Economics* 28 (3): 92–101.

————. 2001. *Trade, Gender, and Poverty.* New York: United Nation Development Programme (UNDP).

————. 2003a. "Engendering Macro-Economics." In *Macroeconomics: Making Gender Matter*, edited by Martha Gutierrez, 22–41. London: Zed Press.

————. 2003b. "Gender Budgets and Beyond: Feminist Fiscal Policy in the Context of Globalisation." *Gender & Development* 11 (1): 15–24.

Çağatay, Nilüfer, and Günseli Berik. 1991. "Transition to Export Led Growth in Turkey: Is There a Feminization of Employment?" *Capital & Class* 43.

Çağatay, Nilüfer, and Şule Özler. 1995. "Feminization of the Labor Force: The Effects of Long-Term Development and Structural Adjustment." *World Development* 23 (11): 1883–94.

Çağatay, Nilüfer, Diane Elson, and Caren Grown. 1995. "Gender, Adjustment and Macroeconomics. Special Issue." *World Development* 23 (11): 1827–36.

Cappelli, Peter. 1999. *The New Deal at Work: Managing the Market-Driven Workforce.* Boston: Harvard Business School Press.

Carney, Judith A. 1992. "Peasant Women and Economic Transformation in the Gambia." *Development and Change* 23 (2): 67–90.

Carr, Marilyn, and Martha Chen. 2008. "Globalization, Social Exclusion and Gender." *International Labour Review* 143 (1–2): 129–60.

Carr, Marilyn, and Mariama Williams. 2010. *Trading Stories: Experiences with Gender and Trade.* London: Commonwealth Secretariat.

Carr, Marilyn, Martha Chen, and Jane Tate. 2000. "Globalization and Home-Based Workers." *Feminist Economics* 6 (3): 123–42.

Carrasco, Cristina, and Marius Dominguez. 2011. "Family Strategies for Meeting Care and Domestic Work Needs: Evidence from Spain." *Feminist Economics* 17 (4): 159–88.

Carter, Michael R., and Elizabeth G. Katz. 1997. "Separate Spheres and the Conjugal Contract: Understanding the Impact of Gender-Biased Development." In *Intra-Household Resource Allocation in Developing Countries: Models, Methods and Policy*. Baltimore, MD: Johns Hopkins University Press.

Cassels, Jamie. 1993. "User Requirements and Data Needs." In *Summary of Proceedings of the International Conference on the Valuation and Measurement of Unpaid Work*, 18–30. Ottawa: Statistics Canada.

Castells, Manuel, and Alejandro Portes. 1989. "World Underneath: The Origins, Dynamics and Effects of the Informal Economy." In *The Informal Economy: Studies in Advanced and Less Developed Countries*, edited by Alejandro Portes, Manuel Castells, and Lauren A. Benton. Baltimore, MD: Johns Hopkins University Press.

CEPAL. 2004. *Panorama Social de América Latina 2004*. Santiago, Chile: Naciones Unidas, CEPAL.

Chadeau, Ann. 1992. *What Is a Households' Non-Market Production Worth*. Paris: Organization for Economic Cooperation and Development.

Chambers, Robert. 2006. "Vulnerability, Coping and Policy." *IDS Bulletin* 37 (4): 33–40.

Chang, Ha-Joon. 2002. *Kicking Away the Ladder: Development Strategy in Historical Perspective*. Anthem Press.

———. 2011. "Hamlet without the Prince of Denmark." In *Towards New Developmentalism: Market as Means rather than Master*, edited by Shahrukh R. Khan and Jens Christiansen, pp. 47–58. Abindgdon, UK and New York: Routledge.

Chang, Ha-Joon, and Ilene Grabel. 2014. "Preface to the Critique Influence Change Edition." In *Reclaiming Development: An Alternative Economic Policy Manual*, edited by Ha-Joon Chang and Ilene Grabel. London and New York: Zed Books. pp. xxvi–xxxi.

Chang, Hongqin, Fiona MacPhail, and Xiao-yuan Dong. 2011. "Feminization of Labor and the Time-Use Gender Gap in Rural China." *Feminist Economics* 17 (4): 93–124.

Chant, Sylvia. 2007. *Gender, Generation and Poverty: Exploring the "Feminisation of Poverty" in Africa, Asia and Latin America*. Cheltenham, UK: Edward Elgar.

———. 2008. "The Feminisation of Poverty and the Feminisation of Anti-Poverty Programmes: Room for Revision?" *Journal of Development Studies* 44 (2): 165–97.

———. 2010. "Gendered Poverty across Space and Time: Introduction and Overview." In *The International Handbook of Gender and Poverty*, edited by Sylvia Chant, 1–28. Cheltenham, UK and Northampton, MA: Edward Elgar.

———. 2012. "The Disappearing of 'Smart Economics'? The World Development Report 2012 on Gender Equality: Some Concerns about the Preparatory Process and the Prospects for Paradigm Change." *Global Social Policy* 12: 198–218.

Chant, Sylvia, and Caroline Sweetman. 2012. "Fixing Women or Fixing the World? 'Smart Economics', Efficiency Approaches, and Gender Equality in Development." *Gender and Development* 20 (3): 517–29.

Charles, Aurelie. 2011. "Fairness and Wages in Mexico's Maquiladora Industry: An Empirical Analysis of Labor Demand and the Gender Wage Gap." *Review of Social Economy* 69 (1): 1–28.

Charmes, Jacques. 1998. *Women Working in the Informal Sector in Africa: New Methods and New Data*. New York: UN Statistics Division, the Gender in Development Programme of UNDP.

———. 2004. *Data Collection on the Informal Sector: A Review of Concepts and Methods Used Since the Adoption of an International Definition Towards a Better Comparability of Available Statistics*. Geneva: ILO.

———. 2012. "The Informal Economy Worldwide: Trends and Characteristics" *Margin: The Journal of Applied Economic Research* 6 (103): 103–132. Available at, http://mar.sagepub.com/content/6/2/103. Accessed on April 11, 2013.

Chen, Martha. 2005. "Rethinking the Informal Economy: Linkages with the Formal Economy and the Formal Regulatory Environment." Research Paper No. 2005/10. UNU-WIDER, United Nations University (UNU).

Chen, Martha, and Marilyn Carr. 2004. "Globalization, Social Exclusion and Work: With Special Reference to Informal Employment and Gender." *International Labour Review* 143 (1–2): 129–60.

Chen, Martha, Joann Vanek, Francie Lund, James Heintz, Renana Jhabvala, and Christine Bonner. 2005. *Progress of the World's Women: Women, Work and Poverty*. New York: United Nations Development Fund for Women.

Chin, Christine. 2013. *Cosmopolitan Sex Workers: Women and Migration in a Global City*. Oxford, UK and New York: Oxford University Press.

Chin, Yoo-Mi. 2012. "Male Backlash, Bargaining, or Exposure Reduction?: Women's Working Status and Spousal Violence in India." *Journal of Population Economics* 25: 175–200.

Cho, Seo-young, Axel Dreher, and Eric Neumayer. 2013. "Does Legalized Prostitution Increase Human Trafficking?" *World Development* 41: 67–82.

Chor, Davin, and Richard B. Freeman. 2005. *The 2004 Global Labor Survey: Workplace Institutions and Practices around the World*. NBER Working Paper 11598, Cambridge, MA: NBER.

Coase, Ronald H. 1937. "The Nature of the Firm." *Economica* 4 (16): 386–405.

Cobham, Alex, and Andy Sumner. 2013. *Is It All About the Tails? The Palma Measure of Income Inequality*. Working Paper. No. 343. Center for Global Development. Available at, http://www.cgdev.org/sites/default/files/it-all-about-tails-palma-measure-income-inequality.pdf

Coleman, Brett E. 2006. "Microfinance in Northeast Thailand: Who Benefits and How Much?" *World Development* 34 (9): 1612–38.

Colgan, Fiona, and Sue Ledwith, eds. 2002. *Gender, Diversity and Trade Unions*. New York: Routledge.

Collins, Mary. 1993. "Opening Remarks." In *Statistics Canada/Status of Women. Summary of Proceedings of the International Conference on the Valuation and Measurement of Unpaid Work. Ottawa, 18–30 April.* Ottawa.

Commonwealth Secretariat. 1989. *Engendering Adjustment for the 1990s.* London: Commonwealth Secretariat.

Connolly, Kate, and Louise Osborne. 2013. "Low-Paid Germans Mind Rich-Poor Gap as Elections Approach." *The Guardian*, August 30. Available at, http://www.the guardian.com/world/2013/aug/30/low-paid-germans-mini-jobs.

Cook, Maria Lorena. 2002. "Cross-Border Labor Solidarity." In *Global Backlash: Citizen Initiatives for a Just World Economy*, edited by Robin Broad, 140–41. New York and Oxford: Rowman & Littlefield.

Cornia, Giovanni Andrea, Richard Jolly, and Frances Stewart. 1987. *Adjustment with a Human Face: Protecting the Vulnerable and Promoting Growth, A Study by UNICEF.* New York: Oxford University Press.

Costanza, Robert. 1989. "What Is Ecological Economics?" *Ecological Economics* 1 (1): 1–7.

Craig, Lyn, and Michael Bittman. 2008. "The Incremental Time Costs of Children: An Analysis of Children's Impact on Adult Time Use in Australia." *Feminist Economics* 14 (2): 59–88.

Craig, Lyn, Killian Mullan, and Megan Blaxland. 2010. "Parenthood, Policy and Work-Family Time in Australia 1992–2006." *Work, Employment & Society* 24 (1): 27–45.

Cravey, Altha. 1997. *Women and Work in Mexico's Maquiladoras.* Lanham, MD: Rowman & Littlefield.

Croll, Elisabeth. 1979. *Women and Rural Development in China: Production and Reproduction.* Geneva: International Labour Office.

———. 1985. *Women and Rural Development in China: Production and Reproduction.* Women, Work and Development Series No. 11. Geneva: International Labour Office.

Crompton, Rosemary, Duncan Gallie, and Kate Purcell. 1996. "Work, Economic Restructuring and Social Regulation." In *Changing Forms of Employment-Organizations, Skills and Gender*, edited by Rosemary Crompton, Duncan Gallie, and Kate Purcell, 1–20. London: Routledge.

Cypher, James M. 2014. *The Process of Economic Development.* 4th ed. Abingdon, UK and New York: Routledge.

Cypher, James M. and James Dietz. 2009. *The Process of Economic Development.* 3rd ed. Abingdon, UK and New York: Routledge.

Da Roit, Barbara, and Bernhard Weicht. 2013. "Migrant Care Work and Care, Migration and Employment Regimes: A Fuzzy-Set Analysis." *Journal of European Social Policy* 23 (5): 469–86.

Daly, Herman E, and Joshua Farley. 2004. *Ecological Economics: Principles and Practice.* Washington DC: Island Press.

Daly, Mary E. 2001. *Care Work: The Quest for Security.* Geneva and London: International Labour Organization.

Daly, Mary E., and Jane Lewis. 2000. "The Concept of Social Care and the Analysis of Contemporary Welfare States." *The British Journal of Sociology* 51 (2): 281–98.

Danby, Colin. 2004. "Toward a Gendered Post Keynesianism: Subjectivity and Time in a Nonmodernist Framework." *Feminist Economics* 10 (3): 55–75.

Dannin, Ellen J. 2006. *Taking Back the Workers' Law: How to Fight the Assault on Labor Rights.* Ithaca, NY: ILR Press.

Darity, William Jr. 1995. "The Formal Structure of a Gender-Segregated Low-Income Economy." *World Development* 23 (11): 1963–68.

Dasgupta, Sukti, and David Williams. 2010. "Women Facing the Economic crisis—The Garment Sector in Cambodia." In *Poverty and Sustainable Development in Asia*, edited by A. Bauer and M. Thant. Manila: Asian Development Bank.

Dash, Anup. 2014. *Toward an Epistemological Foundation for Social and Solidarity Economy.* UNRISD Occasional Paper No. 3. Geneva. UNRISD.

Dayal, Mala. 2002. *Towards Securer Lives: SEWA's Social-Security Programme.* New Delhi: Ravi Dayal Publisher.

DAWN (Development Alternatives for Women in a New Era). 2013. "DAWN Response to High Level Panel Report on Post 2015 Development Agenda." http://www.dawnnet.org/advocacy-appeals.php?id=306.

De Brauw, Alan, Daniel O. Gilligan, John Hoddinott, and Shalini Roy. 2014. "The Impact of Bolsa Família on Women's Decision-Making Power." *World Development* 59: 487–504.

De la O, M. E. 2006. "El Trabajo de Las Mujeres En La Industria Maquiladora de México: Balance de Cuatro Décadas de E/studio." *AIBR: Revista de Antropología Iberoamericana* 1 (3).

De Ruyter, Alex, Ajit Singh, Tonia Warnecke, and Ann Zammit. 2012. "Labor Standards, Gender and Decent Work in Newly Industrialized Countries: Promoting the Good Society." In *Alternative Perspectives of a Good Society*, edited by John Marangos, 121–46. New York: Palgrave Macmillan.

De Vogli, Roberto, and Gretchen L. Birbeck. 2011. "Potential Impact of Adjustment Policies on Vulnerability of Women and Children to HIV/AIDS in Sub-Saharan Africa." *Journal of Health, Population and Nutrition* 23 (2): 105–20.

Dedeoğlu, Saniye. 2010. "Visible Hands–Invisible Women: Garment Production in Turkey." *Feminist Economics* 16 (4): 1–32.

Deere, Carmen Diana. 1976. "Rural Women's Subsistence Production in the Capitalist Periphery." *Review of Radical Political Economics* 8 (1): 9–17.

———. 1977. "Changing Social Relations of Production and Peruvian Peasant Women's Work." *Latin American Perspectives* 4 (12–13): 58–69.

———. 1982. "The Division of Labor by Sex in Agriculture: A Peruvian Case Study." *Economic Development and Cultural Change* 30 (4): 795–811.

———. 2009. "The Feminization of Agriculture?: The Impact of Economic Restructuring in Rural Latin America." In *The Gendered Impacts of Liberalization: Towards Embedded Liberalism?*, edited by Shahra Razavi, 99–127. New York and Abingdon, UK: Routledge.

Deere, Carmen Diana, and Cheryl R. Doss. 2006. "The Gender Asset Gap: What Do We Know and Why Does It Matter?" *Feminist Economics* 12 (1–2): 1–50.

Deere, Carmen Diana, and Magdalena León de Leal. 1987. *Rural Women and State Policy: Feminist Perspectives on Latin American Agricultural Development*. Boulder, CO: Westview Press.

———. 2001a. *Empowering Women. Land and Property Rights in Latin America*. Pittsburgh: University of Pittsburg Press.

———. 2001b. "Institutional Reform of Agriculture under Neoliberalism: The Impact of the Women's and Indigenous Movements." *Latin American Research Review* 36 (2): 31–64.

———. 2003. "The Gender Asset Gap: Land in Latin America." *World Development* 31 (6): 925–47.

Deere, Carmen Diana, Gina E. Alvarado, and Jennifer Twyman. 2012. "Gender Inequality in Asset Ownership in Latin America: Female Owners versus Household Heads." *Development and Change* 43 (2): 505–530.

Deere, Carmen Diana, Abena D. Oduro, Hema Swaminathan, and Cheryl Doss. 2013. "Property Rights and the Gender Distribution of Wealth in Ecuador, Ghana and India." *The Journal of Economic Inequality* 11 (2): 249–65.

Delphy, Christine. 1984. *Close to Home: A Materialist Analysis of Women's Oppression*. Amherst, MA: University of Massachusetts Press.

Delphy, Christine, and D. Leonard. 1992. *Familiar Exploitation: A New Analysis of Marriage in Contemporary Western Societies*. Cambridge: Polity Press.

Departamento Administrativo Nacional de Estadistica (DANE). 2013. *Encuesta Nacional de Uso Del Tiempo (ENUT)*. Boletin de Prensa. Bogota, Colombia. Available at, http://www.dane.gov.co/files/investigaciones/boletines/ENUT/Bol_ENUT_2012_ 2013.pdf. Accessed on July 10, 2014.

———. 2014. *Economia de Cuidado*. Bogotá, Colombia. Available at, http://www.dane. gov.co/index.php/es/cuentas-economicas/cuentas-satelite/77-cuentas-nacionales/ cuentas-anuales/2805-economia-del-cuidado.Accessed on June 25, 2014.

Dijkstra, Geske. 2006. "Towards a Fresh Start in Measuring Gender Equality: A Contribution to the Debate." *Journal of Human Development* 7 (2): 275–83.

———. 2011. "The PRSP Approach and the Illusion of Improved Aid Effectiveness: Lessons from Bolivia, Honduras, and Nicaragua." *Development Policy Review* 29 (S1): S110–33.

Dijkstra, Geske, and Lucia Hanmer. 2000. "Measuring Socio-Economic Gender Inequality: Toward an Alternative to the UNDP Gender-Related Development Index." *Feminist Economics* 6 (2): 41–75.

Doellgast, Virginia, and Ian Greer. 2007. "Vertical Disintegration and the Disorganization of German Industrial Relations." *British Journal of Industrial Relations* 45 (1): 55–76.

Dollar, David, and Roberta Gatti. 1999. *Gender Inequality, Income, and Growth: Are Good Times Good for Women?* Policy Research Report on Gender and Development, Working Paper Series. Washington DC.

Domínguez, Edmé, Rosalba Icaza, Cirila Quintero, Silvia López, and Åsa Stenman. 2010. "Women Workers in the Maquiladoras and the Debate on Global Labor Standards." *Feminist Economics* 16 (4): 185–209.

Domínguez-Villalobos, Lilia, and Flor Brown-Grossman. 2010. "Gender Wage Gap and Trade Liberalization in Mexico." *Feminist Economics* 16 (4): 53–79.

Doraisami, Anita. 2008. "The Gender Implications of Macroeconomic Policy and Performance in Malaysia." In *Social Justice and Gender Equality: Rethinking Development Strategies and Macroeconomic Policies*, edited by Günseli Berik, Yana van der Meulen Rodgers, and Ann Zammit, 187–212. New York and London: Routledge.

Dorman, Peter, Nancy Folbre, Donald McCloskey, and Tom Weisskopf. 1996. "Debating Markets." *Feminist Economics* 2 (1): 69–85.

Doss, Cheryl. 2013. *Intrahousehold Bargaining and Resource Allocation in Developing Countries*. Policy Research Working Paper No. 6337. Washington DC: The World Bank.

Drèze, Jean, and Amartya Sen. 2013. *An Uncertain Glory: India and Its Contradictions*. Princeton, NJ: Princeton University Press.

Duvvury, Nata, and Madhabika B. Nayak. 2003. "The Role of Men in Addressing Domestic Violence: Insights from India." *Development* 46 (2): 45–50.

Duvvury, Nata, Patricia Carney, and Huu Minh Nguyen. 2012. *Estimating the Costs of Domestic Violence against Women in Viet Nam*. Galway: National University of Ireland.

Dwyer, Daisy, and Judith Bruce. 1988. *A Home Divided: Women and Income in the Third World*. Stanford, CA: Stanford University Press.

Dymski, Gary, Jesus Hernandez, and Lisa Mohanty. 2013. "Is This Race, Gender, Power, and the US Subprime Mortgage and Foreclosure Crisis: A Meso Analysis in Feminist Economics." *Feminist Economics* 19 (3): 124–51.

ECA (Economic Comission for Africa). 1989. *Adjustment with Transformation*. Addis Ababa: Economic Commission for Africa, United Nations.

ECLAC (Economic Comission for Latin America). 1990. *Transformación Productiva Con Equidad*. Santiago, Chile: Economic Commission for Latin America.

———. 1995. *Social Panorama of Latin America*. Santiago, Chile: Economic Commission for Latin America.

Edwards, Richard, Michael Reich, and David Gordon. 1973. *Labor Market Segmentation*. Lexington, MA: D.C. Heath and Co.

Egaña, Pablo, and Alejandro Micco. 2011. *Labor Market in Latin America and the Caribbean: The Missing Reform*. 345. Serie Documentos de Trabajo. Santiago, Chile.

Eisenstein, Hester. 2005. "A Dangerous Liaison? Feminism and Corporate Globalization." *Science & Society*, 487–518.

———. 2009. *Feminism Seduced; How Global Elites Use Women's Labor and Ideas to Exploit Women*. Boulder, CO and London: Paradigm Publishers.

Elborgh-Woytek, Katrin, Monique Newiak, Kalpana Kochhar, Stefania Fabrizio, Kangni Kpodar, Philippe Wingender, Benedict Clements, and Gerd Schwartz. 2013.

Women, Work, and the Economy: Macroeconomic Gains from Gender Equity. Staff Discussion Note, International Monetary Fund (IMF).

Elson, Diane. 1991a. *Male Bias in the Development Process.* Manchester, UK: Manchester University Press.

———. 1991b. "Male Bias in Macroeconomics: The Case of Structural Adjustment." In *Male Bias in the Development Process*, edited by Diane Elson, 164–90. Manchester and New York: Manchester University Press.

———. 1999. "Labor Markets as Gendered Institutions: Equality, Efficiency and Empowerment Issues." *World Development* 27 (3): 611–27.

———. 2002a. "Gender Justice, Human Rights and Neo-Liberal Economic Policies." In *Gender Justice, Development and Rights*, edited by Maxine Molyneux and Shahra Razavi. Oxford: Oxford University Press.

———. 2002b. "International Financial Architecture: A View from the Kitchen." *Politica Femina: Zeitschrift Fur Feministische Politik-Wissenschaft* 11 (1): 26–37.

———. 2005. "Unpaid Work, the Millennium Development Goals, and Capital Accumulation." In *Conference on Unpaid Work and the Economy: Gender, Poverty and the Millennium Development Goals, United Nations Development Programme and Levy Economics Institute of Bard College, Annandale-on-Hudson, New York* (1–3 October. 2005).

———. 2012a. "The Reduction of the UK Budget Deficit: A Human Rights Perspective." *International Review of Applied Economics* 26 (2): 177–90.

———. 2012b. "Review of World Development Report 2012: Gender Equality and Development." *Global Social Policy* 12 (2): 178–83.

Elson, Diane, and Nilüfer Çağatay. 2000. "The Social Content of Macroeconomic Policies." *World Development* 28 (7): 1347–64.

Elson, Diane, and Ruth Pearson. 1981. "Nimble Fingers Make Cheap Workers: An Analysis of Women's Employment in Third World Export Manufacturing." *Feminist Review* 7 (1): 87–107.

———, eds. 1989. *Women's Employment in Multinationals in Europe.* London: Macmillan Press.

Elson, Diane, and Tonia Warnecke. 2011. "IMF Policies and Gender Orders. The Case of the Poverty Reduction and the Growth Facility." In *Questioning Financial Governance from a Feminist Perspective*, edited by Brigitte Young, Isa Bakker, and Diane Elson, 110–31. London and New York: Routledge.

Engelhart, Neil A., and Melissa K. Miller. 2014. "The CEDAW Effect: International Law's Impact on Women's Rights." *Journal of Human Rights* 13: 22–47.

Engels, Frederick. [1884] 1981. *The Origin of the Family, Private Property and the State.* New Jersey: New World Paperbacks.

England, Paula. 1993. "The Separative Self: Andocentric Bias in Neoclassical Assumptions." In *Beyond Economic Man: Feminist Theory and Economics*, edited by Julie A. Nelson and Marianne Ferber, 37–53. Chicago: University of Chicago Press.

———. 2003. "Separative and Soluble Selves: Dichotomous Thinking in Economics." In *Feminist Economics Today: Beyond Economic Man*, edited by Marianne Ferber and Julie A. Nelson, 33–60. Chicago: University of Chicago Press.

EPI. 2014. "State of Working America." *2014*. Available at, http://stateofworkingamerica. org/charts/underemployment-gender/. Accessed on September 9.

Ertürk, Korkut, and Nilüfer Çağatay. 1995. "Macroeconomic Consequences of Cyclical and Secular Changes in Feminization: An Experiment at Gendered Macro-modeling." *World Development* 23 (11): 1969–77.

Escobar Latapí, Augustín, and Mercedes González de la Rocha. 2008. "Girls, Mothers and Poverty Reduction in Mexico." In *The Gendered Impacts of Liberalization: Towards Embedded Liberalism?*, edited by Shahrashoub Razavi, 435–68. New York: Routledge/UNRISD.

Esguerra, Emmanuel. 2011. *Microfinance: One Promise Too Many?* School of Economics Working Paper. Quezon City: University of the Philippines.

Esim, Simel. 1997. "Can Feminist Methodology Reduce Power Hierarchies in Research Settings?" *Feminist Economics* 3 (2): 137–39.

———. 2002. *Women's Informal Employment in Transition Economies*. Washington DC: International Center for Research on Women (ICRW), Economic and Social Committee and the Committee of the Regions.

Esping-Andersen, Gøsta. 1990. *The Three Worlds of Welfare Capitalism*. Princeton, NJ: Princeton University Press.

Espino, Alma. 2013. "Gender Dimensions of the Global Economic and Financial Crisis in Central America and the Dominican Republic." *Feminist Economics* 19 (3): 267–88.

Esquivel, Valeria. 2011. "Sixteen Years after Beijing: What Are the New Policy Agendas for Time-Use Data Collection?" *Feminist Economics* 17 (4): 215–38.

Esquivel, Valeria, and Corina Rodríguez Enríquez. 2014. "Addressing the Global Economic Crisis in Mexico, Ecuador and Argentina: Implications for Gender Equality." In *Gender Perspectives and the Gender Impacts of the Global Economic Crisis*, edited by Rania Antonopoulos. New York: Routledge.

Esquivel, Valeria, Debbie Budlender, Nancy Folbre, and Indira Hirway. 2008. "Explorations: Time-Use Surveys in the South." *Feminist Economics* 14 (3): 107–52.

EUbusiness. 2014. "Europeans Move Towards Watered-down 'Tobin' Tax." September 15. Available at, http://www.eubusiness.com/news-eu/finance-economy.xt4.

Eurofound. 2014. "Law to Support Care of Dependent People, Spain." Available at, http://www.eurofound.europa.eu/areas/labourmarket/tackling/cases/es001. htm. Accessed on July 15, 2014.

European Commission. 2012. *The Impact of the Economic Crisis on the Situation of Women and Men and on Gender Equality Policies. Report of the European Network of Experts on Gender Equality*. Available at, http://ec.europa.eu/justice.

Eurostat. 2013. *Trafficking in Human Beings*. Available at, http://ec.europa.eu/dgs/home-affairs/what-is-new/news/news/2013/docs/20130415_thb_stats_report_en.pdf.

Evans, Peter. 2008. "Is an Alternative Globalization Possible?" *Politics and Society* 36 (1): 271–305.

Express Employment Professionals. 2013. "Express Employment Professionals." http://irvineca.expresspros.com/.

Ezquerra, Sandra. 2012. "Acumulación Por Desposesión, Género Y Crisis En El Estado Español." *Revista de Economía Crítica* 14: 124–47.

Farm-to-Consumer Legal Defence Fund. 2013. "Lawsuit over Monsanto GMO Seed Patents and Farmland Contamination." Available at, www.farmtoconsumer.org/news_wp/?p=7764.

Felber, Christian. 2012. *La Economia Del Bien Comun*. Barcelona: Deusto S.A. Ediciones.

Ferber, Marianne A., and Bonnie G. Birnbaum. 1977. "The 'New Home Economics': Retrospects and Prospects." *Journal of Consumer Research*: 19–28.

Ferber, Marianne, and Julie A. Nelson, eds. 1993. *Beyond Economic Man: Feminist Theory and Economics*. Chicago: University of Chicago Press.

———, eds. 2003a. *Feminist Economics Today. Beyond Economic Man*. Chicago and London: University of Chicago Press.

———. 2003b. "Introduction." In *Feminist Economics: Beyond Economic Man*, edited by Marianne Ferber and Julie Nelson, 1–29. Chicago: University of Chicago Press.

Fiala, Robert, and Susan Tiano. 1991. "The World Views of Export Processing Workers in Northern Mexico: A Study of Women, Consciousness, and the New International Division of Labor." *Studies in Comparative International Development* 26 (3): 3–27.

Figart, Deborah M. 1997. "Gender as More than a Dummy Variable: Feminist Approaches to Discrimination." *Review of Social Economy* 55 (1): 1–32.

Figart, Deborah M., Ellen Mutari, and Marilyn Power. 2013. "A Feminist Theory of Labor Markets." In *Models of Labor Markets*, edited by Bruce Kaufman. Palo Alto, CA: Stanford University Press.

Filippin, Antonio, and Paolo Crosetto. 2014. *A Reconsideration of Gender Differences in Risk Attitudes*. 8184. Bonn, Germany: IZA DP.

Fisher, Kimberly, and Jonathan Gershuny. 2013. "Time Use and Time Diary Research." In *Oxford Bibliographies in Sociology*, edited by Jeff Manza. New York: Oxford University Press.

Fisher, Kimberly, Muriel Egerton, Jonathan I. Gershuny, and John P. Robinson. 2007. "Gender Convergence in the American Heritage Time Use Study (AHTUS)." *Social Indicators Research* 82 (1): 1–33.

Fisher, Monica G., Rebecca L. Warner, and William A. Masters. 2000. "Gender and Agricultural Change: Crop-Livestock Integration in Senegal." *Society & Natural Resources* 13 (3): 203–22.

Flecker, Jörg, and Pamela Meil. 2010. "Organisational Restructuring and Emerging Service Value Chains: Implications for Work and Employment." *Work, Employment and Society* 24 (4): 680–98.

Floro, Maria Sagrario. 1995. "Economic Restructuring, Gender and the Allocation of Time." *World Development* 23 (11): 1913–29.

———. 2005. "The Importance of the Gender Dimension in the Finance and Economic Development Nexus." In *Financial Liberalization: Beyond Orthodox Concerns*, edited by P. Arestis and M. Sawyer, 43–89. UK: Palgrave Macmillan.

———. 2012. "The Crisis of Environment and Social Reproduction: Understanding Their Linkages." *Development Dialogue: 50 Years Dag Hammarskjöld Foundation Special Issue* 60: 175–98.

Floro, Maria Sagrario, and Hitomi Komatsu. 2011. "'Labor Force Participation, Gender and Work: What Time Use Data Can Reveal?'" *Feminist Economics* (4): 33–67.

Floro, Maria Sagrario, and John Messier. 2010. "Is There a Link between Quality of Employment and Indebtedness? The Case of Urban Low-Income Households in Ecuador." *Cambridge Journal of Economics* 35 (3): 1–28.

Floro, Maria Sagrario, and Mieke Meurs. 2009. *Global Trends in Women's Access to Decent Work*. 43. Occasional Paper Series. Geneva and Berlin: Friedrich Ebert Stiftung.

Floro, Maria Sagrario, and Marjorie Miles. 2003. "Time Use, Work and Overlapping Activities: Evidence from Australia." *Cambridge Journal of Economics* 27 (6): 881–904.

Floro, Maria Sagrario, and Anant Pichetpongsa. 2010. "Gender, Work Intensity, and Well-Being of Thai Home-Based Workers." *Feminist Economics* 16 (3): 5–44.

Floro, Maria Sagrario, and Ranjula Bali Swain. 2013. "Food Security, Gender, and Occupational Choice among Urban Low-Income Households." *World Development* 42: 89–99.

Floro, Maria Sagrario, and Kendall Schaefer. 1998. "Restructuring of Labor Markets in the Philippines and Zambia: The Gender Dimension." *The Journal of Developing Areas*: 73–98.

Floro, Maria Sagrario, Emcet Oktay Taş, and Annika Törnqvist. 2010. *The Impact of the Global Economic Crisis on Women's Well-Being and Empowerment*. Stockholm: Swedish International Developmen Agency.

Folbre, Nancy. 1982. "Exploitation Comes Home: A Critique of Marxian Theory of Family Labour." *Cambridge Journal of Economics* 6: 317–29.

———. 1994. *Who Pays for the Kids? Gender and the Structures of Constraint*. New York: Routledge.

———. 1995. "'Holding Hands at Midnight': The Paradox of Caring Labor." *Feminist Economics* 1 (1): 73–92.

———. 2006. "Measuring Care: Gender, Empowerment and the Care Economy." *Journal of Human Development* 7 (2): 183–99.

———. 2008. *Valuing Children: Rethinking the Economics of the Family*. Cambridge, MA: Harvard University Press.

———. 2012. "Should Women Care Less? Intrinsic Motivation and Gender Inequality." *British Journal of Industrial Relations* 50 (4): 597–619.

Folbre, Nancy, and Jayoung Yoon. 2007. "#What Is Child Care? Lessons from Time-Use Surveys of Major English-Speaking Countries." *Review of Economics of the Household* 5 (3): 223–48.

———. 2008. "The Value of Unpaid Child Care in the US in 2003." In *Document presented at the meetings of the Allied Social Science Association, Boston, MA*.

Folbre, Nancy, and Julie A. Nelson. 2000. "For Love or Money—Or Both?" *The Journal of Economic Perspectives* 14 (4): 123–40.

Folbre, Nancy, and Michele Pujol. 1996. "A Special Issue in Honor of Margaret Reid." *Feminist Economics* 2 (3): 1–120.

Foley, Duncan K., and Thomas R. Michl. 1999. *Growth and Distribution*. Cambridge, MA: Harvard University Press.

Fontana, Marzia. 2009. "The Gender Effects of Trade Liberalization in Developing Countries: A Review of the Literature." In *Gender Aspects of the Trade and Poverty Nexus: A Macro-Micro Approach*, edited by Maurizio Bussolo and Rafael E. De Hoyos. Washington DC: The World Bank.

Fontana, Marzia, and Adrian Wood. 2000. "Modeling the Effects of Trade on Women, at Work and at Home." *World Development* 28 (7): 1173–90.

Francisco, Josefa. 2012. "Engendering the WTO? What Else?". *Review of Women's Studies* 15 (2): 2–8.

Frank, Dana. 2005. *Bananeras: Women Transforming the Banana Unions of Latin America*. Cambridge, MA: South End Press.

Frank, Robert H. 2004. *What Price the Moral High Ground?: Ethical Dilemmas in Competitive Environments*. Princeton, NJ: Princeton University Press.

Fraser, Nancy. 1997. *Justice Interruptus. Critical Reflections on the "Postcolonialist" Condition*. New York and London: Routledge.

———. 2009. "Feminism, Capitalism and the Cunning of History." *New Left Review* 56.

———. 2010. *Scales of Justice: Reimagining Political Space in a Globalizing World*. New York and Chichester, West Sussex: Columbia University Press.

———. 2013. "How Feminism Became Capitalism's Handmaiden and How to Reclaim It." *The Guardian*, October 14.

Fraumeni, Barbara. 1998. "Expanding Economic Accounts for Productivity Analysis: A Nonmarket and Human Capital Perspective." Paper presented at the Conference on Income and Wealth, organized by the National Bureau for Economic Research, 20–21 Mar. 1998.

Frazis, Harley, and Jay Stewart. 2007. "Where Does the Time Go? Concepts and Measurement in the American Time Use Survey." In *Hard-to-Measure Goods and Services: Essays in Honor of Zvi Griliches*, edited by Ernst Berndt and Charles Hulten, 73–97. University of Chicago Press.

Freeman, Carla. 2000. *High Tech and High Heels in the Global Economy: Women, Work, and Pink-Collar Identities in the Caribbean*. Duke University Press Books.

Friedan, Betty. 1963. *The Feminine Mystique*. New York: W.W. Norton & Company.

Friedemann-Sánchez, Greta. 2006. "Assets in Intrahousehold Bargaining among Women in Colombia's Cut-Flower Industry." *Feminist Economics* 12 (1–2): 247–69.

Friedemann-Sánchez, Greta, and Joan M. Griffin. 2011. "Defining the Boundaries between Unpaid Labor and Unpaid Caregiving: Review of the Social and Health Sciences Literature." *Journal of Human Development and Capabilities* 12 (4): 511–34.

Friedman, Milton, and Rose Friedman. 1980. *Free to Choose: A Personal Statement*. New York: Harcourt Brace Jovanovich.

Fukuda-Parr, Sakiko. 1999. "What Does Feminization of Poverty Mean? It Isn't Just Lack of Income." *Feminist Economics* 5 (2): 99–103.

Fukuda-Parr, Sakiko, James Heintz, and Stephanie Seguino. 2013. "Critical Perspectives on Financial and Economic Crises: Heterodox Macroeconomics Meets Feminist Economics." *Feminist Economics* 19 (3): 4–31.

Fussell, Elizabeth. 2000. "Making Labor More Flexible: The Recomposition of Tijuana's Maquiladora Female Labor Force." *Feminist Economics* 6 (3): 59–80.

Fuwa, Makiko. 2004. "Macro-Level Gender Inequality and the Division of Household Labor in 22 Countries." *American Sociological Review* 69 (6): 751–67.

Galli, Rossana, and David Charles Kucera. 2004. "Labor Standards and Informal Employment in Latin America." *World Development* 32 (5): 809–28.

Gálvez, Lina. 2013. "Una Lectura Feminista Del Austericidio." *Revista de Economía Crítica* 15: 80–110.

Gálvez-Muñoz, Lina, Paula Rodríguez-Modroño, and Monica Domínguez-Serrano. 2011. "Work and Time Use by Gender: A New Clustering of European Welfare Systems." *Feminist Economics* 17 (4): 125–57.

Gammage, Sarah. 2010. "Time Pressed and Time Poor: Unpaid Household Work in Guatemala." *Feminist Economics* 16 (3): 79–112.

Garikipati, Supriya. 2008. "The Impact of Lending to Women on Household Vulnerability and Women's Empowerment: Evidence from India." *World Development* 36 (12): 2620–42.

Garikipati, Supriya, and Stephan Pfaffenzeller. 2012. "The Gendered Burden of Liberalization: The Impact of India's Economic Reforms on Its Female Agricultural Labour." *Journal of International Development* 24: 841–64.

Geier, Kathleen, Kate Bahn, Joelle Gamble, Zillah Eisenstein, and Heather Boushey. 2014. "How Gender Changes Piketty's Capital in the 21st Century." *The Nation*, August 6. http://www.thenation.com/blog/180895/what-pikettys-capital-21st-century-missed

Gereffi, Gary. 1998. "Commodity Chains and Regional Divisions of Labor in East Asia." In *Four Asian Tigers: Economic Development and the Global Political Economy*, edited by Eun Mee Kim, 94–124. London: Academic Press.

Gereffi, Gary, and Miguel Korzeniewicz, eds. 1994. *Commodity Chains and Global Capitalism*. Westport, CT: Praeger.

Gershuny, Jonathan and Kimberly Fisher. 2013. "Exploit and Industry: Why Work Time Will Not Disappear For Our Grandchildren." Paper presented at the 35th International Association for Time Use Research Conference, Rio de Janeiro, Brazil, August 4–6.

Gershuny, Jonathan, and J. P. Robinson. 1988. "Historical Changes in the Household Division of Labor." *Demography* 25 (4): 537–52.

Gershuny, Jonathan, and Oriel Sullivan. 2003. "Time Use, Gender, and Public Policy Regimes." *Social Politics: International Studies in Gender, State & Society* 10 (2): 205–28.

Ghemawat, Pankaj. 2007. *Redefining Global Strategy: Crossing Borders in a World Where Differences Still Matter*. Boston, MA: Harvard Business School Publishing.

Ghosh, Jayati. 2000. "Rules of International Economic Integration and Human Rights." Background Paper for the Human Development Report, UNDP, New York.

Giddings, Lisa, Mieke Meurs, and Tilahun Temesgen. 2007. "Changing Preschool Enrolments in Post-Socialist Central Asia: Causes and Implications." *Comparative Economic Studies* 49 (1): 81–100.

Gill, Stephen. 2000. "Knowledge, Politics, and Neo-Liberal Political Economy." In *Political Economy and the Changing Global Order*, edited by Richard Stubbs and Geoffrey R. D. Underhill, 48–59. Toronto: Oxford University Press.

Global Social Policy. 2012. *GSP Forum on World Bank's World Development Report 2012*, 12 (2).

Goetz, Anne Marie, and Rina Sen Gupta. 1996. "Who Takes the Credit? Gender, Power, and Control over Loan Use in Rural Credit Programs in Bangladesh." *World Development* 24 (1): 45–63.

Goldin, Claudia. 1995. "The U-Shaped Female Labor Force Function in Economic Development and Economic History." In *Investment in Women's Human Capital and Economic Development*, edited by T. Paul Shultz, 61–90. Chicago: University of Chicago Press.

Goldschmidt-Clermont, Luisella. 1983. "Output-Related Evaluations Of Unpaid Household Work: A Challenge for Time Use Studies." *Home Economics Research Journal* 12 (2): 127–32.

———. 1993. "Monetary Valuation of Unpaid Work: Arguing for an Output Measurement." *Bulletin of Labour Statistics* 4: 28–30.

González de la Rocha, Mercedes. 2007. "The Construction of the Myth of Survival." *Development and Change* 38 (1): 45–66.

———. 2012. *Vulnerability, Household Dynamics and Social Policy in Mexico*. Mexico, D.F. Secretaria del Desarrollo Social.

Goodin, Robert E., James Mahmud Rice, Antti Parpo, and Lina Eriksson. 2008. *Discretionary Time: A New Measure of Freedom*. Cambridge University Press.

Gordon, David, Richard Edwards, and Michael Reich. 1982. *Segemented Work, Divided Workers: The Historical Transformation of Labor in the United States*. Cambridge: Cambridge University Press.

Gornick, Janet C., and Marcia K. Meyers. 2003. "Welfare Regimes in Relation to Paid Work and Care Advances in Life Course Research." In *Changing Life Patterns in Western Industrial Societies*, edited by Janet Zollinger Giele and Elke Holst, 45–67. Netherlands: Elsevier Science Press.

Graaf, John De, Ilona Boniwell, and Robert Levine. 2013. *Report of International Expert Working Group on Gross National Happiness*. Unpublished manuscript, Thimphu, Bhutan, February.

Grapard, Ulla. 1995. "Robinson Crusoe: The Quintessential Economic Man?" *Feminist Economics* 1 (1): 33–52.

Greenglass, Esther, Gerrit Antonides, Fabian Christandl, Gigi Fosterd, Joana K. Q. Katter, Bruce E. Kaufman, and Stephen E. G. Lea. 2014. "The Financial Crisis and Its Effects: Perspectives from Economics and Psychology." *Journal of Behavioral and Experimental Economics* 50: 10–12.

Gross, James A. 2010. *A Shameful Business: The Case for Human Rights in the American Workplace*. Ithaca, NY: ILR Press.

Grown, Caren. 2014. *Missing Women: Gender and the Extreme Poverty Debate*. Available at, http://usaidlearninglab.org/library/missing-women-gender-and-extreme-poverty-debate. Accessed on August 20, 2014.

Grown, Caren, Diane Elson, and Nilüfer Çağatay. 2000. "'Introduction' to Special Issue on Growth, Trade, Finance and Gender Inequality." *World Development* 28 (7): 145–56.

Grown, Caren, Maria Sagrario Floro, and Diane Elson. 2010. "Guest Editors' Note." *Feminist Economics* 16 (3): 1–3.

Gunewardena, Dileni, Darshi Abeyrathna, Amalie Ellagala, Kamani Rajakaruna, and Shobana Rajendran. 2008. *Glass Ceilings, Sticky Floors or Sticky Doors? A Quantile Regression Approach to Exploring Gender Wage Gaps in Sri Lanka.* 04. Poverty and Economic Research Network Working Paper.

Gupta, Ruchira. 2014. *Trafficking of Children for Prostitution and the UNICEF Response.* New York: UNICEF.

Hale, Angela. 1996. "The Deregulated Global Economy: Women Workers and Strategies of Resistance." *Gender & Development* 4 (3): 8–15.

Halls, A. S., and M. Johns. 2013. *Assesment of the Vulnerability of the Mekong Delta Pangasius Catfish Industry to Development and Climate Change in the Lower Mekong Basin.* Report prepared for the sustainable fisheries partnership. Bath, UK: ASL Fisheries Management and Development Services, Bath UK. Available at, msdevelopment.sustainablefish.org.s3.amazonaws.com/2013/01/22/Pangasius Mekong Delta-4b2036ad.pdf. Accessed September 9, 2013.

Hampson, Ian, and Anne Junor. 2005. "Invisible Work, Invisible Skills: Interactive Customer Service as Articulation Work." *New Technology, Work and Employment* 20 (2): 166–81.

Haney, Lynne. 2000. "Global Discourses of Need: Mythologizing and Pathologizing Welfare in Hungary." In *Global Ethnography: Forces, Connections, and Imaginations in a Postmodern World*, edited by Michael Burawoy, Joseph A. Blum, Sheba George, Zsuzsa Gille, and Millie Thayer, 48–73. Berkeley: University of California Press.

Harding, Sandra. 1995. "Can Feminist Thought Make Economics More Objective?" *Feminist Economics* 1 (1): 7–32.

Harding, Sandra, and Kathryn Norberg. 2005. "New Feminist Approaches to Social Science Methodologies: An Introduction." *Signs* 30 (4): 2009–15.

Harris, Jonathan M. 2013. "Green Keynesianism: Beyond Standard Growth Paradigms." In *Building a Green Economy: Perspectives from Ecological Economics*, edited by Robert B. Richardson, 69–82. East Lansing, MI: Michigan State University Press.

Harrison, Ann, and Jason Scorse. 2010. "Multinationals and Anti-Sweatshop Activism." *American Economic Review* 100 (1): 247–73.

Harriss-White, Barbara. 2003. "On Understanding Markets as Social and Political Institutions in Developing Economies." In *Rethinking Development Economics*, edited by Ha-Joon Chang. London and New York: Anthem Press.

Hart, Gillian. 1992. "Household Production Reconsidered: Gender, Labor Conflict, and Technological Change in Malaysia's Muda Region." *World Development* 20 (6): 809–23.

Hart, Keith. 1972. *Employment, Income and Inequality: A Strategy for Increasing Productive Employmnet in Kenya.* Geneva: ILO.

Hartmann, Heidi I. 1979a "Capitalism, Patriachy, and Job Segregation by Sex." In *Capitalist Patriarchy and the Case for Socialist Feminism*, edited by Zillah Einstein. New York: Monthly Review Press.

———. 1979b. "The Unhappy Marriage of Marxism and Feminism: Towards a More Progressive Union." *Capital & Class* 3 (2): 1–33.

———. 1981. "The Family as the Locus of Gender, Class, and Political Struggle: The Example of Housework." *Signs: Journal of Women, Culture and Society* 6 (3): 366–94.

Hartsock, Nancy. 1983. "The Feminist Standpoint: Developing the Ground for a Specifically Historical Materialism." In *Discovering Reality: Feminist Perspectives on Epistemology, Metaphysics, Methodology and Philosophy of Science*, edited by Sandra Harding and Merrill B. Hintikka. Dordrecht, Holland: D. Reidel Publishing Company.

Harvey, David. 2007. *A Brief History of Neoliberalism*. Oxford: Oxford University Press.

Hazarika, Gautam, and Rafael Otero. 2004. "Foreign Trade and the Gender Earnings Differential in Urban Mexico." *Journal of Economic Integration* 19 (2): 353–73.

Heckman, James. 2000. "Policies to Foster Human Capital." *Research in Economics* 54 (1): 3–56.

———. 2011. "The Economics of Inequality: The Value of Early Childhood Education." *American Educator* 35 (1): 31–35.

Hegewisch, Ariane, Claudia Williams, and Angela Edwards. 2013. *The Gender Wage Gap: 2012*. Washington DC. http://www.iwpr.org/publications/pubs/the-gender-wage-gap-2012/.

Heilbroner, Robert, and William Milberg. 1995. *The Crisis of Vision in Modern Economic Thought*. Cambridge: Cambridge University Press.

Herrigel, Gary, and Jonathan Zeitilin. 2010. "Inter-Firm Relations in Global Manufacturing: Disintegrated Production and Its Globalization." In *The Oxford Handbook of Comparative Institutional Analysis*, edited by Glenn Morgan, John L. Campbell, Colin Crouch, Ove Kaj Pedersen, and Richard Whitley, 527–61. New York: Oxford University Press.

Herszenhorn, D. M. 2008. "Administration Is Seeking $700 Billion for Wall Street." *The New York Times*, September 20. http://www.nytimes.com/2008/09/21/business/21cong.html?_r=1.

Heston, Alan. 1994. "A Brief Review of Some Problems in Using National Accounts Data in Level of Output Comparisons and Growth Studies." *Journal of Development Economics* 44 (1): 29–52.

Hewitson, Gillian. 1999. "Deconstructing Robinson Crusoe: A Feminist Interrogation of Rational Economic Man." In *Feminist Economics: Interrogating the Masculinity of Rational Economic Man*. Cheltenham, UK: Edward Elgar.

———. 2014. "The Commodified Womb and Neoliberal Families." *Review of Radical Political Economics* 46 (4): 489–95.

Heymann, Jody, Alison Earle, Divya Rajaraman, C. Miller, and Kenneth Bogen. 2007. "Extended Family Caring for Children Orphaned by AIDS: Balancing Essential Work and Caregiving in High HIV Prevalence Nations." *AIDS Care* 19 (3): 337–45.

Himmelweit, Susan. 1995. "The Discovery of 'Unpaid Work': The Social Consequences of the Expansion of 'Work.' *Feminist Economics* 1 (2): 1–19.

Himmelweit, Susan, and Simon Mohun. 1977. "Domestic Labour and Capital." *Cambridge Journal of Economics* 1. JSTOR: 15–31.

Hinrichs, Karl, and Matteo Jessoula, eds. 2012. *Labour Market Flexibility and Pension Reforms: Flexible Today, Secure Tomorrow?* Basingstoke, UK: Palgrave Macmillan.

Hinz, Richard P., David D. McCarthy, and John A. Turner. 1997. "Are Women Conservative Investors? Gender Differences in Participant-Directed Pension Investments." In *Positioning Pensions for the Twenty-First Century*, edited by Michael S. Gordon, Olivia S. Mitchell, and Marc M. Twinney, 91–103. Philadelphia, PA: University of Pennsylvania Press.

Hirway, Indira. 2010. "Understanding Poverty: Insights Emerging from Time Use of the Poor." In *Unpaid Work and the Economy: Gender, Time Use and Poverty*, edited by Rania Antonopoulos and Indira Hirway, 22–57. Basingstoke: Palgrave Macmillan.

Hirway, Indira, and Sunny Jose. 2011. "Understanding Women's Work Using Time-Use Statistics: The Case of India." *Feminist Economics* 17 (4): 67–92.

Hochschild, Arlie R. 2012. *The Outsourced Self: Intimate Life in Market Times*. New York, NY: Metropolitan Books/Henry Holt & Company.

Hoddinott, John, and Lawrence Haddad. 1995. "Does Female Income Share Influence Household Expenditures? Evidence from Côte d'Ivoire." *Oxford Bulletin of Economics and Statistics* 57 (1): 77–96.

Hoff, Karla, Avishay Braverman, and Joseph E. Stiglitz, eds. 1993. *The Economics of Rural Organization*. Oxford University Press.

HomeNet Thailand. 2002. *Impact of the Economic Crisis on Homeworkers in Thailand*. HomeNet Thailand.

Hossain, Md. Ismail, Golam M. Mathbor, and Renata Semenza. 2013. "Feminization and Labor Vulnerability in Global Manufacturing Industries: Does Gendered Discourse Matter?" *Asian Social Work and Policy Review* 7 (3): 197–212.

Howcroft, Debra, and Helen Richardson. 2008. "Gender Matters in the Global Outsourcing of Service Work." *New Technology, Work and Employment* 23 (1–2): 44–60.

Hsiung, Ping-Chun. 1996. *Living Rooms as Factories: Class, Gender, and the Satellite Factory System in Taiwan*. Philadelphia, PA: Temple University Press.

Htun, Mala, and S. Laurel Weldon. 2012. "The Civic Origins of Progressive Policy Change: Combating Violence Against Women in Global Perspective." *American Political Science Review* 106 (3): 548–569.

Huber, Manfred, Ricardo Rodrigues, Frédérique Hoffmann, Katrin Gasior, and Bernd Marin. 2009. *Facts and Figures on Long-Term Care. Europe and North America*. Vienna: European Centre for Social Welfare Policy and Research.

Hugo, A., and E. N. Pistikopoulos. 2005. "Environmentally Conscious Long-Range Planning and Design of Supply Chain Networks." *Journal of Cleaner Production* 13 (15): 1471–91.

Humphries, Jane. 1977. "Class Struggle and the Persistence of the Working-Class Family." *Cambridge Journal of Economics* 1: 241–58.

Humphries, Jane, and Carmen Sarasúa. 2012. "Off the Record: Reconstructing Women's Labor Force Participation Rates in the European Past." *Feminist Economics* 18 (4): 39–67.

Hung, S. 2009. "Lessons Not Learned? Gender, Employment and Social Protection in Asia's Crisis-Affected Export Sectors." Paper presented at conference on "Impact of the Global Economic Slowdown on Poverty and Sustainable Development in Asia and the Pacific," Hanoi, 28–30 September. Available at, www.adb.org/Documents/Events/2009/Poverty-Social-Development/papers.asp. Accessed on October 31, 2013.

Husmanns, Ralf. 2004. *Statistical Definition of Informal Employment: Guidelines Endorsed by the Seventeenth International Conference of Labour Statisticians.* Geneva: International Labour Organization.

Hyder, A., S. Maman, J. Nyoni, S. Khasiani, N. Teoh, Z. Premji, and S Sohani. 2005. "The Pervasive Triad of Food Security, Gender Inequity and Women's Health: Exploratory Research from Sub-Saharan Africa." *African Health Sciences* 5 (4): 328–34.

İlkkaracan, İpek. 2012. "Why so Few Women in the Labor Market in Turkey?" *Feminist Economics* 18 (1): 1–37.

———. 2013a. "Political Economy of Caring Labor, Gender and Deepening Conservatism in a Developing Economy Context: The Case of Turkey." Istanbul Technical University, Women's Studies Center, Working Paper Series. Available at, http://www.kaum.itu.edu.tr/dosyalar/3013WorkingPaper.WorkFamilyBalance.Turkey.pdf

———. 2013b. "The Purple Economy: A Call for a New Economic Order beyond the Green." In *Sustainable Economy and Green Growth: Who Cares? International Workshop Linking Care, Livelihood and Sustainable Economy*, edited by Ulrike Röhr and Conny van Heemstra, 32–37. Berlin: LIFE e.V./German Federal Ministry for the Environment.

ILO (International Labor Organization). 1976. *International Recommendations on Labour Statistics.* Geneva: ILO.

———. 1993. Statistics of employment in the informal sector, Report for the XVth International Conference of Labour Statisticians, Geneva, 19–28 January 1993.

———. 1998. *ILO Declaration on Fundamental Principles and Rights at Work*, http://www.ilo.org/declaration/lang--en/index.htm.

———. 2000a. "Organization, Bargaining and Dialogue for Development in a Globalizing World," GB.279/WP/SDG/2, Geneva: ILO.

———. 2000b. "Report of the Meeting of Experts on Workers in Situations Needing Protection GB.279/2 279th Session. Geneva: ILO. http://www.ilo.org/public/english/standards/relm/gb/docs/gb279/pdf/gb-2.pdf. Accessed on February 13, 2013.

———. 2002a. "Effect to be given to resolutions adopted by the International Labour Conference at its 90th Session (2002), (b) Resolution concerning decent work and the informal economy, ILO Governing Body, 285th Session," Geneva: ILO.

———. 2002b. *Decent Work and the Informal Economy; Report of the Director-General.* Geneva: ILO.

———. 2007. *Equality at Work: Tackling the Challenges. International Labour Conference 96th Session 2007, Report I (B).* Geneva: ILO.

———. 2008. A Manual on the Measurement of Volunteer Work, Exposure Draft. Geneva: ILO.

———. 2009. *World of Work Report 2009: The Global Jobs Crisis and Beyond.* Geneva.

———. 2010. *Women in Labour Markets: Measuring Progress and Identifying Challenge.* Geneva: ILO.

———. 2011a. *Statistical Update on Employment in the Informal Economy.* Geneva: ILO.

———. 2011b. *Manual on the Measurement of Volunteer Work.* Baltimore: ILO and Johns Hopkins University.

———. 2013a. *The Social Dimensions of Free Trade Agreements.* Geneva: ILO.

———. 2013b. *Global Employment Trends: Recovering from a Second Job Dip.* Geneva: ILO.

———. 2013c. *Global Child Labour Trends, 2008–2012.* Geneva: ILO.

———. 2013d. *Measuring Informality: A Statistical Manual on the Informal Sector and Informal Employment.* Geneva: ILO.

———. 2013e. *Resolution Concerning Statistics of Work, Employment and Labour Underutilization.* Geneva: ILO.

———. 2014a. *Maternity and Paternity at Work: Law and Practice around the World.* Geneva. Available at http://www.ilo.org/wcmsp5/groups/public/---dgreports/---dcomm/---publ/documents/publication/wcms_242615.pdf. Accessed on January 13, 2014.

———. 2014b. "Decent Work." http://www.ilo.org/global/topics/decent-work/lang--en/index.htm. Accessed on Sept. 8, 2014.

———. 2014c. *Trade Union Membership Statistics: Industrial Relations Indicators.* Geneva: ILO. Available at, http://www.ilo.org/ifpdial/information-resources/dialogue-data/lang—en/index.htm.

IMF (International Monetary Fund). 2001. "IMF Lending to Poor Countries: How Does the PRGF Differ from the ESAF? Factsheet." Washington DC: International Monetary Fund. Available at, http://www.imf.org/external/np/exr/ib/2001/043001.

———. 2014. "IMF Conditionality. Factsheet." http://www.imf.org/external/np/exr/facts/conditio.htm.

India Ministry of Environment and Forests. 2011. "The Traditional Coastal and Marine Fisherfolk (Protection of Rights) Act 2009." Delhi. Available at, http://www.indiaenvironmentportal.org.in/files/TheTraditionalFisherfolkProtectionofRights_Act2009.pdf. Accessed on January 13, 2015.

IndustriALL Global Union. 2014. *IndustriALL Renews Agreement with World's Largest Fashion Retailer.* July 8. Available at, http://www.industriall-union.org/special-report-inditex-and-industriall-global-union-getting-results-from-a-global-framework.

INSTRAW (United Nations International Research and Training Institute for the Advancement of Women). 1991. *Methods of Collecting and Analysing Statistics on Women in the Informal Sector and Their Contributions to National Product. Results of Regional Workshops.*INSTRAW/BT/CRP.1. Santo Domingo: United Nations.

Ironmonger, Duncan. 1996. "Counting Outputs, Capital Inputs and Caring Labor: Estimating Gross Household Product." *Feminist Economics* 2 (3): 37–64.

———. 2004. "Bringing up Bobby and Betty: The Inputs and Outputs of Childcare Time." In *Family Time: The Social Organization of Care*, edited by Michael Bittman and Nancy Folbre, 93–109. London and New York: Taylor & Francis.

Jackson, Cecile. 2013. "Cooperative Conflicts and Gender Relations: Experimental Evidence from Southeast Uganda." *Feminist Economics* 19 (4): 25–47.

Jacob, Rahul. 2013. "Cambodia Reaps Benefit of China's Rising Wage." *Financial Times*, January 8.

Jaggar, Alison. 1983. *Feminist Politics and Human Nature.* Oxford: Rowman & Littlefield.

Jahiruddin, A. T. M., Patricia Short, Wolfram Dressler, and M. Adil Khan. 2011. "Can Microcredit Worsen Poverty? Cases of Exacerbated Poverty in Bangladesh." *Development in Practice* 21 (8): 1109–21.

Jain, Devaki, and Nirmala Banerjee. 1985. *Women in Poverty. Tyranny of the Household: Investigative Essays on Women's Work.* New Delhi: Shakti Books.

Jain, Devaki, and Malini Chand. 1982. "Report on a Time Allocation Study. Its Methodological Implications." In *Technical Seminar on "Women's Work and Employment" from April 9–11, 1982.* New Delhi.

Jenkins, Jean. 2013. "Organizing 'Spaces of Hope': Union Formation by Indian Garment Workers." *British Journal of Industrial Relations* 51 (3): 623–43.

Jennings, Ann. 1993. "Public or Private? Institutional Economics and Feminism." In *Beyond Economic Man: Feminist Theory and Economics*, edited by Marianne Ferber and Julie A. Nelson, 111–29. Chicago: University of Chicago Press.

Jeyaseelan, L., Shuba Kumar, Nithya Neelakantan, Abraham Peedicayil, Rajamohanam Pillai, and Nata Duvvury. 2007. "Physical Spousal Violence against Women in India: Some Risk Factors." *Journal of Biosocial Science* 39 (5): 657–70.

Jianakoplos, Nancy Ammon, and Alexandra Bernasek. 1998. "Are Women More Risk Averse?" *Economic Inquiry* 36 (4): 620–30.

Johnsson-Latham, Gerd. 2010. "Power, Privilege and Gender as Reflected in Poverty Analysis and Development Goals." In *The International Handbook of Gender and Poverty*, edited by Sylvia Chant, 41–46. Cheltenham, UK: Edward Elgar.

Johnston, David Cay. 2006. "New Rise in Numbers of Millionaires." *New York Times*, April 5.

Juliano, Dolores. 2004. *Excluidas Y Marginadas. Una Aproximación Antropológica.* Madrid: Ediciones Cátedra.

Juster, Thomas, and Frank Stafford. 1985. *Time, Goods, and Well-being.* Ann Arbor, MI: University of Michigan Press.

———. 1991. "The Allocation of Time: Empirical Findings, Behavioral Models, and Problems of Measurement." *Journal of Economic Literature* 29 (2): 471–522.

Kabeer, Naila. 1994. *Reversed Realities: Gender Hierarchies in Development Thought.* London and New York: Verso.

———. 2000. *The Power to Choose: Bangladeshi Women and Labor Market Decisions in London and Dhaka.* London and New York: Verso.

———. 2001. "Conflicts over Credit: Re-Evaluating the Empowerment Potential of Loans to Women in Rural Bangladesh." *World Development* 29 (1): 63–84.

———. 2004. "Globalization, Labor Standards, and Women's Rights: Dilemmas of Collective (In)action in an Interdependent World." *Feminist Economics* 10 (1): 3–35.

Kabeer, Naila, and Simeen Mahmud. 2004. "Globalization, Gender and Poverty: Bangladeshi Women Workers in Export and Local Markets." *Journal of International Development* 16 (1): 93–109.

Kahn, Lawrence M. 2010. "Employment Protection Reforms, Employment and the Incidence of Temporary Jobs in Europe: 1996–2001." *Labour Economics* 17 (1): 1–15.

Kamas, Linda, Anne Preston, and Dandy Baum. 2008. "Altruism in Individual and Joint-Giving Decisions: What's Gender Got to Do With It?" *Feminist Economics* 14 (3): 23–50.

Kamler, Erin. 2014. "Trafficking and Coerced Prostitution in Thailand: Reconceptualizing International Law in the Age of Globalization." In *Contemporary Socio-Cultural and Political Perspectives in Thailand*, edited by Pranee Liamputtong, 363–79. The Netherlands: Springer.

Kan, Man Yee, Oriel Sullivan, and Jonathan Gershuny. 2011. "Gender Convergence in Domestic Work: Discerning the Effects of Interactional and Institutional Barriers from Large-Scale Data." *Sociology* 45 (2): 234–51.

Kanbur, Ravi. 2002. "Economics, Social Science and Development." *World Development* 30 (3): 477–86.

Kandiyoti, Deniz. 1988. "Bargaining with Patriarchy." *Gender & Society* 2 (3): 274–90.

Kapadia, Karin. 2002. *The Violence of Development. The Politics of Identity, Gender and Social Inequalities in India.* London and New York: Zed Books.

Karanikolos, Marina, Philipa Mladovsky, Jonathan Cylus, Sarah Thomson, Sanjay Basu, David Stuckler, Johan P. McKenbach, and Martin McKee. 2013. "Financial Crisis, Austerity, and Health in Europe." *The Lancet* 381 (9874): 1323–31.

Karim, Lamia. 2011. *Microfinance and Its Discontents: Women in Debt in Bangladesh.* University of Minnesota Press.

Kasante, Deborah, Matthew Lockwood, Jessica Vivian, and Ann Whitehead. 2001. "Gender and the Expansion of Non-traditional Agricultural Exports in Uganda." In *Shifting Burdens: Gender and Agrarian Change under Neo-Liberalism*, edited by Shahrashoub Razavi. Bloomfield, CT: Kumarian Press.

Katz, Elizabeth G. 1991. "Breaking the Myth of Harmony: Theoretical and Methodological Guidelines to the Study of Rural Third World Households." *Review of Radical Political Economics* 23 (3–4): 37–56.

———. 1995. "Gender and Trade within the Household: Observations from Rural Guatemala." *World Development* 23 (2): 327–42.

Keck, Margaret, and Kathryn Sikkink. 1998. *Activists beyond Borders: Advocacy Networks in International Politics.* Ithaca, NY: Cornell University Press.

Khan, Shahrukh R., and Jens Christiansen, eds. 2011. *Towards New Developmentalism: Market as Means rather than Master*. New York: Routledge.

Khatun, Fahmida, Debapriya Bhattacharya, Mustafizur Rahman, and Khondaker Golam Moazzem. 2008. *Gender and Trade Liberalization in Bangladesh: The Case of the Ready-Made Garments*. Dhaka: Centre for Policy Dialogue.

Kiefer, David, and Codrina Rada. 2014. "Profit Maximizing Goes Global: The Race to the Bottom." *Cambridge Journal of Economics*. doi: 10.1093/cje/beu040.

King, John E. 2013. "A Case for Pluralism in Economics." *Economic and Labour Relations Review* 24 (1): 17–31.

King, Mary C. 2008. "What Sustainability Should Mean." *Challenge* 51 (2): 27–39.

King, Richard, and Caroline Sweetman. 2010. *Gender Perspectives on the Global Economic Crisis*. Discussion Paper. Oxfam International.

Klasen, Stephan, and Janneke Pieters. 2013. *What Explains the Stagnation of Female Labor Force Participation in Urban India?* Discussion Paper No. 7597. IZA (Institute for the Study of Labor).

Klasen, Stephan, and Dana Schüler. 2011. "Reforming the Gender-Related Index (GDI) and the Gender Empowerment Measure (GEM): Some Specific Proposals." *Feminist Economics* 17 (1): 1–30.

Koenig, Michael A., Saifuddin Ahmed, Mian Bazle Hossain, and A. B. M. Khorshed Alam Mozumder. 2003. "Women's Status and Domestic Violence in Rural Bangladesh: Individual- and Community-Level Effects." *Demography* 40 (2): 269–88.

Koggel, Christine. 2003. "Globalization and Women's Paid Work: Expanding Freedom." *Feminist Economics. Special Issue: Amartya Sen's Work and Ideas* 9 (2 & 3): 163–83.

Kongar, Ebru. 2007. "Importing Equality or Exporting Jobs? Competition and Gender Wage and Employment Differentials in US Manufacturing." In *The Feminist Economics of Trade*, edited by Irene Van Staveren, Diane Elson, Caren Grown, and Nilüfer Çağatay. Oxon and New York: Routledge.

———. 2008. "Is Deindustrialization Good for Women?" *Feminist Economics* (14) 1: 73–92.

Koopman, Jeanne. 1991. "Neoclassical Household Models and Models of Household Production: Problems in the Analysis of African Agricultural Households." *Review of Radical Political Economics* 23 (3 & 4): 148–73.

———. 2009. "Globalization, Gender, and Poverty in the Senegal River Valley." *Feminist Economics* 15 (3): 253–86.

Kotz, David. 1995. "Lessons for a Future Socialism from the Soviet Collapse." *Review of Radical Political Economics* 27 (3): 1–11.

Krishnan, Suneeta, Corinne H. Rocca, Alan E. Hubbard, Kalyani Subbiah, Jeffrey Edmeades, and Nancy S. Padian. 2010. "Do Changes in Spousal Employment Status Lead to Domestic Violence? Insights from a Prospective Study in Bangalore, India." *Social Science & Medicine* 70 (1): 136–43.

Krugman, Paul. 2009. *The Return of Depression Economics and the Crisis of 2008*. New York: W.W. Norton and Co.

———. 2012. *End This Depression Now*. New York and London: W.W. Norton and Co.

————. 2013a. "What A Real External Bank Bailout Looks Like." *New York Times*, July 16.

————. 2013b. "Another Bank Bailout." *New York Times*, July 16.

Kucera, David. 2002. "Core Labour Standards and Foreign Direct Investment." *International Labour Review* 141 (1–2): 31–69.

Kucera, David Charles, and Anne Chataignier. 2005. *Labour Developments in Dynamic East Asia: What Do the Data Show?* Working Paper No. 61. Geneva: Policy Integration Department, ILO.

Kucera, David, and Marco Principi. 2014. "Democracy and Foreign Direct Investment at the Industry Level: Evidence for US Multinationals." *Review of World Economics* 150 (3): 595–617.

Kucera, David Charles, and Sheba Tejani. 2014. "Feminization, Defeminization, and Structural Change in Manufacturing." *World Development* 64: 569–82.

Kuruvilla, Sarosh, and Aruna Ranganathan. 2010. "Globalisation and Outsourcing: Confronting New Human Resource Challenges in India's Business Process Outsourcing Industry." *Industrial Relations Journal* 41 (2): 136–53.

Kyrili, Katerina, and Matthew Martin. 2010. *The Impact of the Global Financial Crisis on the Budgets of Low-Income Countries*. Research Report for Oxfam. UK: Oxfam International. http://www.oxfam.org.uk/resources/policy/economic_crisis/down loads/rr_gec_impactbudget_lics_200710.pdf.

Lamers, Patrick, Ric Hoefnagels, Martin Junginger, Carlo Hamelinck, and André Faaij. 2014. "Global Solid Biomass Trade for Energy by 2020: An Assessment of Potential Import Streams and Supply Costs to North-West Europe under Different Sustainability Constraints." *GCB Bioenergy*. DOI: 10.1111/gcbb.12162

Lastarria-Cornhiel, Susana. 1997. "Impact of Privatization on Gender and Property Rights in Africa." *World Development* 25 (8): 1317–33.

Laufer, Jacqueline. 1998. "Equal Opportunities and Employment Change in West European Economies." *Feminist Economics* 4 (1): 53–69.

Lazear, Edward. 2000. "Economic Imperialism." *The Quarterly Journal of Economics* 115 (1): 99–146.

League of Nations. 1938. *Statistics of the Gainfully Occupied Population: Definitions and Classifications Recommended by the Committees of Statistical Experts. Studies and Reports on Statistical Methods*. No.1. Geneva.

LeClair, M. S. 2002. "Fighting the Tide: Alternative Trade Organizations in the Era of Global Free Trade." *World Development* 30 (6): 949–58.

Leigh, Duane E. 1995. *Assisting Workers Displaced by Structural Change: An International Perspective*. Kalamzoo, MI: Upjohn Institute Press.

Lilly, Meredith B., Audrey Laporte, and Peter C. Coyte. 2007. "Labor Market Work and Home Care's Unpaid Caregivers: A Systematic Review of Labor Force Participation Rates, Predictors of Labor Market Withdrawal, and Hours of Work." *Milbank Quarterly* 85 (4): 641–90.

Lim, Joseph Y. 2000. "The Effects of the East Asian Crisis on the Employment of Women and Men: The Philippine Case." *World Development* 28 (7): 1285–306.

Lim, Linda. 1983. "Capitalism, Imperialism and Patriarchy: The Dilemma of Third World Women Workers in Multinational Factories." In *Women, Men and the International Division of Labor*, edited by June C. Nash and María Patricia Fernández-Kelly, 70–92. Albany, NY: State University of New York Press.

———. 1990. "Women's Work in Export Factories: The Politics of a Cause." In *Persistent Inequalities: Women and World Development*, edited by Irene Tinker, 101–19. New York: Oxford University Press.

Lind, Amy. 1997. "Gender, Development and Urban Social Change: Women's Community Action in Global Cities." *World Development* 25 (8): 1205–23.

Liu, Jie-yu. 2007. "Gender Dynamics and Redundancy in Urban China." *Feminist Economics* 13 (3–4): 125–58.

Liu, Lan, Xiao-yuan Dong, and Xiaoying Zheng. 2010. "Parental Care and Married Women's Labor Supply in Urban China." *Feminist Economics* 16 (3): 169–92.

Liu, Minquan, Luodan Xu, and Liu Liu. 2004. "Wage-Related Labour Standards and FDI in China: Some Survey Findings From Guangdong Province." *Pacific Economic Review* 9 (3): 225–43.

Lloyd, Cynthia. 1975. *Sex, Discrimination and the Division of Labor*. New York: Columbia University Press.

Lloyd, Cynthia, and Beth Niemi. 1979. *Economics of Sex Differentials*. New York: Columbia University Press.

Locke, Richard, Fei Qin, and Alberto Brause. 2006. *Does Monitoring Improve Labor Standards? Lessons from Nike*. 24. Corporate Social Responsibility Initiative Working Paper. Cambridge, MA.

Longino, Helen. 1993. "Economics for Whom?" In *Beyond Economic Man: Feminist Theory and Economics*, edited by Julie A. Nelson and Mariane Ferber. Chicago: University of Chicago Press.

López, Ramón, and Sebastian J. Miller. 2008. "Chile: The Unbearable Burden of Inequality." *World Development* 36 (12): 2679–95.

López-Montaño, Cecilia. 2013. "Care Economy: A Way to Women's Autonomy and Political Leadership." Paper presented at the Different Perspectives on Economic Empowerment Conference, WPSP Institute for Women's Leadership in Latin America, Scripps College, USA, March 17, 2013.

Lora, Eduardo A. 2001. *Structural Reforms in Latin America: What Has Been Reformed and How to Measure It*. 466. Inter-American Development Bank Working Paper. Washington D.C.: Inter-American Development Bank.

Lorde, Audre. 1984. "The Master's Tools Will Never Dismantle the Master's House," pp. 94–101 in Cherríe Moraga and Gloria Anzaldúa, eds. *This Bridge Called My Back: Writings by Radical Women of Color*, New York: Kitchen Table Press.

Lund-Thomsen, Peter, Khalid Nadvi, Anita Chan, Navjote Khara, and Hong Xue. 2012. "Labour in Global Value Chains: Work Conditions in Football Manufacturing in China, India and Pakistan." *Development and Change* 43 (6): 1211–37.

Lyberaki, Antigone. 2008. "Migrant Women, Care Work, and Women's Employment in Greece." *Feminist Economics* 17 (3): 101–31.

Mabsout, Ramzi, and Irene Van Staveren. 2010. "Disentangling Bargaining Power from Individual and Household Level to Institutions: Evidence on Women's Position in Ethiopia." *World Development* 38 (5): 783–96.

MacDonald, Martha. 1995. "Feminist Economics: From Theory to Research." *Canadian Journal of Economics* 28 (1): 159–75.

MacKintosh, Maureen. 1978. "Domestic Labor and the Household." In *Feminism and Materialism*, edited by Annette Kuhn and Annemarie Wolpe. London: Routledge.

Maes, Kenneth C., Craig Hadley, Fikru Tesfaye, and Selamawit Shifferaw. 2010. "Food Insecurity and Mental Health: Surprising Trends among Community Health Volunteers in Addis Ababa, Ethiopia during the 2008 Food Crisis." *Social Science & Medicine* 70 (9): 1450–57.

Mankiw, N. Gregory. 2012. *Principles of Macroeconomics*. Mason, OH: South-Western Cengage Learning.

Manser, Marilyn, and Murray Brown. 1980. "Marriage and Household Decision-Making: A Bargaining Analysis." *International Economic Review* 21 (1): 31–44.

Marchington, Mick, Damien Grimshaw, Jill Rubery, and Hugh Wilmott, eds. 2005. *Fragmenting Work, Blurring Organizational Boundaries and Disordering Hierarchies*. Oxford: Oxford University Press.

Marques, Joana S. 2014. *Between Emancipation and Reproduction*. UNRISD Occasional Paper No. 2. Geneva: UNRISD.

Martinez-Tablas, Angel. 2012. "La Crisis Del Euro: Interpretación Contextual y Salidas." *Revista de Economia Crítica* 13: 5–29.

Marx, Karl. [1887] 1967. *Capital: A Critique of Political Economy, Vol. 1*. New York: International Publishers.

———. 1904. "Preface." In *A Contribution to the Critique of Political Economy*. Chicago: Charles H. Kerr & Company.

Maurer-Fazio, Margaret, Thomas G. Rawski, and Wei Zhang. 1999. "Inequality in the Rewards for Holding up Half the Sky: Gender Wage Gaps in China's Urban Labour Market, 1988–1994." *China Journal* 41: 55–88.

Mayoux, Linda. 2000. *Micro-Finance and the Empowerment of Women: A Review of the Key Issues*. Geneva: International Labour Office.

McCloskey, Deirdre. 1996. "Love and Money: A Comment on the Markets Debate." *Feminist Economics* 2 (2): 137–40.

McCloskey, Donald N., Robert M. Solow, and Arjo Klamer. 1989. *The Consequences of Economic Rhetoric*. Cambridge University Press.

McCrate, Elaine. 1987. "Trade, Merger and Employment: Economic Theory on Marriage." *Review of Radical Political Economics* 19 (1): 73–89.

McElroy, Marjorie B., and Mary Jean Horney. 1981. "Nash-Bargained Household Decisions: Toward a Generalization of the Theory of Demand." *International Economic Review* 22 (2): 333–49.

McKay, Ailsa. 2001. "Rethinking Work and Income Maintenance Policy: Promoting Gender Equality through a Citizens' Basic Income." *Feminist Economics* 7 (1): 97–118.

McMichael, Philip. 2012. "The Land Grab and Corporate Food Regime Restructuring." *Journal of Peasant Studies* 39 (3–4): 681–701.

Mead, Margaret. 1958. *Male and Female: A Study of the Sexes in the Changing World*. New York: Mentor.

Melber, Henning. 2012. "No Future without Justice; Report of the Civil Society Reflection Group on Global Development Perspectives." Uppsala, Sweden: *Development Dialogue* 59.

Menon, Nidhiya, and Yana van der Meulen Rodgers. 2009. "International Trade and the Gender Wage Gap: New Evidence from India's Manufacturing Sector." *World Development* 37 (5): 965–81.

Mersland, Roy, and Reidar Øystein Strøm. 2010. "Microfinance Mission Drift?" *World Development* 38 (1): 28–36.

Mesch, Debra J., Patrick M. Rooney, Kathryn S. Steinberg, and Brian Denton. 2006. "The Effects of Race, Gender, and Marital Status on Giving and Volunteering in Indiana." *Quarterly, Nonprofit and Voluntary Sector* 35 (4): 565–87.

Messier, John. 2005. "Dynamics of Poverty Trap and the Role of Credit." PhD. Dissertation. American University, Washington DC.

Mies, Maria. 1982. *The Lace Makers of Narsapur: Indian Housewives Produce for the World Market*. London: Zed Press.

Milanovic, Branko. 2012. "Global Inequality Recalculated and Updated: The Effect of New PPP Estimates on Global Inequality and 2005 Estimates." *The Journal of Economic Inequality* 10 (1): 1–18.

Milberg, William, and Matthew Amengual. 2008. *Economic Development and Working Conditions in Export Processing Zones: A Survey of Trends*. Geneva: International Labor Office.

Mill, John Stuart. [1848] 1965. *Principles of Political Economy with some of their Applications to Social Philosophy*. London: John W. Parker West Strand.

———. [1869] 1970. *The Subjection of Women*. Cambridge, MA: MIT Press.

Miller, Doug, Veasna Nuon, Charlene Aprill, and Ramon Certeza. 2008. *"Business—as Usual?" Governing the Supply Chain in Clothing—Post MFA Phase Out. The Case of Cambodia*. Discussion Paper No. 6. Global Union Research Network (GURN). http://www.gurn.info/papers/dp6.pdf.

Mills, David, and Richard. Ssewakiryanga. 2002. "That Beijing Thing: Challenging Transnational Feminisms in Kampala." *Gender, Place and Culture: A Journal of Feminist Geography* 9 (4): 385–98.

Mincer, Jacob. 1962. "Labor Force Participation of Married Women: A Study of Labor Supply." In *Aspects of Labor Economics*, 63–106. Princeton, NJ: Princeton University Press.

Minnich, Elizabeth Karmarck. 1990. *Transforming Knowledge*. Philadelphia: Temple University Press.

Mishel, Lawrence. 2012. *The Wedges between Productivity and Median Compensation Growth*. Washington DC: Economic Policy Institute. http://www.epi.org/publication/ib330-productivity-vs-compensation/.

Mishel, Lawrence, John Schmitt, and Heidi Shierholz. 2013. *Assessing The Job Polarization Explanation of Growing Wage Inequality*. Washington DC: Economic Policy Institute.

Mitra, Arup. 2005. "Women in the Urban Informal Sector: Perpetuation of Meagre Earnings." *Development and Change* 36 (2): 291–316.

Moghadam, Valentine M. 2001. "Women, Work, and Economic Restructuring: A Regional Overview." In *The Economics of Women and Work in the Middle East and North Africa (Research in Middle East Economics, Volume 4)*, edited by Jennifer Olmstead, 93–116. Emerald Group Publishing Limited.

Moghissi, Haideh. 1999. *Feminism and Islamic Fundamentalism: The Limits of Postmodern Analysis*. London: Zed Books.

Mohanty, Chandra. 1988. "Under Western Eyes: Feminist Scholarship and Colonial Discourses." *Feminist Review* 30: 61–88.

Molyneux, Maxine. 1979. "Beyond the Domestic Labour Debate." *New Left Review* 115: 3–28.

———. 1985. "Mobilisation Without Emancipation? Women's Interests, the State and Revolution in Nicaragua." *Feminist Studies* 11: 227–54.

———. 2006. "Mothers at the Service of the New Poverty Agenda." In *Gender and Social Policy in a Global Context*, edited by Shahra Razavi and Shireen Hassim, 43–68. Basingtoke, UK and New York: Palgrave Macmillan.

Molyneux, Maxine and Marilyn Thomson. 2011. "Cash Transfers, Gender Equity and Women's Empowerment in Peru, Ecuador and Bolivia." *Gender and Development* 19(2): 195-212..

Morrissey, Oliver, and Manop Udomkerdmongkol. 2012. "Governance, Private Investment and Foreign Direct Investment in Developing Countries." *World Development* 40 (3): 437–45.

Moser, Caroline. 1981. "Surviving in the Suburbios." *The IDS Bulletin* 12 (3): 1–11.

———. 1989. "Gender Planning in the Third World: Meeting Practical and Strategic Gender Needs." *World Development* 17 (11): 1799–825.

Mosley, Layna. 2011. *Labor Rights and Multinational Production*. Cambridge, UK: Cambridge University Press.

Mukherjee, Sucharita Sinha. 2013. "Women's Empowerment and Gender Bias in the Birth and Survival of Girls in Urban India." *Feminist Economics* 19 (1): 1–28.

Mukhopadhyay, Maitrayee. 2004. "Mainstreaming Gender or 'Streaming' Gender Away: Feminists Marooned in the Development Business." *IDS Bulletin* 35 (4): 95–103.

———. 2013. "Mainstreaming Gender or Reconstituting the Mainstream? Gender Knowledge in Development." *Journal of International Development* 26 (3): 356–67.

Mullan, Killian. 2010. "Valuing Parental Childcare in the United Kingdom." *Feminist Economics* 16 (3): 113–39.

Muturi, Nancy. 2006. "Gender Empowerment through ICTs: Potential and Challenges for Women in the Caribbean." *Revista de Estudios Para El Desarrollo Social de La Comunicación* 3: 133–48.

Nash, June, and Helen Safa. 1985. *Women and Change in Latin America*. South Hadley, MA: Bergin and Garvey Publishers.

Nassar, Heba. 2007. *Addressing Gender and Trade within Human Rights Framework*. Working Paper. Cairo: Social Research Center, American University.

National Women's Law Center. 2014. *Fair Pay for Women Requires Increasing the Minimum Wage and Tipped Minimum Wage.* Available at, http://www.nwlc.org/resource/fair-pay-women-requires-increasing-minimum-wage-and-tipped-minimum-wage#thirteen.

Naylor, Rosamond. 1994. "Culture and Agriculture: Employment Practices Affecting Women in Java's Rice Economy." *Economic Development and Cultural Change* 42 (3): 509–35.

Nayyar, Deepak. 2013. "The Millennium Development Goals Beyond 2015: Old Frameworks and New Constructs." *Journal of Human Development and Capabilities* 14 (3): 371–92.

Nelson, Julie A. 1992. "Gender, Metaphor, and the Definition of Economics." *Economics and Philosophy* 8 (1): 103–25.

———. 1993. "The Study of Choice or the Study of Provisioning? Gender and the Definition of Economics." In *Beyond Economic Man: Feminist Theory and Economics,* edited by Marianne Ferber and Julie A. Nelson, 23–36. Chicago: University of Chicago Press.

———. 1995. "Feminism and Economics." *The Journal of Economic Perspectives* 9 (2): 131–48.

———. 1997. "Feminism, Ecology and the Philosophy of Economics." *Ecological Economics* 20 (2): 155–62.

———. 2008. "Economists, Value Judgments, and Climate Change: A View from Feminist Economics." *Ecological Economics* 65 (3): 441–47.

———. 2010. "Getting Past 'Rational Man/Emotional Woman': Comments on Research Programs in Happiness Economics and Interpersonal Relations." *International Review of Economics* 57 (2): 233–53.

———. 2013. "Ethics and the Economist: What Climate Change Demands of Us." *Ecological Economics* 85: 145–54.

———. 2014. "The Power of Stereotyping and Confirmation Bias to Overwhelm Accurate Assessment: The Case of Economics, Gender, and Risk Aversion." *Journal of Economic Methodology* 21 (3): 211–31.

———. 2015. "Poisoning the Well, or How Economic Theory Damages Moral Imagination" In *Oxford Handbook on Professional Economic Ethics,* edited by George DeMartino and Deirdre McCloskey. Oxford University Press.

———. Forthcoming. "Are Women Really More Risk-Averse than Men? A Re-Analysis of the Literature Using Expanded Methods." *Journal of Economic Surveys.*

Neumayer, Eric, and Indra de Soysa. 2006. "Globalization and the Right to Free Association and Collective Bargaining: An Empirical Analysis." *World Development* 34 (1): 31–49.

———. 2007. "Globalisation, Women's Economic Rights and Forced Labour." *World Economy* 30 (10): 1510–35.

Neumayer, Eric, and Thomas Plümper. 2007. "The Gendered Nature of Natural Disasters: The Impact of Catastrophic Events on the Gender Gap in Life Expectancies, 1981-2002." *Annals of the Association of American Geographers* 9 (3): 551–66.

Ng, Cecilia, and Swasti Mitter. 2005. "Valuing Women's Voices: Call Center Workers in Malaysia and India." *Gender, Technology and Development* 9 (2): 209–33.

Ngai, Pun. 2007. "Gendering the Dormitory Labor System: Production, Reproduction, and Migrant Labor in South China." *Feminist Economics* 13 (3–4): 239–58.

Niño-Zarazúa, M., A. Barrientos, S. Hickey, and D. Hulme. 2012. "Social Protection in Sub-Saharan Africa: Getting the Politics Right." *World Development* 40 (1): 163–76.

Nolan Garcia, Kimberly A. 2011. "Transnational Advocates and Labor Rights Enforcement in the North American Free Trade Agreement." *Latin American Politics and Society* 53 (2): 29–60.

Ñopo, Hugo. 2012. *New Century, Old Disparities: Gender and Ethnic Earnings Gaps in Latin America and the Caribbean.* Washington DC: The World Bank.

Nordhaus, William D. 2006. "Principles of National Accounting for Nonmarket Accounts." In *A New Architecture for the US National Accounts*, edited by Dale W. Jorgenson, J. Steven Landefeld, and William D. Nordhaus, 143–60. Chicago: University of Chicago Press.

North, Douglass. 1990. *Institutions, Institutional Change and Economic Performance.* Cambridge, MA: Cambridge University Press.

Nussbaum, Martha. 2000a. *Women and Human Development: The Capabilities Approach.* Cambridge: Cambridge University Press.

———. 2000b. "Women's Capabilities and Social Justice." *Journal of Human Development* 1 (2): 219–47.

———. 2003. "Capabilities as Fundamental Entitlements: Sen and Social Justice." *Feminist Economics* 9 (2–3): 33–59.

———. 2004. "Promoting Women's Capabilities." In *Global Tensions*, edited by Lourdes Benería and Savitri Bisnath, 241–56. New York: Routledge.

———. 2011a. "Capabilities, Entitlements, Rights: Supplementation and Critique." *Journal of Human Development and Capabilities* 12 (1): 23–37.

———. 2011b. *Creating Capabilities: The Human Development Approach.* Cambridge, MA: Harvard University Press.

Nwagbara, Eucheria N. 2011. "The Story of Structural Adjustment Programme in Nigeria from the Perspective of the Organized Labor." *Australian Journal of Business and Management Research* 1 (7): 30–41.

Nzomo, Maria. 1995. "Women and Democratization Struggles in Africa: What Relevance to Postmodernist Discourse?" In *Feminism/Postmodernism/Development*, edited by Marianne H. Marchand and Jane L. Parpart, 131–41. London and New York: Routledge.

O'Hara, Sabine. 2009. "Feminist Ecological Economics Theory and Practice." In *Eco-Sufficiency and Global Justice*, edited by A. Salleh, 152–75. New York: Pluto Press.

OECD (Organization for Economic Co-operation and Development). 2004. *Employment Outlook: 2004.* Paris: Organization for Economic Cooperation and Development.

———. 2009. Data on Informal Employment and Self-Employment from *Is Informal Normal? Towards More and Better Jobs in Developing Countries*. Paris: Organization for Economic Cooperation and Development. http://www.oecd.org/dataoecd/4/49/42863997.pdf.

———. 2011. "Part-Time Employment." In *OECD Factbook 2011–2012: Economic, Environmental and Social Statistics*. Paris: Organization for Economic Cooperation and Development.

———. 2013. *African Economic Outlook: Structural Transformation and Natural Resources*. Paris: OECD Publishing.

———. 2014a. "Part Time Employment/Work." Paris: Organization for Economic Cooperation and Development. Available at, http://stats.oecd.org/glossary/detail.asp?ID=3046.

Olmsted, Jennifer C. 1997. "Telling Palestinian Women's Economic Stories." *Feminist Economics* 3 (2): 141–51.

Ong, Aiwa. 1987. *Spirits of Resistance and Capitalist Discipline: Women Factory Workers in Malaysia*. Albany, NY: State University of New York Press.

Oostendorp, Remco H. 2009. "Globalization and the Gender Wage Gap." *The World Bank Economic Review*. World Bank.

Ortiz, Isabel, and Matthew Cummins. 2011. *Global Inequality: Beyond the Bottom Billion. A Rapid Review of Income Distribution in 141 Countries*. UNICEF Social and Economic Working Paper. New York: UNICEF.

———. 2013. "Austerity Measures in Developing Countries: Public Expenditure Trends and the Risks to Children and Women." *Feminist Economics* 19 (3): 55–81.

Ostrom, Elinor. 1990. *Governing the Commons: The Evolution of Institutions for Collective Action*. Cambridge, UK: Cambridge University Press.

Ostry, Jonathan D., Andrew Berg, and Charalambos G. Tsangarides. 2014. *Redistribution, Inequality and Growth*. IMF Staff Discussion Note, SDN/14/02, Washington, DC: International Monetary Fund.

Otobe, Naoko. 2008. *The Impact of Globalization and Macroeconomic Change on Employment in Mauritius: What Next in the Post-MFA Era?* Employment Working Paper No. 9. Geneva: Employment Policy Department, International Labour Office.

Özler, Şule. 2007. "Export-Led Industrialization and Gender Differences in Job Creation and Destruction: Micro Evidence from the Turkish Manufacturing Sector." In *The Feminist Economics of Trade*, edited by Irene Van Staveren, Caren Grown, Diane Elson, and Nilüfer Çağatay, 164–84. London and New York: Routledge.

Padhi, Kulamani. 2007. "Agricultural Labour in India: A Close Look." *Orissa Review*: 23–28.

Palma, José Gabriel. 2011. "Homogenous Middles vs. Heterogenous Tails, and the End of the 'Inverted-U': It's All about the Share of the Rich." *Development and Change* 42 (1): 87–153.

Panda, Pradeep, and Bina Agarwal. 2005. "Marital Violence, Human Development and Women's Property Status in India." *World Development* 33 (5): 823–50.

Park, Nowook. 2010. "Gender and Economic Policy Management in Korea." Paper presented at the UNDP Gender and Economic Policy Management Initiative Expert Workshop, Seoul, Korea, May 8–10.

Parmar, Aradhana. 2003. "Micro-Credit, Empowerment, and Agency: Re-evaluating the Discourse." *Canadian Journal of Development Studies/Revue Canadienne D'étude Du Développement* 24 (3): 461–76.

Parpart, Jane L. 1995. "Deconstructing the Development 'Expert': Gender, Development and the 'Vulnerable Groups.'" In *Feminism/Postmodernism/Development*, edited by Marianne H. Marchand and Jane L. Parpart, 221–43. London and New York: Routledge.

Parpart, Jane L., and Marianne H. Marchand. 1995. "Exploding the Canon: An Introduction/Conclusion." In *Feminism/Postmodernism/Development*, edited by Marianne H. Marchand and Jane L. Parpart, 1–22. London and New York: Routledge.

Pastore, Francesco, and Alina Verashchagina. 2011. "When Does Transition Increase the Gender Wage Gap?" *Economics of Transition* 19 (2): 333–69.

Patel, Leila. 2012. "Poverty, Gender and Social Protection: Child Support Grants in Soweto, South Africa." *Journal of Policy Practice* 11 (1–2): 106–29.

Paul-Majumder, Pratima, and Anwara Begum. 2000. *The Gender Imbalances in the Export Oriented Garment Industry in Bangladesh*. Policy Research Working Paper No. 12. Washington DC: The World Bank.

Pearson, Ruth. 1995. "Male Bias and Women's Work in Mexico's Boarder Industries." In *Male Bias in the Development Process*, edited by Diane Elson, 2nd ed., 133–63. Manchester and New York: Manchester University Press.

———. 2005. "The Rise and Rise of Gender and Development." In *A Radical History of Development Studies: Individuals, Institutions and Ideologies*, edited by U. Kothari, 157–79. London: Zed Books.

Pearson, Ruth, and Kyoko Kusakabe. 2012. "Who Cares? Gender, Reproduction, and Care Chains of Burmese Migrant Workers in Thailand." *Feminist Economics* 18 (2): 149–75

Peet, Richard. 2011. "Inequality, Crisis and Austerity in Finance Capitalism." *Cambridge Journal of Regions, Economy and Society* 4 (3): 383–99.

Pérez, Mamerto, Sergio Schlesinger, and Timothy A. Wise. 2008. *The Promise and the Perils of Agricultural Trade Liberalization: Lessons from Latin America*. Washington DC and Medford, MA: Washington Office on Latin America (WOLA) and Global Development and Environment Institute (GDAE). http://ase.tufts.edu/gdae/Pubs/rp/AgricWGReportJuly08.pdf.

Pérez, Marta. 2012. "Emergency Frames: Gender Violence and Immigration Status in Spain." *Feminist Economics* 18 (2): 265–90.

Perkins, Ellie, Edith Kuiper, Rayen Quiroga-Martinez, Terisa E. Turner, Leigh S. Brownhill, Mary Mellor, Zdravka Todorova, Maren A. Jochimsen, and Martha McMahon. 2005. "Introduction: Exploring Feminist Ecological Economics." *Feminist Economics* 11 (3): 107–50.

Perkins, Patricia Ellie. 1997. "Introduction: Women, Ecology, and Economics: New Models and Theories." *Ecological Economics* 20 (2): 105–6.

———. 2007. "Feminist Ecological Economics and Sustainability." *Journal of Bioeconomics* 9 (3): 227–44.

Permanyer, Iñaki. 2013. "A Critical Assessment of UNDP's Gender Inequality Index." *Feminist Economics* 19 (2): 1–32.

Peterman, Amber, Julia Behrman, and Agnes Quisumbing. 2010. *A Review of Empirical Evidence on Gender Differences in Nonland Agricultural Inputs, Technology, and Services in Developing Countries.* Working Paper No. 975. Washington DC: International Food Policy Research Institute (IFPRI).

Phelps, Charlotte D. 1972. "Is the Household Obsolete?" *The American Economic Review* 62 (1–2): 167–74.

Phillips, Anne. 2004. "Defending Equality of Outcome." *Journal of Political Philosophy* 12 (1): 1–19.

Picchio, Antonella. 1992. *Social Reproduction: The Political Economy of the Labour Market.* Cambridge: Cambridge University Press.

Pietilä, Hilkka, and Jeanne Vickers. 1990. *Making Women Matter. The Role of the United Nations.* London: Zed Books.

Piketty, Thomas. 2014. *Capital in the Twenty-First Century.* Cambridge, MA: Harvard University Press.

Piketty, Thomas, and Emmanuel Saez. 2014. "Inequality in the Long Run." *Science* 344 (6186): 838–42.

Piore, Michael. 2004. "Rethinking International Labor Standards." In *Labor and the Globalization of Production: Causes and Consequences of Industrial Upgrading,* edited by William Milberg. Basingstoke: Palgrave Macmillan.

Piras, Claudia, ed. 2004. *Women at Work: Challenges for Latin America.* Washington DC: Inter-American Development Bank.

Poch-de-Feliu, R. 2013. "Alemania en la gram desigualdad." In *La quinta Alemania. Un modelo hacia el Fracaso europeo,* edited by R. Poch-de-Felie, A. Guerrero, and C. Negrete, 15–144. Barcelona: Icaria.

Polanyi, Karl. 1944. *The Great Transformation: Economic and Political Origins of Our Time.* New York: Rinehart.

Polaski, Sandra. 2006. "Combining Global and Local Forces: The Case of Labor Rights in Cambodia." *World Development* 34 (5): 919–32.

Pollin, Robert. 2003. *Contours of Descent: U.S. Economic Fractures and the Landscape of Global Austerity.* London and New York: Verso Books.

Population Reference Bureau. 2011. *The World's Women and Girls 2011 Data Sheet.* Washington DC.

Porro, Noemi Miyasaka, and Joaquim Shiraishi Neto. 2014. "Coercive Harmony in Land Acquisition: The Gendered Impact of Corporate 'Responsibility' in the Brazilian Amazon." *Feminist Economics* 20 (1): 227–48.

Portes, Alejandro, Manual Castells, and Lauren Benton, eds. 1989. *The Informal Economy: Studies in Advanced and Less Developed Countries.* Baltimore, MD: Johns Hopkins University Press.

Power, Marilyn, and Sam Rosenberg. 1995. "Race, Class, and Occupational Mobility: Black and White Women in Service Work in the United States." *Feminist Economics* 1 (3): 40–59.

Power, Marilyn. 2004. "Social Provisioning as a Starting Point for Feminist Economics." *Feminist Economics* 10 (3): 3–19.

———. 2009. "Global Climate Policy and Climate Justice: A Feminist Social Provisioning Approach." *Challenge* 52 (1): 47–66.

———. 2013. "A Social Provisioning Approach to Gender and Economic Life." In *Handbook of Research on Gender and Economic Life*, edited by Deborah M. Figart and Tonia L. Warnecke, 7–17. Cheltenham, UK: Edward Elgar.

Pronk, Jan. 2012. "Addressing the Defaults of Globalization." In *Justice, Not Greed*, edited by Pamela Brubaker and Rogate Mshana, 17–30. Geneva: WCC Publications.

Prügl, Elisabeth. 1999. *The Global Construction of Gender: Home-Based Work in the Political Economy of the 20th Century*. New York: Columbia University Press.

Pujol, Michèle A. 1992. *Feminism and Anti-Feminism in Early Economic Thought*. Aldershot, England: Edward Elgar.

Qian, Yingyi. 2003. "How Reform Worked in China." In *Search of Prosperity: Analytic Narratives on Economic Growth*, edited by Dani Rodrik. Princeton, NJ: Princeton University Press.

Quinlan, Michael. 2012. "The 'Pre-Invention' of Precarious Employment: The Changing World of Work in Context." *The Economic and Labour Relations Review* 23 (4): 3–24.

Quisumbing, Agnes and John Maluccio, 2000. *Intrahousehold Allocation and Gender Relations: New Empirical Evidence from Four Developing Countries*. Washington, DC: International Food Policy Research Institute.

Quisumbing, Agnes, Kelly Hallman, and Marie T. Ruel. 2003. "Maquiladoras and Market Mamas: Women's Work and Childcare in Guatemala City and Accra." *Journal of Development Studies* 43 (3): 420–55.

Radin, Margaret J. 1996. *Contested Commodities: The Trouble with Trade in Sex, Children, Body Parts, and Other Things*. Cambridge, MA: Harvard University Press.

Rai, Shirin. 2002. *Gender and Political Economy of Development: From Nationalism to Globalisation*. Cambridge: Polity Press.

Rajan, Ramkishen S., and Sadhana Srivastava. 2007. "Global Outsourcing of Services: Issues and Implications." *Harvard Asia Pacific Review* 9 (1): 39–40.

Ramírez, A. L., and P. Rosés. 2005. *Conciliation of Work and Family Life: Costa Rica*. Conditions of Work and Employment Programme Working Paper. Geneva: ILO.

Ranis, Gustav, and Frances Stewart. 1999. "V-Goods and the Role of the Urban Informal Sector in Development." *Economic Development and Cultural Change* 47 (2): 259–88.

Rankin, Katherine. 2002. "Social Capital, Microfinance, and the Politics of Development." *Feminist Economics* 8 (1): 1–24.

Rao, Smriti, and Christina Parenti. 2012. "Understanding Human Trafficking Origin: A Cross-Country Empirical Analysis." *Feminist Economics* 18 (2): 231–63.

Raunikar, Ronald, Joseph Buongiorno, James A. Turner, and Shushuai Zhu. 2010. "Global Outlook for Wood and Forests with the Bioenergy Demand Implied by Scenarios of the Intergovernmental Panel on Climate Change." *Forest Policy and Economics* 12 (1): 48–56.

Raynolds, Laura T., Douglas R. Murray, and John Wilkinson, eds. 2007. *Fair Trade: The Challenges of Transforming Globalization.* New York and Abingdon, UK: Routledge.

Razavi, Shahra. 1999. "Export-Oriented Employment, Poverty and Gender: Contested Accounts." *Development and Change* 30 (3): 653–83.

———. 2007. *The Political and Social Economy of Care in a Development Context: Conceptual Issues, Research Questions and Policy Options.* Gender and Development Programme Paper No. 3. Geneva: UNRISD.

———. 2012. "World Development Report: Gender Equality and Development – A Commentary." *Development and Change* 43 (1): 423–37.

Razavi, Shahrashoub, and Carol Miller. 1995. *From WID to GAD: Conceptual Shifts in the Women and Development Discourse.* Occasional Paper No. 1. Geneva: UNRISD.

Razavi, Shahra, and Silke Staab. 2012. *Global Variations in the Political and Social Economy of Care: Worlds Apart.* New York and Abingdon, UK: Routledge.

Razavi, Shahrashoub, Camila Arza, Elissa Braunstein, Sarah Cook, and Kristine Goulding. 2012. *Gendered Impacts of Globalization, Employment and Social Protection.* Geneva: UNRISD.

Reich, Michael, David Gordon, and Richard Edwards. 1980. "A Theory of Labor Market Segmentation." In *The Economics of Women and Work*, edited by Alice Amsden, 232–41. New York: St. Martin's Press.

Reich, Robert B. 2012. *Beyond Outrage: What Has Gone Wrong with Our Economy and Our Democracy and How to Fix It.* New York: Vintage.

Rey de Marulanda, Nohra. 2012. "Politicas Públicas Y Economia Del Cuidado." *IB Magazin de La Gestión Estadística: Numero Especial Sobre El Seminario Internacional*, 46–49.

Reynolds, Sarah. 2008. "Intergenerational Intra-Household Bargaining with an Application to Teen Mothers and Their Mothers in Salvador, Brazil." PhD. Dissertation. Cornell University.

Rice, Robert A. 2001. "Noble Goals and Challenging Terrain: Organic and Fair Trade Coffee Movements in the Global Marketplace." *Journal of Agricultural and Environmental Ethics* 14 (1): 39–66.

Rio, Coral Del, and Olga Alonso-Villar. 2012. "Occupational Segregation of Immigrant Women in Spain." *Feminist Economics* 18 (2): 91–124.

Ritzen, Jo, and Klaus F. Zimmermann. 2014. "A Vibrant European Labor Market with Full Employment." *IZA Journal of European Labor Studies* 3 (1): 1–24.

Roberts, Adrienne. 2012. "Financing Social Reproduction: The Gendered Relations of Debt and Mortgage Finance in 21st Century America." *New Political Economy* 8(1): 21-42.

Robeyns, Ingrid. 2000. "Is There a Feminist Economic Methodology?" Italian translation published as 'Esiste Una Metodologia Economica Feminista? In *Gli Studi Delle Donne in Italia: Una Guida Critica*, edited by Paola Di Cori and Donatella Barazzetti, 119–145. Roma: Carocci Editore.

———. 2003a. "The Capability Approach: An Interdisciplinary Introduction." Available at, http://www.ingridrobeyns.nl/. Accessed on August 30, 2014.

———. 2003b. "Sen's Capability Approach and Gender Inequality: Selecting Relevant Capabilities." *Feminist Economics* 9 (2–3): 61–92.

———. 2005. "The Capability Approach: A Theoretical Survey." *Journal of Human Development* 6 (1): 93–117.

Rochester, Colin, Angela Ellis Paine, and Steven Howlett. 2009. *Volunteering and Society in the 21st Century*. Basingstoke: Palgrave Macmillan.

Rodrik, Dani. 1996. "Labor Standards in International Trade: Do They Matter and What Do We Do about Them?" In *Emerging Agenda For Global Trade: High Stakes for Developing Countries*, edited by Robert Z. Lawrence, Dani Rodrik, and John Whalley, 35–80. Baltimore, MD: Johns Hopkins University Press.

Roldán, Martha. 1985. "Industrial Outworking, Struggles for the Reproduction of Working Class Families and Gender Subordination." In *Beyond Employment: Household, Gender and Subsistence*, 248–85. Oxford: Basil Blackwell.

Roncolato, Leann. 2014. "Essays on Economic Structure, Employment and Development". PhD. Dissertation. American University, Washington DC.

Roodman, David, and Jonathan Morduch. 2009. *The Impact of Microcredit on the Poor in Bangladesh: Revisiting the Evidence*. 174. CGD Working Paper. Washington DC: Center for Global Development.

Rosewarne, Stuart. 2012. "Temporary International Labor Migration and Development in South and Southeast Asia." *Feminist Economics* 18 (2): 63–90.

Rubery, Jill, and Damian Grimshaw. 2003. *The Organization of Employment: An International Perspective*. Basingstoke: Palgrave Macmillan.

———. 2011. "Gender and the Minimum Wage." In *Regulating for Decent Work. New Directions in Labour Market Regulation*, edited by Sangheon Lee and Deirdre McCann, 226–54. Geneva and Basingstoke: ILO and Palgrave Macmillan.

Rubery, Jill, Mark Smith, and Colette Fagan. 1998. "National Working-Time Regimes and Equal Opportunities." *Feminist Economics* 4 (1): 71–101.

Rubery, Jill, Mark Smith, Dominique Anxo, and Lennart Flood. 2001. "The Future European Labor Supply: The Critical Role of the Family." *Feminist Economics* 7 (3): 33–69.

Rugh, Jacob S., and Douglas S. Massey. 2010. "Racial Segregation and the American Foreclosure Crisis." *American Sociological Review* 75 (5): 629–51.

Sachs, Jeffrey. 1991. *The Economic Transformation of Eastern Europe: The Case of Poland*. Memphis, TN: P.K. Seidman Foundation.

Safa, Helen. 1986. "Runaway Shops and Female Employment: The Search for Cheap Labor." In *Women's Work*, edited by Eleanor Leacock and Helen Safa, 58–71. South Hadley, MA: Bergin and Garvey Publishers.

Saffioti, Heleieth. 1986. "Technological Change in Brazil: Its Effect on Men and Women in Two Firms." In *Women and Change in Latin America*, edited by June Nash and Helen Safa, 109–35. South Hadley, MA: Bergin and Garvey Publishers.

Salamon, Lester M., S. Wojciech Sokolowski, and Megan A. Haddock. 2011. "Measuring the Economic Value of Volunteer Work Globally: Concepts, Estimates, and a Roadmap to the Future." *Annals of Public and Cooperative Economics* 82 (3): 217–52.

Salzinger, Leslie. 2003. *Genders in Production: Making Workers in Mexico's Global Factories.* Berkeley: University of California Press.

Samarasinghe, Vidyamali. 1998. "The Feminization of Foreign Currency Earnings: Women's Labor in Sri Lanka." *Journal of Developing Areas* 32 (3): 303–26.

———. 2009. *Female Sex Trafficking in Asia: Resilience of Patriarchy in a Changing World London.* New York: Routledge.

Sánchez López, Gabriela, and Daniela Jiménez Rodríguez. 2012. "Trayectorias Juveniles: Escolaridad, Empleo y Formación de Nuevos Hogares." In *Pobreza, Transferencias Condicionadas Y Sociedad*, edited by Mercedes González de la Rocha and Agustín Escobar Latapí. México, D.F.: Publicaciones de la Casa Chata, CIESAS.

Saunders, Kriemild. 2002. *Feminist Development Thought. Rethinking Modernity, Postcolonialism and Representation.* London and New York: Zed Books.

Sawhill, Isabel V. 1977. "Economic Perspectives on the Family." *Daedalus* 106 (2): 115–25.

Sayer, Liana C. 2005. "Gender, Time and Inequality: Trends in Women's and Men's Paid Work, Unpaid Work and Free Time." *Social Forces* 84 (1): 285–303.

Schandl, Heinz, and Jim West. 2010. "Resource Use and Resource Efficiency in the Asia–Pacific Region." *Global Environmental Change* 20 (4): 636–47.

Schneider, Cédric. 2011. "The Battle for Patent Rights in Plant Biotechnology: Evidence from Opposition Fillings." *The Journal of Technology Transfer* 36 (5): 565–79.

Schuberth, Helene, and Brigitte Young. 2011. "The Role of Gender in Governance of the Financial Sector." In *Questioning Financial Governance from a Feminist Perspective*, edited by Brigitte Young, Isabella Bakker, and Diane Elson, 132–54. Abingdon, UK and New York: Routledge.

Schüler, Dana. 2006. "The Uses and Misuses of the Gender-Related Development Index and Gender Empowerment Measure: A Review of the Literature." *Journal of Human Development* 7 (2): 161–81.

Schuler, Sidney Ruth, Syed M. Hashemi, and Shamsul Huda Badal. 1998. "Men's Violence against Women in Rural Bangladesh: Undermined or Exacerbated by Microcredit Programmes?" *Development in Practice* 8 (2): 148–57.

Scott, Joan W. 1986. "Gender: A Useful Category of Historical Analysis." *American Historical Review* 91 (5): 1053–75.

Seguino, Stephanie. 1997. "Gender Wage Inequality and Export-Led Growth in South Korea." *Journal of Development Studies* 34 (2): 102–32.

———. 2000a. "The Effects of Structural Change and Economic Liberalisation on Gender Wage Differentials in South Korea and Taiwan." *Cambridge Journal of Economics* 24 (4): 437–59.

———. 2000b. "Gender Inequality and Economic Growth: A Cross-Country Analysis." *World Development* 28 (7): 1211–30.

———. 2000c. "Accounting for Gender in Asian Economic Growth." *Feminist Economics* 6 (3): 27–58.

———. 2002. "Gender, Quality of Life, and Growth in Asia 1970–90." *The Pacific Review* 15 (2): 245–78.

———. 2008. "Micro-Macro Linkages Between Gender, Development, and Growth: Implications for the Caribbean Region." *Journal of Eastern Caribbean Studies* 33 (4): 8–42.

———. 2012. "Macroeconomics, Human Development, and Distribution." *Journal of Human Development and Capabilities* 13 (1): 59–81.

Seguino, Stephanie, and Caren Grown. 2006. "Gender Equity and Globalization: Macroeconomic Policy for Developing Countries." *Journal of International Development* 18 (8): 1081–104.

Seiz, Janet A. 1991. "The Bargaining Approach and Feminist Methodology." *Review of Radical Political Economics* 23 (1–2): 22–29.

Sen, Amartya. 1985. "Women, Technology and Sexual Divisions." *Trade and Development*, 195–223.

———. 1990a. "Gender and Cooperative Conflicts." In *Persistent Inequalities: Women and World Development*, edited by Irene Tinker, 195–223. New York: Oxford University Press.

———. 1990b. "More than 100 Million Women are Missing." *The New York Review of Books* 37.

———. 1992. "Missing Women." *British Medical Journal* 304.

———. 1999. *Development As Freedom*. New York: Knopf.

———. 2001. "The Many Faces of Gender Inequality." *Frontline: India's National Magazine* 18 (22), November 9.

Sen Amartya and Jean Drèze. 2013. *An Uncertain Glory: India and its Contradictions*. Princeton, NJ: Princeton University Press.

Sen, Gita. 2010. "Poor Households or Poor Women: Is There a Difference?" In *International Handbook of Gender and Poverty*, edited by Sylvia Chant, 101–4. Cheltenham, UK and Northampton, MA: Edward Elgar.

Sen, Gita, and Caren Grown. 1987. *Development, Crises, and Alternative Visions: Third World Women's Perspectives*. New York: Monthly Review Press.

Sender, John, Carlos Oya, and Christopher Cramer. 2006. "Women Working for Wages: Putting Flesh on the Bones of a Rural Labour Market Survey in Mozambique." *Journal of Southern African Studies* 32 (2): 313–34.

Sevilla-Sanz, Almudena, José Ignacio Giménez-Nadal, and Cristina Fernández. 2010. "Gender Roles and the Division of Unpaid Work in Spanish Households." *Feminist Economics* 16 (40): 137–84.

Sharp, Rhonda, and Ray Broomhill. 2002. "Budgeting for Equality: The Australian Experience." *Feminist Economics* 8 (1): 25–47.

Shiva, Vandana. 1988. *Staying Alive: Women, Ecology and Development*. London: Zed Books.

Shivakumar, Sujai. 1996. "Valuing women's work: Theoretical constraints in determining the worth of household and other non-market activity." In Workshop on Integrating Paid and Unpaid Work into National Policies, May 28–30, organized by UNDP, United Nations Statistical Division, UNIFEM, the Ministry of Foreign Affairs of the Republic of Korea, and the Women's Development Institute, Seoul.

Shlay, Anne B. 2006. "Low-Income Homeownership: American Dream or Delusion?" *Urban Studies* 43 (3): 511–31.

Simmons, Beth. 2009. *Mobilizing for Rights: International Law in Domestic Politics.* Cambridge: Cambridge University Press.

Simonazzi, Annamaria. 2009. "Care Regimes and National Employment Models." *Cambridge Journal of Economics* 33 (2): 211–32.

Singh, Ajit, and Ann Zammit. 2000. "International Capital Flows: Identifying the Gender Dimension." *World Development* 28 (7): 1249–68.

———. 2001. *The Global Labor Standards Controversy: Critical Issues for Developing Countries.* Geneva: South Centre.

———. 2004. "Labour Standards and the 'Race to the Bottom': Rethinking Globalization and Workers' Rights from Developmental and Solidaristic Perspectives." *Oxford Review of Economic Policy* 20 (1): 85–104.

Sirimanne, Shamika. 2009. The Interactive Expert Panel. Written statement. UN Commission of the Status of Women, Fifty-third session, New York, 2–13 March.

Skidelsky, Robert, and Edward Skidelsky. 2012. *How Much Is Enough?: The Love of Money and the Case for the Good Life.* Harmondsworth, UK: Penguin.

Slater, Rachel, Rebecca Holmes, Nicola Jones, and Matseliso Mphale. 2010. "Conceptual and Practical Issues for Gender and Social Protection: Lessons from Lesotho." In *The International Handbook of Gender and Poverty*, edited by Sylvia Chant, 399–408. Cheltenham, UK and Northampton, MA: Edward Elgar.

Soros, George. 1998. *The Crisis of Global Capitalism: Open Society Endangered.* New York: Public Affairs Press.

South Centre. 2014. "SDGs: Economic Issues at National and Global Levels" South Views. No. 107, Available at, www.southcentre.int. Accessed on July 30, 2014.

Sparr, Pamela. 1994. *Mortgaging Women's Lives: Feminist Critiques of Structural Adjustment.* London and New Jersey: Zed Books.

Srinivasan, Sharada, and Arjun Singh Bedi. 2008. "Daughter Elimination in Tamil Nadu, India: A Tale of Two Ratios." *The Journal of Development Studies* 44 (7): 961–90.

Standing, Guy. 1989. "Global Feminization through Flexible Labor." *World Development* 17 (7): 1077–95.

———. 1999. "Global Feminization through Flexible Labor: A Theme Revisited." *World Development* 27 (3): 583–602.

———. 2011a. *The Precariat: The New Dangerous Class.* Bloomsbury Academic.

———. 2011b. "Responding to the Crisis: Economic Stabilisation Grants." *Policy & Politics* 39 (1): 9–25.

Starr, Martha A. 2014. "Qualitative and Mixed-Methods Research in Economics: Surprising Growth, Promising Future." *Journal of Economic Surveys* 28 (2): 238–64.

Stern, Nicholas. 2011. "How Should We Think About the Economics of Climate Change?" Lecture for the Leontief Prize Medford, Global Development and Environment Institute. Available at, http://www.ase.tufts.edu/gdae/about_us/leontief/SternLecture.pdf. Accessed on Novemeber 6, 2011.

Stiglitz, Joseph. 2012. *The Price of Inequality: How Today's Divided Society Endangers Our Future.* New York and London: W.W. Norton and Co.

———. 2013. "Inequality Is a Choice." *New York Times,* October 13.

Stolcke, Verena. 2012. "Homo Clonicus." In *Clones, Fakes and Posthumans: Cultures of Replication,* edited by P. Essed and G. Schwab, 25–43. Amsterdam and New York: Editions Rodopi.

Strassmann, Diana. 1993. "Not a Free Market: The Rhetoric of Disciplinary Authority in Economics." In *Beyond Economic Man: Feminist Theory and Economics,* 54–68. Chicago: University of Chicago Press.

Strober, Myra H. 1984. "Towards a General Theory of Occupational Segregation: The Case of Public School Teaching." In *Sex Segregation in the Workplace: Trends, Explanations, Remedies,* edited by Barbara Reskin, 144–56. Washington DC: National Academy Press.

———. 1994. "Rethinking Economics through a Feminist Lens." *The American Economic Review* 84 (2): 143–47.

———. 2003. "The Application of Mainstream Economics Constructs to Education: A Feminist Analysis." In *Beyond Economic Man: Feminist Theory and Economics,* edited by Julie A. Nelson and Marianne Ferber, 135–56. Chicago: University of Chicago Press.

Sunden, Annika E, and Brian J Surette. 1998. "Gender Differences in the Allocation of Assets in Retirement Savings Plans." *American Economic Review*: 207–11.

Sweetman, Caroline. 2010. "A Woman and an Empty House Are Never Alone for Long: Autonomy, Control, Marriage and Microfinance in Women's Livelihoods in Addis Ababa, Ethiopia." In *The International Handbook of Gender and Poverty,* edited by Sylvia Chant, 575–80. Cheltenham, UK and Northampton, MA: Edward Elgar.

Takenoshita, Hirohisa. 2012. "Family, Labour Market Structures and the Dynamics of Self-Employment in Three Asian Countries: Gender Differences in Self-Employment Entry in Japan, Korea and Taiwan." *Comparative Social Research* 29: 85–112.

Taylor, Marcus. 2011. "'Freedom from Poverty Is Not for Free': Rural Development and the Microfinance Crisis in Andhra Pradesh, India." *Journal of Agrarian Change* 11 (4): 484–504.

———. 2012. "The Antinomies of 'Financial Inclusion': Debt, Distress and the Workings of Indian Microfinance." *Journal of Agrarian Change* 12 (4): 601–10.

Tejani, Sheba, and William Milberg. 2010. *Global Defeminization? Industrial Upgrading, Occupational Segmentation and Manufacturing Employment in Middle-Income Countries.* SCEPA Working Paper No. 2010–1. New York: New School for Social Research.

Tett, Gillian. 2007. *Fool's Gold: How Unrestrained Greed Corrupted a Dream, Shattered Global Markets and Unleashed a Catastrophe*. New York: Simon and Schuster.

Thomas, Duncan. 1990. "Intra-Household Resource Allocation: An Inferential Approach." *Journal of Human Resources* 25 (4): 635–64.

Tiano, Susan. 1994. *Patriarchy on the Line: Labor, Gender, and Ideology in the Mexican Maquila Industry*. Philadelphia: Temple University Press.

Tilly, Charles. 1995. "Globalization Threatens Labor's Rights." *International Labor and Working-Class History* 47 (spring): 1–23.

Tinker, Irene. 1990. "The Making of a Field: Advocates, Practitioners, and Scholars." In *Persistent Inequalities*, edited by Irene Tinker, 27–53. New York: Oxford University Press.

Touza, A. L., and O. L. Pineda. 2010. "Mujeres Hondureñas en Crisis: Estudio de Caso de los Impactos Económicos del Golpe de Estado y de la Crisis Internacional." Paper presented at the 19th Annual Conference of the International Association for Feminist Economics, Buenos Aires, 22–24 July.

Trzcinski, Eileen. 2000. "Family Policy in Germany: A Feminist Dilemma?" *Feminist Economics* 6 (1): 21–44.

Udayagiri, Mridula. 1995. "Challenging Modernization: Gender and Development, Postmodern Feminism and Activism." In *Feminism/Postmodernism/Development*, edited by Marianne H. Marchand and Jane L. Parpart, 159–77. London and New York: Routledge.

UN Department of Economic and Social Affairs (2010), Table 4c, p. 211.

UN Statistical Office/ECA/INSTRAW. 1991a. *Handbook on Compilation of Statistics on Women in the Informal Sector in Industry, Trade and Services in Africa*. Santo Domingo and New York: United Nations.

———. 1991b. *Synthesis of Pilot Studies on Compilation of Statistics on Women in the Informal Sector in Industry, Trade and Services in African Countries*. Santo Domingo and New York: United Nations.

UN Women. 2013. *A Transformative Stand-alone Goal on Achieving Gender Equality, Women's Rights and Women's Empowerment: Imperatives and Key Components*. Position Paper. Available at, http://www.unwomen.org/lo/digital-library/publica tions/2013/7/post-2015-long-paper#sthash.FJADieaf.dpuf. Accessed on March 3, 2014.

———. 2014. Convention for the Elimination of All Forms of Discrimination Against Women, Women Watch. Available at, http://www.un.org/womenwatch/daw/cedaw/text/econvention.htm. Accessed on September 21, 2014.

UNCTAD (United Nations Conferences on Trade and Development). 2013. *World Investment Report*. Geneva: UNCTAD.

UNDP (United Nations Development Programme). 2010. *Human Development Report 2010. The Real Wealth of Nations: Pathways to Human Development*. New York: UNDP.

UNDP (United Nations Development Programme). 2011. *Human Development Report 2011. Sustainability and Equity: A Better Future for All*. New York: UNDP.

UNFPA (United Nations Population Fund). 2006. *A Passage of Hope: Women and International Migration, State of the World Population*. New York: UNFPA.

UNICEF (United Nations Children's Fund). 2008. *TransMONEE database.,* Florence: UNICEF Innocenti Research Centre, Florence. Available at, http://www.unicef-irc.org/databases/transmonee/. Accessed on June 27, 2013.

UN Department of Economic and Social Affairs. 2010. *The World's Women 2010.* New York: United Nations.

United Nations. 1989. *1989 World Survey on the Role of Women in Development.* Centre for Social Development and Humanitarian Affairs. United Nations Office at Vienna. Document ST/CSDHA/6. New York: United Nations.

———. 1996. *Beijing Declaration and Platform for Action,* Report of the Fourth World Conference on Women, Beijing, September, 4–15 1995, UN Document No. A/CONF.177/20/REV.1. New York: United Nations.

———. 2003. *Handbook on Nonprofit Institutions in the System of National Accounts.* New York: United Nations.

United Nations Statistical Commission. 1983. *Demographic and Social Statistics: Social Indicators and Links among Social, Demographic and Related Economic and Environmental Statistics.* New York: United Nations.

———. 1993. *Towards the 1993 SNA.* New York: United Nations.

———. 2004. *Treatment of the Informal Sector in the 1993 SNA,* Advisory Expert Group on National Accounts Report, SNA/M2.04/12, New York: United Nations.

United Nations, European Communities, International Monetary Fund, Organization for Economic Cooperation and Development, and the World Bank. 2009. *System of National Accounts 2008.* New York: United Nations.

United States Bureau of Labor Statistics. 2010. *Volunteers by Annual Hours of Volunteer Activities and Selected Characteristics.* Washington DC.

———. 2014. "News Release: The employment situation–Aug 2014." Available at, http://www.bls.gov/news.release/pdf/empsit.pdf. Accessed on Sept. 9, 2014.

Valiani, Salimah. 2011. *Rethinking Unequal Exchange: The Global Integration of Nursing Labour Markets.* Toronto: University of Toronto Press.

Van der Hoeven, Rolph. 2010. *Labour Markets Trends, Financial Globalization and the Current Crisis in Developing Countries.* New York: United Nations.

Van Staveren, Irene. 1997. "Focus Groups: Contributing to a Gender-Aware Methodology." *Feminist Economics* 3 (2): 131–35.

———. 2008. "The Gender Bias of the Poverty Reduction Strategy Framework." *Review of International Political Economy* 15 (2): 289–313.

———. 2010. "Post-Keynesianism Meets Feminist Economics." *Cambridge Journal of Economics* 34 (6): 1123–44.

———. 2013. "To Measure is to Know? A Comparative Analysis of Gender Indices." *Review of Social Economy* 71 (3): 339–72.

Van Staveren, Irene, and Olasunbo Odebode. 2007. "Gender Norms as Asymmetric Institutions: A Case Study of Yoruba Women in Nigeria." *Journal of Economic Issues* 41 (4): 903–25.

Van Staveren, Irene, Diane Elson, Caren Grown, and Nilüfer Çağatay, eds. 2007. *The Feminist Economics of Trade.* Abingdon, UK and New York: Routledge.

Veblen, Thorstein. [1899] 1973. *The Theory of the Leisure Class*. Gutenberg: Oxford University Press.

Venn, Danielle. 2009. *Legislation, Collective Bargaining and Enforcement: Updating the OECD Employment Protection Indicators*. Paris: OECD.

Veras, Fabio, Rafael Perez Ribas, and Rafael Guerreiro Osório. 2010. "Evaluating the Impact of Brazil's Bolsa Familia: Cash Transfers Programs in Comparative Perspective." *Latin America Research Review* 45 (2): 173–90.

Veuthey, Sandra, and Julien-François Gerber. 2010. "Logging Conflicts in Southern Cameroon: A Feminist Ecological Economics Perspective." *Ecological Economics* 70 (2): 170–77.

Vickery, Claire. 1977. "The Time-Poor: A New Look at Poverty." *The Journal of Human Resources* 12 (1): 27–48.

Visser, Jelle. 2006. "Union Membership Statistics in 24 Countries." *Monthly Labour Review* 129: 38–49.

Vo, Phuong. H., Kate Penrose, and Jody Heymann. 2007. "Working to Exit Poverty While Caring for Children's Health and Development in Vietnam." *Community, Work and Family* 10: 179–99.

Vosko, Leah F. 2002. "Decent Work The Shifting Role of the ILO and the Struggle for Global Social Justice." *Global Social Policy* 2(1): 19–46.

Wade, Robert. 2011. "Market as Means Rather than a Master: The Crisis of Development and the Future Role of the State." In *Towards New Developmentalism*, edited by S. R. Khan and J. Christiansen, 22–46. New York: Routledge.

Walters, Bernard. 1995. "Engendering macroeconomics: A reconsideration of growth theory." *World Development* 23 (11): 1869–880.

Wanyama, Fredrick O. 2014. *Cooperatives and the Sustainable Development Goals: A Contribution to the Post-2015 Development Debate*. Geneva: ILO.

Waring, Marilyn. 1988. *If Women Counted: A New Feminist Economics*. San Francisco: Harper & Row.

Weldon, S. Laurel, and Mala Htun. 2013. "Feminist Mobilization and Progressive Policy Change: Why Governments Take Action to Combat Violence against Women." *Gender and Development* 21 (2): 231–47.

Werner, Marion. 2012. "Beyond Upgrading: Gendered Labor and the Restructuring of Firms in the Dominican Republic." *Economic Geography* 88 (4): 403–22.

Western, Bruce, and Jake Rosenfeld. 2011. "Unions, Norms, and the Rise in U.S. Wage Inequality." *American Sociological Review* 76 (4): 513–37.

WHO (World Health Organization). 2013. *Global and Regional Estimates of Violence against Women: Prevalence and Health Effects of Intimate Partner Violence and Non-Partner Sexual Violence*. Geneva: WHO. http://apps.who.int/iris/bitstream/10665/85239/1/9789241564625_eng.pdf?ua=1

Wichterich, Christa. 2012. "The Other Financial Crisis: Growth and Crash of the Microfinance Sector in India." *Development* 55 (3): 406–12.

Williams, Mariama. 2001. *Imbalances, Inequities and the WTO Mantra*. DAWN Discussion Paper II on the WTO, Development Alternatives with Women for a New Era (DAWN). Manila: University of the Philippines.

———. 2004. "Gender, the Doha Development Agenda, and the Post-Cancun Trade Negotiations." *Gender & Development* 12 (2): 73–81.

———. 2007. "Gender Issues in the Multilateral Trading System. Irene van Staveren, Diane Elson, Caren Grown, and Nilufer Cagatay." In *The Feminist Economics of Trade*, edited by Irene Van Staveren, Caren Grown, and Nilüfer Çağatay, 277–91. London and New York: Routledge.

Williamson, Oliver. 1985. *The Economic Institutions of Capitalism: Firms, Markets, Relational Contracting.* New York: Free Press.

Wisman, Jon. 2011. "Inequality, Social Respectability, Political Power and Environmental Devastation." *Journal of Economic Issues* 45 (4): 877–900.

Wolf, Diane L. 1992. *Factory Daughters: Gender, Household Dynamics, and Rural Industrialization in Java.* Berkeley: University of California Press.

Woo, Wing Thye, Stephen Parker, and Jeffrey Sachs, eds. 1997. *Economies in Transition: Comparing Asia and Eastern Europe.* Cambridge, MA: MIT Press.

Wood, Cynthia A. 1997. "The First World/Third Party Criterion: A Feminist Critique of Production Boundaries in Economics." *Feminist Economics* 3 (3): 47–68.

World Bank. 2001. *Engendering Development through Gender Equality in Rights, Resources, and Voice.* Washington DC: The World Bank.

———. 2006. *Gender Equality as Smart Economics: A World Bank Group Gender Action Plan (Fiscal Years 2007–10).* Washington DC: The World Bank.

———. 2011. *World Development Report 2012: Gender Inequality and Development.* Washington DC: The World Bank.

———. 2012. *World Development Report 2013: Jobs.* Washington DC: The World Bank.

———. 2014a *Gender at Work: A Companion to the World Development Report on Jobs* Washington DC http://www.worldbank.org/content/dam/Worldbank/document/Gender/GenderAtWork_web.pdf.

———. 2014b. *Voice and Agency: Empowering Women and Girls for Shared Prosperity.* Washington DC: The World Bank.

Wray, L. Randall. 2008. "A Minskyan Road to Financial Reform." In *The Handbook of the Political Economy of Financial Crises*, edited by Martin H. Wolfson and Gerald A. Epstein, 696–710. New York: Oxford University Press.

Wright, Angus Lindsay, and Wendy Wolford. 2003. *To Inherit the Earth: The Landless Movement and the Struggle for a New Brazil.* Oakland, CA: Food First Books.

Wymer Jr., Walter. 2011. "The Implications of Sex Differences on Volunteer Preferences." *Voluntas: International Journal of Voluntary and Nonprofit Organizations* 22 (4): 831–51.

Wymer Jr., Walter W., and Sridhar Samu. 2002. "Volunteer Service as Symbolic Consumption: Gender and Occupational Differences in Volunteering." *Journal of Marketing Management* 18 (9–10): 971–89.

Yokokawa, Nobuharu, Jayati Ghosh, and Bob Rowthorn. 2013. *Industrialization of China and India: Their Impacts on the World Economy.* Abingdon, UK and New York: Routledge.

Yoon, Jayoung. 2014. "Counting Care Work in Social Policy: Unpaid Child- and Eldercare in Korea." *Feminist Economics* 20(2): 65–89.

Young, Brigitte, Isabella Bakker, and Diane Elson. 2011. "Introduction." In *Questioning Financial Governance from a Feminist Perspective*, edited by Brigitte Young, Isabella Bakker, and Diane Elson, 1–10. Abingdon, UK and New York: Routledge.

Young, Kate. 1992. "Gender and Development." In *Gender and Development Reader*. Ottawa: Canadian Council for International Cooperation.

Yu, Xiaomin. 2008. "Impacts of Corporate Code of Conduct on Labor Standards: A Case Study of Reebok's Athletic Footwear Supplier Factory in China." *Journal of Business Ethics* 81 (3): 513–29.

Zacharias, Ajit, Rania Antonopoulos, and Thomas Masterson. 2012. *Why Time Deficit Matter: Implications for the Measurement of Poverty.* Research Project Report of LEVY Economics Institute of Bard College. Anandale-on-Hudson, NY: Levy Economics Institute. Available at, http://www.levyinstitute.org/files/download.php?file=rpr_08_12.pdf&pubid=1566. Accessed on June 21, 2014.

Zarsky, Lyuba. 2011. "Climate-Resilient Industrial Development Paths: Design Principles and Alternative Models." In *Towards New Developmentalism: Market as Means rather than Master*, edited by Shahrukh R. Khan and Jens Christiansen, 227–251. New York: Routledge.

Zein-Elabdin, Eiman. 1999. "Economic History of Sub-Saharan Africa." In *Elgar Companion to Feminist Economics*, edited by Janice Peterson and Margaret Lewis, 257–64. Cheltenham, UK: Edward Elgar Publishing.

Zein-Elabdin, Eiman, and S. Charusheela. 2004. "Introduction: Economics and Postcolonial Thought." In *Postcolonialism Meets Economics*, 1–18. London and New York: Routledge.

Zielenziger, David. 2012. "Chinese Contractors: Foxconn's Underage Worker Use Affects Sony, Google, Apple, Amazon, Nokia." *International Business Times*, October 17. Available at, http://www.ibtimes.com/chinese-contractors-foxconns-underage-worker-use-affects-sony-google-apple-amazon-nokia-847987.

Index